Computer Applications
for Anthropologists

D1601408

The Wadsworth Modern Anthropology Library

Margaret S. Boone and John J. Wood: Computer Applications for Anthropologists

Richard de Mille: The Don Juan Papers: Further Castaneda Controversies

Philip R. DeVita: The Humbled Anthropologist: Tales from the Pacific

Philip R. DeVita: The Naked Anthropologist: Tales from Around the World

Conrad Phillip Kottak: Prime-Time Society: An Anthropological Analysis of Television and Culture

Mac Marshall and Leslie B. Marshall: Silent Voices Speak: Women and Prohibition in Truk

R. Jon McGee: Life, Ritual, and Religion Among the Lacandon Maya

Serena Nanda: Neither Man nor Woman: The Hijras of India

Alice Pomponio: Seagulls Don't Fly Into the Bush: Cultural Identity and Development in Melanesia

Computer Applications for Anthropologists

Edited by

Margaret S. Boone
George Washington University School of Medicine

John J. Wood
Northern Arizona University

Wadsworth Publishing Company
Belmont, California
A Division of Wadsworth, Inc.

Anthropology Editor: *Peggy Adams*
Editorial Assistant: *Tammy Goldfeld*
Production Editor: *Angela Mann*
Managing Designer: *Cynthia Schultz*
Print Buyer: *Barbara Britton*
Art Editor: *Nancy Spellman*
Permissions Editor: *Jeanne Bosschart*
Designer: *Donna Davis*
Copy Editor: *Melissa Andrews*
Illustrator: *Kathryn Werhane*
Cover Illustration: *Adriann Dinihanian*
Compositor: *Bookends Typesetting, Ashland, Oregon*
Printer: *Malloy Lithographing*

1 2 3 4 5 6 7 8 9 10—96 95 94 93 92

Library of Congress Cataloging-in-Publication Data

Computer applications for anthropologists / edited by Margaret S.
  Boone and John J. Wood.
      p.   cm. — (The Wadsworth modern anthropology library)
   Includes bibliographical references (p.   ) and index.
   ISBN 0-534-17166-4
   1. Anthropology—Data processing.   2. Anthropology—Computer
programs.   I. Boone, Margaret S.   II. Wood, John J.   III. Series.
GN34.3.D36C66 1992   91-29700
301'.0285—dc20

This book is dedicated to Harold E. Driver and Stanislaw Klimek, two models for us all

 # Contents

🪷 List of Figures

List of Tables

Foreword to the Series

Modern cultural anthropology encompasses the full diversity of all humankind with a mix of methods, styles, ideas, and approaches. No longer is the subject matter of this field confined to exotic cultures, the "primitive," or small rural folk communities. Today, students are as likely to find an anthropologist at work in an urban school setting or a corporate boardroom as among a band of African hunters and gatherers. To a large degree, the currents in modern anthropology reflect changes in the world over the past century. Today there are no isolated archaic societies available for study. All the world's peoples have become enveloped in widespread regional social, political, and economic systems. The daughters and sons of yesterday's yam gardeners and reindeer hunters are operating computers, organizing marketing cooperatives, serving as delegates to parliaments, and watching television news. The lesson of cultural anthropology, and this series, is that such peoples, when transformed, are no less interesting and no less culturally different because of such dramatic changes.

Cultural anthropology's scope has grown to encompass more than simply the changes in the primitive or peasant world, its original subject matter. The methods and ideas developed for the study of small-scale societies are now creatively applied to the most complex of social and cultural systems, giving us a new and stronger understanding of the full diversity of human living. Increasingly, cultural anthropologists also work toward solving practical problems of the cultures they study, in addition to pursuing more traditional basic research endeavors.

Yet cultural anthropology's enlarged agenda has not meant abandonment of its own heritage. The ethnographic case study remains the bedrock of the cultural anthropologist's methods for gathering knowledge of the peoples of the world, although today's case study may focus on a British urban neighborhood or a new American cult as often as on efforts of a formerly isolated Pacific island people to cope with bureaucracy. Similarly, systematic comparison of the experiences and adaptations of different societies is an old approach that is increasingly applied to new issues.

The books in the Wadsworth Modern Anthropology Library reflect cultural anthropology's greater breadth of interests. They include introductory texts and supporting anthologies of readings, as well as advanced texts dealing with more specialized fields and methods of cultural anthropology.

However, the hub of the series consists of topical studies that concentrate on either a single community or a number of communities. Each of these topical studies is strongly issue-focused. As anthropology has always done, these topical studies raise far-reaching questions about the problems people confront and the variety of human experience. They do so through close face-to-face study of people in many places and settings. In these studies, the core idiom of cultural anthropology lies exposed. Cultural anthropologists still, as always, go forth among the cultures of the world and return to inform. Only where they go and what they report has changed.

James A. Clifton
Series Editor

🪷 Preface

Computers are becoming indispensable tools for anthropologists. Computer use can open new perspectives and often make work less tedious, but computer use nearly always makes our work different. Students and practicing professionals today, more than ever, need to learn how computers can assist them in their practice and how computers make their work different. *Computer Applications for Anthropologists* draws together a variety of experiences by anthropologists who all use research designs that involve a modern mainframe computer or microcomputer. It is primarily a methodology text whose chapters illustrate applications of anthropological theory and method in problem-solving projects.

Each project shows how computers assisted legitimate research goals. Applications range from the simple use of a computer to store and display research results to complex examples involving multivariate analysis. The contributors show how the use of a computer made their work less laborious, or more complex, or just different, and they illustrate ways that computer-assisted methods can be integrated with the use of more traditional anthropological approaches. Anthropological research projects on a wide range of topics are included. Research populations include Native Americans, Sri Lankans, farmers in Cameroon, inner-city African-Americans, and migrant farm workers. The chapters include topics in ethnology, archaeology, and physical anthropology. There are two chapters on skeletal analysis and one on a historic preservation project. Language use is also illustrated in a chapter on kinship analysis and a chapter on multidimensional analysis.

This book is designed for use with both undergraduate and graduate students in anthropology and as a reference for professionals. Most of the techniques for storage, display, analysis, and expert decision making (artificial intelligence) can be used equally well in all of anthropology's subdisciplines. The text is also ideal for applied anthropology students, since many chapters have a practical, applied component, and the authors of these chapters show program and policy implications of their work. It will serve as a supplementary reader for any methods course in anthropology. It complements a broader methodology text well, since methodology texts do not concentrate on computer use. As the major text for a course in computer applications, it could be supplemented by a statistics text or other general methods texts. The book will be useful in courses on methods, statistics, and computer use for students in other programs with strong fieldwork components, for example, sociology, rural sociology, Third World development, public health, and even international business. All students who will be collecting, storing, and analyzing information in and from fieldwork will find the text helpful.

Chapters 1 through 3 provide background and discussions of the disciplinary and sociocultural context of computer use. Chapters 4 through 15 are arranged in increasing order of complexity and difficulty. Chapter 16 reviews some considerations in teaching computer applications for anthropologists and provides example curricula for a course emphasizing quantitative applications and a course on qualitative applications. Chapter 17 offers suggestions for new directions. A Software Appendix provides information on software availability, and a Resources Appendix and Computer Databases Available to Anthropologists section reference applications that expand and augment those discussed in the text. The reference list includes references cited as well as suggested readings.

We would like to thank reviewer James W. Carey, Georgia State University, for his helpful comments.

🌿 About the Contributors

ROBERT L. BEE is Professor of Anthropology at the University of Connecticut. He received his MA from UCLA and his PhD from the University of Kansas, both in anthropology. He has done extensive ethnographic fieldwork on a Native American reservation in California over the past twenty-six years, along with ethnographic research on a Native American reservation in Kansas, in Native American communities of the central Mexican highlands, and in Washington, DC. He continues his interests in community-level processes of sociocultural change, national-level processes of policy formulation and implementation, and the dynamic interaction between these local and national processes.

CLIFFORD A. BEHRENS holds a PhD in anthropology from UCLA and has specialized in the mathematical modeling of Amazonian Indian decision making. His experience with mainframe and microcomputers includes knowledge of numerous statistical software libraries and programming languages and the application of artificial intelligence systems in the social sciences. He is a Visiting Investigator at NASA's Science and Technology Lab at the Stennis Space Center. Through committee participation and teaching, he has worked to improve computer literacy in UCLA social science departments by integrating computing and quantitative research methodologies into social science curricula. He is Research Coordinator for the Office of Information Studies at the UCLA Latin American Center.

BENJAMIN F. CRABTREE is Assistant Professor and Associate Director of Research in the Department of Family Medicine at the University of Connecticut and holds an MA in applied anthropology from the University of South Florida and a PhD in medical anthropology from the University of Connecticut. He has written several methodological papers on topics ranging from log-linear models to time-series analysis. More recently he has taught the use of microcomputers to researchers from developing countries as a consultant to the Center for International Community Health Studies and to graduate students in medical anthropology with Pertti J. Pelto. He is coeditor of a forthcoming book on methodologies for qualitative research and primary care.

JAMES DOW, Professor of Anthropology at Oakland University, holds a PhD in anthropology from Brandeis University. His experience with computers covers thirty years, going back to his early work in engineering science after graduation from MIT with a BS in mathematics. He is the author of three books on anthropological subjects, and his interests range from quantitative mathematical models of cultural evolution to the anthropology of religion. He has done extensive fieldwork with the sierra Otomi Indians in Mexico. His most recent book (*The Shaman's Touch*, University of Utah Press, 1986) resulted from work in which computers were used to compile and organize shamanic teachings. His other recent research deals with evolutionary biology and human social behavior. He is the editor of the *Computer Assisted Anthropology News,* has helped to organize conferences on the uses of computers in anthropology, and has served as chairperson of the Electronic Communications Committee of the Society for Applied Anthropology.

MARC R. FELDESMAN is Professor and Chairman of the Department of Anthropology at Portland State University. His PhD is from the University of Oregon. His computer experience spans over twenty years. Since 1971 he has been focusing his research in the area of morphometrics, the application of statistical (and computer) methodologies to problems in comparative morphology. His university draws on his computer expertise in numerous ways. He is on the College of Liberal Arts and Sciences Computer Applications Committee, served on the University Computer Advisory Committee, and has participated in the high-level decision making involved in acquiring several different mainframe and minicomputers.

JOHN B. GATEWOOD received his PhD in cultural anthropology from the University of Illinois at Urbana-Champaign in 1978 and is currently a Professor and Chair of the Department of Social Relations at Lehigh University. His primary interests are cognitive anthropology (decision making; relations among talking about, knowing how, and doing) and maritime anthropology (worker satisfaction; causes of fishing success; appropriate policy). He acquired a personal computer in 1984 and since that time has been dabbling in the "black art" of computer simulation. The GODZILLA program, described in this volume, was his first effort in that direction.

JEFFREY C. JOHNSON is with the Institute for Coastal and Marine Resources and is an Associate Professor in the Department of Sociology and Anthropology, East Carolina University, Greenville, NC. His interests include cognitive anthropology, methods, and the organization of work. Much of his past work has focused on social network analysis and its application to solving human problems and informing marine policy in the United States. He is editor of the *Journal of Quantitative Anthropology* and received his PhD from the University of California, Irvine, in 1981.

ADAM KOONS received his doctorate from the American University. He is an applied anthropologist based in Washington, DC, and his work focuses primarily on rural development in Africa. At the time of publication of this book, he is serving with an A.I.D.-sponsored development project in the Sudan. His interests are cross-cultural and interpersonal communication and their effects on development projects, especially with regard to the exchange of technical information. He is also very active in public education about world hunger issues and has been associated with the Presidential Commission on World Hunger during the Carter administration.

KATY MORAN is an applied anthropologist who specializes in development and conservation. She received an MA in applied anthropology in 1987 from the American University. She is currently press secretary for Congressman James Scheuer of New York and formerly was a legislative assistant who helped to write, pass, and implement conservation legislation for the U.S. House of Representatives. Her fieldwork assignments in development anthropology have taken her to Sri Lanka to study elephant management; to Kenya to study desertification and camel pastoralism; and to Brazil to lecture on and study deforestation and population. In 1987 she organized a Smithsonian Institution Symposium on Culture and Conservation and will edit an upcoming volume of papers on this topic with Robert Hoage of the National Zoological Park in Washington, DC.

KEN NOVAK is a development consultant who specializes in telecommunications and computer systems. He has concentrated his work on assisting developing countries and institutions involved in agricultural and development research. His primary interests are in the implementation of electronic data exchange systems that allow organizations to retrieve and share research information worldwide. Recently, he has been setting up a system of this type in the Philippines and neighboring countries.

MICHAEL K. ORBACH received his PhD from the University of California, San Diego, in 1975. His interests focus on maritime anthropology, economic anthropology and development, natural resource management, North America, and the Pacific. He is currently Professor of Sociology and Anthropology at East Carolina University. He authored the book *Hunters, Seamen and Entrepreneurs* and has written extensively on matters concerning marine policy and anthropology.

DWIGHT W. READ is Professor of Anthropology at UCLA and professor-in-residence at the IBM Los Angeles Scientific Center, with degrees in mathematics from Reed College, the University of Wisconsin, and UCLA. He is a mathematician/anthropologist who has worked extensively on the application of formal methods of reasoning to anthropological and archaeological problems. His work in cultural anthropology has centered on the problem of modeling conceptual structures, and he has published a number of papers on the modeling of kinship terminology structures. His most recent work has focused on the development of computer-assisted research for the analysis of the structure of kinship terminologies. He is also the faculty associate director of Social Science Computing at UCLA.

BARBARA J. SIBLEY, ND, RN, is a nurse-anthropologist with a doctorate from the Case Western Reserve University. She is a psychiatric nurse with the University Hospitals of Cleveland and is involved in direct inpatient care. Her previous experience includes work in hospital planning, community drug education, cross-cultural child training in the Philippines, research in cognitive dissonance among children, and federal environmental impact assessment.

ROBERT T. TROTTER II is Professor and Chair of the Anthropology Department at Northern Arizona University. He is a medical anthropologist and has worked extensively on cross-cultural access barriers to modern health care, as well as ethnomedicine in Mexican-American communities. He also has a research interest in alcohol use and abuse and in ethnopharmacology. He received his MA and PhD from Southern Methodist University and has an undergraduate degree in Zoology and Physiology from the University of Nebraska, Lincoln. He has served as president of the National Association for the Practice of Anthropology (NAPA), as well as co-chair of the Electronic Communications Committee for that organization. His research has focused on the U.S.-Mexico border, with short projects in Puerto Rico, as well. His computer interests are in the areas of electronic communications, computer management of field notes, and microcomputer statistical applications to ethnographic data.

GREGORY F. TRUEX teaches anthropology at California State University, Northridge. He received his MA at Tulane University and his PhD at the University of California, Irvine. He also holds an MBA from UCLA. His principal fieldwork has been in Oaxaca, Mexico, where he began working twenty years ago. He also has done fieldwork in Ensenada, Baja California, Mexico, where he is an adjunct research professor at Xochicalco Center for University Studies. His current research interests are in two major areas: economic anthropology and cognition. He has a paper on the role of crime (particularly economic crime) in the development process in press. He recently completed fieldwork on male and female perceptions of kin relations in Santa Maria, which is part of ongoing research on interhousehold reciprocal exchanges in the maintenance and use of kinship networks.

WILLIAM WILSON has worked as a freelance computer consultant specializing in database applications and data conversions. He received an MA in anthropology from Northern Arizona University in 1985 and taught FORTRAN and Pascal in the Computer Science Department of NAU from 1983 to 1986. His research interests include microcomputer applications in the social sciences, artificial intelligence, and Native American education.

PART ONE

Introduction to Computers for Anthropologists

In this first section we review the role that computers play in the development of new methods and new ways of doing old tasks. Computer technologies will have an increasingly important effect on the way that anthropologists do their work. The focus here is positive. Computers encourage new research techniques, new analytical paradigms, and even new modes of thought.

CHAPTER ONE

Use and Study of Computer Systems in the Development of Anthropological Methodologies

MARGARET S. BOONE
JAMES DOW
JOHN J. WOOD

This volume illustrates a wide variety of projects by anthropologists who all use research designs that involve a modern mainframe or microcomputer. Each chapter is set firmly on a foundation of anthropological theory, and each project shows how computers assist legitimate research goals. The computer applications illustrated in the following chapters describe methodologies that are typical for anthropologists: field research (including interviewing and participant observation), analysis of research results, and the drawing together of research results into a final paper or report. Research activities range from participant observation in new high-tech social settings (Chapters 2 and 3), to the simple use of a computer to store and display research results (Chapters 6 and 7), to complex examples involving multivariate analysis (Chapters 12 to 14). Sometimes the use of a computer makes the anthropologist's work less laborious, or more complex, or just different. All chapters illustrate the ways in which computer-assisted methods can supplement more traditional approaches such as interviewing, use of secondary records, participant observation, classification of museum specimens, laboratory analysis, kinship analysis, linguistic analysis, role analysis, and functional analysis. In many cases, the use of computers expands the range of a traditional method.

In most ways, the methodologies described in the following chapters are not new, except for their use of, or focus on, a new technology. However, in some ways they are new. What is new about the approaches of these anthropologists?

First, a large number of the projects use a mixed methodological approach to achieve their research goals. The use of computers encourages combination approaches that mix quantitative and qualitative methods.

Second, the methodological approaches tend to be creative. Contrary to many fears and expectations that computer use would restrict innovation, it has, so far, usually encouraged anthropologists to be innovative and to experiment with combinations of facts and factors to explain a phenomenon. A great deal of creativity can be displayed in the computer programming required for use of standard statistical packages, in the adaptation of a qualitative analysis program to the particular requirements of a project, or in the writing of specialized software. We see examples of all these in the following chapters.

Third, use of computers tends to blur the traditional stages of anthropological research, so that fieldwork, analysis, and writing become more of a single, interactive, ongoing process. Analysis and write-up of either quantitative or qualitative results can begin in the field on portable computers and then be transmitted back to a research office over telephone wires or mailed on diskettes. Similarly, analysis and write-up tend to become an iterative process rather than two distinct stages in a research project. Computers allow an anthropologist to repeat trials as new hypotheses arise in the course of writing. Computer use allows analysis and report production at the same time, on the same machine or terminal.

This volume includes anthropological research projects on a wide range of topics. Research populations include Native Americans, Sri Lankans, farmers in Cameroon, inner-city African Americans, migrant farm workers, and fishermen. The chapters include topics in ethnology, archaeology, and physical anthropology. There are two chapters on skeletal analysis and one on a historic preservation project. Language use is also examined in the chapter on kinship analysis and the chapter on multidimensional scaling (research on naming and perceiving). Most of the techniques for storage, display, analysis, and expert decision making (artificial intelligence) can be used equally well in all of anthropology's subdisciplines. Many of the chapters have a practical, applied component, and authors have taken pains to point out program and policy implications of their work.

THE INTRODUCTION OF A NEW HUMAN TOOL

The electronic computer is one of the latest in a long line of energy-capturing, energy-controlling devices. Computing devices are not new. The earliest known computing devices may be the markings scratched into the bones of animals killed by Paleolithic hunters to calculate the moon's phases and to devise a method of predicting the seasonal migration of game animals. The transcription of language and mathematics came later, and these recordings on paper or clay were also computing devices. Information storage and retrieval—which are part of modern computing—began with these kinds of inventions. Computing, as we think of it today, follows a long history of technological inventions for extending the human intellectual capacity.

Tools for computing are probably as old as any other type of tool. What is new in computing technology today is the electronic computer, which appeared only after World War II. The ideas implemented by electronic data processing technology were, at first, old ones. However, new types of symbolic manipulation gradually were developed to take advantage of the electronic medium. The implications of these developments are substantial for training, practice, research, and the theoretical development of all scientific disciplines, including anthropology. The technological characteristics of computers—their speed, storage capacity, flexibility, and (now) portability—are all important in bringing to anthropologists the full methodological capabilities of modern social science. The use of the modern computer affects the development of the discipline and the anthropologists who use computers, in a reflexive fashion similar in some ways to the fieldwork experience itself. Just as the anthropologist is a "tool" in filtering information gained through participant observation, the computer filters information, too. Computer technology translates information and thereby transforms anthropological methods and gives them added dimensions. These changes carry potential benefits and costs.

The Mediating Position of Computer Technology

In 1965, Hymes published the first major synthesis of computer use in anthropology. He compares the potential future impact of computers to the historical impact of the telescope and the microscope.[1] Like the telescope and the microscope, computers are destined to become "indispensable adjuncts." They enable us to "see"—to envision—complex relationships that might otherwise be unavailable or incomprehensible. Hymes's analogy, his visual metaphors, and his forecast all raise interesting and important issues about computer technology.

The use of the telescope and the microscope are good examples of a reflexive, dual process in research. Both tools magnify parts of the visual field while simultaneously reducing its scope. Because of their amplificatory-reductive dimensions, technologies are essentially ambiguous and, hence, transformative. Ihde writes that "precisely because this ambiguity is inescapable, it makes the use and development of technologies simultaneously fascinating, threatening and in need of serious reflection."[2] We act toward and within the world, and as we come to know the world we come to know ourselves.[3] An artifact, says Ihde, is taken into this reflexive intentionality and occupies a mediating position between us and the world. In this mediating position, the artifact both amplifies and diminishes our experience. The computer, like the camera, can help us to see detail and to identify complex relationships—but sometimes at the expense of seeing the larger whole. Information is filtered by computer use, just as it is by the camera, the microscope, or the telescope. Interpretation still falls to the anthropologist, and it is still the task of the anthropologist to integrate the patterns discovered through field research and to use them to develop sound theory.

The use of computer technology amplifies and reduces our experience, much like the use of the telescope and the microscope. For example, as an "indispensable adjunct"—in Hymes's words—computer technology also becomes transformative and, coincidently, stressful and mesmerizing. The latter has been described as "technostress" in an absorbing book of the same title by Brod. He writes that technostress may be seen in "the struggle to accept computer technology, and in the more specialized form of overidentification with computer technology."[4] This theme is touched on in several chapters in this book. This transformative aspect of computer technology is a fertile field for anthropological research, as illustrated by Koons and Novak's studies and by Sibley's studies of changes that occur when computers are introduced and used in modern social settings (Chapters 2 and 3).

The issues raised in adding computers to the methodological toolkit of anthropologists counsel us to reflect on our experience with other technologies. The best example that comes to mind is film. Have the predictions about film technology proved to be true? Bateson and Mead's work in Bali in the late 1930s portended a breakthrough in anthropological uses of film. However, comparable projects were, and are, uncommon.[5] Increased use of film some thirty years later led Asch, Marshall, and Spier to believe that "the use of camera and film, particularly over the last five years, has grown to the point where they might be considered as important as the notebook in any research project."[6] Yet, five years later, MacDougall offered a more cautious assessment of the role of ethnographic film.[7] Anticipating our position, MacDougall said, "We know that films often render the specific at the expense of the general" and that, furthermore, "the camera, through its positioning and framing, continues to see selectively, and the burden of interpretation falls with a new immediacy upon the film-maker at the time of filming."[8]

It has been almost thirty years since computer technology was heralded as a breakthrough in anthropological methodology, and the mid 1990s are seeing an unprecedented growth in personal computing. Will personal computers "be considered as important as the notebook in any research project"? In our haste to overidentify with computer technology or in our struggle to accept it, we should not lose sight of its mediating position between us and the world.

Historical Development

Most computer applications in anthropology take traditional tasks, automate them, and make them easier and more precise. Because tasks can be done quickly and accurately with little effort, the potential for creative use of the computer is high—as is the potential for abuse. A taxonomy of computer applications based on the primary language of description includes two categories: numbers and text or quantitative and qualitative. Numerical applications are the earliest and the most common. The early work with text on computers—which came under the rubric of content analysis—also involved counting.[9]

Quantitative research has a long history in American anthropology. Kidder, Kroeber, and Spier seriated potsherds in the second decade of this century, and Kroeber and others continued their taxonomic work with culture element distributions and language classification through the 1930s.[10] Particularly impressive in this era were hand computations of discriminant functions by Howells and cluster analyses by Klimek.[11,12] Computers were not widely available until the late 1950s and early 1960s. Some of us remember, not too fondly, the rotary calculators of our graduate student days and, later, the endless stacks of real "punched" IBM cards that we would load in boxes and drag to early campus computer centers.

Not surprisingly, when the Burg Wartenstein conference on "The Use of Computers in Anthropology" was being planned in 1960 and 1961, "little use of the computer in anthropology was apparent."[13] However, by the time the conference was convened in 1962, the organizers were able to bring together an impressive list of projects and participants. About the same time, research reports that incorporated computing began to appear in major professional journals and books with some frequency. Many of the applications were numerical, or quantitative, and continued earlier traditions of taxonomy and statistical analysis. Some applications involved simulation and modeling; others reported the results of content analysis, or the linguistic analysis of texts, or the study of themes in folklore. Still others demonstrated the utility of managing large amounts of data. The literature of this period portrays a sense of excitement and promise and a great deal of sophistication and creativity.

Much of the literature on computer use in anthropology since the 1960s continues earlier traditions. Easy-to-use data analysis packages for mainframe and microcomputers have assured the continuance and prominence of statistical applications. Multivariate analyses and network analyses are more frequent, however, and newer techniques, such as exploratory data analysis, have joined the repertoire (see Chapters 7 to 9 and 12 to 14). The development of full-screen editors and word processors, with search and "cut-and-paste" functions and simple but powerful database managers for personal computers, have accompanied a renaissance of qualitative research in the social sciences (Chapters 4 to 6).

The use of computer simulation models has continued. For example, the analysis of the demographic impact of marriage patterns makes heavy use of computer simulation, and in so doing, patterns bridge cultural and physical anthropology.[14] Computer simulation has provided an unparalleled means for investigating human demography and has led to many advances in population anthropology.[15] Computer simulation has made important contributions to theoretical archaeology.[16] General programs have been written to carry out computer simulations in anthropology.[17,18] Computer simulation continues to be a prominent use of computer technology in the field.

Portable computers are now used commonly in anthropological fieldwork to enter data and to record field notes. Field-note management and analysis have gone beyond the word frequency counts of early text analysis (see Chapters 4 to 6). There are also new genres of computer software, such as the spreadsheet (a concept borrowed from financial analysis) and the expert system (an outgrowth of artificial intelligence research) (see Chapters 10 and 15 and Software Appendix). Many of the computer applications in social and cultural anthropology in the 1960s reflect interest in traditional topics such as kinship, marriage, and social organization. These are interests that abide today but that have found new modes of analysis with computer-assisted methods (see Chapter 15).

In 1965, Hymes saw the development of computer use as an opportunity for anthropology *if* two demands could be met: the demand for "formalization of analysis," and the demand for "exchange of data."[19] It is evident in the chapters in this book and in the current literature that the first demand—the demand for increased attention to "the logic and practice of quantitative and qualitative analysis" is being met. The possibility of satisfying Hymes's second requirement, the exchange of information among anthropologists, is enhanced today by the potential sharing of data and manuscripts on mailable computer disks or along worldwide communication networks using electronic message systems, in which computer terminals or personal computers serve as nodes (see "Computer-Based Opportunities for Professional Collaboration" later in this chapter and the Resources Appendix). A research management application that builds on this concept is discussed in Chapter 4.

In the past two decades, computer use in anthropology has increased enormously, although it is still not routinized in the discipline. Computers are not yet "indispensable adjuncts." They are still best described as "useful adjuncts." However, the mass computing phenomenon that has developed since the successful marketing of the personal computer starting around 1982 promises to enhance the "indispensability" of the computer as its mediating position becomes more salient and as the technological transformation continues its trajectory.

Pitfalls and Promises

The use of computer technology simultaneously augments and diminishes experience. It does not simply extend the capabilities of the human mind. Looking at a computer screen is like looking through a window. It presents the possibility of seeing something beyond our immediate space, but it frames the world at the same time, making it harder to pay attention to the whole.

Unlike a window, the computer screen is connected to the electronic circuitry of a machine that can execute coded instructions and perform a simple series of tasks and that, when combined and recombined in innumerable ways, can calculate discriminant functions[20]; write the chapters in this book; "talk" to colleagues in Carbondale, Illinois, or Berne, Switzerland; or keep a research budget up to date. These are all significant enhancements for anthropologists. However, computers often render the specific at the expense of the general, and because computers are programmed to work selectively, the burden of interpretation falls with new immediacy on the user at the time the information is entered.

If computers extend the capabilities of the human mind, we should remember that those capabilities include our best and our worst tendencies. For example, researchers sometimes have a tendency to treat the assumptions required by statistical tests cavalierly. It is far easier to obtain endless yards of computer output than to interpret the results with an appropriate understanding of the assumptions underlying the particular statistical tests being used. Without forethought and a clear understanding of the restrictions of both the data and the procedures, an anthropologist—like any other researcher—can end up with what Milke so aptly describes as a *Zahlenfriedhof,* a "graveyard of numbers."[21]

There is also a tendency to see the promise of riches in any new technique. Not all of the possibilities imagined for any technology are borne out in actual use. At the same time, other possibilities emerge that were never envisioned. To date, computer technology has served anthropology well, and we have not yet begun to exhaust its potential. We need to invent new alternatives and new ways of looking at data without sacrificing the discipline's implicit standard of extended engagement with data and without forgetting the implications of computer technology's mediating position.

To better comprehend the full capabilities of computers for research, teaching, and practice and for changing the type and quality of the research experience, it will be useful to review a more technical description of this particular human technology—both the "hardware" and the "software." In the development of computers, we can see parallels in the evolution of human biology, human language, and social organization. These developments also hinged on speed, flexibility, growing complexity, and the recombination of basic, arbitrary units.

THE TECHNOLOGY ITSELF

Hardware: The Machine

Early electronic computers were somewhat like calculators and mainly completed arithmetic operations on numbers in the memory. From the very beginning, computers have carried out logical operations in order to interpret instructions. However, as the cost of memory and other electronic components has dropped, processors have performed many other symbolic operations as well as arithmetic ones.

The power of the electronic computer derives from the fact that its operational instructions are stored in high-speed memory along with the symbols on which it operates. A computer takes its instructions from the memory as fast as it takes the data, at a speed that now hovers around a million times a second. In fact, electronically stored computer instructions look exactly like the data and exist in the form of binary numbers. However, they are interpreted differently. They can be changed by the computer itself, and thus, from this capability, the new manipulative power of the electronic computer arises. The machine can change its own instructions based on what it finds in the symbolic data. It can perform a variety of tasks with the data it is given. Modern computers are highly coordinated sequential interpreters of instructions, and although they can modify these instructions, they do so only in a rigidly controlled, programmed fashion. The program—an original set of instructions—covers all contingencies for its own modification, and if the computer faces a decision for which it is not programmed, it ceases to function properly.

The advance of computer technology has relied to a great extent on the speed and flexibility allowed by the development of integrated circuits—electronic devices that are like little computers within computers. The architectural units of the computer technology produce a kind of inertia in the development of new hardware. An engineer must think not only of a new way of making an integrated circuit but also of a way of getting it to work with the other chips that will interface with it and perhaps design some of those other chips, too. Further out from the computer in this network of electronic circuit connections are other devices that are part of the broader field of computer technology. By making use of their own internal, "dedicated" central processing units that take their instructions from fixed programs, many other devices besides computers have been simplified and made cheaper. For example, the following types of devices are now available at moderate cost: dot-matrix printers with high resolution, plotters that draw lines, scanners that read pictures, speech analyzers, speech synthesizers, and music generators. By combining video recording technology with computer technology, inexpensive mass symbolic storage is appearing in the form of tapes and optical disks. The combination of the electrostatic copying machine with computer technology has resulted in the laser printer. As a greater variety of microelectronic devices appears, innovative machinery resulting from the vastly increased number of combinations becomes possible.

In some ways, the above process resembles biological or linguistic evolution. Computer technology—having settled on a standard code of signals between devices (analogous to the genetic code or phonemes and morphemes) and the integrated circuit (analogous to the eucaryotic cell or the word and sentence)—involves increasingly complex combinations of elementary units.

Software: The Instructions

The program (the original instruction set) is the most important part of the computer. Without it, the computer can do nothing. Programs are called "software" because they reside in the high-speed memory of the computer and can be rapidly changed or erased. When the computer is turned off, the programs disappear and have to be reloaded again from some type of permanent storage (such as a floppy disk) before they can be used again. On the other hand, hardware (the circuits that form the different physical parts of the computer) does not disappear when the power is shut off. So, software is ephemeral in a sense, but its development is critical for new computer applications.

Software is the most frequent limiting factor in most anthropological applications at present. The full potential of computer hardware is usually not realized before it is abandoned in favor of faster, smaller, cheaper, and more cleverly designed hardware. Meanwhile, the development of software plods along trying to keep up with the better hardware being sold to run it. The process of "software development chasing hardware development" creates an interesting, interactive effect on new computer technologies and their applications: Because the power of a computer depends greatly on the software available for it, the "most powerful computer" may be the one that is available to the largest number of motivated programmers! This need not be the most expensive or the fastest machine. A collective effort can generate a larger body of software and enhance the power of all the standardized computers if electronics and operating systems are also standardized.

Computers can be programmed to translate programs (instructions) from one computer language to another. "Compiler programs" translate very basic general-language programs into languages for specific computers. Interpreter programs run general-language programs on different computers by interpreting the instructions for the computer as they are taken from memory. Mass computing does not have to arrive at the use of a single standardized computer to be efficient. It merely has to evolve enough standardization to make the translation of programs economic.

Our software heritage consists now of several common types of symbol-manipulating programs that still need a brief description because they are so new. Most ubiquitous among these today are spreadsheets, editors, and databases. The spreadsheet arranges text and numbers spatially in rows and columns. The data in the resulting "cells" can be used in calculations with data in other cells and so set up a chain of calculations, each one dependent on the next. The spreadsheet differs from earlier symbol manipulators in that portions of the matrix of cells can be constantly displayed on a video screen. The spreadsheet has a direct and useful user interface. Modern spreadsheets have the ability to display numerical data in graphic form such as bar charts. Most spreadsheets are two-dimensional, working only with cells in rows and columns. There is a three-dimensional experimental spreadsheet that offers new possibilities and that is available as shareware.[22] The creation of the string-manipulating spreadsheet is another development that would be of potential use in cultural anthropology. Besides their usefulness in displaying data and doing simpler statistical calculations, spreadsheets have been used by anthropologists to record field data.

Editors—software that allows the typing of words and symbols into a computer file—are used by practically all computer users today. Editors differ according to their purpose. There are two major types: document-creating editors and program-creating editors. Often the former are called word processors, since they evolved from an earlier line of electronic machines that replaced typewriters. They tend to have built-in text-formatting capabilities. The program-creating editors manipulate input to other programs and tend to have powerful macro and search capabilities. Editors are essential for creating input and recording data. Many microcomputer programs have their own built-in editing capability. These features usually have less power than a full editor and are often based on an early microcomputer editor. Operating systems, the basic computer programming that allows input and output in a regular fashion, often have their own standard editors.

A database stores categorized pieces of data (usually numbers or text) that are easily retrievable by category. There are two types of databases, fixed form and free form. The fixed-form database specifies the size and type of the data for each field of a record. The free-form database does not require a particular type or length of data in a particular field. Most of the databases used in business are fixed form and designed to hold descriptions of customers, orders, and machine parts. Anthropologists use databases to record scientific data on people, material artifacts, words, genes, and human settlements, and databases now even store images (see Chapters 6 and 17). Fixed-form databases can be used for fully coded and organized data. However, they are not as useful when the input is textual and not fully categorized. Mainframe computers have free-form list-processing databases that are quite useful for partially analyzed data, and microcomputers are being equipped with free-form databases that allow the typing of text directly into the database.

ANTHROPOLOGICAL USES OF COMPUTERS

During the 1980s, both the amount of anthropological data stored on electronic storage media and the software to analyze the data began to increase exponentially. For example, a vast library of cross-cultural codes is now being published on computer disks as the World Cultures

Database,[23] and these codes can be used, for example, in exploratory data analysis and statistical analysis, which are described below. The Human Relations Area Files has also begun to publish data on disk (see Resources Appendix). New types of software are being written at an increasing rate, for example, programs that can be used to analyze texts such field notes and lengthy interviews, programs to develop outlines of ideas, and programs to simulate changes in complex systems in society and the environment. Finally, more and more anthropologists are learning to write their own specialized computer programs that are tailor-made for their own particular analytical needs. Together, all of these changes broaden the capabilities of traditional anthropological methodologies and create new ones.

Exploratory Data Analysis

The first step in the analysis of either quantitative or qualitative data is to discover their basic parameters. Computers simplify the task of initially exploring both text and numerical measurements, but they are especially useful in analyzing relatively large quantitative databases. "Exploratory data analysis" refers most often to the discovery of the basic dimensions of all variables in a database and interesting trends and patterns that may be worth exploring in detail with more sophisticated techniques. Exploration of a quantitative database provides the foundation for later decisions concerning appropriate statistical tests or more complex exploratory procedures.

Exploratory data analysis proceeds from a univariate, to a bivariate, to a multivariate stage. Using whatever statistical (or spreadsheet) software is available, a researcher determines ranges, measures of central tendency, and approximate shape of the distribution of each variable (using quartiles, or standard deviation, skewness, and kurtosis). It is also a good idea to determine the amount of missing data at this stage. The univariate stage frequently includes graphing or tabulating important variables to better understand their importance (see Chapter 7). The next stage, the bivariate stage, involves producing cross-tabulations or a correlation matrix of all variables to get a rough notion of relationships among all the variables. Finally, multivariate procedures are used to develop a statistical model, as with a log-linear or regression procedure (see Chapter 9), or, to continue to explore the data, as with cluster analysis, factor analysis, and multidimensional scaling (see Chapters 13 and 14).

Statistical Analysis

The electronic computer stimulated the rapid development of new statistical techniques in the late 1970s and 1980s because they compressed calculations that could take (literally) days to complete into several seconds. Most statistical techniques—even the simplest, such as the computation of a Chi-square statistic—can be laborious and time consuming by hand. The computer can reduce the time taken, for example, to compute a step-wise regression analysis by several magnitudes, from hours to seconds. Complex statistical procedures that are themselves new—techniques such as log-linear analysis and covariance structure modeling—are practically impossible without the use of a computer. These newer techniques are only now beginning to be applied in anthropology.

All types of statistical analysis procedures are being programmed for microcomputers and made available in the form of widely used statistical packages for the personal computer. In this way, teachers and researchers will have sophisticated statistical tools at their fingertips.[24] At the same time, universities are beginning to install local area networks that hook up research offices to university mainframe computers and provide easier access to the larger storage capacities needed to analyze very large data sets with the most sophisticated statistical software that includes all available programming and report-producing options. The result of all these rapid new trends is the broad application of statistical techniques in anthropological research. A good sign of this increased activity is the emergence of a new publication, *The Journal of Quantitative Anthropology* (see Resources Appendix).

Statistical analysis is being used in all of anthropology's subdisciplines with an increasing frequency. Statistical testing, like the use of computers itself, holds great promise in evaluating hypotheses that develop before or during fieldwork. However, there are also dangers in using inferential statistics (tests based on a probability model) without thorough grounding in the assumptions and restrictions imposed by the theory behind the procedures. There are also conventional restrictions that make the reporting of statistical results standard throughout the social and behavioral sciences, and these—like the theoretical assumptions underlying the techniques—must be considered by anthropologists as they design their research projects and choose appropriate statistical tests. The use of computers to perform statistical testing can save research time and dollars, allow research to be more creative, and provide a powerful tool for anthropologists if, and only if, the assumptions behind statistical testing are adhered to, and reported, with great care (see, Chapters 8 and 9, on the Chi-square test and linear regression, respectively).

Taxonomic Analysis, Mapping, and Optical Applications

One of the most basic and useful types of scientific analysis that is facilitated by the computer is taxonomic analysis, and some of the best examples of this application come from archaeology and museum studies. High-speed computers can store, classify, and analyze large amounts of data on material culture and search for "types" with similar combinations of characteristics. Computers have been taken to excavation sites where archaeologists enter data directly into a computer while an excavation is taking place. A variety of sensors are used to input data, including satellite sensors, magnetometers, and automated recording devices, which produce maps that locate above-ground and underground features. Once all the data on a site have been recorded, computer graphics programs can produce three-dimensional views of selected natural features and artifact distributions, which help the archaeologist test various hypotheses about the site. On a larger scale, mapping techniques can help to explain the way in which earlier cultures were functioning within entire ecosystems. Computer programs for the production of simple frequency distributions, a numerical taxonomy, a cluster analysis, and statistical tests have all been used to pursue the basic scientific task of classification.

Archeological applications benefit from incorporating computer developments from various fields of engineering. For example, new computer applications programs in the field of computer-automated design (CAD) are capable of storing and rendering different views of all the locational data at an archaeological site. CAD programs can be interfaced with databases for combined graphic, textual, and numerical analysis of data. Commonly available devices called "digitizers" can input line drawings and maps into a microcomputer. Off-the-shelf hardware can produce outlines from a video camera, and even color pictures can be stored in computer memory.

Museums have problems keeping track of all their collections, and computerized documentation is an excellent solution (see Chapter 6 on the Arizona State Historic Preservation Project). Databases can now include visual representations of objects in a database, as well as identification codes and characteristics. The problem of massive, permanent memory required for visual information is now being overcome by developments in hardware technology. Optical disk recordings now store digital data very much like a compact disk stores a musical recording or a video disk stores a movie. An optical disk contains thousands of optical tracks per inch. The difference between computer optical disks and other common recordings is that the computer can write on the disk as well as read it. A typical computer optical disk contains 3 gigabytes (3×10^9 bytes) of information. There are technical problems in developing optical disks that can be written more than once, and it is possible that cassette tapes will replace them. Standard video cassettes are now being used to store over five gigabytes of digital data and are another way for museums to store pictures of artifacts.

There are many advantages of computerized museum catalogs, and a number of text-video databases are now being set up for museums (see Computer Databases Available to Anthropologists). Items can be located very rapidly, summary data can be produced, and data can be analyzed on the computer for research purposes. Video data are analyzed to produce basic measurements of the artifacts, and more sophisticated analyses will probably be produced in the future. One can imagine that, as more studies are completed and as the data are continuously entered into central databases, valuable analytical, computerized databases from museum collections will be developed and shared.

Qualitative or Text Analysis

The data with which anthropologists are dealing is becoming rapidly digitized. Even the simple written field note, which used to be hand-written or typed, is more conveniently typed into a portable word processor or a lap-top computer. One of the impediments to fully digitized field data that remains is the moderate, but not insignificant, cost of the equipment. Another impediment is that direct computer entry in some field situations may be too intrusive for effective interviewing and participant observation. On the other hand, informant reactions to field computers can be enlightening, and their elicitation can be integrated into field research.

Text data processing is aided by microcomputer packages (see Chapter 5 and Software Appendix) or by integrated operating systems, containing a number of string-processing programs useful in qualitative data analysis. Word-crunching programs now exist that can improve the speed, quality, and complexity of searching and analyzing textual data. If data are left as one or more text files with keywords and codes, then other programs can scan and index them and produce summaries. Programs can count words or produce a concordance keyed to lines or paragraphs, a keyword-in-context index, and a bi-level index.[25] Common word processors now produce tables of contents and indexes. A set of text notes processed this way constitutes a valuable database. Programs can pull a text apart and group together areas that cover similar subjects. However, splitting and grouping can be done more rapidly in a free-form database.

A keyword-in-context (KWIC) index shows each important word in the text surrounded by words that accompany it before and after in the text. A more readable type of KWIC index shows the word followed by the sentence in which it occurs. The location is indexed by line number to the text. A concordance shows the locations of important words in the text by page number, paragraph number, or line number. Existing software comes in two varieties: programs that require the user to specify the keywords for each section of text (including standard word-processing indexes) and programs that find the keywords themselves from a list of significant words. Running the latter type of program before indexing the text for the first type of program saves some time.

Idea Processing

"Idea processors" are essentially word-processing programs that work in an outline structure. Blocks of text can be moved from one level of the outline to another. The headings become tags by which the text can be moved around and placed in its proper position in an outline. This type of program can be especially useful when a microcomputer is being used as a notebook to organize data or ideas. A text-processing spreadsheet is just a step away and could be used in a number of qualitative data analysis applications like those advocated by Miles and Huberman.[26] The outline processors group text in a tree structure, whereas the text spreadsheet would group it in a matrix structure. Coupling this type of text-processing program with word-processing, clipboard, and notepad software makes the microcomputer a more convenient tool than paper for handling notes and text. Clipboard software takes text from one file, stores it in memory, and inserts it in another file without writing an intermediate file. It belongs to a genus of software commonly called "pop-up" software because the user pushes a certain key and the clipboard pops up on the screen. Notepad software is similar except that it is set up primarily to record notes on a popped-up window. On large-screen video displays, popped-up windows can be kept in a corner of the display. Optical scanners of text pages can go one step further: They "read" pages of text, store it as digitized data, and file it directly in memory or format it with currently used word-processing instructions.

The development of large-size, high-resolution video screens now makes possible the inclusion of several documents and drawings on the same screen simultaneously. This is of great value to translators and people analyzing text—perhaps for coding or inclusion in another database. The ability of these graphic devices to use exotic scripts like Korean or Arabic is just around the corner, and direct voice transcription of field interviews in native tongues is just beyond that. Databases of raw ethnographic notes and properly indexed transcripts can be coded for statistical analysis much easier with these devices. These capabilities illustrate yet other advantages for having all field notes in electronic form.

Simulation

It is much more difficult to develop a meaningful, useful model of a human phenomenon than it is to find a computer to run a dynamic model of it. Some of the heaviest computational loads are in the area of computerized modeling, so the capacity of extremely fast "supercomputers" will probably extend the range of the types of models that can be considered in anthropology—as they have in other scientific fields like chemistry and pharmaceuticals and "Star Wars" defense systems.

There have been some successful anthropological models of ecological dynamics, cultural cognition, motion of the human body, social phenomena, population growth, the evolution of economic systems, and organic evolution. Models can be developed that will improve our understanding of the cultural, biological, and sociobiological aspects of evolution. In as much as these models are important to the theoretical understanding of human behavior, they will be developed further. The wide availability of computers, their increasing power, and developments in applied mathematics related to computer modeling will very likely make modeling approaches more popular in the future.

Artificial Intelligence

Artificial intelligence (AI) is a branch of computer science that focuses on developing ways to describe and imitate the intellectual capacities of human beings. At the simplest level, AI deals with (culturally based) cognitive processes such as recognizing printed characters. This work has lead to a number of text-scanning devices that can read text into a computer.

At more complex levels, AI is concerned with "banking" knowledge of an expert, for example, a physician. This type of AI "knowledge bank" might be examined by other professionals to aid them in their work. In anthropology, AI has been used to analyze kinship terminology (see Chapter 15 for an application in kinship terminology and Chapter 10 for an application in skeletal typing). Pattern recognition and classification methods in artificial intelligence can lead to other models of cultural cognition that can describe the culturally transmitted, intellectual aspects of a culture.

COMPUTER-BASED OPPORTUNITIES FOR PROFESSIONAL COLLABORATION

Computers have a significant impact on the professional lives of anthropologists in the way they enhance professional communications. Two communications areas that are developing fast are computer networks and desktop publishing. For other resources, see the Resources Appendix.

Computer Networks

Among the problems that anthropology shares with a number of other academic disciplines is that it is small and its practitioners are widely scattered. Anthropologists meet periodically at meetings and seminars. However, they do not often have the privilege of working in large teams. The advent of computer communication can bring together widely separated colleagues to share ideas. One way to do this is to share data and manuscripts on mailable computer disks. This is particularly valuable for persons collaborating on a single project.

There are now a number of computer message systems that permit the rapid sending of messages between computers. Bitnet is a favorite academic computer network. It is not the only one available, but it is the one that tends to be used most often by anthropologists in academic settings. It is available to anyone who works at an academic institution with a computer connected to the network system. It permits the sending of mail messages that take from five to thirty minutes to arrive. It also permits the sending of brief high-priority messages and the transfer of files. Bitnet is a network of regular academic computers connected by dedicated phone lines. There are also commercial, computer-amateur, and radio-amateur computer networks. The computer-amateur networks make use of phone calls, and the radio-amateur networks make use of radio communication.

There are several advantages in using electronic mail in professional collaboration. The recipient does not have to be at the telephone when the message is sent; the message arrives within minutes; the underlying costs are quite low; and the text is available for electronic editing when it arrives. It is an ideal system for people who are collaborating on a joint project. For example, text files can be sent via Bitnet, then programs that compare two texts and extract the differences can be sent. Only the update of a text needs to be sent by electronic mail. In this way, electronic coediting can take place.

UNIX operating systems, which are now available on microcomputers, have inspired some interesting software developments that could be more widely used in all the sciences. For example, in many of the engineering sciences, electronic journals circulate on the UNIX networks. A UNIX computer provides an electronic journal subscription in a subject area. Unfortunately, anthropology is not now included. The great advantages of these newsletters are that the articles are distributed within days of their final editing, and readers can make public comments. The comments circulate back through the network to be read by all the readers of the original article. Essentially, this is similar to the system started by the journal *Current Anthropology,* in which comments as well as original articles are published. However, all the publishing, reading, and commenting can take place in a week. Universities and their supporters see the advantages of paying for and otherwise supporting electronic mail systems.

Desktop Publishing and Journals on Diskette

The term *desktop publishing* refers to small-scale, high-quality printing made possible by microcomputers and laser printers. A number of word-processing and text-formatting programs are now available that enable very good-looking documents to be produced. The latest software developments are page formatters that format each page of text instead of the whole document at once and that can include graphics with the text. If manuscripts are submitted in proofread electronic form, much of the typing and proofreading that were previously required can be eliminated. Computers are opening up the possibility of producing reports with technical data more rapidly and accurately and distributing them more effectively. However, hard editorial work is still needed to produce good publications.

Another interesting development is the publication of electronic journals on disks. A floppy disk with text is now cheaper than the paper required to print the text, and the disk can be easily copied. Furthermore, the disk-based journal can contain data that the reader can then reformat and use directly. See the Resources Appendix for examples of anthropological journals on diskette.

COMPUTER TRAINING FOR NEW AND TRADITIONAL ANTHROPOLOGICAL ROLES

According to David Givens, Director of Programs and Information Services for the American Anthropological Association, "There is a very good chance that in the foreseeable future, virtually every department will have some kind of introductory course in computers and anthropology. Computer use makes learning methodology 'fun.' There are more and more anthropologists writing their own software." The use of computers in anthropology will grow rapidly in the immediate future, based on information from a 1987 Survey of Departments of Anthropology. Between 57 and 65 percent of BA, MA, and PhD departments are expected to grow by the year 2000, and 25 to 32 percent are expected to stay the same. Enrollments will increase as the total college population once again climbs after declines in the 1970s and 1980s.

Computer use will be increasingly favored by departments that expect themselves to be "leaner and meaner," that is, more efficient in the use of resources; interdisciplinary in focus; responsive to new directions in the discipline; more flexible in incorporating innovations; increasingly visible; and strongly competitive for innovative new colleagues. Computer use is favored by, and favorable for, departments with changes in these directions. Younger colleagues are more likely to be those with computer training and work experience with computers and those who can write their own specialized software. Computers allow high visibility for research projects and courses that make ample use of graphics, desktop publishing, database management, and innovative and experiential computer programs for teaching. Departments that can afford special equipment like "workstations" will be in a favorable position for attracting students. Interdisciplinary activities in research and teaching are encouraged by the use of standard statistical programs, as anthropologists, sociologists, economists, and psychologists learn increasingly to "speak the same language." For those departments whose goal is to become more efficient, computer-assisted methods are perhaps the most widely accessible for the entire array of courses in the department, thanks not only to quantitative analysis programs but also to qualitative analysis programs.

The 1987 Survey of Departments of the American Anthropological Association also asked specifically about computer use today. A third of the departments are "totally" computerized, with all faculty members having computers in their offices. Not a single PhD department of anthropology noted "no computers in the department" in 1987. Of the wide variety of applied careers now being pursued by anthropology graduates, almost all could today typically involve computer use (from computer programmer to librarian, to consultant for the Agency for International Development). It is difficult to envision a future career in applied anthropology that would not make use of computer-assisted methods.

SUMMARY

The use of computer systems in anthropological methods represents an area of tremendous growth in the future. Anthropologists will be able to readily develop their own special applications and introduce them to colleagues and students. They will also continue to learn and to adapt methods developed in the other social science disciplines, mainly through common use of statistical packages like SPSS-X and SAS. However, in spite of any common ground provided by the use of computer technologies, anthropologists' use of computers will continue to be based uniquely on anthropological theory. The use of computerized methods has the potential of helping to contribute to a more solid theoretical base for the discipline.

NOTES

1. Dell Hymes, ed., *The Use of Computers in Anthropology* (The Hague: Mouton & Co., 1965), pp. 29–30.

2. Don Ihde, *Existential Technics* (Albany, NY: State University of New York Press, 1983), p. 56.

3. Ihde, 1983, pp. 52–63. Don Ihde, *Consequences of Phenomenology* (Albany, NY: State University of New York Press, 1986), pp. 79–136.

4. Craig Brod, *Technostress: The Human Cost of the Computer Revolution* (Menlo Park, CA: Addison-Wesley, 1984), p. 16.

5. David MacDougall, "Ethnographic Film: Failure and Promise," in *Annual Review of Anthropology,* edited by B. J. Siegel, A. R. Beals, and S. A. Tyler, vol. 7 (Menlo Park, CA: Annual Reviews, Inc., 1978), pp. 405–425.

6. Timothy Asch, John Marshall, and Peter Spier, "Ethnographic Film: Structure and Function," in *Annual Review of Anthropology,* edited by B. J. Siegel, A. R. Beals, and S. A. Tyler, vol. 2 (Menlo Park, CA: Annual Reviews, Inc., 1973), p. 179.

7. MacDougall, 1978.

8. MacDougall, 1978, pp. 416, 418.

9. In content analysis, the researcher develops a coding scheme for themes and topics of interest, tallies frequencies of their occurrence, and generalizes from the results.

10. Harold E. Driver, "Survey of Numerical Classification in Anthropology," in *The Use of Computers in Anthropology,* edited by Dell Hymes (The Hague: Mouton & Co., 1965), pp. 301–304.

11. W. W. Howells, "Introduction," in *Multivariate Statistical Methods in Physical Anthropology: A Review of Recent Advances and Current Developments,* edited by G. N. Van Vark and W. W. Howells (Boston, MA: D. Reidel, 1984), pp. 1–11.

12. Stanislaw Klimek, "The Structure of California Indian Culture," *University of California Publications in American Archaeology and Ethnology* 37 (1935): 1–70.

13. Hymes, 1965, p. 507.

14. Douglas White, "Mathematical Anthropology," in *Handbook of Social and Cultural Anthropology,* edited by John J. Honigmann (Chicago, IL: Rand McNally, 1973), pp. 377–402.

15. Bennet Dyke and Jean W. MacCluer, eds., *Computer Simulation in Human Population Studies* (New York, NY: Academic Press, 1973).

16. Colin Renfrew and Kenneth L. Cooke, *Transformations: Mathematical Approaches to Culture Change* (New York, NY: Academic Press, 1979).

17. Nancy Howell, *The Demography of the Dobe !Kung* (New York, NY: Academic Press, 1979), pp. 277–304.

18. Eugene A. Hammel, "The SOCSIM Demographic-Sociological Microsimulation Program Operating Manual," in *Research Series* 27 (Berkeley, CA: University of California, 1976).

19. Hymes, 1965, p. 31.

20. Discriminant analysis is a statistical technique that searches for linear combinations of independent variables that discriminate between predefined groups.

21. Hymes, 1965, p. 198.

22. One of these is Qubecalc and is available as "shareware," which are programs that are available for noncommercial use without licensing fees.

23. Data on diskette are available from WORLD CULTURES, P.O. Box 12524, La Jolla, CA 92037-0650. The editor is Douglas White, School of Social Sciences, University of California, Irvine, CA 92717. See Resources Appendix.

24. A list of some microcomputer statistical packages appears in the Software Appendix. Various reviews have appeared: Robert T. Trotter II, "Statistical Packages for Micro-Computers," *Computer-Assisted Anthropology News* 2, no. 2 (1986): 15–17. Marc R. Feldesman, "A Review of Selected Microcomputer Statistical Software Packages: A Cautionary Tale," *Computer-Assisted Anthropology News* 2, no. 1 (1986): 3–26. Timothy A. Kohler, "Statistical Packages for the Macintosh," *Computer-Assisted Anthropology News* 2, no. 3 (1987): 1–26. John J. Wood, "Some Tools for the Mangement and Analysis of Test: A Pedagogic Review," *Computer-Assisted Anthropology News* 2, no. 4 (1987): 2–26.

25. A bilevel indexing program, NEEDLE-IN-THE-HAYSTACK, is available for personal computers from Aurora Software, Drawer A, 12591 Beachcomber, Anchorage, AK 99515.

26. Matthew B. Miles, and A. Michael Huberman, *Qualitative Data Analysis: A Sourcebook of New Methods* (Beverly Hills, CA: Sage Publications, 1984).

PART TWO

Ethnography and Organizational Analysis in Computer-Assisted Environments

Anthropologists have a long tradition of analyzing change and trying to understand how new technologies affect social relationships. In the chapters in this section, two anthropologists use participant observation, interviews, and structural-functional analysis to explore organizations that are changing because of the introduction of new, computer-based technologies. Sometimes, an anthropologist's first introduction to computers is not at a keyboard but in contexts where computers have brought about major social change— as these two chapters illustrate. Readers who want to go directly to keyboard applications can go directly to Part Three.

CHAPTER TWO

🌀 The Ethnography of a Computer Workplace in Cameroon

ADAM KOONS
KEN NOVAK

In this chapter, Adam Koons and Ken Novak explore the changes in hierarchical relations and worker morale at a telecommunications facility in Africa. Their original goal was to provide advice as management consultants. Koons's training as a cultural anthropologist helps to analyze the effect that a computerized system has on the maintenance of rules and the improvement of social relations in the workplace.

How do computers change the workplace? How do computers affect bureaucratic operations and human relationships? What procedural and social adaptations occur? How does the computer-centered environment mold culture and vice versa? It is often said that computers dehumanize their operators, that the computer workplace is sterile and unfriendly, and that workers in high-technology environments can become merely appendages of their machines. One way of testing these propositions is to examine a computer workplace using traditional anthropological participant observation.

This chapter illustrates that, far from dehumanizing the workplace and constricting personal interaction, computers can encourage cooperation and enhance morale. In a telecommunications workplace in Cameroon, the mechanical system for handling telegrams was replaced with a computerized system, which resulted in several changes in social interaction. Some formal bureaucratic rules became more rigid because they were automatically enforced by the computer. However, the automatic enforcement of rules provided by the computerized system served to decrease authority-based tension within the staff hierarchy and ultimately resulted in the relaxation of formal and informal social relations. All jobs were tied directly to one computer system, so staff with different roles and functions came to regard their activities and responsibilities as part of a single operation. Employees came to see themselves as team members whose different functions were all necessary for organizational success. The result of computerizing the workplace was a development of social relationships based on cooperation rather than authority and formal position.

BACKGROUND

In recent years, some anthropologists have focused their attention on the workplace and on bureaucracies. Research in these settings provides new insights into human interaction and an understanding of how formally designed environments affect the same aspects of behavior and society that anthropologists have studied in other settings, such as social structure, authority, status, and communication. In the anthropological study of work, questions have been asked about how the broader cultural context affects and is affected by the modern workplace and how social interaction changes in new forms of organization.[1] Ultimately, the answers to these questions can lead to increased efficiency and better working conditions.

This brief study of the changes in social structure and social interaction in a newly computerized work environment provides an example of a fertile field for primary research. To date, there are few studies that are grounded firmly in social science theory and based primarily on participant observation. Popular works such as Naisbitt's *Megatrends* and *Megatrends 2000* foretell striking changes in human interactions and work patterns in high-technology environments.[2,3] However, most primary research focuses on the stress induced by computer use, both within the individual person[4] and between different people.[5] There have been calls to investigate the effects of workplace technologies in the broad field of human resource management, with the goal of increasing productivity and understanding organizational structure,[6] but most works remain problem oriented in nature.[7]

The newly developing field of ergonomics considers the effects of computers and other forms of high-technology on the workplace.[8] Some of this literature considers ergonomic issues and computers in the workplaces of developing nations.[9,10] Relatively few studies explore the positive, creative changes in social structures and relations that are encouraged by computers. There are some studies in the sociology of computer network operations. Percival and Noonan examine the process of system monitoring its impact on social interaction.[11] However, their study primarily provides recommendations for improving human performance and is not intended to address the evolution of new structures in a social science context. Similarly, Kraut, Galegher, and Egido offer guidelines that help employers provide computer technologies that foster collaborative work groups.[12]

Some research examines the effect of technology on social status and organization. Mandon explores the effects of an improvement in the technical skills of office support staff on their standing in an office social hierarchy.[13] Long et al. examine, among other issues, the spread of computer knowledge and various social roles after the introduction of an interactive computer system in the workplace.[14] A significant amount of research has been completed on the effects of introducing computers in educational environments, especially the positive effects of computer use on facilitating social interaction among students.[15] For example, McInerney examines the social and organizational effects of introducing computing into academic and administrative offices of schools.[16] He highlights control issues such as the individual's control over other people, the individual's control by others, and the individual's control over work. There are studies of the effects of computer use on instruction that involves creativity—especially writing.[17] A substantial body of literature examines the use of new technologies to assist handicapped students and adults and the benefits they impart in terms of increased social interaction.[18]

METHODS

To examine the relationship between man and machines in the computer-based workplace it is necessary to examine the goals of the organization, the structure of roles and authority, and the interaction among individuals and between them and the computer. This chapter explores the influence of a computer on formal and informal behavior in a telecommunications facility in Cameroon. The research took place at the government-operated central communications facility, during the early stages of transition from manual to computer-assisted telegram-receiving and telegram-sending operations. The principal method for investigation was participant observation, which took place as a part of our technical work in introducing a computerized telecommunications system and in providing management consultant advice. The work was part of a broader development assistance project and like many similar projects provided an opportunity for both applied and basic research. We interviewed and interacted with many individuals in the workplace, in the pursuit of our primary goal, that is, the successful introduction of a new technology and its effective management. One of the authors was a member of the team that developed and programmed the computer system. He spent ten months working in Cameroon with the local staff. The other author was in Cameroon at the same time and was involved in examining interpersonal relationships in organizational settings. Our work included a number of return visits that allowed us to examine changes over time.

INTRODUCTION OF A COMPUTER-ASSISTED SYSTEM IN A DEVELOPING NATION

The Reason for Automation

The computer-assisted workplace was dominated by three closely interrelated components: (1) the task of the organization, (2) the procedures used to accomplish the task, and (3) social interaction, both formal and informal. The task of the workplace consisted of the goals and objectives of the activities performed by the staff. The computer center was responsible for routing all telegrams coming into Cameroon to the proper remote printers throughout the country and for receiving telegrams from all over the country and routing them to their destinations within the country and around the world. The way in which this task was carried out determined specific jobs, procedures, and responsibilities. The task required, and defined, a set of formal mechanical procedures, a set of roles, and a hierarchy of responsibility and authority.

The major goal of automating the process with a computer was to save management time. Skillful management was a scarce resource that could be used most profitably in expanding the facilities and services. It was not effective to have management skills tied only to maintaining operations. The computer was financed by revenues of the communications agency. A French firm was hired to take charge of the transition to a computerized system. However, an American-made computer was purchased, so both American and French programmers worked together developing the communications management control system.

The Automation

Before the arrival of the computer system, all operations were done entirely by hand, and each message required human attention and motion. Every telegram had to be read before it could be sent out, to determine (1) its category and destination, (2) whether there were any errors that needed special attention, and (3) conditions that needed special approval—as in the case of money orders. Telegrams came in from all over Cameroon and from other countries in the form of punched tape spewing from a row of teletype machines. Employees tore off the tape for each message, read it, and decided where to send it. They then carried the tape across the room to the proper machine and fed it in, so that it could be sent on the appropriate telegraph line.

The computer made the process more automatic. There were no longer any teletype machines or punched paper tapes. All incoming messages were received by the computer, which automatically placed each message in one of three categories: (1) messages containing no ambiguities or mistakes and needing no approval or verification, which the computer sent to their destinations immediately without any human intervention; (2) messages involving money orders, which had to be verified and approved, but involving no other action; and (3) messages with an error that needed to be corrected. The computer recognized money orders by a specific combination of characters near the beginning of the telegram, and messages were sent to designated computer terminals where they were read on screens by "traffic operators" who verified them and sent them to their destinations by tapping a single 'Send' key on their keyboards. All of the messages needing corrections contained some element that the computer could not identify and that it could not send out automatically or could not send directly for verification. There were format errors, which were portions of the telegram that were typed incorrectly—such as an address that ran into the text. There were address errors in which a destination was inadvertently misspelled at the originating teletypewriter so that the computer could not identify the city or country. The computer rejected these messages, and they appeared on an operator's computer screen. Although the two types of mistakes made messages unintelligible to the computer, the problems could usually be immediately identified and deciphered by human operators. The operators made the spelling or format corrections on their keyboards and hit a "Send" key, and the message was sent to a destination somewhere in Cameroon or in another country.

Changes in the Organization of the Workplace

The structure of the telegram operation was composed of four sets of hierarchical roles and responsibilities, each of which occupied a specific physical location in the computer center. The roles were filled by sixteen people. The physical placement of the personnel enhanced the ease of communication and interaction. The computer center was divided into four rooms separated by glass partitions. Everyone could view the action in all four rooms. Conversations from moment to moment would tend to happen within a room, but it was also easy to signal other people or see where they were and meet with them. As a result of the computer-based activities and roles, the hierarchy was built on job responsibility and training rather than direction or authority. Relations between people at different levels in the hierarchy functioned on the basis of mutual respect and a sense of teamwork and cooperation rather than subordination and acquiescence.

At the bottom of the hierarchy were ten "traffic operators." They had worked in the manual operation and were retrained for the computerized operation. Their responsibility was to do something with every message sent to their screens—either approve it, correct it, or send it forward to a supervisor if an approval or correction could not be easily made. The operators sat on both sides of a long table in front of the computer terminals with keyboards and screens. As the computer detected messages that needed to be checked, they were sent to one of these terminals. There was some role specialization, in that money orders, format errors, and address errors were routed to different operators. The traffic operators' daily activities usually proceeded at a leisurely pace. There were several peak periods: after lunch and at certain hours when traffic from Europe was heavy. The computer program was designed so that messages stacked up in an orderly way during busy periods, and they could be taken care of, in turn, during several hours of concentrated work. However, during most of the day there were several seconds between messages at any terminal. This gave operators plenty of time to get up and stretch or converse.

At the next level of the office hierarchy were the line supervisor and the traffic supervisor. Together they were responsible for the functioning of the entire message-handling system. They made sure that all messages that came in during a day went out during that same day. The line operator had counterparts in every city, and together, this network of operators ensured that international traffic kept flowing, partly by pinpointing the location of problems in the entire system. Traffic supervisors worked directly with the traffic operators. The supervisors received messages on their screens that were forwarded to them by the traffic operators when they were uncertain about correcting or approving them. The supervisors did not have the authority to order the operators to do things. However, when the supervisors wanted the operators to do something, their requests were obeyed out of respect and cooperation. The supervisors were regarded not as bosses but as foremen.

Three technicians occupied another unit (but not a clearly defined level) in the hierarchy. Their job was maintenance and repair of the computer system. In addition to periodic repairs, the technicians had ongoing, scheduled duties that included making backup computer tapes, generating reports about computer output, and creating billing reports. The technicians were crucial to the operation of the entire organization, since there were no other repair facilities in Cameroon, and the only other repair option would be to bring in specialists from France or the United States. The technicians had received a year of training in France and the United States, where they learned to fix the computer hardware. After many of the initial problems with the system in Cameroon had been worked out, the technicians were less busy, and they began to train apprentice technicians, thereby adding to local human resources and further repaying the company's investment in their own education. Gradually, the apprentices performed more of the straightforward, tedious maintenance tasks. They had no formal authority over staff or operations. They could not make procedural or policy decisions, and they could not order staff about or reprimand them. However, everyone realized that the technicians were responsible for maintaining the system on which everyone's job depended. When repairs were needed, the technicians' judgment and decisions were respected. During maintenance and repairs the technicians took charge and told others in the organization what to do. For instance, they told operators and supervisors to shut down certain lines or to change a certain way of doing things. There were never any questions or resistance to these requests. The technicians occupied a position outside of the normal hierarchy. Although they had no formally assigned authority over others, they were given a high level of authority and status because of their importance to the organization. In contrast, their equivalent position in the United States would not have carried as much prestige and power because of differences in the availability of their services and the relative level of their education in the two countries. The company had invested a large amount of money in their training, so they had a high level of credibility. They had substantial clout with the operations manager in charge of the entire department. This enabled them to suggest procedural and policy changes. The higher status of the technicians was clearly demonstrated in their Western-style suits and ties. Supervisors and operators wore more casual clothing. The technicians were also young (in their late twenties) compared to the others, whose ages ranged from the mid-thirties to the late fifties.

At the top of the office hierarchy was the operations manager. He was in charge of all aspects of the computerized telegram center, including personnel and hardware. His role was administrative rather than technical, and he was the only one with hiring and firing authority. Although his educational level was high, he was not educated in management or computer science. He had to depend on the supervisors, technicians, and periodic visits from consultant programmers for knowledge of what could and could not be done with the computer system. Not surprisingly, his clothing was the most expensive, and he was slightly older than everyone else. In his dealings with the staff, even while handling problems, he always appeared very relaxed and self-assured. He was well respected and very popular with all of the employees.

The Effect of the Computerized System on Social Patterns

With some background on workplace roles and procedures, it is now possible to examine how the introduction of the computer affected social structure, hierarchy, authority, personal relations, and attitudes. The mechanical requirements of the major task of the facility required a specific set of roles. Together, the formal roles and the mechanical procedures at times allowed, and at other times required, certain types of formal and informal relationships and interaction. When the mechanical operations changed with the computer, so did other aspects of the work environment. One of the most immediately apparent changes was in the nature of the formal rules governing employee activities. They became more rigid because many of them were automatically enforced by the computer. The employees had always used mechanical equipment before—the teletype machines. However, the computer, through its programming, imposed a pattern on its human operators. It required much more structured activity. Before the introduction of the computer, someone decided how the messages should be handled according to a set of procedural rules. For example, all money orders had to be approved by particular traffic operators, but no money order above a certain value was allowed to be sent. Operators would either let a money order go through or transfer it to a supervisor who decided whether or not to send it. Many of the rules were maintained by word of mouth and were implemented as a function of bureaucratic authority. Some of the rules were commonly regarded as outdated and therefore were not systematically applied or enforced—although they may have still been "on the books." A supervisor or the operations manager could order certain rules to be followed or allow them to be broken. In the manual system, individual operators who were faced with a situation in which a rule should be invoked could decide either to obey it, disregard it, or call for a ruling from above. Rules were regularly broken for reasons of expediency. An operator could decide that a money order was only a little above the limit and send it, or he might decide not to bother the supervisor at the moment. Similarly, a supervisor might decide the money order was within an acceptable range over the limit.

With the computer, the rules were strictly enforced. The computer programming was guided by the rule book rather than by the day-to-day activities of the staff. A money order that was too high would simply not go through. With a great deal of trouble a supervisor could force it through the system, but the computer would record the incident, along with the name of the person who overrode the program. Similarly, if an operator did not make the proper corrections or sent a message forward to a supervisor when there were spelling or format errors, he simply could not send it to its destination. One result of the computerized system was that the rules that were regularly circumvented in the past now showed up very clearly. Far more money orders were prevented from being sent because their value was beyond the limit. This led to reviews and changes in rules and policies that were no longer relevant.

More important, the computer system, and particularly the way in which it took over many of the organizational details and decisions about rules, caused changes in human interaction and in the nature of the hierarchical structure itself. Job-related communication decreased significantly. When it did occur, it was between neighboring levels of the hierarchy. In general, it took place to a far lesser extent than with the previously used manual system. The operations manager now came out of his office only once a day. He had far less need to deal directly with the staff, especially with the supervisors, in making decisions about how to handle problems. When the manager did come out, it was to talk to the supervisors so that he could keep track of how things were going. Usually the conversation focused on what could be done to refine and improve the system, in light of the way that the programming was working in relation to the way things had been done in the past—as in the case of money orders. The operations manager rarely needed to speak with the traffic operators, and he was not approached by them often.

Changes Resulting in Greater Efficiency

The significant decrease in interaction between the manager and the staff was a primary reason for installing the computer. The manager was given more time for longer-range, broader-scope activities. Supervisors and traffic operators still spoke with the manager about matters concerning schedules, money, and personal problems, but this occupied relatively little time. The supervisors' jobs became centered more around managing machines than people, so their interaction with others was reduced significantly. The computer made many of the decisions that traffic operators had previously brought to the supervisors. Even the process of bringing a problem to a supervisor's attention had been automated. Problem messages were sent between computer terminals and appeared on screens rather than being hand carried and shown while asking questions and waiting for answers. Because both supervisors were trained in both supervisory roles (and they sometimes traded posts), when questions about the system occurred they often worked them out together instead of going to other personnel.

The traffic operators had little formal contact with other staff. Their closest and most frequent interaction was with the supervisors, although this was greatly reduced because of the automatic message transfer system. They sometimes asked supervisors for clarifications or pointed out to them that a particular type of problem was occurring frequently, or that a certain telegraph outpost was regularly making a specific kind of error. There was little contact between operators and technicians, and when there was, the technicians initiated it. There was no formal reason for the traffic operators to confer among themselves.

In contrast, the technicians' responsibilities were structured so that work-related interaction between them was frequent. When part of the system broke down—even something simple enough for one person to fix—all three technicians would confer and cooperate in the repair. All three wanted to be there from start to finish to make sure they were up to date and fully apprised of changes and problems concerning the system. The three technicians composed their own autonomous unit. They normally did not receive or give orders. Their authority was limited to taking any actions that ensured continued operation of the computer hardware. They usually spoke only to other staff when there were problems for which they needed actions to be taken in order to complete their repairs. They spoke to the supervisors a fair amount. Each of the three maintenance people spoke to the operations manager about every other day. There were also days when there was no interaction because there were no computer system problems. They rarely needed to speak with the operators.

The type of interaction between the different staff levels changed. Each job became far more involved with managing the machines and making decisions that kept the system running than with managing and being managed by others. The manager and the supervisors were no longer required to enforce the rules personally, nor did they need to reprimand employees for breaking them. Authority itself became less important, both as a means of keeping the system operating and as a means of maintaining a position in the office hierarchy. Although true authority remained important, the infrequent need for it made it appear to decline. The hierarchy remained intact, as did the differences in status. These were held in place by clearly recognized differences in level of training, responsibilities, and capabilities. This was overtly illustrated by the differences in clothing of the different staff.

The nature of interaction between different levels in the hierarchy changed. Communication was based primarily on requests and explanations. For example, because the manager was not trained in computer technology, his conversations with supervisors and technicians did not begin, "Do this," but rather, "Can this be done?" Therefore, relations were based not on compliance with orders but rather on guidance and cooperation that used workers' different, interdependent skills to make the system work properly. There was an increase in the level of enthusiasm, job dedication, and team spirit. It was not uncommon for technicians to stay late into the night making a repair, to ensure that the system would be working in the morning and that other staff would not be forced to be idle. This sort of dedication was rarely seen in other local organizations.

Changes in the Relationship between Humans and Machines

The enthusiasm among employees at the telecommunications facility was due partly to the greater autonomy that employees felt as a result of the decreased use of authority and partly because of the new human-to-machine relationship. In sharp contrast to the previous manual operation, the new operation used the computer to do most of the tedious and trivial work such as sorting, carrying, and checking for errors. There was a clear awareness among the operators that they now did what the computer could not do, that is, make decisions based on knowledge and experience. All of the jobs required certain skills that were both indispensable and irreplaceable by the computer. In contrast to any fears about "men becoming machines," there was a clear awareness that the staff operated the computer and that the computer was nothing more than a tool.

Although the computer made formal interaction between workers less necessary, the change in the tone of the formal relations allowed for a greater amount of informal contact and a more relaxed atmosphere in general. At the beginning of the day, workers usually shook hands with the others in their group and with whomever else they saw from the organization. The morning greeting was also performed between the operations manager and the staff. Throughout the day there was a great deal of social communication between people of the same status, such as between traffic operators, between supervisors, and between maintenance people. There was an especially large amount of interaction among the traffic operators. In a half-hour, each operator usually spoke at least a dozen social sentences. They were free to get up and move around and to talk to someone for a moment. Because of the automation of the system, there was usually a little time between messages on a terminal, and workers used this time to talk to each other. There were no rules about this interaction or any attempt to prohibit it as long as the messages did not become backlogged.

SUMMARY AND CONCLUSIONS

Staff relations in the computer-assisted workplace were based on cooperation in achieving the smooth operation of the entire system rather than on a chain of authority for the protection of individual position and status, as has been noted elsewhere.[19] The staff acted as a unified team whose members had different roles with the same ultimate purpose. As a result of the enforcement of rules by the computer, there was a decrease in formal interaction between levels of the hierarchy. The decrease in the use of authority enhanced personal dedication and satisfaction and allowed informal interaction to become more relaxed. The computer facility in Cameroon was a case in which, instead of people becoming lost behind their machines, the machines allowed people to become more human.

NOTES

1. Gerald M. Britan and Ronald Cohen, "Toward an Anthropology of Formal Organizations," in *Hierarchy and Society,* edited by Gerald M. Britan and Ronald Cohen (Philadelphia, PA: Institute for the Study of Human Issues, 1980).

2. John Naisbitt, *Megatrends: Ten New Directions Transforming Our Lives* (New York, NY: Warner Books, 1982).

3. John Naisbitt (with Patricia Aburdene), *Megatrends 2000: Ten New Directions for the 1990s* (New York, NY: Morrow Books, 1990).

4. Paul H. Faerstein, "Fighting Computer Anxiety," *Personnel* 63, no. 1 (1986): 12–17.

5. Werner Kuhmann, W. Boucsein, F. Shaefer, and J. Alexander, "Experimental Investigation of Psychophysiological Stress-Reactions Induced by Different System Response Times in Human-Computer Interaction," *Ergonomics* 30, no. 6 (1987): 933–943.

6. Janet J. Turnage, "The Challenge of New Workplace Technology for Psychology. Special Issue: Organizational Psychology," *American Psychologist* 45, no. 2 (1990): 171–178.

7. Archie Kleingartner and Carolyn S. Anderson, eds., *Human Resource Management in High Technology Firms* (Lexington, MA: Lexington Books, 1987).

8. Eric D. Sundstrom, *Work Places: The Psychology of the Physical Environment in Offices and Factories* (New York, NY: Cambridge University Press, 1986).

9. International Symposium on Ergonomics in Developing Countries, *Ergonomics in Developing Countries. Symposium Held in Jakarta, Indonesia, November, 1985* (Geneva, Switzerland: International Labour Office, 1987).

10. National Research Council, Board on Science and Technology for International Development, *Cutting Edge Technologies and Microcomputer Applications for Developing Countries. Report of an Ad Hoc Panel on the Use of Microcomputers in Developing Countries* (Boulder, CO: Westview Press, 1988).

11. Lynn C. Percival and Thomas K. Noonan, "Computer Network Operations: Applicability of the Vigilance Paradigm to Key Tasks. Special Issue: Vigilance; Basic and Applied Research," *Human Factors* 29, no. 6 (1987): 685–694.

12. Robert E. Kraut, Jolene Galegher, and Carmen Egido, "Relationships and Tasks in Scientific Research Collaboration. Special Issue: Computer-Supported Cooperative Work," *Human Computer Interaction* 3, no. 1 (1987–1988): 31–58.

13. Nicole Mandon, "La Bureautique des Enjeux Sociaux," *Connexions* 35 (1981): 83–91.

14. J. Long et al., "Gentrification as Urban Reinvasion: Some Preliminary Definitional and Theoretical Considerations," in *Back to the City: Issues in Neighborhood Renovation,* edited by S. B. Laska and D. Spain (New York, NY: Pergamon Press, 1983), pp. 77–92.

15. Steven B. Silvern, "Classroom Use of Video Games. Special Issue: Computers in the Classroom," *Educational Research Quarterly* 10, no. 1 (1985–1986): 10–16.

16. William D. McInerney, "Social and Organizational Effects of Educational Computing," *Journal of Educational Computing Research* 5, no. 4 (1989): 487–506.

17. Colette Daiute, "Issues in Using Computers to Socialize the Writing Process. Special Issue," *Social Aspects of Educational Communication and Technology* 33, no. 1 (1985): 41–50.

18. Stephen A. Pisano, "The Potential of the Word Pocessor for the Writing of Maladjusted Students," *Maladjustment and Therapeutic Education* 7, no. 1 (1989): 47–53.

19. Britan and Cohen, 1980.

CHAPTER THREE

Computerized Information Networks in a Complex Organization: Patient-Related Data in an Urban Teaching Hospital

BARBARA J. SIBLEY

Barbara Sibley takes a new approach to a standard analytical task in cultural anthropology. She proposes a method of understanding structure and function by "mapping" social relationships—in this case, the computer networks in a modern hospital complex. She also demonstrates that graphics software help to illustrate an analysis by keeping track of organizational changes through time.

AN INITIAL APPROACH FOR PURE AND APPLIED RESEARCH

Anthropologists can take advantage of a relatively new approach in the study of modern agencies, organizations, and corporations, namely, an intial description and analysis of an organization's information systems. This chapter takes a descriptive approach in analyzing the flow of information and the manipulation and analysis of data in the rapidly changing network of computers in a large hospital complex of a major urban area in the United States. The following description illustrates a new type of starting point for a structural-functional analysis. The study of information systems in any large and complex organization can be useful in developing hypotheses, which can then be tested using data from a series of interviews and extended participant observation in selected parts of the organization.

There are advantages in initiating the anthropological study of a complex organization with an examination of its flow of information. A summary of computer systems is a relatively neutral and nonthreatening entry into an organization, just as making a map is a good beginning for fieldwork in a community or village. The components of an organization, such as leadership, values, physical layout, and ownership of the symbols of power, have long been studied by anthropologists interested in how an organization is structured and how it functions. An analysis of the use of information, the importance of computers, the access that computer systems provide, and their role in symbolizing power in bureaucratic structures can be a good beginning for a more in-depth analysis. The old adage "Knowledge is power" takes on increased significance when applied to anthropologists studying computer-assisted organizations and to the use of knowledge within the organizations themselves. Expertise in hardware and software is usually not necessary in this type of initial exploration. The explanation of technical systems and the organization of people who use them can serve as a focal point in follow-up interviews. The process of discovering who needs what data, who has access to them, and where the various terminals and mainframes are located can contribute to an understanding of the history, goals, and decision-making structure of an organization that might appear initially too complex and large for an anthropologist's holistic analysis.

THE MODERN HOSPITAL AS AN EXAMPLE OF A COMPLEX ORGANIZATION

The modern American hospital serves as a reasonably self-contained complex organization that is worthy of anthropological inquiry. Analysis of its information systems provides a good place to begin research of either a pure or an applied nature. Researchers interested in developing ethnographic profiles of patient groups or summaries of illness episodes or of a specific mode of treatment can examine the categories in a disaggregated, summary form using the many computerized databases available in the modern hospital. Similarly, the applied anthropologist working as a management consultant can describe the computer systems and software available for the financial and administrative staff, as compared, for example, to those available for the nursing staff, the medical staff, or the top executive managers. One can trace the history and evolution of staff organization by initially noting which offices and experts acquire the first computers and then later noting who obtains the updated models—and why. Hospital information systems are now often linked together into single systems. It may be of interest to note when, by whom, and how in the planning process the need for linking computers in a local area network is first acknowledged. The implications of these historical facts for the structure of the organization and the distribution of power and authority can be fundamental.

This chapter provides a brief examination of the flow of patient information, chiefly by computer, throughout a hospital complex and its centralized administration. The complex consisted of five adjoining private hospitals that treated women, children, adult and adolescent psychiatry patients, and adult medical and surgical patients. There were a total of 874 beds and almost 5,000 employees. The hospitals were affiliated with the nursing, medical, and dental schools of a contiguous private university. The growth of information systems fulfills specific needs and functions in the history of American hospitals and the health care field in general.

DEVELOPMENT OF COMPUTER USE IN HOSPITALS

Historically, hospital administration in the United States has been based on a military model or a religious model, or on a combination of both. The former is based on a line-and-staff pattern with responsibilities divided hierarchically, whereas the latter has a less rigid structure, with service and charity as primary goals. Until recently, hospitals focused on the needs of physicians and invested in new medical technologies to satisfy the demands of physicians and their patients. Hospitals charged fees based on what they believed it should cost their patients for the services, treatment, and supplies they received. Individuals and third parties like Medicaid, Medicare, and private insurance companies usually paid those fees.

The federal reimbursement system for Medicare and Medicaid patients was instituted in 1983, after passage of the Tax Equity and Fiscal Responsibility Act of 1982 (TEFRA). Fees are now based on schedules that are in line with Diagnostic Related Groups (DRGs), so hospitals know ahead of time how much they will be reimbursed for the care of patients covered by federal programs. Many insurance companies have adopted similar approaches. Simply put, if a hospital can treat patients with a given diagnosis for less cost than the DRG listing for the geographical area and type of hospital, then the hospital can keep the difference. If the cost is higher, the hospital must absorb the loss. Because of the cost-saving function of the new law, hospitals found that they needed to look closely at their fiscal management and billing systems and at all phases of their operations to see where they could reduce inefficiencies and cut costs. Data collection, analysis, and information management became essential means to discover where expenses are generated and how they are related to revenue-producing activities. The new model for hospital administration became the corporate or industrial model, and it has largely superseded the military and religious models.

The influence of the corporate model resulted in demands by managers—who now sometimes come from industrial and corporate worlds and have no previous health care experience—for more information and new computer hardware and software to furnish data on costs, services, and diagnoses that they need for reporting requirements.

"Capturing costs," increasing reimbursable activities, and reducing over-head are major goals that the new managers have adopted to achieve the economic survival of their hospitals in an increasingly competitive health care market.

METHODS

Two major departments, nursing and medicine, are discussed here in relation to the patient data they generate and the incorporation of those data into information systems. Hospital managers monitor physicians' treatment patterns and patient outcomes by computer and use the data to evaluate physicians' needs instead of automatically complying with their requests for advanced medical equipment. Nurses, like physicians, assess and diagnose patients and write orders as part of their parallel care of patients. Nursing administrators have noted that nursing diag-noses are frequently better predictors of a patient's length of stay in the hospital than are the medical diagnoses on which the DRGs are based for reimbursement purposes.[1] Because length of stay is a primary cost factor, nursing data take on an increasing importance. At the hospital complex in the present study, the registered nurses selected all the diag-noses that applied to each of their patients and entered them daily into hand-held computers that are located at each nursing station. The com-bined database is used to produce the "Nurse/Patient Summary." This system is discussed in detail in Halloran, Patterson, and Kiley[2] and in Kiley.[3]

An understanding of the independent and linked systems containing data on patients was developed by using both primary and secondary research approaches. It began with a thorough study of an internal report[4] and a colleague's draft sketch.[5] An early version of Figure 3.1 was drawn, and then the content and relationships were revised substan-tially. The model was verified and redrawn several times after a series of interviews with selected individuals who were active in various parts of the system.[6] When information from all knowledgeable parties was assembled, the final figure was generated with MacPaint graphics soft-ware on a Macintosh Apple computer and printed with an Apple laser printer.

CAPTURING THE FLOW OF PATIENT INFORMATION

The flow chart in Figure 3.1 is a static model representing structural com-ponents of two rapidly changing fields—health care and information science. Researchers who are attempting to capture the changes in in-formation systems and bureaucratic organizations can make good use of graphics software that allows easy updating. The research that led

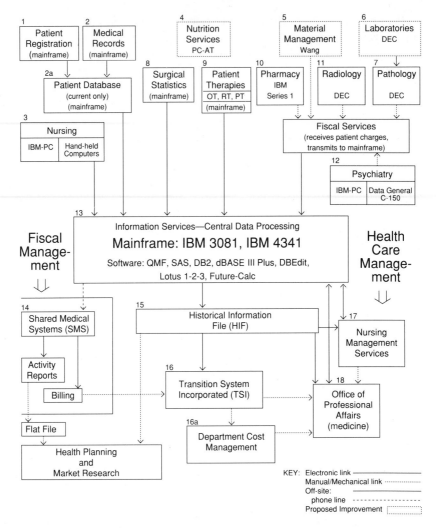

FIGURE 3.1 *Patient-related computer information linkages in an urban hospital complex.*

to the model in Figure 3.1 was a dynamic process because it integrated the views of many people into a single deign. However, the model was out of date very quickly. By the time the research ended, some parts of the model had already changed, making it necessary to revise the information gained in earlier interviews. Other changes in the hospital's information systems were scheduled for implementation in the future. When anthropologists examine the configurations of information systems, they should be prepared to document the changing versions of a structural organization. It is useful to develop a single template—as with a Macintosh graphics package—so that serial changes can be illustrated with ease.

The flow of patient information begins with Patient Registration (Box 1, Figure 3.1), when basic demographic data, next of kin, insurance, and other billing information are entered. The Medical Records Department (Box 2) is consulted about previous admissions and asked to assign a permanent patient hospital number. These initial data, plus the records of patient encounters and services from the various hospitals and outpatient clinics during hospitalization, make up the current Patient Database (Box 2a). This database changes daily as patients are admitted and discharged. Computer terminals have been installed so that nursing unit secretaries can continually enter data on patient admissions, discharges, transfers, and diet changes directly into the mainframe. The data are available in aggregated, condensed, printed tables, by day, week, and patient location within the hospital complex.

Nursing diagnoses are entered each day from hand-held computers (Box 3). The Nurse/Patient Summary data go directly into the mainframe computer (Box 13). Other departments, including Nutrition Services (Box 4), Material Management (Box 5), the Laboratories (Box 6), Pathology (Box 7), Surgical Statistics (Box 8), Patient Therapies (Occupational, Recreational, and Physical) (Box 9), Pharmacy Services (Box 10), and Radiology (Box 11), also feed patient data into the mainframe or to the Fiscal Services Department. The departments also maintain smaller, independent computer systems. As patients have contact with departments that do not have direct links to the hospital mainframe, data on charges are downloaded from the various systems or hand-delivered to the hospital's centralized Fiscal Services Department for billing purposes. The initial purpose for departmental linkage to the hospital's mainframe was to centralize the billing system. Except for some surgical statistics and pharmacy data, little medical information is transmitted directly to the mainframe. Laboratory printouts of clinical findings, test results, reports of consultations, examinations, and radiology readings are sent via the hospital's internal hand-delivered mail system to the hospital floor for manual insertion into a patient's chart. Terminals allow laboratory results to be retrieved as they are entered into the system by the various laboratories. Hard copies of lab results are still hand-delivered for inclusion in a patient's chart. When patients are released and all charges have been entered for billing, the patient data are no longer kept in the temporary information base (Box 2a). The data are stored in condensed form in the mainframe computer, and they are retrievable via the permanent Historical Information File (Box 15).

There is an independent computer (Box 12) in the psychiatric hospital that contains demographic, clinical, and treatment data about psychiatric patients at the time of discharge. These data are used to prepare annual reports and to provide quality assurance information. Psychiatry's computer is also used for research projects. Charges generated by the psychiatric outpatient clinics are hand-delivered to Fiscal Services for entry into the mainframe computer for accounting purposes.

TRACKING COSTS AND QUALITY OF CARE

Linkages are illustrated between a fiscal component (Box 14 and others), a health care component (Boxes 17 and 18), and some components that are of value to both financial and health care managers (Boxes 15, 16, and 16a). Nursing Management Services (Box 17) uses data available from the Nurse/Patient Summary (from Box 3), and the Historical Information File (Box 15). These provide a huge amount of information about patients and their nurses, individually and collectively, which can be assembled in a variety of matrices for administrative, clinical, personnel allocation, cost accounting, and research purposes, including studies on length of stay.[7] Staff throughout the hospital complex have access to the mainframe via the Information Services Department (Box 13) and to its various software packages.

The medical profession is encouraged by corporate hospital management to strive for increased efficiency. Toward this end, the Office of Professional Affairs (Box 18) monitors and assesses the quality of patient care provided by physicians in the medical services throughout the five hospitals. The staff of the Professional Affairs Office look at length of patient stay, use of medications, severity of illness, and infection and death rates, by medical diagnosis and by treating physician, via access to the mainframe, the Historical Information File (Box 15), the surgical log (Surgical Statistics, Box 8), and the cost accounting (Shared Medical Systems, Box 14) and cost management (Boxes 16 and 16a) systems. The hospital can determine where changes may be required to reach the cost-containment goals set by corporate managers. Within the hospital, there are many plans for continued use and expansion of the various computers systems described. A major goal of the hospital's financial managers is to link the functions of the independent departmental computers together so that patient charges can be entered immediately and only once, at the source of the charge. This will reduce errors and the time it takes to manually handle the figures.

A more distant goal is to have bedside terminals, one for each patient, which would be used by nurses to enter patient-care findings directly and create instant charting and storage in the main computer. Nursing managers envision other benefits of better patient information systems. They could provide continuity of care as a patient progresses back and forth through a variety of settings, including home health care after discharge and outpatient facilities, in addition to care in the hospital.

Some clinical managers are looking forward to having all clinical services and treatment results entered into the mainframe and accessible via terminals at each nursing station. This would provide an up-to-date clinical picture of each patient. However, physicians would have to be willing to reduce their dependence on hardcopy charts in exchange for the advantages of quicker data profiles via computer. Patient chart summaries are already being entered into the computer system experimentally by one group of nurses, with the goal of making the chart review process quicker, and hence more cost-efficient, for physicians. Similar computerization is taking place to greater or lesser degrees in hospitals throughout the United States[8-12] and in England.[13,14]

FUTURE GOALS FOR THE ANTHROPOLOGICAL STUDY OF INFORMATION SYSTEMS

Researchers who are interested in exploring the structure and functioning of modern bureaucratic agencies and organizations like the health care complex described in this chapter can use an information systems approach as a beginning point for their work. Electronic information systems provide an infrastructure for the examination of large social structures that may at first appear unapproachable using traditional anthropological methodologies. The descriptive procedure presented in this chapter could be followed either in pure research—for example, on social roles or on the diagnosis of disease in urban hospitals—or in applied research—for example, for a management consulting firm.

The structure and functioning of computer systems reflect social status, prestige, the organization of resources, and the fundamental social and cultural values represented by a complex bureaucracy. The study of the way an organization manages its information flow provides a window on the most important functions of the organization. Social relationships and social interaction will be increasingly reflected in the organization of information systems. Their study also provides a relatively nonthreatening approach to a rich source of data. One could begin by learning about the overt goals and functions of the organization and then look at the kind of data collected and transmitted—as in the above research on patient information flow. This approach will ultimately lead to a pinpointing of the crucial conflicts and incongruities between overt and covert functions. A researcher can investigate the history of the organization's computer use and the evolution of its various systems as new and updated hardware and software are acquired. In the process, there will be much to learn indirectly about the organization's goals and decision-making structure. One could discover who within the organization does, or does not, have access to hardware and software, and who gets, or does not get, updated and improved computer capabilities, as well as when and why. The human characteristics of the organization and its members are revealed through its information technology, and new insights can be gained that would not have been readily apparent by initially using a more traditional approach.

NOTES

1. E. J. Halloran, "Nursing Workload, Medical Diagnosis Related Groups, and Nursing Diagnoses," *Research in Nursing and Health* 8, no. 4 (1985): 421–433.

2. E. J. Halloran, C. Patterson, and M. Kiley, "Case Mix: Matching Patient Need with Nursing Resource," *Nursing Management* 18, no. 3 (1987): 27–42.

3. Marylou Kiley, "Applications of Nurse/Patient Summary Information," *In Touch* (University Hospitals of Cleveland Department of Nursing Quarterly) 2, no. 4 (1986): 22.

4. Intech Incorporated, "In-House Private Report. Analysis of the Division of Psychiatry Information Systems. University Hospitals of Cleveland," 1986.

5. Laura Nosek, Personal Inteview. Unpublished Sketch. Information Services, University Hospitals of Cleveland, 1986.

6. Vicki Freiberger, Personal Interview. Office of Information Services, University Hospitals of Cleveland, April 6, 1987.

7. Halloren, Patterson, and Kiley, 1987.

8. R. A. Korpman, "Patient Care Information Systems: Looking to the Future," *Software in Healthcare* Parts 1–5, April/May–December/January (1984–1985).

9. D. M. Steinwachs, "Management Information Systems: New Challenges to Meet Changing Needs," *Medical Care* 23 (1985): 607.

10. E. B. Roberts, "Commentary, Health Information Systems, Management Information Systems: New Challenges to Meet Changing Needs," *Medical Care* 23, no. 5 (1985): 672–673.

11. C. L. Packer, "Medical Records Automation Comes Up to Speed," *Hospitals* October 20 (1986): 98–99.

12. W. I. Bullers, R. A. Reid, and H. L. Smith, "Computer Oriented Hospital Systems," *Health Topics* March/April (1986): 16–20.

13. J. Gabbay and P. Drury, "Getting the Data Recipe Right," *The Health Service Journal* March 20 (1986): 388–389.

14. L. Ijebor et al., "What Happens to the Strategy Debate?" *The Health Service Journal* October 16 (1986): 1360–1362.

PART THREE

Getting Friendly with the Computer

In this part we are introduced to computer use through applications that help to solve old, but relatively simple, problems in fieldwork, classification, and analysis. For example, we learn how the fieldworker makes and stores field notes using computer technologies and how he or she communicates with other members of a field team. We also see how a fieldworker sorts field notes into meaningful categories and how items of material culture are cataloged. For all these tasks, anthropologists accustom themselves to the keyboards of microcomputers and special software applications. Communications software, database software, and text analysis are among the applications that many anthropologists first use.

CHAPTER FOUR

Ethnographic Data Management: A Model from a Dispersed Multi-Ethnographer Project

ROBERT T. TROTTER II

In this chapter, Trotter introduces us to the notion of team field project that relies on effective communications between widely separated field sites. He shows us how a number of communication, transmission, and data storage problems can be solved through good planning and the use of the right field equipment.

New computer applications can free anthropologists from much of the drudgery inherent in ethnography. Programs are available for field data management that take us well beyond the pen-and-pad-in-pocket days of early anthropology. They can provide solutions for three problems facing ethnographers: (1) rapid and convenient data recording and storage, (2) safe data transport, and (3) easy data retrieval and manipulation for analysis and write up. Computer use can also significantly speed up the ethnographic research process—sometimes from time spans measured in years to those measured in only months or weeks. This chapter addresses data management considerations that field researchers should anticipate before beginning their projects.

BACKGROUND FOR THE MODEL

Three other ethnographers[1] and I recently completed a project that called for convenient, rapid turnaround of ethnographic research data (Trotter et al. 1989). The project was called the "Pennsylvania Identification and Recruitment Project"[2] (I and R Project) and will serve to illustrate the data management model presented in this chapter.

The I and R Project was designed to provide an ethnographic database for the development of migrant education program administrative models and training materials. The project ethnographers worked in nine states in each of the three migrant streams (East Coast, Midwest, and West Coast) to produce data focused on the problems surrounding the recruitment of migrant children into migrant educational programs. The project included ten people in addition to the ethnographers. The non-ethnographic personnel's functions were dependent on having rapid access to summaries of the ethnographic data.

One unusual feature of the project was that it was designed from inception to depend on the content of the ethnographic data. It did not follow the more common practice of using ethnography as an evaluation tool. Instead, the data were collected and summarized prior to each non-ethnographic step of the overall program objectives. Those objectives were (1) the development of a training manual for migrant recruiters, (2) another manual for administrators who supervise migrant recruiters, and (3) the development of a model training package using the manuals, videos constructed out of the ethnographic findings, and oral presentations of the ethnographic information. The data were also used to assist in congressional hearings on the reauthorization of the migrant education legislation.[3]

There were severe time constraints imposed on the project. The program's overall objectives could be met only after the ethnographic data were available. This meant that recording, moving, and summarizing the data had to be completed at a much faster rate and in more convenient formats than is common in most ethnographic research. The project was a success, from the point of view of the people involved in using the ethnographic data, so most of the elements of the model presented in this chapter can be considered to have withstood a serious field test. Modifications or alternatives to the model are also suggested, as a result of that test.

DATA-RECORDING PHASE

The volume of potential field notes for an ethnographic project can virtually overwhelm the other problems discussed in this chapter (storage, transportation, and data manipulation). For example, in a seven-month period, the I and R Project ethnographers produced over 1,400 single-spaced (12-pitch type) computer paper pages of field notes. In computer storage terms, this was approximately 12 megabytes of text stored on forty-seven, 5-1/4 inch floppy computer disks. It is not uncommon for a single ethnographer, in a twelve- to eighteen-month field project, to produce as much as 10,000 pages of 8×12 field notes, or approximately 80 megabytes of computer storage needs.

Given the nature of ethnography, there will always be a problem of which data an ethnographer should record and which to leave unrecorded. Computers cannot alleviate the necessity of good ethnographic judgment. However, once that judgment is made, computers do allow the ethnographer to record a higher volume of information in a shorter length of time than is possible with pen-and-paper techniques. This gives the ethnographer time to spend on other activities, such as observation, interviewing, or even occasionally getting enough sleep to maintain the alert condition that leads to serendipitous discoveries.

If the researcher is guilty of poor planning (that is, does not anticipate the capabilities and limits of computers), he or she will merely duplicate past field note management mistakes by substituting a computer and printer for a typewriter (with the caveat that computer-stored field notes can be transformed at a later date into a more manageable database). As a first step, the researcher needs to recognize that computer-aided ethnographic data recording can involve elaborate predetermined coding schemes, recording systems developed in the field, and postfieldwork coding schemes. All three benefit from prefieldwork planning.

The basic components necessary for field note recording and storage are a microcomputer (hardware) and a word processor (software). A printer, to create "hard copy" of the field notes is useful but not absolutely necessary.[4] The word-processing software allows ethnographers to record field notes and store them on magnetic media. This has the advantage of being at least as rapid a method of recording data as a typewriter and allows more rapid editing and duplication of field notes.

Computers may also be used to enter and store observational data without first recording, then retyping, that data. It is possible, with some preparation, to directly record informants' responses to questions in standardized interviews. The ethnographer can then create summary descriptions or statistics without having to retype or recode the data. The example in this chapter is restricted to the more conventional model of using a computer to record (1) field note transcriptions of conversations, (2) direct observations, and (3) theoretical speculations and the daily log of the ethnographer.

A word processor is the tool that a researcher uses to get the data into storage. Once the words are available in a file, they can be manipulated by other programs that are more powerful tools for ethnographic analysis. These tools are the reason that it is necessary to be able to create ASCII files. Most of the more powerful tools have trouble with the program features that are used to create special effects in word-processing programs. The types of programs that go beyond simple data entry and storage are discussed in the third section of this chapter, Data Manipulation. It is necessary to plan for their use prior to the creation of the field notes, in order to use them most effectively.

Choices among the most advanced types of word-processing software are highly personalized and should be based on individual needs and preferences. Virtually any decent word-processing software is adequate, and virtually any has problems.

The use of electronically stored field notes prepared with different computer software is the most commonly encountered problem in trying to interface two computer programs in an ethnography project. The basic rule of thumb for choosing a word processor is that the program should be in common use. This means that its "quirks" will be reasonably well known, and help will be available. At a minimum, the program should allow a researcher to create what is called a "straight

ASCII file." This is a file that does not have any computer code in it that is specific to a particular computer or an individual computer program. An ASCII file can normally be exported easily from computer to computer and from program to program. In Chapter 7, Koons illustrates file transfer from a microcomputer to a mainframe computer by converting to ASCII files.

In the I and R Project, the ethnographers used a small portable computer with two floppy disk drives. One floppy drive ran the word processor,[5] and the other stored the field note files on a separate floppy disk. The content of each field note file varied. Some were chronological accounts of direct observations; others were transcriptions of recorded interviews; and still others were the ethnographer's daily log. File structure, including number and content, needs to be determined on a project-by-project, or even an ethnographer-by-ethnographer, basis. The size of the individual files for the I and R Project was determined by the program, which does not allow for files larger than 60 kilobytes (about twelve pages, single spaced). For some anthropological projects, files of this size would have been a serious inconvenience. Our files were merged later when another word processor was used to help summarize the data; therefore, the file size became a solvable problem.

Once the field notes are saved on a computer disk, they must be stored for later use. A concern was expressed before the beginning of the I and R Project about the security of the data, since virtually all data collection, recording, and transportation were to be computer based from the inception of the project. Two types of security issues were discussed: physical vulnerability and unauthorized access.

The problems of unauthorized access to computer files are virtually identical with those involved with protecting paper versions of field notes, with the added protection that one cannot simply glance at a computer disk and gain information. The disk must be placed in a compatible computer to be read. For ethnographers who have particularly sensitive data, or who are more than ordinarily concerned about confidentiality, computers offer security systems that are not possible with physical files. One measure built into many word processors is the capacity to create "locked files," where a password must be used to open the file. Another simple computer security measure is the availability of encrypted files. Free, public domain programs are available that can scramble a computer file, using a code word chosen by the person doing the encrypting. Both the program and the code word must be used to unscramble the file successfully. The only problem with these extreme measures—since they only take a few seconds or minutes to set up—is that any loss of the code words means a loss of the data, for all practical purposes.

The physical security problems of computer disks are very similar to those encountered with paper. A 5-1/4 inch disk used for computers contains about thirty pages of notes (single spaced), and newer disks contain twice to four times that much. Therefore, the physical space requirements for computerized field notes are far below those of paper-based field notes. A shoe box can contain 6,000 pages of notes and is easier to grab than 50 pounds of paper, should a fire break out. Paper can stand somewhat higher and lower temperatures than floppy disks, but the disks are more resistant to mold and to being dumped in water. Magnets can destroy magnetically stored data, but, like damaged paper, some data can be recovered from partially damaged disks. For all practical purposes, if paper storage of data is possible at a research site, then computer disk storage will also be possible with intelligent use. It may even be more convenient.

The storage of computer data involves the same precautions that should be a part of any data collection effort, regardless of the way that the data are collected and stored. Duplicate, if not triplicate, copies of all data should be kept. One set should be kept at a geographical location that is altogether different from the primary data storage location. Computer data have the advantage that they can be copied cheaply and very rapidly. Computer disks cost (on average) from thirty-five to seventy-five cents each when purchased in bulk. It takes from thirty seconds to a couple of minutes to copy a disk that has from 30 to 120 pages of field notes on it. The cost and the time involved are below those needed for conventional paper copying. Other than foolishness, carelessness, or an occasional uncontrollable disaster (which can also occur to paper-stored data), there is no reason to experience data loss from computer-based ethnographic data storage. The safest method for avoiding loss is to back-up (copy) all new data at the end of each data entry session.

Another concern in the I and R Project was the durability of the computers themselves. Computers are turning out to be tougher than people at first thought possible. There are rational limits to the abuse a computer can survive, but the basic rule of thumb is, "if a human can live reasonably comfortably with it, so can a microcomputer." The computers used by the I and R ethnographers survived minor falls and airport x-ray machines with no problem at all. One computer was used as a stepladder by a 3-year-old, with no ill effects, and one was the object of a male dog's attention. After being wiped off, the computer worked with no glitches that we have been able to discover, several months after the deed was done.

DATA TRANSPORTATION

In the past, beyond a few commonsense options, ethnographers had little choice about data transportation or any other communication from a field site. Data transportation consisted of putting field notes in a box and lugging them home or, for security's sake, mailing one or two copies of the notes home and carrying another set back. Communication consisted primarily of mail and telephone, when available. These possibilities still exist, but now there are additional options.

A single ethnographer may find it sufficient to simply put his or her computer disks in a box and head home, avoiding damage from airport security and other environmental hazards along the way. But, for projects with multiple researchers who need access to one another's data, the logistics are much more complicated.

In the I and R Project we had four anthropologists who needed access to the data, and other professionals who needed access to data summaries. We could not wait until everyone got out of the field to look at the data. We needed to share insights, discoveries of key questions, and data trends so that comparable data could be collected in each of the migrant streams. We also needed to assemble the information rapidly so that it could be summarized as a coherent whole rather than piecemeal.

We intended to solve this problem through electronic communication linkages to a central location from the remote sites. The model was to set up a central computer bulletin board system (CBBS) that was accessible through telephone hookups for all of the ethnographers (see Trotter 1986 for CBBS details and Chapter 17 in this book for future communication trends). The CBBS part of the model was not tested during the I and R Project because of budget cuts that prevented the purchase of a necessary piece of equipment. However, all of the separate parts of the model have been tested.

An electronic bulletin board program allows a microcomputer to accept incoming calls from another computer. The CBBS lets the user of a remote computer (1) receive or leave messages for any other person with access to the CBBS and (2) send text or program language files to the CBBS or receive them from it. Access to the CBBS can be open or restricted. The simplest restriction is to keep the telephone number for the CBBS private, but beyond that it is possible to restrict access by means of passwords and other devices.

The equipment needed to set up an electronic communications network for an ethnographic research project is (1) a microcomputer for each person who needs to communicate (or at least one at each site), (2) an electronic communications software package, (3) a modem, and (4) telephone access. The communication package contains programming that allows the ethnographer to compose messages then send or receive files and to configure a computer's communication parameters to those of the computer that is to receive the messages. The modem is a computer device that changes the computer's internal signals into signals that can be sent over the telephone. At the other end, another modem decodes the telephone communication and allows that computer to respond to messages sent from the remote site. In order to use a CBBS, someone at a "central location" hooks a computer and modem into a telephone line and starts up the bulletin board package. The computer waits for a call. When a call comes in, the CBBS allows or prevents access. The successful caller has the opportunity to pick up (and store on his or her computer) any messages that have been left and to leave messages for one or more persons that he or she needs to contact. The person also has the opportunity to "pick up" any files that have been left and to leave files that need to be stored in the central location or transferred to someone else in the network.

The ideal situation for the I and R contract would have been to have had the ethnographers call in about every three days and "download" a copy of their field notes for that time period. They would have received messages from other individuals on the project asking for specific types of information, or responding to queries about earlier information. They would also have been able to leave messages any time the CBBS was running (that is, up to twenty-four hours a day) about what resources they needed, to ask the other ethnographers questions, or to request help on a particular topic or on a nonemergency basis. In addition to the rapid communication and responsiveness to the project needs it enabled, it was also thought that a CBBS system would have alleviated some of the unnecessary stress of fieldwork that comes from isolation.

Instead of fully implementing this model at the ideal level, we ended up compromising. We used telephone communication to pass on verbal requests for information and help. The ethnographers mailed their computer disks with field notes to the central office. The telephone part of this communication system depended on both parties being there at the same time (in some cases we were involved in conference calls that had eight people hooked together). This made communication much more difficult to accomplish on a regular basis. Using the CBBS model, long messages can be composed on any microcomputer and sent at electronic speeds over the phone at a time when the other person is not available. Then the other party can call in at his or her convenience, get the message, and reply without a significant delay. The asynchronous communication of the CBBS would have increased the frequency and the quality of communication in the I and R Project and would do so in any other multiple researcher project where sharing is the key to success.

The CBBS does not eliminate the need for occasional voice communication and a rare letter or package of printed materials. Some things are easier to discuss or resolve directly. However, having most of the facts or issues transmitted through a CBBS system beforehand can make the occasional call much more productive.

Mailing in the computer disks worked for the I and R Project. It did slow our ability to share information because the ethnographers tended to wait and send in several disks at a time rather than sending a steady stream of files. That increased the amount of time it took to print and return the hard copies of the files, and it increased the amount of material that had to be read and summarized, rather than keeping it in more manageable pieces. Our system worked, but the CBBS system should stand as the ideal model—with mail and voice communication retained as an important backup.

The CBBS system can also work for single ethnographer projects. For example, we have set up a CBBS at our university that can be used by graduate students and faculty doing remote research projects.[6] They can leave messages, store data files for safekeeping, send calls for help, and so on. There is no reason, with time, money, and a friend to regularly turn the system on, that this system could not work for virtually anyone. Even overseas communication is possible, although expensive.

Sophisticated alternatives to the CBBS system of data transportation are also available. These alternatives involve the use of computer tele-communications networks. Some are regional, but most are either national or international in scope. Cost varies, but anthropologists can maintain linkages with colleagues through communications systems such as Bitnet (a network linking over 500 universities in the United States and in many foreign countries), instead of setting up their own CBBS network. The decision about which type of computer communication system to use depends on the project. The funding level of the project and the location where it will take place are probably the two key variables that shape the decision about the type of data transportation system that can and should be used.

DATA MANIPULATION

The issue of data manipulation brings this chapter full circle. It would be unwise to plan for data analysis without carefully considering how it is going to be collected, stored, and transported—and vice versa. Before computers are taken into the field, the structure that the field notes will take must be at least partially decided, with some natural room left for modifications required by the reality of the fieldwork itself (Bernard et al. 1986; Wood 1987).

One of the most common things that anthropologists do with data after they record it is to take descriptive chunks of it from one place or another and bring all of the pertinent pieces together for both analysis and write-up. This is the "cut-and-paste" stage of data manipulation. It is often a time-consuming mess. Virtually every ethnographer I know has sat in a blizzard of paper shards trying to create coherent piles for analysis, for an article or a book. I, myself, have experienced serious (if only temporary) psychic damage and loss of valuable time when some well-meaning person opened the door to my workroom at the wrong time, usually just after I opened the window to get some fresh air. The resulting draft unpiled three days' work.

One of the simplest advantages of computerized field notes is that the cutting and pasting can be done without filling a room with pieces of paper (see Wood 1987 and Chapter 5 in this volume for examples). With the proper computer software tools, all of the references to a particular cultural domain can be found and copied into a separate file for analysis or other use. One can collect all of the utterances of a particular informant into a single file or the utterances of all people of type X about subject Y. Or, the researcher can speedily accomplish complex searches that look for the occurrence of one variable (for example, economics) in conjunction with another variable somewhere in close proximity (for example, women's organizations). Files can be put into (or out of) chronological order. Superfluous parts can be eliminated. Observations can be grouped according to an important theoretical structure. What is done with the data depends on the ethnographer's theoretical orientation, data needs, and imagination. The computer accomplishes all of the time-consuming operations of ethnographic research much more rapidly than they could be done by hand.

Speeding up those operations alone is worth the investment in computerizing field notes. However, with ASCII files there are several other types of operations that can enhance the analysis of the data. Indexes of files or groups of files can help uncover the occurrences of particular words, phrases, and sequences of symbols. Existing programs can produce a concordance, create an index or concordance that retains contextual material around it (Wood 1984), count words, number lines, and interpose codes into various segments of existing field notes to aid analysis and cut-and-paste operations. Other programs allow files to be sent to a mainframe computer for many other aspects of content analysis.[7] Using some of the text-oriented databases that are now available, ethnographers can even perform some text-oriented statistical operations on the data.

There are several philosophies, or preferences, for managing anthropological field notes once they are created. All require that the ethnographer have some useful structure in mind for breaking down the data into usable units. One approach is to break up the units by chronology (dates, time of day, and so on). Another is to place codes at convenient points in the data as they are collected, so all of the information of a particular type can be found later. Another technique is to number pages, lines, and even words within the text for future reference. And another is to create separate files for certain types of information and give each type a label that identifies its key content. Computer-based field notes allow all of these to be done at the same time and allow for additional modifications to be made at a later date.

Once the units are set up, the philosophies for handling the data take over. Bernard and Evans (1983) recommend one of the simplest methods. They suggest printing out files with paragraphs and pages numbered. They then suggest setting up a separate computerized database that includes all of the key information found on each page and in each paragraph of the printed text. To recover data, the researcher queries the database, and the database program prints out the appropriate page and line of your physical field notes. The researcher flips through the pages to find the appropriate segments of data for analysis and write-up and if necessary copies them. This method is a fast way to find where the information is, but the speed of using the data depends on how fast the pages can be physically turned. This procedure is probably one of the more effective ways of employing computer-assisted access to field note files that are already typed on paper, since retyping up to 10,000 or more pages is a Herculean task that might have limited return. On the other hand, for as yet uncollected field data, the other options that are available may be more appropriate—ones that use the full power of the computer.

A second method of working with field notes is incorporated into the philosophy of computer programs that allow ethnographers to compose field notes, number the lines, and code segments of the data, all as a part of a data manipulation program (Wood 1987). Searching the data and copying the data out into a separate file for other use can all be accomplished in the same operation.

The first option involves setting up a database of appropriate codes separate from your field notes, and the second involves having a program that allows you to code alongside the field notes as a part of the same file. A third approach is also possible. In this option, codes are embedded in the text of the field notes at appropriate intervals, and the total field note file is imported into a text-oriented database program (Wood 1987). The text-oriented database supports searches (including Boolean commands), cut-and-paste, some counts and indexing operations, and other similar options for data manipulation. In many ways, this option allows the power of a computer to be brought more fully to bear on field note management than either of the first two options. It, combined with indexing, concordance, and other content analysis features, points the direction that the software will take in the near future.

SUMMARY AND CONCLUSIONS

Based on the field tests conducted as a part of the Pennsylvania I and R Project, we conclude that existing computer-based technology is a successful tool for ethnographic data recording, storage, transportation, and analysis. Although we recommend printed copies of field notes in addition to multiple copies of computer-filed field notes (a case of wearing both belt and suspenders), it would be possible to conduct a "safe" ethnography virtually without the use of pen and paper. In the case of the I and R Project, the field notes were entered directly into computers and not printed until much later. Summaries of the field notes were recorded by the ethnographers on computer disk, combined with background information (also on computer disk), and edited several times before they were printed out as the draft final report. After review, corrections were made to the computer file, and the final report was sent for typesetting—again on computer disk and without the need for hard copy. It would have been possible to conduct the entire project without ever putting anything on paper until the final report was printed.

The enormous time savings we gained from the use of computers on the project made our experiment worthwhile. The data are now readily available for further analysis and easy write-up, which would not be as true of paper files. We can do future linguistic analyses of migrants' utterances, and we can test hypotheses with content analysis. We can provide summaries of data not covered in the project report (data not directly germane to the education of migrant children but certainly vital information for understanding migrant life-styles). Almost daily we are finding other potential uses of the data—projects that are feasible because the information is already stored in computer-accessible form.

The physical piles of data I have collected during other projects are daunting. After a couple of articles, there is a certain amount of burnout from simply handling the data. I predict that the same will be true of the migrant data but not as soon. The migrant data will see more use, in an anthropological sense of pursuing theoretical issues, than it would have seen if not already in computer storage. In the meantime, the overall experiment of using computers as the primary data recording tool for an extensive ethnography can be considered a success.

NOTES

1. The other ethnographers were, in alphabetical order, Mary Felegy, Marcela Gutierrez-Mayka, and Anita Wood.

2. The I and R Project was a Chapter I (Migrant), 143c project of the U.S. Office of Education was funded through the Pennsylvania State Department of Education, Migrant Education Division. Project reports and the training products for the project can be requested from Dr. Manuel Recio, Director, Migrant Education Division, Pennsylvania State Department of Education, 333 Market Street, Harrisburg, PA 17108.

3. The final report for the project was a ninety-seven-page ethnography. It was first presented at the twentieth anniversary celebration for the Migrant Education Program, in Washington, DC. That occasion was used to brief staff members from various federal agencies that provide services to migrant farm workers, brief congressional staffs and congressional leaders from key states, support the reauthorization of the program, and prepare the way for congressional hearings later in the year. The next day the information was presented in a key policy forum. The individuals present included the

Assistant Secretary of Education, U.S. Office of Education, and all of the State Directors of Migrant Education in the United States, as well as members of their staffs. In addition, the staff of the federal program office were present.

4. The three ethnographers involved in the field collection for the I and R Project did not take printers with them. Printers were not compatible with the mobility needed for the project—although mobile printers now exist and are widely used—and the project suffered from a limited amount of capital equipment funds. The ethnographers submitted field notes to the central office where data summaries were made and printed copies of the notes were shipped back to their remote sites.

5. The word processor used for field note creation and storage on the I and R Project was a "freeware" program called PCWRITE. It is easy to learn, has lots of academic users (so help is readily available), and creates straight ASCII files. We are now providing copies of it to our graduate students and requiring that they use it or some other program to turn in assignments for selected graduate classes in our applied anthropology program.

6. There are both commercial and public domain (free) bulletin board programs available. The one set up in Northern Arizona University's Anthropology Department is called Fido and is a very sophisticated public domain program that allows electronic mail and file transfer functions to be accomplished easily.

7. There are a number of sources of suggestions for computer-based content analysis, such as Agar (1983), Dennis (1984), Eguchi (1987), Gillespie (1986), J. Wood (1987), M. Wood (1980, 1984), and Werner (1982), among others.

CHAPTER FIVE

Using ETHNOGRAPH in Field Note Management

ROBERT L. BEE
BENJAMIN F. CRABTREE

Bee and Crabtree use a type of text analysis software that is made possible by the rapid search capabilities of the computer. They show us clearly how the organization of field notes can be simplified and, at the same time, made more meaningful. The type of software they use can even suggest ways of looking at field notes that might not have been so obvious when using index cards and handwritten notes.

In the premicrocomputer era, the typing, coding, storage, and retrieval of ethnographic data, particularly qualitative data, were major logistical hassles that few novices thought much about. Only when they sat down to work over their first day's scribbled field notes, or perhaps later when they tried to find that perfect quote from an informant's monologue, did they feel an unanticipated sense of frustration. The qualitative ethnographic data that concern us here are those derived from such sources as structured or unstructured interviews with informants, detailed observations of events, or daily journal entries—anything, in short, that involves fairly extensive written or tape-recorded narrative. If these data are to be useful at all, then they must be repeatedly accessible and, above all, coded or indexed so that needed portions can be quickly identified without having to plow through an entire narrative.

QUALITATIVE RESEARCH OPERATIONS

There are at least three variants of basic qualitative research operations using narrative material. First, an analyst can use several raters who independently score or code a particular text for indications of described qualities, patterns, or themes, such as affect (for example, "pleasure," "pain," "hostility," "nurturance"). Typically, the raters infer the quality from described behavior, feelings, or the context of particular comments in the text. Such analysis can yield subtle insights into significant, if sometimes unintentional, social messages sent by individuals or groups in particular social settings. They can also lead to the development of hypotheses to be tested using other segments of text or from further fieldwork. Such analysis demands a high level of interrater reliability.

A second research operation centers more directly on the context within which comments or particular types of interaction occur. Analysts can gain insights into linkages between events or informants' perceptions of events—perhaps several basic themes—that would otherwise not be apparent. For example, texts from a study of a Native American community might reveal that informants' mention of community factions almost always leads to ruminations about native leaders' ability to speak the native language. This contextual analysis suggests a linkage between factionalism and a preoccupation with the persistence of traditional ways. The linkage might be less apparent if the comments on the factions and the language ability had been assigned to separate coded categories. In this type of qualitative operation, interrater reliability is less an issue because inference about the quality or the affect being conveyed is not as basic for assigning coded categories.

A third type of qualitative research operation is more general and straightforward: coding the text according to readily apparent descriptive categories such as "kinship terminology," "funeral ceremony," or "Community Health Representative activities." Here the objective is to gain quick access to all portions of the narrative that fit a particular category. There is no concern with the frequency of certain expressions or affect or with contextual linkage.

These three types of operations—searching for (1) qualities or patterns, (2) contexts, and (3) descriptive categories—can all be used with the same basic narrative. They might form an analytical sequence beginning with the creation of a codebook of basic categories, expanding the codebook to include patterns and themes, and moving the analysis of categories and patterns within contexts (Miles and Huberman 1984). The type of operation may depend on the stage of investigation in the fieldwork process. Conducting ongoing fieldwork may impose different demands than analysis of field notes and interview transcripts after the researcher has left the field. Data manipulation may be simply searching for key words, or it may be part of an iterative process of hypothesis formation and testing (Agar 1982, 1986; Bernard 1988; Lincoln and Guba 1985; Miles and Huberman 1984; Werner and Schoepfle 1987a, 1987b). Depending on the type of operation, computer software requirements may vary.

Qualitative ethnographic data collection has been a basic ingredient in sociocultural anthropology since its emergence as a discipline in the nineteenth century. The voluminous notes accumulated by scholars like Franz Boas and Margaret Mead demanded an organizational and retrieval scheme. However, they relied mainly on ethnographic insight. We think that it is largely this insight that continues to make anthropology unique among the social sciences. Detailed qualitative observations create a necessary context within which to evaluate quantitative data. Extensive personal narratives can reveal insights and relationships that quantitative data could not possibly detect or analyze. These functions are apart from the fundamental importance of the analysis of qualitative data for endeavors such as cross-cultural comparisons, ethnohistory, assessment of developmental change, folklore, and more. Analysis can come only after the data have been organized and made easily accessible.

USING ETHNOGRAPH TO ANALYZE TEXT

In this chapter we explore the use of the computer for organizing ethnographic field notes and the subsequent search and retrieval of specific passages. We focus on a software program called ETHNOGRAPH, which is familiar to us and meets our needs well. With some variation in syntax, the basic functions of this program may be transferable to similar programs on the market.

The examples used in this chapter come from a long-term study of federal programs and community development on a Native American reservation. The research data come from extensive structured and unstructured interviews with numerous individuals over a twenty-five-year period, as well as documentary materials and government and tribal statistics. A major task in any effort to analyze these data is to retrieve relevant portions—*all* relevant portions—bearing on a particular subject quickly. These portions might include all interviews with a single informant such as "John Dooley" that span several years or all information on a particular program such as the Community Health Representative (CHR) effort. Below we will follow a segment from a single interview with "Dooley" from the typing through the coding processes in ETHNOGRAPH format, in order to illustrate how the computer can, and sometimes cannot, relieve some of the drudgery that precedes actual ethnographic analysis.

THE MECHANICS OF FIELD NOTE MANAGEMENT: OLD AND NEW

In all cases the material must first be typed from the original handwritten or tape-recorded field notes to make it easier to read, code, and retrieve. Before the availability of microcomputers, the typing operation could not begin *without* deciding how the material was to be organized for coding. There were two options: Either the narrative could be coded before typing, then broken up into separate typed sheets, each with its own subject code, or the narrative could be typed as a unit, then coded.

Typing the narrative as a unit is far more useful. It preserves the context within which remarks, incidents, or observations are made. However, if the narrative covers more than three or four subjects and one uses standard 8-1/2 × 11 inch typing paper, then the need for multiple copies creates a serious logistical logjam: Does one photocopy multiple copies of the narrative and code each differently, for example? In time, this puts a tremendous strain on storage space for larger studies. Retrieval is also time consuming and cumbersome: One must go to the file drawer, pull the proper file, and search through the documents to find the narrative and the coded portion of the narrative one wishes to use.

Index cards with preprinted numbers along perforated margins solve some of the problems of keeping notes on standard manu-script paper. The entire narrative can be typed on a series of cards, then coded, and the codes can be punched into the numbered per-forations on the margins. There are several alternatives available commercially,[1] but the basic principle involves using a special punch tool to cut a clear channel from a perforation to the edge of the card so that, when a large needle is passed through a stack of cards at that particular numbered perforation, the cards bearing that code will fall free when the stack is lifted by the needle. This method avoids the multiple-copy problem (except as needed for protecting against accidental loss of the data). This drastically reduces the amount of re-quired storage space. Once a researcher becomes adept at wielding the needle, the retrieval is relatively fast. The marked perforations along the margins do not permit much coding complexity, so two or three or more passes with the needle might be needed to find the wanted passage.

One of the present authors (Bee) has used the card system for years. The coding system is based on Murdock's *Outline of Cultural Materials* subject file (1961) and is amended to fit particular cir-cumstances not covered in the *Outline*. It involves a two-digit general category code, then a one-digit subcategory code. For example, 66 is the general category code for "Political Behavior," which is de-fined in a short introductory paragraph. Codes 664 and 665 refer to "pressure politics" and "political parties," respectively, each with a brief paragraph of description of the sorts of behavior belonging in that category (Murdock 1961:97–98). The narrative is coded using indelible red ink in the left margin of the cards as well as cutting channels to the perforations around the margin. Any card typically contains several codes because the entire narrative is typed as a unit. Therefore, after the needle sort, it is necessary to scan the written codes to find the particular one desired. This is time consuming, but in the precomputer days it was worth the price of keeping the narrative as a unit.

COMPUTER-AIDED SOLUTIONS

The microcomputer dramatically speeds the process of preparing, coding, and retrieving the narrative. The inevitable chore of typing field notes is made easier with a word-processing program, and beyond the word processor are text management programs with more refined indexing capabilities that add further dimensions to processing field notes and interview transcripts.

There are several basic types of text management programs: (1) those that conduct word searches with varying levels of sophistication, (2) text-oriented database managers, and (3) those that operate on the basis of coding categories and patterns imposed on the narrative text by analysts (Brent et al. 1987; Gerson 1986; Pfaffenberger 1988). Keeping in mind the types of qualitative data operations mentioned at the outset, one kind of text management program may be better than another for some types of operations. Word-search programs (for example, askSam, WORDCRUNCHER) can be quite good for locating expressions of affect or other qualities *as long as the same or similar words are used to express the quality.* Some of the word-search programs also offer sophisticated contextual analysis—again, as long as the focus is on particular words rather than semantic homologies that use a wide variety of alternative words.[2] Some coding can even be added to the text to include patterns and themes, but generally, unless the more obvious descriptive categories are clearly indicated by key words in the text, the word-search alternative is not particularly efficient at identifying content categories. Pfaffenberger (1988) provides useful descriptions of many of these programs and points out both the advantages and the disadvantages.

Although word-search programs can be a real boon for literary or legal research, the major disadvantage of these types of programs for ethnographers is the possibility that important data will be overlooked simply because the searched-for word is not included in the passage. An informant could give an extremely hostile portrayal of a particular medical crisis, but unless *criticism* or *anger* or *crisis* or *shortcoming* or some other anticipated synonym actually occurs in the monologue, the passage would not be retrieved for analysis.

The word-search programs do allow an analyst to move fairly quickly from field note typing to the process of extracting portions of the narrative for analysis. This is a significant advantage over the second type of data-retrieval program that requires a fairly lengthy process of coding the entire text before it can be analyzed.

Text-oriented database management programs, such as Notebook II, are discussed by Pfaffenberger (1988) and resemble database managers used in business. "Fields" are expanded so that large amounts of text can be entered. However, their inability to search beyond a single file at a time seems like a tremendous constraint. Pfaffenberger advises caution in selecting these programs (1988:47). A review of Notebook II by Becker (1985) should be read before considering this type of program.

We have found that the added time and effort required for the coding of text are usually worth it for the sorts of data we typically use. There is greater flexibility and retrieval reliability because the codes are based on content, not just the words used. Typically, in extensive research projects the coding of the same material can be successively refined to accomplish increasingly abstract facets of the analysis: The basis for the codes and the codes themselves both change (Miles and Huberman 1984:56–57). This means that the narrative must inevitably be coded at some point, whether earlier or later in the analysis. Why, then, invest in two separate kinds of software packages when one—the analyst-coded program—will accomplish the same objectives? Again, this applies to ethnographic data used in a particular analytical manner; other sorts of data and/or other analytical objectives may be best served by word-search programs.

As noted earlier, our discussion is based on the use of ETHNOGRAPH, a data-coding and retrieval software marketed by Qualis Research Associates (Seidel et al. 1988). We use an IBM-XT compatible microcomputer with 640K RAM memory that has a single 5-1/4 inch floppy disk drive and a 20-megabyte hard drive.[3]

ETHNOGRAPH is strictly an indexing program and includes no word-processing functions. Field notes must first be typed using a word-processing program or an editor. We use a common word processor, WordPerfect (Version 4.1), for purposes of this discussion. We will also look at some advantages offered by a general purpose editor, Kedit (Version 3.51).

Field Note Typing

The maximum record length (the number of characters allowed in a line, or the line length) permissible in ETHNOGRAPH is 40 bytes or characters, so as to allow inclusion of codes in the right margins. Therefore, the margins in WordPerfect were set at 3 on the left and 39 on the right. When the text is printed or appears on the screen it will be less than half a page wide; the field notes after typing would look something like Table 5.1.

The completed field notes are then saved as a DOS text file designated with a file extension of .ETH. In this case we use "C:\ETHNO\DOOLEY86.ETH" (a file with the name Dooley86 and an extension of ETH in the ETHNO subdirectory on drive C). This file must not contain any non-ASCII characters, such as those produced by many word-processing programs when specifying printing functions (for example, underscoring and boldfacing text). Most programs are capable of "stripping out" these special characters. For example, in WordPerfect you use CTRL-F5 and Option 2.

TABLE 5.1 *Sample field notes in .ETH format*

```
Jim Dooley  8 July 1982   Telecon at ca 10 PM

CHR program is "going out." Funding
to be cut (allegedly) on 1 Sept.  The
local grant people are trying to look
for block grants.  Would like to see
the alcohol halfway house and CHR as
one program.  ADAP program has gone
down quite a bit.  "Friendship
(halfway) house is doing pretty good,
but it's also under IHS."

The local grantsman (non-Indian) is
hired by ANA; will be phasing out at
the end of this month.  By 1 October
1982 perhaps there will be a new
budget outlook.  (Apparently the
September cut is a rumor; by October
the picture may be much brighter.)
```

After typing field notes it is a good idea to back up these .ETH files on a floppy disk. We do *not* recommend an erasure of the .ETH document once it has been numbered and coded by the ETHNOGRAPH procedure (as suggested in the manual) unless it has been backed up. The ETHNOGRAPH manual suggests erasure as a way to cut down on storage, but we have found the .ETH document to be invaluable even after numbering and coding. The reason is that when the ETHNOGRAPH numbering and coding procedures have been performed, the .ETH version of the document can be legibly retrieved by WordPerfect without numbers or codes and is therefore easily incorporated into later text. It also allows for a clean text to be independently audited.

Once the field notes have been entered using a word-processing program or editor, the operations shift to the ETHNOGRAPH program. The first step is to create a numbered version of the field note document, in which each line of text is numbered. This is fairly rapid and straightforward, since the ETHNOGRAPH menu does a good job of leading one through the process. This numbered version (Table 5.2) must be printed so that the user has a hard copy of the document for the next step.

Field Note Coding

Next is the coding operation, probably the most time consuming and critical of all the operations except for typing the final draft of the field notes themselves. The user pencils in the codes for the various segments of the document directly on the printed copy of the numbered version.

T A B L E 5.2 *Numbered version (.NUM) of an EHTNOGRAPH file.*

```
Jim Dooley 8 July 1982   Telecon           1
at ca. 10 PM.                              2

CHR program is "going out."  Funding       4
to be cut (allegedly) on 1 Sept.  The      5
local grant people are trying to look      6
for block grants.  Would like to see       7
the alcohol halfway house and CHR as       8
one program.  ADAP program has gone        9
down quite a bit.  "Friendship            10
{halfway} house is doing pretty good,     11
but it's also under IHS."                 12

The local grantsman (non-Indian) is       14
hired by ANA; will be phasing out at      15
the end of this month.  By 1 October      16
1982 perhaps there will be a new          17
budget outlook.  (Apparently the          18
September cut is a rumor; by October       19
the picture may be much brighter.)        20

CETA is out except for some state         22
involvement.  Apparently there's          23
still some training for nurses' aide      24
positions.                                25
```

This is done on the right side of the text, using brackets to indicate the lines of the text to be given a particular code. ETHNOGRAPH permits multiple coding of a single segment, as well as "nesting" of segments using one or more codes within the longer segments bearing a different code. Table 5.3 illustrates both the multiple coding of a single segment and the "nesting" feature. For example, in our sample text in Table 5.4 lines 4 through 25 cover material in two different coding categories, M478 and M659 (designated with the #). Within that segment are three other categories—M733 (lines 4–12), M647 (lines 14–20), and M464 (lines 22–25)—that are "nested" within the longer coded segment extending from line 4 to line 25. Naturally, even more specific categories could be "nested" within these as shown in Table 5.3; coded segments can range in size from one line ot the total number of lines in the file.

The codes themselves can be whatever the user devises. Those in the examples are an adaptation of Murdock's *Outline of Cultural Materials* code; the "M" preceding the numbers is a device to get around ETHNOGRAPH's unwillingness to accept a digit as the first character of a code.[4] Except for this, any combination of letters and numbers or letters alone will serve as codes. Some analysts may prefer to use key

TABLE 5.3 *Schematic diagram of overlapping/nested codes*

```
------------------------- 52 -|1
------------------------- 53  |-------|5
------------------------- 54  |-|2     |-|6
------------------------- 55  | |-|3   | |
------------------------- 56  | | |-|4| |-|7
------------------------- 57  | | | | | | |
------------------------- 58 -| | | | | | |
------------------------- 59    | | | | | |
------------------------- 60    | | | |-|-|
------------------------- 61    |-| | |
------------------------- 62    |   | |
------------------------- 63    |   | |
------------------------- 64    |---| |
------------------------- 65    |-----|
------------------------- 66 ---|
```

SOURCE: *The ETHNOGRAPH Manual,* p. 6-4.

TABLE 5.4 *Coded version of an ETHNOGRAPH file*

```
Jim Dooley 8 July 1982   Telecon        1
at ca. 10 PM.                           2

#-M478       #-M659          $-M733
CHR program is "going out." Funding     4  -#-$
to be cut (allegedly) on 1 Sept.  The   5   | |
local grant people are trying to look   6   | |
for block grants.  Would like to see    7   | |
the alcohol halfway house and CHR as    8   | |
one program.  ADAP program has gone     9   | |
down quite a bit.  "Friendship         10   | |
{halfway} house is doing pretty good,  11   | |
but it's also under IHS."              12   |-$
                                             |
$-M647
The local grantsman (non-Indian) is    14   |-$
hired by ANA; will be phasing out at   15   | |
the end of this month.  By 1 October   16   | |
1982 perhaps there will be a new       17   | |
budget outlook.  (Apparently the       18   | |
September cut is a rumor; by October   19   | |
the picture may be much brighter.)     20   |-$
                                             |
$-M464
CETA is out except for some state      22   |-$
involvement.  Apparently there's       23   | |
still some training for nurses' aide   24   | |
positions.                             25  -#-$
```

words rather than number/letter codes (see Miles and Huberman 1984, for some codebook alternatives). Here we use M647 as a code for "administrative agencies," M652 as a code for "public finance-budget," M659 as a code for "miscellaneous government activities," and M478 as a code for "economic development programs–general." ETHNOGRAPH codes can be up to ten characters long and can contain embedded blanks.

Once this penciling process—called "code mapping"—has been completed, the codes are typed into the ETHNOGRAPH for the document. Again, the menu makes this relatively easy. The program gives users frequent opportunities to recheck their entries to be sure the codes have been typed accurately.[5] Table 5.4 illustrates the coded version when it is printed.

The coding process using ETHNOGRAPH is not unlike the action required to code index cards. In both cases the coder must decide which codes apply to a particular segment, then write those codes by hand in the margin of the document. The codes must then be entered a second time—by punching openings in the proper perforations on the margin of the cards or by typing the codes and the inclusive line numbers into the computer. This similarity helps make the transition from cards to computer less traumatic, even if no less time consuming. However, once the codes are entered, the similarity ends.

Searching and Retrieving Text Segments

Searching this coded document and others for particular segments of coded data is relatively simple and fast. ETHNOGRAPH's on-screen sequence of instructions is clear. The analyst enters the names of all files to be searched, then the codes for the needed data. According to its producers, in a single search ETHNOGRAPH can cover up to eighty files and look for up to eighty single codes. We have never come close to requiring those maximums in our search procedures.

With Version 3.0 of ETHNOGRAPH, a user may either view the searched segments on the monitor screen or send them directly to the printer or disk. One can also have it both ways: view the searched segments in sequence on the monitor, and decide as each segment appears whether to print it, send it to a disk file, or simply move on to the next segment. This is a real improvement over earlier versions, which simply printed all segments bearing the same code without first sending them to the monitor screen for viewing. This built up a pile of wasted paper and actively discouraged users from searching several documents in a single sweep.

We asked to search the DOOLEY86 file for all data coded "M647" (administrative agencies), and the ETHNOGRAPH produced Table 5.5. The first line identitities the document file name and the first words of the segment. The next two lines of numbers note that the segment bears

T A B L E 5 . 5 *Segment file (.SEG) produced by a search*

```
  DOOLEY86    The local

  E: #-M478        #-M659

  C: $-M647        $-M652

  SV: M647


  : The local grantsman (non-Indian) is    14 |-$
  : hired by ANA; will be phasing out at   15 |  $
  : the end of this month.  By 1 October   16 |  $
  : 1982 perhaps there will be a new       17 |  $
  : budget outlook.  (Apparently the       18 |  $
  : September cut is a rumor; by October    19 |  $
  : the picture may be much brighter.)     20 |-$
```

other codes as well and gives all the codes that apply to the segment along with their symbols. The "SV" line shows the particular code(s) ("sort variables") entered to locate this segment. To the right of the segment text are the line numbers and the symbol for code "M647."

Opting to send the segment to disk preserves it on the hard disk as a "SEG" subfile of the file being searched. (The user is not asked to supply a different file name or to designate which disk is to receive the segment.) Later the entire segment can be incorporated directly into a manuscript by creating a second window in WordPerfect, retrieving the segment from ETHNOGRAPH as a second document, blocking the text of the segment, cutting the block, returning to the first document, and retrieving the blocked-out text. The coding symbols will have to be deleted, but the whole operation is still faster and more accurate than retyping lengthy segments from hard copy. Alternatively, as noted earlier, one could note the file name and line numbers of the segments and then retrieve from the original .ETH file.

The need for retrieving segments and quotes from field notes presents some special problems. The ideal system is one with the smallest break in concentration, that is, where the field notes can be searched and specific quotes rapidly located. The microcomputer provides excellent facilities in this regard. In a word-processing program such as Word-Perfect, it is possible to "drop back" into DOS, run another program, and then return to the original program and job.[6] In the newer 3.0 Version of ETHNOGRAPH it is possible to search a file, look at the results of the search on the screen, save needed segments as a disk file, return

to DOS, and reenter WordPerfect. By editing the ETHNOGRAPH segment as a second document (placed at the lower half of the screen),
or simply retrieving the lines you want into your file, it is possible to
quote directly without retyping.

DISCUSSION

Here we have focused on just one type of operation on a data set, the
most basic or "descriptive" type. As others have noted, the typical analytical process passes through several phases and more than one operation. Thus, the most basic descriptive operation covered in this chapter
would conceivably come early in the analytical process. As the analysis
proceeds, the bases for the codes and the codes themselves typically
change, becoming more "pattern seeking" and "context oriented." However, the machine tasks remain largely the same. To illustrate, one might
add to the codes for the narrative passage shown in Table 5.4 a more
general and inferential "pattern code" such as FUNDANX (for "funding
anxiety"). This would not be in the Murdock system but would flag
a passage that fits a more general analytical pattern that a user wants
to describe.

One problem faced by ETHNOGRAPH users is storage. The text files
are narrow and thus take up more space. The number of pages of paper
printed from the numbered and coded files is a particular problem. For
example, we downloaded onto a floppy disk a twenty-page, double-
spaced, mainframe word-processing SCRIPT file, which had 533 lines
extending as far as column 74. Using Kedit, we transformed it, using
a format command, into a file with a maximum record length of sixty-
four columns, which could be read by WordPerfect as a normal-size
WordPerfect file. This file was reduced to 506 lines by omitting the lines
for the SCRIPT word-processing commands. In order to transform this
file into an .ETH file, the line lengths were further reduced to forty columns. As a result, a file that began with 506 lines on eighteen double-
spaced pages ended up as a document of 778 lines that was close to
twenty-eight double-spaced pages long. As mentioned earlier, the
ETHNOGRAPH manual suggests that the .ETH file be erased. However,
for segment retrieval, the .ETH file is the easiest to work with, since
it is identical to the .NUM file but does not have all the codes that come
with the .SEG file. Unfortunately, the line numbers of a normal line
length file (for example, WordPerfect's sixty-four columns) differ
dramatically from the .ETH file because of the forty-column constraint.

Many potential users of ETHNOGRAPH will also be mainframe users
who will wish to upload or download files to and from PCs. It is becoming increasingly common for documents to be sent from one university to another, or even to publishers, via computer networks such as
Bitnet. However, documents received through Bitnet will be standard

ASCII files, so the record length can be wider than the sixty-four columns used by word processors such as WordPerfect. We found a general purpose editor, such as Kedit, to be invaluable in reformatting text to conform to the constraints of an ETHNOGRAPH .ETH file. It was simple to edit a mainframe file and reformat text to margin requirements.

A general purpose editor can also be integrated with ETHNOGRAPH, although word-processing functions are limited. In Kedit it is possible to give DOS commands (for example, running the ETHNOGRAPH program) without leaving the editor. It also has the capability of cutting blocks of text from the bottom file of a split screen and copying them into the top file without the need for editing out the codes in a .SEG file. For example, in Table 5.4 we could transfer only the field note text without the other information provided.

There is no way to avoid the mechanics of typing the field notes from handwritten or tape-recorded originals. And, there is no automatic method of coding the typed notes, so "code mapping" or a similar task must inevitably be performed manually—unless one is content with the word-search alternatives. What the computer can do is combine these two chores and dramatically speed up the sorting and retrieval processes of data management. The computer's speed and efficiency in incorporating large segments directly from coded field notes into manuscript drafts are noteworthy, as is the tremendous potential reduction in field data storage space. In short, the computer can simplify and greatly accelerate the logistics of getting to the analysis stage of ethnographic data. However, the computer will not analyze the data. That is still up to the anthropologist who, using the computer, can spend far less time sorting and more time analyzing than Lewis Henry Morgan, Franz Boas, or Alfred L. Kroeber would have imagined possible.

NOTES

1. The McBee system is perhaps the best known. One of the present writers (Bee) has used the E-Z Sort system with generally good results. The cards are available in several sizes and varieties of marginal markings/perforations.

2. Reviews of the various text analysis software programs regularly appear in journals such as *Qualitative Sociology* and *Computers and the Humanities*. For example, Brown (1987) reviews askSam Version 2.3 and Olsen (1987) WORDCRUNCHER. See Software Appendix and Resources Appendix for further information.

3. It should be noted that the program will function acceptably without a hard drive. We did find, however, that the number of diskettes required on a floppy drive system became excessive. The manual notes that although the maximum file size that can be handled is 9,999 lines, they recommend keeping files below 2,000 lines (or forty pages) because a floppy diskette can fill up because of the multiple files required by ETHNOGRAPH.

4. The Murdock code was used in these notes to make them compatible with other field notes from this same community entered on cards that date back to 1961. The coding has been elaborated and adapted to specific concerns, but it remains essentially Murdock's, with any changes carefully noted on the master coding list.

5. The numbered and coded versions of the document should be backed up on floppy disks and stored in separate locations for security.

6. In WordPerfect, for example, the F1 key puts you into DOS, where ETHNOGRAPH can then be run.

CHAPTER SIX

Data Entry and Management Techniques for Anthropologists: An Example Using dBASE IV in a Historic Preservation Project

WILLIAM WILSON

Cultural anthropologists, physical anthropologists, and archaeologists all collect specimens—of words, tools, bones, customs, or potsherds. In this chapter, Wilson shows us how to keep track of information about many items of the same general type and how we can find them, sort them, re-arrange them, and display them in the variety of ways made possible by database management software.

This chapter explores the use of microcomputer-based data management software programs for anthropological research and writing. Anthropologists, like other scientists, are often inundated with extremely large amounts of data that must be managed efficiently. Data entry and management can be simplified with the microcomputer-based tools that are now available. One of the most commonly used software packages is dBASE. The current release of dBASE at this writing is dBASE IV (DB4). Its use is examined in this chapter by addressing the following topics: (1) data entry techniques, (2) report generation, and (3) integration of dBASE IV with other software packages. Other database management programs are also described, including special data management programs called "spreadsheets."

BACKGROUND ON THE HISTORIC PRESERVATION PROJECT

In 1984, I was involved with Charles Hoffman of Northern Arizona University (NAU) in a historic preservation project. The purpose of the project was to study and identify potential historic resources existing in the residential areas of West Flagstaff, Arizona. This project was part of an ongoing study to help designate and nominate a section of West Flagstaff as a Historic District with the National Register of Historic Places.

During the course of the study, I became aware of the difficulties involved in retrieving information from the files. The file system was based on an NAU inventory number, which was, in turn, based on the year that the property was inventoried. If that year was unknown, the file had to be searched in its entirety to locate the required information. To solve this problem, I wrote an application program[1] to carry out the task of entering and maintaining the information that is contained on the Arizona State Historic Property form.[2] This form is submitted to the State Historic Preservation Office when a site is nominated for consideration by the National Register of Historic Places. It was also used as the starting point when researching a property that had been surveyed.

Figure 6.1 is a sample of the property information portion of page one of the Arizona State Historic Property Inventory (ASHPI) form. This form will be used as a reference in the discussion of how dBASE IV or a dBASE compatible product can be used to help track a historic property.

THE PURPOSE OF DATABASE MANAGEMENT PROGRAMS

Database management programs are intended to help organize and manipulate data. A database is simply a collection of related pieces of information. Database programs facilitate data entry for later statistical analysis, and some even provide minimal descriptive statistics, such as the calculation of means. They are not useful for more sophisticated statistical analyses that involve the interaction of several variables and the development of statistical models.

Tracking and managing historic properties (or any other type of museum information) can be more efficient with a computer-based filing system than with a manual filing system. When using a package like dBASE IV, a researcher can quickly find a specific piece of data, based on the information contained in the database. It is also possible to sort the information and produce detailed reports for use by government agencies, students, other researchers, museum specialists, or private contractors and benefactors.

SETTING UP A COMPUTER-BASED FILING SYSTEM USING dBASE IV

When a researcher considers using a database package to manage information, there are a number of terms that are useful in understanding how a database program works and in deciding whether such a program will be helpful. The following terms are used when defining and

ARIZONA STATE
HISTORIC PROPERTY INVENTORY

HISTORIC PROPERTY NAME	COUNTY	INVENTORY NO.
COMMON PROPERTY NAME	QUAD/COUNTY MAP	
PROPERTY LOCATION-STREET & NO.	CURRENT BLACK & WHITE PHOTOGRAPH	

CITY, TOWN/VICINITY OF	ASSESSOR'S PARCEL NO.
OWNER OF PROPERTY	PHONE
STREET & NO./P.O. BOX	
CITY, TOWN STATE ZIP	
FORM PREPARED BY	DATE
STREET & NO./P.O. BOX	PHONE
CITY, TOWN STATE ZIP	
PHOTO BY	DATE
VIEW	
HISTORIC USE	
PRESENT USE	ACREAGE
ARCHITECT/BUILDER	
CONSTRUCTION/MODIFICATION DATES	

PHYSICAL DESCRIPTION

FIGURE 6.1 *Arizona State Historic Property Inventory (ASHPI) form*

organizing the information that is to be stored in the database. Illustrations come from the Arizona State Historic computerized database of historic properties.

Character: A character is a single letter (upper or lowercase), number, or special symbol (that is, !@#$% and so on)

Field: A field is a collection of characters that describe or represent a specific type of information. On the ASHPI form, the historic property's name, county, dates, and acreage are examples of fields.

Record: A record is a collection of fields. When working with statistical packages, a record is also called a "case." Each record is composed of fields that will fully describe a specific item or person. For example, all of the information contained on the ASHPI form for a specific historic property would constitute a single record.

File: A file is a collection of records. For example, the state historic preservation file could contain all of the records or "forms" for a given group of historic sites in an area.

Database: A database is a collection of related files that are used to maintain the data for a given topic.

COMPUTERIZING THE DATA

A major concern when switching from a manual to a computer-based filing system or when setting up a new computerized system is how the data are to be stored in the computer. The Arizona State Historic Property Inventory form contains a number of different types of information. Each specific piece of information must be defined as an individual field in the database, and each field must be one of the data types listed below. All of the examples are from the Arizona State Historic Property Inventory form.

Numeric: This type of field is used to hold decimal or integer numbers. A decimal number is one that contains a decimal or fractional portion, and an integer is a number that contains only the whole part of the number. Acreage is a good example of a numeric type of field.

Date: A date field can only contain a date in the form of MM/DD/YY (month/date/year). Photo and preparation dates would be candidates for this type of field.

Char: Char or character fields contain normal printable information. This information includes the letters of the alphabet, digits, and special characters. Most fields, including names and addresses, would be of this type.

T A B L E 6.1 *ASHPI database definition*

Field Name	Type	Width	Usage
HPN	Char	30	Historic property name
CPN	Char	30	Common property name
STREET	Char	25	Street address
CITY	Char	20	City
APN	Char	10	Assessor parcel number
OWNER	Char	20	Owner name
Phone	Char	12	Owner phone
O_STREET	Char	25	Owner street address
O_CITY	Char	20	Owner city
O_STATE	Char	2	Owner state
O_ZIP	Char	5	Owner ZIP
PREPARER	Char	20	Preparer of forms
D_OF_PREP	Date	8	Date of preparation
P_PHONE	Char	12	Preparer's phone number
P_STREET	Char	25	Preparer's address
P_CITY	Char	20	Preparer's city
P_STATE	Char	2	Preparer's state
P_ZIP	Char	5	Preparer's ZIP
PHOTO_BY	Char	20	Photo taken by?
PHOTO_DATE	Date	8	Date photo taken
VIEW	Char	2	View of photo
HIST_USE	Char	80	Historic use
PRES_USE	Char	80	Present use
ACREAGE	Num	4.2	Size of lot
ARCH_BLDR	Char	40	Architect/builder
CON_MOD_DT	Char	20	Construction/modification dates
COUNTY	Char	10	County of location
INV_NUM	Char	10	Inventory number
QUAD	Char	40	Quadrangle of location
PHYS_DESC	Memo	10	Physical description
SIG_HIST	Memo	10	Significant history
BIBLIO	Memo	10	Bibliography
GEODAT	Memo	10	Geographical data
COMMENTS	Memo	10	General comments

Logical: This type of field can only contain a value that represents a true or false condition. This type of field is not currently used in the State Historic Preservation Inventory program.

Memo: Memo fields are used to store large blocks of text. The only limitation is that the field can hold only 4,000 characters. This type of field was most appropriate for textual descriptions of historic properties.

There is no strict rule on how to translate information into fields in a database, although there are a few guidelines that can be used. First, consider how much space is available for storage. This will limit the size of the data fields. A data field is an area in the database where a specific piece of information is stored. The size of the field must be set when defining the database for a specific project.

When data are then added to the field, the data can occupy any size up to the size of the field. For example, the Historic Property Name (HPN) field is set at thirty characters (Table 6.1 shows the database layout). This means that a property name can be up to thirty characters long. All of the lengths of the fields added together make up the record length. The record length will affect how much data can be stored on a disk. In the Arizona State Historic Preservation Inventory database, each record occupies 656 bytes (characters). This may seem to be adequate, but, because this must also include the memo fields, if all of the memo fields are full (4,000 characters of information per memo), the disk would hold only seventeen records. To solve a problem like this, a database can be split over multiple floppy disks. However, this can sometimes be inconvenient.

Selection of the type of data fields is also important. In general, the following rules apply: (1) Names, addresses, phone numbers, and short descriptions should be character fields. (2) Long descriptions should be memo fields. (3) All dates should be the date type of field. (4) Any numeric information such as counts, acreage, ages, or any field requiring calculations should be numeric fields. Data fields should be "mapped out" by hand on paper when first planning a database. Once the database structure has been laid out on paper, DB4 can then be used to create the database, and data entry can begin. When the DB4 program is started, the user will normally see a copyright for the program and then will be presented with the dBASE "DOT prompt," which signals a ready state when dBASE will take a new command.

DATA COLLECTION AND ENTRY

In order to enter and manage the data, the database must be defined, or created. Table 6.1 shows the file format (with the use of each field) of the Arizona State Historic Preservation Inventory database.[3] To fully illustrate the process of defining a database, the commands for creating the Arizona State Historic Preservation Inventory database, entering the data, and producing a property report will be discussed. These property reports can then be used for submission to the State Historic Preservation Office or for further research.

From the "DOT prompt," the CREATE command is the correct choice for building a new database. This command leads to the database definition screen where the field name, data type, and field size must be entered (Table 6.2). After defining the fields in the database, the next step is to start entering data. When APPEND is selected, a list of the previously defined variables is displayed down the left-hand side of the screen,[4] and the cursor[5] is placed next to the first field, indicating that data may be entered. When data entry is completed, control is returned to the "DOT prompt."

As with most data-entry operations, errors or omissions in data entry will need to be corrected and entries updated. The EDIT command is used to change the information already entered into a record.

T A B L E 6.2 *Database definition screen*

```
          Field Name  Type      Width  Dec
                      ─────────────────────
       1  HPN         Character  30
       2  CPN         Character  30
       3  STREET      Character  25
       4  CITY        Character  20
       5  APN         Character  10
       6  OWNER       Character  20
       7  PHONE       Character  12
       8  O_STREET    Character



   CREATE           |<G:>|ASHPI                   |Field: 8/8
                                Enter the field name.
```

RETRIEVING INFORMATION FROM THE DATABASE

When the data are entered correctly, the database may be queried for requested information. There are three basic ways of querying, or looking at, the information in the database, and they use the following three commands.

List: The LIST command compiles a list of the information that is housed in the database.

Display: The DISPLAY command is similar to the list command in that it prints out the information contained in the database. However, the DISPLAY command pauses at each screen full of information, whereas the LIST command does not.

Report: The REPORT command is used to compile a formatted report. This includes sorting, subtotals, totals, groups, and so on.

The main limitation of these commands is that they do not handle memo fields very well when directing output to the screen or printer. In order to handle memo fields efficiently, special custom reports must be written in the dBASE application development language (ADL), or with a special relational database report writer, which can be used in combination with dBASE. Except for quick queries to check the data (using the LIST or DISPLAY commands), the REPORT command is the most useful data output feature. Table 6.3 shows a sample report. Reports may be either displayed on the screen or printed.

T A B L E 6.3 *ASHPI sample report*

```
Page No. 1
07/07/87

            Structure Locations and Site Numbers

Historic Property Name     Address              Inventory
                                                Number

E. E. Ellinwood House     105 N. Park Ave.      NAU-83011
Coffin House              503 N. Leroux         NAU-79026
England House             624 W. Santa Fe
```

SORTING THE INFORMATION IN THE DATABASE

At times it is useful to produce reports with data in an order other than the order in which the information was entered. The INDEX command allows the sorting of database records into a specified order. Using the Arizona State Historic Preservation Inventory database, the records could be sorted by Historic Property Name, Owner of the Property, County, or Inventory or by any of the other fields.

Under dBASE there are two ways to sort information—using the INDEX and SORT commands. These two sorting procedures work in slightly different ways and produce different results. Indexing is a process where the user produces an index of the database, based on a specific field. (This is similar to card catalogs in a library where index cards are used by subject, title, or author.) For example, if a list of the properties based on the county and property name were required, and a permanent change to the order of the database were not necessary, INDEX would be appropriate to use. If a new order in the database were required—as in physically ordering the database by inventory number—then SORT would be most appropriate. Indexing does not physically alter the database, whereas sorting does. The SORT command is used to create a totally new file in the sorted order. With indexing, a separate file consisting of the index is created.

At any time, new information can be added to the database or old information can be updated. This process is similar to first entering information into the database. The APPEND or EDIT options can be selected to either add or edit information.

THE ASHPI PROGRAM

The Arizona State Historic Preservation Inventory computer program was developed to automate the process of data entry and retrieval. This program was written in the dBASE application development language (ADL). ADL permits the writing of customized applications (that is,

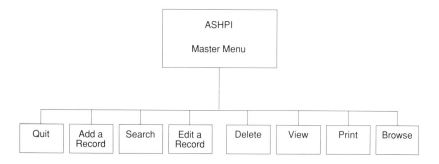

F I G U R E 6 . 2 *ASHPI program layout*

programs) and is much easier than using conventional programming languages.[6]

The commands shown earlier (such as LIST, DISPLAY, and REPORT) are actually part of ADL. If a series of commands are repeatedly used, then a program can be written to automate the process and cut down on the researcher's work. For example, specially tailored programs can be written for using a database, reindexing it (to sort the information on a specific field), adding or updating information, or producing reports. For full information on programs, refer to a manual on dBASE programming or to the documentation for a "relational report writer," which is a program package designed to produce dBASE reports quickly and easily.[7]

The Arizona State Historic Preservation Inventory program was written in ADL to provide a menu-driven facility for managing and reporting on historic properties.[8] The main menu has seven options, not including the exit facility. As is shown in Figure 6.2 and Table 6.4, the options for the menu include adding a record to the database, searching for a specific record in the database, editing a record, deleting a record, viewing a record, printing a record, or browsing through the database. When using the program for the first time, records must be added before using any of the other options.

The Arizona State Historic Preservation Inventory database was set up to pattern the Arizona State Historic Property Inventory forms, and the goal was to be able to print the forms directly using the program. Option 1 (add a record) leads to the Arizona State Historic Preservation Inventory data-entry screens (Table 6.5 shows the first of the entry screens). Like the RECORD ADD facility, the EDIT facility is for modifying the information on a property in the same layout used in the ADD screens. The only difficulty in using this facility is that the record number of the property must be known.[9] The Arizona State Historic Preservation Inventory provides three ways to find the record number. The first and most flexible is the SEARCH option on the main menu. Under the

T A B L E 6.4 *ASHPI program, main menu*

```
                 Arizona State Historic Property Inventory

                       Northern Arizona University
                         written by W. E. Wilson

                                 MENU

         1 - ADD A RECORD
         2 - SEARCH FOR A RECORD
         3 - EDIT A RECORD
         4 - DELETE A RECORD
         5 - VIEW A RECORD
         6 - PRINT A RECORD
         7 - BROWSE

                 ENTER NUMBER OF SELECTION OR Q TO QUIT


         Selection :
```

T A B L E 6.5 *ASHPI data entry screen*

```
              ***     ASHPI ENTRY SCREEN     ***

      HISTORIC PROPERTY NAME :
      COMMON PROPERTY NAME    :
      STREET LOCATION         :
      CITY  :                            ASSESSOR PARCEL NUMBER  :

              ***    OWNER INFORMATION    ***
      OWNER :                           PHONE :

      STREET :
      CITY    :                    STATE :         ZIP :

      ***     PREPARED BY     ***
      PREPARER :
      DATE OF PREP :    /  /
                              PHONE :
      STREET :                          CITY :
      STATE :              ZIP :
      PHOTO BY  :              DATE :    /  /      VIEW (I.E.
      NW,SE) :
```

SEARCH option there are two suboptions: to search on a single field or to search on multiple fields. A search can be made using many of the fields in the database, including inventory number, property name, county, address, and so on. Although it is possible to search memo fields using ADL, this feature was not implemented int he Arizona State Historic Preservation Inventory because of the difficulty involved. Two other facilities were included that can help in finding a record number: BROWSE and VIEW. The BROWSE facility is a standard dBASE feature. The VIEW facility for the Arizona State Historic Preservation Inventory displays only one record at a time and does not allow any data modification.

dBASE IV AND SQL

Structured Query Language (SQL) was originally developed by IBM in the mid-1970s. Since that time a number of other companies have adopted the SQL standard. This allows the user to create programs that can be easily moved from one machine to another, including mainframes.

SQL is a special database language that allows a researcher to work with the data as logical sets called relations (tables). SQL supplies a very small, yet concise, set of commands that will allow the manipulation of these tables (in dBASE a table can equate to a single database that has been created). These manipulations include adding new information to a table, updating a table, relating multiple tables, and viewing information in a table(s). SQL was not used for the ASHPI because it was not available at the project's inception. For more information on SQL, refer to the dBASE IV manual or a manual on SQL.

ALTERNATIVES TO USING dBASE IV

Although the dBASE IV package is expensive, it can be purchased for instruction and class work for about one-third of the retail price. There are a number of less expensive alternatives, including shareware, public domain database managers, and spreadsheet packages, that perform some of the features of dBASE IV.[10] Most of the packages allow data entry, modification, and report generation but normally lack an application development language or sophisticated sorting and selection criteria. They are usually limited in the amount and types of data that can be handled.

At the present there are two packages that perform in the same fashion as dBASE IV (DB4) (that is, they use the same commands, and the databases are interchangeable): DBXL and VP-Info. DBXL is functionally equivalent to DB4 in non-SQL mode, whereas VP-Info is not.[11] They are both considerably cheaper.

Another alternative to using a database manager is to use a spreadsheet package. Spreadsheet packages are the equivalent of using a ledger on a computer, and data are set up to be managed in columns and rows.[12] In certain respects spreadsheet packages are not as flexible as database managers. Importing data can become a problem for anything but numeric information, as character information is not handled well by a spreadsheet package.[13] The benefit of using a spreadsheet package is the ability to perform complex descriptive and statistical functions on numeric information quickly and easily. Also, it is usually easier to learn how to use a spreadsheet. Quick data entry and simple analysis are possible when using a spreadsheet package. Data export is normally easier than data import for spreadsheets.

The most widely used spreadsheet package is Lotus 1-2-3, Versions 1a and 2. SuperCalc and PlanPerfect are two other good spreadsheet packages. Like database managers, shareware spreadsheet packages also exist that perform the same functions. AsEasy (a package similar to Lotus) is a good and frequently used product. VP-Planner (by the authors of VP-Info, PaperBack Software) is an inexpensive Lotus 1-2-3, Version 1a, alternative. VP-Planner Plus and Quattro Pro (by Borland) are Lotus 1-2-3, Version 2, compatible products. Spreadsheets created under Lotus can be used with any of these packages and vice versa.[14] The advantage in using VP-Planner and Planner Plus is in their database manipulation facilities. Lotus 1-2-3 will read dBASE II type files, but VP-Planner not only reads dBASE II, III, and IV files but also creates, updates, browses through, selects from, and easily imports and exports data from these types of files. Like VP-Planner, Quattro will read and write various different file formats, including dBASE IV files.

SUMMARY

The ASHPI program was intended to introduce the feasibility of maintaining the inventory on a computer instead of using a manual filing system. The computer application appeared to work well as a storage and retrieval device and also facilitated an uncomplicated means for creating reports on selected properties. The exercise itself was worthwhile in displaying the capabilities for using existing microcomputer database management software to set up a historic property tracking system. However, at the same time, it was not practical because of cost. At the time that the project was developed, the price of equipment and software was prohibitive. In order to set up a fully working system at that time would have cost approximately $3,000 to $4,000. Today the same system can be set up for approximately $1,000. The experience gained from developing this system was beneficial and helped to demonstrate the practicality of a system of this nature.

At this time it would be appropriate to again pursue the project and to continue to study the feasibility of using a computer-based property tracking system—not only for historic preservation but also for other applications in anthropology. Programs like DB4 (or Paradox, Rbase for DOS, dBXL, or VP-Info) help a researcher set up streamlined applications. These applications can be menu-driven to allow quick learning by research assistants or other colleagues. Database packages can also be used to facilitate data entry for further analysis. Statistical packages, including Abstat, SAS-PC, and Systat, will read dBASE files directly and take advantage of the power of dBASE in the area of controlled data entry. In a similar fashion, spreadsheet packages can also be used for data entry. A database package should be included along with statistical, word-processing, and any of the other microcomputer-based tools available for anthropological research, analysis, museum, and field activities.

NOTES

1. An application program is a specific set of instructions given to a computer to perform a specific task. Under dBASE, instructions can be linked together to form a program that will be used repeatedly. This enables a programmer (application developer) to produce a usable menu-driven system that automates the tasks that must be performed.

2. At the time I was enrolled in a historic preservation class at Northern Arizona University. The project was used to track some of the information collected by the class.

3. ASHPI stands for Arizona State Historic Preservation Inventory, the name of the database system that was set up for the project.

4. The names of the fields displayed are as originally defined. If there are more variables than lines on the screen, dBASE will show only as many as will fit. When the ENTER key is hit after the last field on the screen, the next screen of information will be displayed.

5. The cursor is the symbol (normally a flashing underline symbol) on the screen that indicates where you are.

6. A program is a specific set of instructions that will accomplish a specific task. This may be compared to a recipe in cooking.

7. A good relational report writer is R & R Relational Report Writer, Version 3, from Concentric Data Systems.

8. If you would like a copy of this program, send a self-addressed, stamped envelope and IBM formatted floppy disk to William Wilson, 624 W. Santa Fe, Flagstaff, AZ 86001.

9. The record number is the actual physical record number of the record for the piece of property that you are looking for in the database file.

10. Shareware is a relatively new concept for the marketing of software. Software authors allow the copying and dissemination of their product and ask that individuals who like the product and decide to use it send in a registration fee.

11. Any programs that you write can be used directly under DBXL (SQL commands are not included in this blanket statement). It is a true clone of dBASE III Plus (the release previous to dBASE IV), where only VP-Info is compatible. The database file structures are the same for VP-Info, but the

programs will need to be rewritten. Luckily, the language is close, so the user should have a minimum number of changes to make.

12. VP-Planner, Planner Plus, and Quattro are inexpensive Lotus 1-2-3 compatible products.

13. Importing data refers to bringing already existing information into the program. For example: A researcher has been using a mainframe and has an existing data set that needs to be downloaded and used with a spreadsheet. Incorporating the file into the spreadsheet program is importing.

14. A spreadsheet or worksheet is a file where the data are housed. A spreadsheet package is the program that manages a spreadsheet or worksheet.

PART FOUR

Using Computers for Anthropological Analysis

The nine chapters in this part range from the elementary first steps of the research process to complex forms for the analysis of cultural constructs and culture-based decision making. The continuum is from basic to more advanced forms of analysis. The first chapters in this part (Chapters 7–9) illustrate the usual steps in the analysis of a database stored on an electronic medium—analysis of univariate, then bivariate statistics. These chapters set the stage for the chapters on multivariate statistical analyses (Chapters 12–14). Chapters 10 and 15 describe a new type of software program that seems ideally suited to the analysis of emic data: the "expert system." Chapter 11 features a special application that was programmed by the anthropologist to illustrate an important evolutionary process, genetic drift. Finally, Chapter 15 gives us a glimpse of a computer application on the "cutting edge" and the use of computer programming not as method for achieving results quickly and easily but as a tool for basic research and theoretical discovery.

CHAPTER SEVEN

First Steps in the Computer-Assisted Research Process: An Example from Development Anthropology

ADAM KOONS

In this chapter, Koons takes us through the intial steps in a quantitative analysis of research results. He begins with the design of an interview questionnaire and goes on to the coding of qualitative responses in quantitative form, the creation of an electronic file, and analysis of the results using one of the standard statistical packages. His keyboard work begins in the field, continues at his university's computer center, and ends in his office, where he analyzes the computer output. In his final report, Koons mixes quantitative results from the computer-assisted analysis with quotes taken directly from his field interviews.

USE OF THE COMPUTER IN ANTHROPOLOGICAL RESEARCH

This chapter illustrates the flexibility, ease, and applicability of computer-assisted research for development anthropologists and other anthropologists working in remote field sites. It is addressed to beginning users who need to know some of the basic steps in preparing data for analysis using a computer. The step-by-step approach in this chapter will be especially useful for researchers who have access to a mainframe or microcomputer and statistical software such as SAS, SPSS-X, SYSTAT, or MICROSTAT but have not yet used them. It should serve as an introductory programming guide but primarily as encouragement for further exploration and experimentation in the collection, storage, transmittal, and analysis of data gathered in developing countries and other field sites. Anthropologists who are just beginning to learn computer-assisted methods will soon go beyond the techniques illustrated here to tailor their own research needs to developing technologies for the field, office, and lab.

The research described here is part of a development project that was designed, sponsored, and financed by the International Fund for Agricultural Development (IFAD) and the government of Cameroon. The research was financed by the Breakthrough Foundation because of its interest in fostering successful interpersonal relations in development projects. In this project, as in many others, economic and agricultural development involved planned and directed culture change that had profound effects on many aspects of the people's lives, sometimes including those not intentionally addressed by the projects. In general, development anthropologists try to understand the process of rapid cultural change and to improve it by helping to maintain the quality of people's lives with the least amount of unplanned and unexpected disruption of their sociocultural systems. Anthropological perspectives and ethnographic methods have helped development project personnel understand the interaction between local economies, the environment, and the social, political, and cultural systems into which the projects are placed. Anthropologists have shown that many project failures previously blamed on uncooperative recipients, were often the result of misunderstanding the vastly different cultural world view of the people—their needs, expectations, and concerns about project personnel and intended project beneficiaries. Anthropologists have often been involved in team planning, implementation, and evaluation of development projects, as well as sometimes "troubleshooting" on their own. They are also frequently assigned certain segments of the necessary research that should precede any well-planned development project.[1]

The purpose of the research described here was to examine the implementation of a large, integrated, rural development project in Cameroon and to understand the dynamics of cross-cultural and intergroup relationships in the delivery of technical, agricultural information to farmers. It was hoped that this understanding would help to design approaches for information delivery and improve the ability of project personnel to locate and evaluate problems caused by social and cultural factors. The results of this research showed clearly that some farmers were not being served well by the development project. In the end, new approaches were developed and recommended that would help correct deficiencies in the project.

The methods used to analyze interviews with Cameroonian farmers were both qualitative and descriptive (in the use of graphic display) and quantitative (in the use of univariate statistics to derive generalizations). The SAS software package was used for both qualitative and quantitative methods to produce clear documentation to support research conclusions. The interview data originally contained little quantitative information. Interview results consisted primarily of descriptive responses, for example, farmers' responses to "Why" and "What" questions as opposed to "How many" and "How often." I used SAS software to translate, or "code," some of the descriptive answers into a quantitative form that the computer software could manipulate more easily. For example, instead of claiming that "most farmers said this and that," the use of SAS allowed me to say, "X percent of the farmers said this, and Y percent said that." These responses were analyzed in relation to other characteristics of the farmers, such as age and sex. In the final analysis, the documentation of research results was presented for specific subgroups of farmers. Their results could be more accurately specified, and the conclusions of our research could be more firmly supported, than they could have been using handwritten methods only. One advantage of using computer-assisted methods is that both the raw data and the computer output used to draw conclusions—such as the tables and charts produced by SAS procedures—were readily available for detailed examination by others who might want to double-check the conclusions or use the data to write their own reports.

The interview results of this research were collected in the field, and, while I was still in the field, the interview data were coded and entered into a microcomputer file to create the research "database." The database was later transferred to, or "uploaded to," a mainframe computer so that SAS software for the mainframe could be used with the data for the univariate analysis. After the analysis, the resulting statistics, tables, graphs, and charts were finally integrated into a discussion that included the original verbal responses from the interviews for the final report. The same analysis could have been completed using SAS software for the personal computer (PC): I used a mainframe computer simply because it and SAS software for the mainframe were available at my university. For relatively simple analysis, a PC is usually sufficient. However, for very complicated analysis that requires less common programming options, or for analysis that involves very large databases or many merged databases, a mainframe is often necessary.

The most time-consuming phases of the research were data collection and data preparation. The time for data collection in the field can be measured in weeks, and for data preparation it can be measured in days. However, the time for writing and entering programs at a computer keyboard can be measured in minutes, and the time for running the programs can be measured in milliseconds. Back at the office, the analysis of the computer output can take hours or days. The steps in the methodology I used are illustrated in Figure 7.1. Each step in the analysis is relatively simple, but when it is viewed all at once, the entire process can seem confusing or unmanageable. The actual use of the computer software is anticlimactically easy. Novices can achieve useful results with the statistical packages with little or no formal preparation. Learning and explaining the statistical principles behind the procedures requires classroom instruction and careful analysis of the results in a final report.

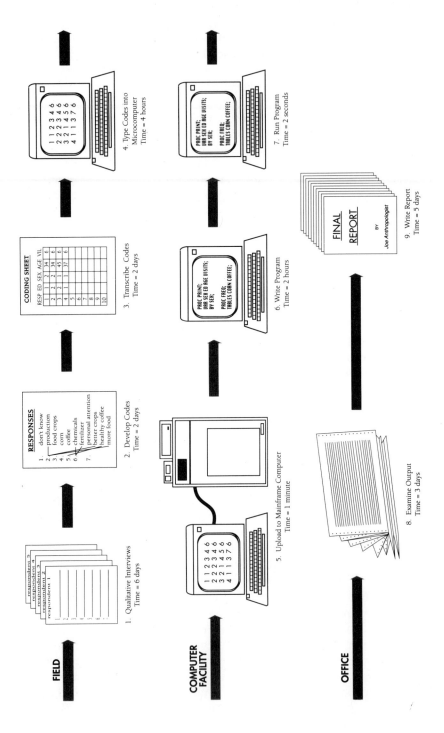

RESPONSES

1. don't know
2. production
3. food crops
4. corn
5. coffee
6. chemicals
   fertilizer
7. personal attention
   better crops
   healthy coffee
   more food

2. Develop Codes
   Time = 2 days

CODING SHEET

RESP	ED	SEX	AGE	VIL
1	2	2	34	6
2	2	2	34	6
3	2	1	45	6
4	1	1	37	6
5				
6				
7				
8				
9				
10				

3. Transcribe Codes
   Time = 2 days

```
1 1 2 3 4 6
2 2 1 4 5 6
3 2 1 1 2 1
4 1 1 3 7 6
```

4. Type Codes into
   Microcomputer
   Time = 4 hours

```
PROC PRINT;
VAR SEX ED AGE VISITS;
BY SEX;

PROC FREQ;
TABLES CORN COFFEE;
```

6. Write Program
   Time = 2 hours

```
PROC PRINT;
VAR SEX ED AGE VISITS;
BY SEX;

PROC FREQ;
TABLES CORN COFFEE;
```

7. Run Program
   Time = 2 seconds

FIELD

1. Qualitative Interviews
   Time = 6 days

COMPUTER FACILITY

5. Upload to Mainframe Computer
   Time = 1 minute

OFFICE

8. Examine Output
   Time = 3 days

FINAL REPORT

BY

Joe Anthropologist

9. Write Report
   Time = 5 days

FIGURE 7.1 *The steps for computer analysis of interviews*

THE RESEARCH PROBLEM

The goal of the research was to understand the relationship that was developing between newly trained agricultural extension agents and Cameroonian farmers and to diagnose early problems and predict possible future problems. One approach was to interview the farmers, so an interview questionnaire was designed to tap the farmers' attitudes and receptivity to agricultural extension and their view of interactions with extension workers. The questionnaire also recorded the extension recommendations that farmers could recall, and this enabled us to count the recalled recommendations. Simply put, the interview would help us to determine which factors hindered or helped extension. We needed to know if the farmers were receiving the extension assistance that the project intended them to receive and whether this is what farmers really wanted.

Interviews were conducted with fifty-two farmers (twenty-seven men and twenty-five women) who were members of mixed-gender farming groups visited by the new extension agents. The interview questionnaire contained eighty-four questions, divided into seven categories according to type and focus. Some were answered with one or several words or numbers. For example, we asked, "Have you belonged to a farmers' group before?" and, "How many meetings has the extension worker held with your group?" Other questions were descriptive or focused on attitudes, and the responses to these ranged from one word to several paragraphs. Examples of questions that elicited longer responses were "What advice did the extension worker give you about fertilizing maize?" and, "Why do you think the government started this new program?" These interviews were not originally designed for quantitative analysis. However, the use of computer-assisted analysis allowed us to use the interview results in a new way, by coding them and analyzing them using simple SAS programs. Anthropologists have a variety of options for reanalyzing notes from interviews and participant observation. The type of analysis in this chapter is one approach, and use of programs like ETHNOGRAPH is another (see Chapter 5).

Many questions elicited multiple responses, so in the final analysis there were 140 separate variables coded for each farmer and entered into the database. For example, farmers were asked "What benefits have you received so far from the new extension program?" Many farmers mentioned several things, and for this question there were up to four variables allowed in the coding. The final database consisted of 140 variables for fifty-two observations, that is, fifty-two farmers. The data file was a rectangular grid with the observations (the farmers) listed at the left side and the variables listed across the top, as in Table 7.1.

TABLE 7.1 *Coding sheet for transcription of interview responses (also, configuration for data file)*

```
                          CODING SHEET

RESP   ED   SEX AGE BNFTS1 BNFTS2 BNFTS3 BNFTS4 ...BNFTS7...
 1._____
 2._____
 3._____
 4._____
 5._____
  ._____
  ._____
  ._____
52._____

KEY
RESP    = respondent
ED      = education
BNFTS_  = benefit type
```

THE METHODOLOGY

There were three place-specific stages in the research: (1) field activities, from asking the interview questions to creating the database; (2) activities at the computer facility, including running and rerunning SAS programs; and (3) office activities, including final analysis and writing a final report (Figure 7.1). The first stage was the most time consuming and took place in the field. This was the collection and coding of raw data and entry of the data into a microcomputer file for later uploading to a mainframe computer (or, in some other project, for direct use on a microcomputer with statistical analysis programs for the PC). The second stage was using the mainframe computer. Using a large computer for the first time was both very exciting and sometimes very frustrating. The first step consisted of uploading the data from the microcomputer to the mainframe using a special transmission program provided by the university computer facility. Then, I wrote the SAS programs and ran them using the interview data. The third stage, back at the office, was using the computer output to examine findings and draw conclusions. At this point, the charts, tables, and graphs from the computer output were integrated with some of the original interview text to help illustrate the report.

To summarize, I converted words and phrases from interviews into numbers, manipulated them using the SAS software package, and translated the results into report text. Then I illustrated conclusions with the

T A B L E 7 . 2 *Reduction of interview responses to phrases*

```
FARMER BENEFITS (PARTIAL LIST)

nothing yet but expected soon
chemicals available
coffee medicine
fertilizer is cheaper
new varieties maize and potato
can reach gov't now for problems
workers visit farms
workers live in village
better planting methods
learn about medicines
treat diseases
fertilizer on maize
learn about livestock
```

farmers' own words. The use of SAS allowed me to quantify the farmers' responses and then enabled me to compare and describe the responses in a number of different ways.

IN THE FIELD

Step 1: Interviewing

During the interviews, responses were written verbatim (or as close as possible) onto prepared response forms. The result was a great deal of handwritten text, much of it in Pidgin English.

Step 2: Data Reduction and the Determination of Codes

Text could not be entered directly into a computer file for quantitative analysis.[2] Therefore, decisions had to be made for each question that elicited a nonnumeric type of response. I needed a coding scheme that would reduce and transform the set of non-numeric text responses to a set of numerically coded categories. In the field office, after all the interviews were completed, the responses for half of the farmers' questions were transcribed as descriptive phrases or quotes from the completed questionnaires onto lists—one for each question (see Table 7.2). The responses on these lists were sufficient to indicate the approximate range of responses for each question. Some differences in responses were substantive, so they were coded as different numbers. Other differences were grammatical, so responses could be considered equivalent and coded with the same number. Recurring similarities in many of the responses allowed them to be grouped into categories, and each category

TABLE 7.3 *Coding scheme for benefits of extension*

Code	Category
0	none
2	inputs
3	extension contact
4	advice: coffee
5	advice: maize
6	advice: foodcrops
7	advice: chemicals
8	increased production
9	non-project sphere
10	farmer groups
11	advice: non-specific
12	money, credit, loans

was assigned a code. A word processor was used to facilitate the experimental process of moving responses around to arrange them into categories.

Decisions had to be made about what constituted a useful category. Too many categories for a single set of responses would make the analysis unwieldy and weak, and too few would hide potentially important information. For example, the question about the personal benefits of extension yielded sixty-five responses for half of the respondents. Twelve subject categories were created and twelve codes assigned (Table 7.3). Because the types of advice were important, each type was given a separate code. Financial matters were less important, so they were lumped together. For questions that involved greater subjectivity in determining categories, a second analyst was asked to propose categories from the same list of responses. The two sets were then compared and reconciled. Other coding schemes based on different research interests would have been possible.

A slightly different coding process was used for the questions that yielded quantitatively measurable or ranked responses. One set of questions was intended to measure the quantity, detail, and accuracy of advice that farmers had received at recent meetings with extension agents. Categories were created to indicate ranked degrees of correctness of the responses (Table 7.4). Using this coding scheme, each respondent was assigned a score for each question about coffee and maize, concerning advice on techniques such as planting, pruning, and fertilizing methods. A response that was correct in precise detail was given 6 points, and one that was correct in general was given 4 points. Incorrect information was judged by the project agronomist as more damaging than no information, so it was given a negative value.

TABLE 7.4 *Measurement codes for accuracy of recall of extension recommendations*

Code/score	Category
6	correct precisely
4	correct in general
2	correct partially
-6	incorrect totally
1	no info yet -- expected later
0	don't know/no info given

TABLE 7.5 *Adding codes while coding the full data set*

FARMER CRITERIA FOR RECOGNIZING SUCCESSFUL DEVELOPMENT

Initial Codes and Categories		Final Codes and Categories	
1	Transportation	1	Transportation
2	Education	2	Education
3	Health	3	Health
4	Money	4	Money
5	Housing	5	Housing
6	Agricultural Productivity	6	Agricultural Productivity
7	Electricity	7	Electricity
		8	Agricultural Assistance
		9	Markets
		10	People Working Together

Step 3: Coding Interviews

While still in the field, I coded each question for each interview and entered them on a coding sheet by hand (Table 7.1). A total of eighty-four questions gave rise to 140 separate variables. Coding began with the assignment of a case number for each respondent. Several other baseline characteristics such as age and sex were also coded. For example, male = 1 and female = 2; age was coded as number of years old. Variables were given unique labels, and a codebook was used to keep track of the labels and code values for variables in the computer data file. SAS programs identify variables by their assigned labels.

As coding proceeded, sometimes new variables and codes had to be added. For instance, the coding for one question began with seven categories and ended with ten because there were responses on some interviews that did not occur in the half-sample initially used for determining codes (Table 7.5). Many questions produced multiple responses

TABLE 7.6 *Coding for multiple responses*

CODING SHEET SECTION FOR FARMER BENEFITS

RESP	BNFTS1	BNFTS2	BNFTS3	BNFTS4
1.	2	12	4	5
2.	8	7	12	4
3.	2	.	.	.
4.	5	8	7	.
5.	9	8	.	.

or responses that gave rise to several coded categories.[3] In these cases each category was entered on the sheet as a separate variable. Some respondents had one coded response, whereas others had up to seven (Table 7.6).

Step 4: Data Entry

After coding all interview responses, data were transcribed from the coding sheets into a computer data file by typing the codes on a computer keyboard. For this step there are normally two options. At a computer facility, the data can be typed directly from the coding sheets into the same mainframe computer that will run the SAS programs for the analysis. This saves the step of "uploading" (that is, transferring) the data from a file on a microcomputer diskette. Typing in codes is a time-consuming process that can take several to many hours depending on the size of the database generated. It is a clerical task that can be completed by a secretary or research assistant, and in some large projects, the task is contracted out to a separate company that is paid to key in the data.

The option used here was to type the data from the coding sheets into a microcomputer for storage on a diskette. This method is useful because it can be accomplished in the field or at home or in the office instead of at a computer facility. When data are entered this way, some types of preliminary analysis can take place using the large variety of statistical analysis software available for microcomputers.[4] Having the data on a microcomputer diskette in the field or at home also allows it to be used by others because the data can easily be copied, mailed, and/or electronically transmitted (for example, over telephone wires). (See Chapter 4 in this volume on computer-assisted data management and research coordination from several field sites.)

In my research the coded interview data were transcribed from the coding sheets into an IBM compatible microcomputer file by using the popular word-processing and editing software WORDSTAR. Using the "nontext option" (Standard ASCII) for this software, the data were typed into a file exactly as they appeared on the coding sheets. All of the codes for a respondent were entered in order, in a row, so that each respondent had a separate row of codes. Some preliminary statistical analysis was completed on the microcomputer using this data file with MICROSTAT software. The data were then ready for the next stage in the analysis, which took place at the computer facility.

AT THE COMPUTER CENTER

Step 5: Uploading

Transferring the database from a microcomputer diskette to a mainframe computer file can be carried out either at a computer center or via telephone from anywhere in the world with the use of a modem and telecommunications software consisting of transmission programs. My data were uploaded at the computer center with the help of a staff member. This was done using a microcomputer that was directly connected to ("hard-wired to") the mainframe computer and transmission software supplied by the computer center. SAS software requires that data files have a specific configuration that is described in the SAS manual. Some files are fine from the start because they are already properly formatted. Others, depending on the number of variables and records, must be altered slightly. The reformatting of my data file was also performed at the computer center by a staff member who assured me that it was not necessary for the average SAS user to learn all of these details initially.

Step 6: Writing SAS Programs

Writing SAS programs to display univariate statistics is not difficult. The process is one of following the SAS manual and trying out variations of programs that work, or "run." In my office, I first decided what kind of analysis would answer my research questions. Then, sitting with the manual and the list of variables, I chose program functions and wrote drafts of programs that analyzed the variables I was most interested in. At the computer center I typed the programs into a mainframe computer file and ran them using the interview data—which in this case were appended to the SAS program in the same computer file. If there was an error in the program it would not run. The error had to be found and corrected. This was usually a very simple, but sometimes difficult to find, syntax problem such as a slash in the wrong place, a misspelled variable, or a missing semicolon, which ends all SAS statements much like periods end sentences.

When programs ran, I took the printouts back to the office where I had to decide whether the results, the "output," was useful. In research involving bivariate and/or multivariate analysis (as in Chapters 9, 12, 13, and 14 in this volume), a researcher usually "goes back and forth" between running programs, analyzing the output, and running new programs for further analysis. In my research it was important to remember that much of the database was in number form only so that it could be most easily manipulated by the computer programs. The codes represented alpha-numeric information, or words, and ultimately ideas, perceptions, and attitudes. For example, analysis of the numbers, or codes, representing types of farming benefits included determination of the frequency of each type of benefit (Table 7.3). However, it would have been meaningless to use the numbers to calculate an "average benefit." On the other hand, an average could be meaningfully determined for variables such as age and socioeconomic level. It is important to keep in mind the kinds of analysis that are meaningful with different types of information.

My very first SAS program, which was written with the assistance of a computer center staff member, was a program that initially directed the mainframe computer to use the SAS software. The program then directed SAS where to find the data file and identified the names and locations of all the variables in the database. This short program segment (called the "Data Step") was used at the beginning of every subsequent SAS program. It had to be typed on the keyboard only once. Thereafter it was just copied to the beginning of other programs by using the computer system's editing capabilities. The SAS manual provides a complete and detailed description of how to set up a Data Step. However, the best way to learn is side by side with another programmer. After the data are located and identified in a "Data Step," they are then manipulated in a second step(s) called the "Proc (procedure) Step."

Step 7: Running SAS Programs for the Research Analysis

Below are some examples of SAS statements and parts of programs that I used to examine the interview data on Cameroonian farmers. Brief descriptions are given of how the output from these programs are used in the research analysis. These examples are not a comprehensive guide to SAS, but they should provide some idea of the simplicity and utility of using SAS. The SAS INTRODUCTORY GUIDE also provides very clear examples of programs and output and easily followed instructions.

Step 7a: Printing

The following PROC statement simply requests the computer to print the data. On the next line are the individual variables from the data set that are to be printed. The list of variables is preceded by the VAR statement, for "variable."

```
PROC PRINT;
    VAR SEX ED VISITS CORN COFFEE INFOSCOR;
```

The computer prints out the values for each variable requested, for each observation—in this case, each interviewed farmer (see Table 7.7). It is useful to take a look at the data in this way, as a first step in the research analysis. PROC PRINT is more useful than simply "dumping the data," that is, printing the data exactly as they appear in the database, with no labels or headings. PROC PRINT allows the data to be printed in specified orders and groupings.

Additional lines of SAS commands can instruct the computer to produce output divided into segments according to specified variables in the data set. For example, when a third line is added to the above program lines, two tables are printed out rather than one.

```
PROC PRINT;
    VAR SEX ED VISITS CORN COFFEE INFOSCOR;
    BY SEX;
```

Since there are two values for sex, the output will list the variables for all observations, first for males (when SEX = 1), and then for females (when SEX = 2), thereby dividing and printing the data in two tables. Table 7.8 shows the output for males only.

Because printing an entire data set, or parts of it, provides a look at the printed values at once, in one place, next to each other, it offers a broad overview of possible relationships and initial patterns that can be pursued later with a more focused analysis. For example, Table 7.7 shows that the most zeroes came from female respondents. Table 7.7 shows that women tended to have no farm visits from extension workers, no scores for recalled recommendations about coffee farming, often low scores for maize recommendations, low coffee and maize cumulative scores, and less formal education than men. These initial observations suggest some possible connections and patterns that were later examined more carefully. Some relationships turned out to be central in the final research analysis and the development of recommendations.

A great deal can be learned from the data set by printing parts of it in particular arrangements or groupings. For example, Table 7.8 displays male respondents' answers about personal project benefits. This type of display allows comparison between respondents' multiple answers. Table 7.8 points to certain attitudes or beliefs about extension and their relationship to production. Using the key to the variable codes (Table 7.3), Table 7.8 suggests that many of the same farmers who said they benefited from advice (codes 4, 5, 6, 7) also noted they

TABLE 7.7 *Example of outcome from PROC PRINT, including original and recoded variables*

OBS	SEX	ED	VISITS	CORN	COFFEE	INFOSCOR
1	1	2	0	34	32	33.0
2	1	1	0	23	40	31.5
3	1	1	0	36	36	36.0
4	1	1	0	3	39	21.0
5	1	2	10	46	55	50.5
6	2	1	4	43	0	21.5
7	2	1	0	35	0	17.5
8	2	1	0	26	0	13.0
9	1	2	4	27	0	13.5
10	1	2	2	22	57	39.5
11	1	4	1	−6	28	11.0
12	1	2	2	6	49	27.5
13	2	1	0	0	0	0.0
14	1	2	1	−4	41	18.5
15	1	2	2	0	57	28.5
16	1	2	4	−8	68	30.0
17	1	1	5	18	42	30.0
18	2	1	0	4	−6	−1.0
19	2	1	0	0	8	4.0
20	2	1	2	37	26	31.5
21	1	2	0	45	37	41.0
22	1	2	2	64	0	32.0
23	1	2	6	28	85	56.5
24	1	2	10	36	0	18.0
25	1	1	5	3	0	1.5
26	1	1	0	24	23	23.5
27	1	2	3	17	37	27.0
28	1	1	4	42	0	21.0
29	1	1	6	62	0	31.0
30	1	1	4	21	68	44.5
31	2	1	3	15	0	7.5
32	1	1	8	−3	0	−1.5
33	2	2	0	1	0	0.5
34	1	2	10	19	0	9.5
35	2	2	1	74	0	37.5
36	2	1	0	2	9	5.5
37	2	1	0	23	0	11.5
38	1	2	2	4	0	2.0
39	1	2	4	18	46	32.0
40	2	1	0	0	0	0.0
41	2	1	0	8	0	4.0
42	2	2	0	17	0	8.5
43	2	1	0	39	0	19.5
44	2	1	0	20	0	10.0
45	2	1	0	19	49	34.0
46	2	1	1	41	0	4.0
47	2	1	0	−5	0	−2.5
48	2	2	0	−11	0	−5.5
49	2	2	0	47	0	23.5
50	2	1	0	21	11	16.0
51	2	1	0	0	0	0.0
52	2	1	1	12	7	9.5

T A B L E 7 . 8 *Output from PROC PRINT for males only, on the benefits of extension*

OBS	BNFTS1	BNFTS2	BNFTS3	BNFTS4
\- SPX = 1 \-				
1	10	4	•	•
2	3	2	3	•
3	3	7	5	•
4	8	4	2	•
5	11	7	10	•
6	2	3	11	9
7	8	5	•	•
8	5	7	2	6
9	11	8	9	•
10	2	4	•	•
11	8	7	•	•
12	8	4	5	•
13	8	4	6	7
14	0	•	•	•
15	8	4	•	•
16	2	12	4	5
17	8	7	12	4
18	2	•	•	•
19	5	8	7	•
20	9	•	•	•
21	3	8	•	•
22	2	8	4	•
23	2	4	•	•
24	8	5	6	9
25	8	2	12	4
26	8	6	•	•
27	2	4	5	•

had recognized increased production (code 8). This hypothesis could be tested using one of the SAS statistical programs such as those that test for correlation.

Step 7b: Recoding

It is often useful to create new variables before an analysis begins or in the middle of the analysis after more hypotheses have been developed. In my database, each respondent had a score for each response about extension information he reported. Recoding the scores meant combining them so that each farmer had a total score for "corn questions," a total for "coffee questions," and an overall total score for extension recommendations that I called INFOSCOR. This new variable was created through addition, but SAS can also manipulate variables with subtraction, multiplication, division, and special formulas. Recoding is done in the Data Step of the SAS program with the following simple SAS statements. The SAS manual also gives instructions on recoding.

```
COFFEE = NURSE + REPLT + DISEASE + PRUNE +
    CARE + VARIETY + SPRAY + CHEMMIX + CHEMAPP;
CORN = SPACING + SEEDS + FERT + WHEN +
    AMOUNT + WEEDS + STORE + USED + STORCHEM;
INFOSCOR = (COFFEE + CORN)*.5;
```

In the first two operations, shown above, the values for each variable in the equation were added, and the sums became recoded values for variables that I called COFFEE and CORN. The computer repeated this for each respondent. Next, the two recodes were first added and then multiplied by 0.5, to produce a third recode for each respondent. The recodes became new variables named COFFEE, CORN, and INFOSCOR, which could be used in SAS procedures just like the original variables.

Step 7c: Univariate Statistics

The determination of "univariate statistics" can be a complete research analysis or the beginning of a more in-depth analysis involving bivariate and/or multivariate statistics. One of the primary means for obtaining univariate statistics for an analysis is by using a SAS procedure that prints frequencies (that is, how often a particular value occurs for a variable) and the associated percentages. Frequencies can be printed in the form of tables, charts, and graphs for any variable in the data file. Table 7.9 illustrates a table of frequencies for the variable representing the aggregate "corn score" created by recoding its components. The program also lists the scores for the respondents in ascending order and

T A B L E 7 . 9 *Output from PROC FREQ (partial)*

CORN	FREQUENCY	CUM FREQ	PERCENT	CUM PERCENT
-11	1	1	1.923	1.923
-8	1	2	1.923	3.846
-6	1	3	1.923	5.769
-5	1	4	1.923	7.692
-4	1	5	1.923	9.615
-3	1	6	1.923	11.538
0	5	11	9.615	21.154
1	1	12	1.923	23.077
2	1	13	1.923	25.000
3	2	15	3.846	28.846
4	2	17	3.846	32.692
6	1	18	1.923	34.615
8	1	19	1.923	36.538
12	1	20	1.923	38.462
15	1	21	1.923	40.385

shows how often each score occurred. This is done simply by typing and running the following instructions:

```
PROC FREQ;
    TABLES CORN;
```

The output provides a more orderly and concise view of the range of scores for the entire set of responses. The next step might be to display score frequencies grouped by gender to determine if high or low scores seem to be gender related. Although research usually involves some major hypothesis for testing, it also can involve this iterative, exploratory process of running statistics, developing a hypothesis, and running further statistics. Even at the univariate stage of analysis, this iterative process would be extremely laborious and time consuming without the use of a computer.

Another example of frequency tables (Table 7.10) uses the same variables referred to in Table 7.8, but this time, the data were divided by gender. The table shows males' responses only, and they are divided into separate tables for each variable, or benefit. The table displays the frequency of a particular answer as it occurred first, second, third, or fourth in the list of responses. The table indicates that 37 percent of men's first answers claim increased production as a project benefit. They also show that none of men's first answers were specifically about receiving advice on coffee production, although they named this in subsequent responses (see Table 7.3 for the key to these codes). From this type of initial reading of the printout, the analyst must find patterns and ask questions that can be pursued further. Using a computer for this task is vastly more flexible than writing out the very same data by hand. Different data displays can be printed out in a matter of seconds or minutes.

SAS programming easily provides a standard statistical overview of quantitative variables. SAS output is similar to that generated by most other mainframe or microcomputer statistical packages. The numerical data were coded from the interviews in order to provide a profile of the farmers' responses and to suggest any possible trends by age, education, socioeconomic level, or past extension experience. A single SAS procedure produces the mean, standard deviation, minimum and maximum values (the range), and error of mean for all the selected variables. Table 7.11 gives the output by gender subgroup. To obtain subgroups, the data must be sorted with a simple SORT procedure and a BY statement that order the data by the specified variable. Table 7.11 was achieved by running the following procedures:

```
PROC SORT;
    BY SEX;
PROC MEANS;
    VAR AGE POSSES EQUIP { . . . other variables . . . };
    BY SEX;
```

TABLE 7.10 *Output from PROC FREQ (partial) for males only*

		SEX=1		
BNFTS1	FREQUENCY	CUM FREQ	PERCENT	CUM PERCENT
0	1	1	3.704	3.704
2	7	8	25.926	29.630
3	3	11	11.111	40.741
5	2	13	7.407	48.148
8	10	23	37.037	85.185
9	1	24	3.704	88.889
10	1	25	3.704	92.593
11	2	27	7.407	100.000
BNFTS2	FREQUENCY	CUM FREQ	PERCENT	CUM PERCENT
.	3	.	.	.
2	2	2	8.333	8.333
3	1	3	4.167	12.500
4	8	11	33.333	45.833
5	2	13	8.333	54.167
6	1	14	4.167	58.333
7	5	19	20.833	79.167
8	4	23	16.667	95.833
12	1	24	4.167	100.000
BNFTS3	FREQUENCY	CUM FREQ	PERCENT	CUM PERCENT
.	11	.	.	.
2	2	2	12.500	12.500
3	1	3	6.250	18.750
4	2	5	12.500	31.250
5	3	8	18.750	50.000
6	2	10	12.500	62.500
7	1	11	6.250	68.750
9	1	12	6.250	75.000
10	1	13	6.250	81.250
11	1	14	6.250	87.500
12	2	16	12.500	100.000
BNFTS4	FREQUENCY	CUM FREQ	PERCENT	CUM PERCENT
.	20	.	.	.
4	2	2	28.571	28.571
5	1	3	14.286	42.857
6	1	4	14.286	57.143
7	1	5	14.286	71.429
9	2	7	28.571	100.000

Step 7d: Charts

Frequency bar charts are very useful visual tools for examining and analyzing data and in producing research reports. Turning again to variables suggested by the initial overview (Table 7.7), horizontal bar charts (Figure 7.2) allow comparison of men's and women's visits from extension workers—as does the vertical bar chart in Figure 7.3. Whereas Figure 7.3 compares cumulative visits (the total number of visits received

T A B L E 7 . 1 1 *Output from PROC SORT and PROC MEANS*

VARIABLE	N	MEAN	STANDARD DEVIATION	MINIMUM VALUE	MAXIMUM VALUE	STD ERROR OF MEAN
---	---	---	---	SEX = 1	---	---
AGE	27	49.222222	10.184201	27.0000000	66.000000	1.959950
POSSES	27	7.185185	5.568020	0.0000000	19.000000	1.071500
EQUIP	27	13.074074	7.595170	2.0000000	27.000000	1.461691
COFFEE	18	66.444444	90.467558	23.0000000	424.000000	21.323406
CORN	27	21.370370	19.901968	−8.0000000	64.000000	3.830135
INFOSCOR	18	42.194444	46.271939	11.0000000	222.500000	10.906401
STEMS	27	2607.037037	1942.824698	300.0000000	7000.000000	373.896787
VISITS	23	4.130435	3.049655	0.0000000	10.000000	0.635897
MTGS	12	22.250000	32.833256	2.0000000	99.000000	9.478145
---	---	---	---	SEX = 2	---	---
AGE	25	41.2000000	10.665365	22.00000000	75.000000	2.133078
POSSES	24	4.6875000	4.481393	0.00000000	18.000000	0.914760
EQUIP	24	6.6250000	5.139891	1.00000000	18.000000	1.049176
COFFEE	12	8.6666667	15.155757	−6.0000000	49.000000	4.375090
CORN	25	18.7200000	20.274204	−11.00000000	74.000000	4.054841
INFOSCOR	12	14.8750000	13.170430	−1.00000000	37.000000	3.801976
STEMS	25	552.4400000	1074.522610	0.00000000	4000.000000	214.904522
VISITS	21	0.5714286	1.121224	0.00000000	4.000000	0.244671
MTGS	18	12.6111111	28.249183	0.00000000	99.000000	6.658396

for all members of each group), Figure 7.2 shows specifically the numbers of individuals receiving each number of visits. The men's chart shows that most men had one or more visits, three men had ten, and a few had none. In clearly visible contrast, the women's chart shows that a few women had some visits, but most had none. Although Figure 7.2 presents the same data found in Table 7.7, it isolates the relationship between sex and the pattern of visits and therefore presents it much more sharply and with greater visual impact. These findings, in addition to scores and other findings, were the basis for the conclusion that women were not getting equal or sufficient attention and benefits from the project, compared to men.

Creating cumulative bar charts is another useful SAS feature that allows data to be divided in a number of ways for display and analysis. Again using the scores of farmers' recall of extension recommendations, Figures 7.3 and 7.4 illustrate vertical bar charts that are grouped according to selected variables. Figure 7.4 compares the total scores of all respondents from four villages (labeled as posts). If a particular bar were much higher or lower, one might hypothesize an unusually successful or unsuccessful extension worker or other reasons for the success of selected villages. This could lead to a more detailed, comparative analysis of specific villages. It could also be an important part of a program evaluation, that is, what makes a development program work well.

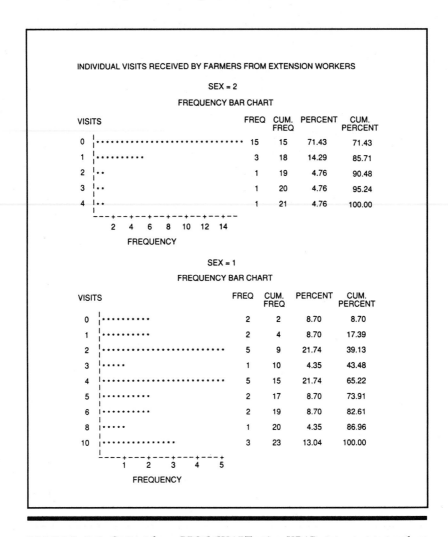

F I G U R E   7.2   *Output from PROC CHART using HBAR statement to produce a horizontal bar chart and associated statistics*

Figure 7.5 further divides the data by looking only at recall of corn recommendations and by separating men and women in each village. Here a great deal of variation is illustrated. This leads to additional examination, especially of the differences between men and women at Village Three. Anthropological analysis using computer output will lead back and forth from the focused output to the original, textual interview material for particular farmers or villages. The task of interweaving quantitative output and qualitative interview text is made easier, faster, and more meaningful with the use of a computer. In light of new questions raised by the computer output, the text becomes newly illuminating and illustrative.

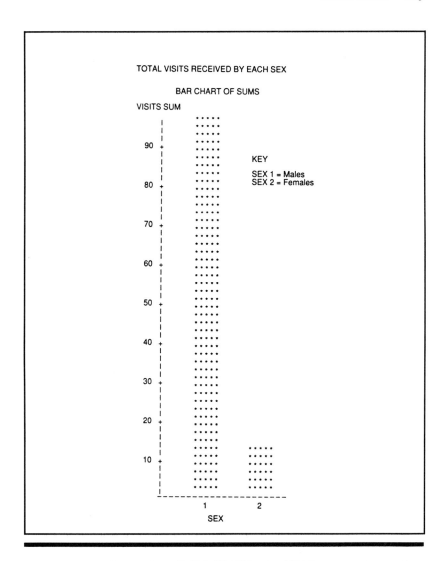

FIGURE 7.3 *Output from PROC CHART using VBAR statement to produce a vertical bar chart*

IN THE OFFICE

Step 8: Examining Output and Drawing Conclusions
Step 9: Writing the Report

These steps require little explanation for simple, univariate analysis. They are familiar steps for any type of anthropological analysis using any type of database, whether it exists as a computer file or as a handwritten tally sheet. However, because the computer can produce and rearrange univariate output much faster, the conclusions and report can potentially

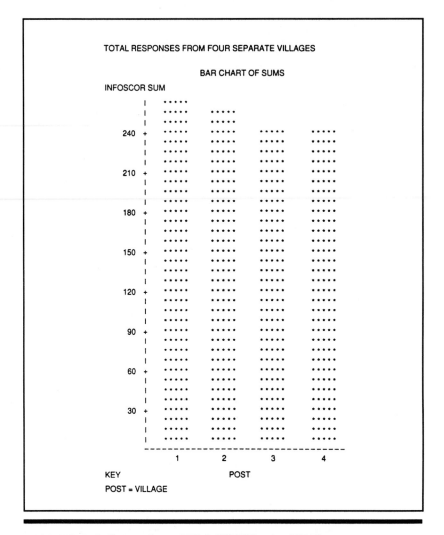

F I G U R E   7.4   *Output from PROC CHART using VBAR statement*

take on added dimensions. Instead of inhibiting creativity, use of a computer can foster it.

Some initial analysis has already been described as it relates to specific types of output. There was no discrete step in which all printouts were analyzed. The analysis moved back and forth from programming to examination and generalization. As the outputs from the individual programs were printed, they were inspected. The inspection led to preliminary conclusions and questions that invoked further computer runs or to final conclusions. The final report integrated both the computer printouts and the original text to illustrate and substantiate

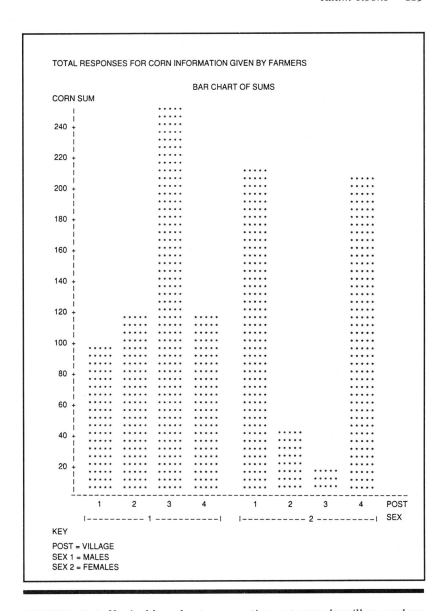

FIGURE 7.5 *Vertical bar charts segregating responses by village and sex*

the findings and conclusions. SAS-generated tables, charts, and graphs were reproduced in the report along with examples of verbal responses and often longer quotes from the interviews—lest the tables lose their original connections to interviews with real, live farmers. The combination of quantitative figures and qualitative interviews is very powerful and persuasive in research reports.

RESEARCH CONCLUSIONS

The final report showed that both men and women were equally receptive to assistance, but men were receiving most of the attention. The interview analysis showed that men knew far more of the extension recommendations than did women. Although men and women both met with extension workers in group settings, women had virtually no individual contact with extension agents and men had a great deal (twelve instances compared to ninety-five). Figure 7.3 shows the comparison quite dramatically. The interviews also showed that farmers were equally concerned with information assistance and material assistance. This contradicted many project officials who claimed that farmers mostly wanted material assistance.

The interviews led to further investigation of gender attitudes that influence agricultural extension in development contexts. In later stages of the research, it was found that both farmers and extension agents subscribed to beliefs about women's lack of interest, resistance to change, inability to understand new techniques, and avoidance of so-called "modern" information and assistance. These attitudes virtually shut women out of the extension program. The system operates with the perspective that once farmers are invited to participate, interested farmers will step forward. Men do; women do not. The situation is self-perpetuating. The women are left out, they feel left out, they do not initiate interaction, and extension workers await women's requests, which do not come. So, women are viewed as resistant and remain ignored.

A change in approach was recommended in the final report, which targets women more directly. Extension workers and the women, themselves, need to realize that women are entitled to, and must have access to, extension services. Extension workers need to encourage women actively to participate.

THE USE OF SAS PROGRAMMING IN ANTHROPOLOGICAL ANALYSIS

The procedures described in this chapter do not convert subjectivity into objectivity or vice versa. What they do is convert qualitative data into quantitative data and thereby greatly speed the process of analysis. The computer distills, isolates, combines, and reorganizes categories of data that are relevant to the analysis. The computer lends itself to experimentation and productive play. One is able to combine and compare variables in ways that never would have been considered if they required more time. The researcher is able to see tables, frequencies, charts, and plots immediately and thereby determine the relationships of variables and their potential relevance. Patterns appear that might have taken far more lengthy and more intense investigation to discover—or might not have been found at all.

NOTES

1. For readers interested in the theory and practice of development anthropology, several good collections are Green 1987; Horowitz and Painter 1986; and Jones and Wallace 1986.

2. Qualitative text material from interviews can, however, be entered into files for analysis with a program such as ETHNOGRAPH. See Bee and Crabtree's example in Chapter 5 of this volume.

3. The SPSS-X software package contains a MULTIPLE RESPONSE program that is specially designed to display the results of this type of question, including percentages of all responses.

4. SAS and SPSS-X now both have smaller, more limited versions for PCs. SYSTAT is another popular, widely used statistical program for microcomputers. For an example of an introductory class on SYSTAT, see Crabtree and Pelto 1988.

CHAPTER EIGHT

Introducing Statistical Testing to Standard Ethnography: An Example from Elephant Management in Sri Lanka

KATY MORAN

Moran, like Koons in Chapter 7, tackles a problem in development anthropology by combining quantitative and qualitative methods. She takes her analysis one step beyond tables of univariate statistics and performs a statistical test to explore a specific hypothesis. The result of the test helps her to interpret her findings in an ethnohistorical context and to frame a recommendation for conservation management. Moran illustrates the statistical test both by hand and in computer programming—reminding us that behind each statistical procedure performed by the computer are mathematical calculations that can be performed by hand.

A COMBINED METHODOLOGY

In this chapter, qualitative methods are combined with quantitative methods to investigate the traditional management of Asian elephants (*Elephas maximus maximus*) in Sri Lanka. The Smithsonian Institution's National Zoo supported this anthropological fieldwork in 1985 to learn if traditional Sri Lankan elephant management could be used to save wild elephants that are endangered because of agricultural development that has encroached on their habitats. The complex relationships among humans, animals, land, and government policy provided a rich research arena that was well suited to a combined approach of ethnohistorical analysis, participant observation, field interviews with questionnaires, graphic tabulation of trends and profiles using Lotus software and a microcomputer, and the testing of a research hypothesis using the Chi-square statistic and SAS software on a mainframe computer.

A RESEARCH PROBLEM IN
APPLIED ANTHROPOLOGY

Approximately 4,000 of the remaining 40,000 Asian elephants in the world today live in Sri Lanka, where the Smithsonian Institution's National Zoo has concentrated conservation efforts for the species. Since 1972, zoologists, wildlife biologists, and ecologists from the zoo have studied the behavior and ecology of elephants in Sri Lanka. More recently, zoo scientists have planned parks, preserves, and buffer zones for wild elephants that compete with humans for scarce land on this small island. In 1985, more than fifty wild Asian elephants were shot and killed by farmers in Sri Lanka, even though most of the farmers are Buddhists who regard elephants as quasi-sacred animals. Elephant meat and hides have never been harvested by Buddhists, and only 5 percent of the elephants in Sri Lanka have tusks. Therefore, the cause of the elephant killings is not poaching but defense of property. Small elephant herds become stranded in habitats that have recently been developed for agriculture. Hungry elephants invade farms for food, forcing farmers to defend their crops, their homes, and often their lives from the destructive power of 4-ton invaders.

Conservation policy does not address these problems but further exacerbates the plight of the farmer and accelerates the extinction of Asian elephants. The policy was set after political independence in 1948, when the new government instituted legislation to save the wild elephants that survived the British colonial gentry who shot the animals for sport. National parks were created to protect remnant herds of approximately 3,500 wild elephants, and as a further conservation measure, the traditional capture of elephants for domestication was also forbidden.

The size of parks and reserves shrank as the human population increased and more elephant habitats were developed into farmland. Parks have reached their carrying capacity, and today there is no room for 800 doomed elephants that are stranded in developed areas where they destroy farmland and disrupt economic progress. These problems can only increase as agricultural development continues to encroach on wild elephant habitats.

The conservation strategy explored in this chapter would solve these complex problems by using traditional methods to domesticate many of the stranded elephants, so that both humans and elephants could share rather than compete for scarce land. Ethnohistoric research on this strategy revealed that elephant domestication has a long and venerable history in Sri Lankan culture. Domesticated elephants were exported in trade and trained for war and work but were used primarily in religious ceremonies. Elephant owners gained religious merit and were publicly recognized as members of the elite when their animals were displayed in Buddhist ceremonies. However, although Sri Lankans have domesticated elephants for over twenty-three centuries, capture of any wild elephants for domestication is now restricted for conservation reasons. On the island today, there are from 400 to 500 elephants that were domesticated before capture was banned or domesticated after being orphaned or injured by farmers and rescued by the Department of Wild Life Conservation.

My goal was to discover if the domestication of more stranded elephants is feasible as a conservation strategy. Two basic questions were asked: (1) What are the incentives for, and constraints against, owning domesticated elephants? (2) Can more elephants be domesticated and used in Sri Lanka today? To answer these questions, I contacted the owners and keepers of these domesticated elephants to be interviewees in this study. Because no one knows exactly how many of these individuals live in Sri Lanka, I took an "opportunistic sample": I interviewed all the owners and keepers that I encountered inside of a six-month period. In this way, the number of interviewees was determined by the period of study time allowed by research funding.

On return from the field, I spent three months coding and entering data from 197 questionnaires, with sixteen to thirty-three questions each, into computer files for use with two types of software and two types of computers. Interviews with elephant owners and keepers provided a wealth of information to develop and test hypotheses about elephant management. I used a computer to quantify, recode, and display their verbal responses. I created three different data files from the questionnaires. The first data file was based on responses from forty-six elephant owners who were asked about the number of elephants they owned; the elephants' value—monetary or in kind; and the profits and losses involved in owning elephants. The second file was based on responses from the same forty-six owners to questions about the types of work each of their elephants performed. Responses were given on a total of 141 domesticated elephants. The third data file represented responses from 110 elephant keepers who were asked how they manage elephants and the number of hours their elephants worked and rested daily.

I used Lotus 1-2-3 and a microcomputer to organize and display the data so that I could make some initial comparisons and form hypotheses for later follow-up. Lotus is basically a "spreadsheet" program that allows entry of figures into columns and rows in a rectangular format. It can be very useful when only univariate statistics are needed and only a microcomputer is available. A certain amount of "programming" is possible with Lotus, by associating formulas (standard, or your own tailor-made) with cells or groups of cells in the rectangular grid. Lotus also has simple, but good, graphics capabilities that allow quantities and percentages of categories to be displayed in pie charts and bar charts (Figures 8.1 through 8.6).

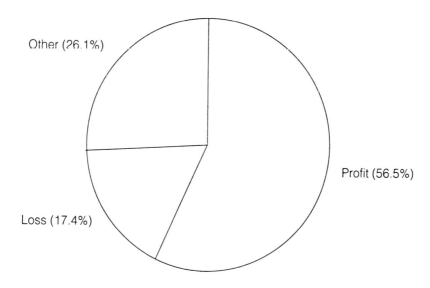

FIGURE 8.1 *Elephant owners' responses on profitability (Lotus pie chart)*

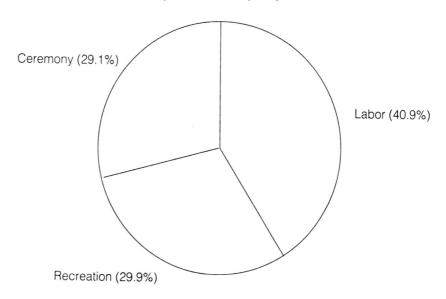

FIGURE 8.2 *Elephant owners' responses on elephant uses. The total is less than 100.0 because of rounding (Lotus pie chart)*

USING LOTUS SOFTWARE
TO PROFILE ELEPHANT USES

Using an IBM microcomputer, Lotus 1-2-3 software, and a dot matrix printer, I created graphic printouts based on percent and frequency distributions of the coded responses to a number of the interview questions. Lotus has the ability to turn rows and columns of data into several kinds of graphs. Figure 8.1 is a pie chart that gives the percent distribution for one of the variables in one of the databases I created. The variable is coded from responses from the sample of forty-six elephant owners to the following question: "Last year, did you have an economic (A) PROFIT (B) LOSS (C) OTHER from your elephant(s)?" The percent distribution shows that 56.5 percent of the owners made an economic profit. A little over 26 percent of the owners worked their animals only enough to pay for their maintenance. They did not net a profit or a loss but kept elephants for the elite status and religious merit still associated with elephant ownership. Another 17.4 percent of the elephant owners responded that they lost money by owning elephants. Interviews disclosed that these owners could afford the loss and that they owned elephants only for the status and merit they gained when their animals participated in religious ceremonies.

Similarly, Figure 8.2, on "Elephant Employment," is a pie chart that shows the percent distribution of primary, paid use of elephants, as indicated by elephant owners. Almost 41 percent of the respondents ranked labor—such as timbering, agriculture, road work, construction, transport, and training other work elephants—as the most frequent use of their domesticated elephants. However, a little over 29 percent ranked ceremonial use of their animals as most frequent, and almost 30 percent ranked recreational use, such as tourism, first.

Lotus 1-2-3 presents a series of menus in a branching fashion that enable a researcher to perform a wide range of manipulations of the research data. One of the commands that allows some of the most creative exploration of the data is the "/Graph" command. Lotus was used to create Figures 8.1 through 8.6 by using the /Graph command and two main specifications: type of chart and the range of cells that contained the data. The "Main Menu" for the /Graph command looks like this:

Type X A B C D E F Reset View Save Options Name Quit

When "Type" is selected, a new menu appears that allows selection of the graph type:

Line Bar Stacked Pie XY

Figures 8.1 and 8.2 in this chapter were created by selecting "Pie," and Figures 8.3 through 8.6 were created by selecting "Bar." The data used in these charts were specified as "cell ranges" in the grids of data in

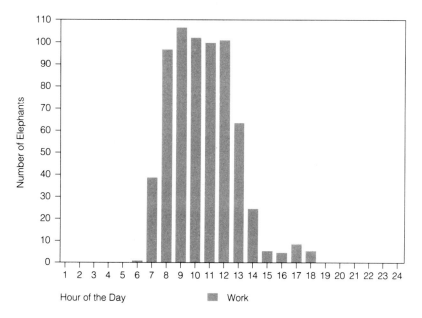

FIGURE 8.3 *Working elephants' daily schedule (working)*

the data file. The program prompts the user each step of the way, and when all specifications are made (including labels using several different methods), then "/Graph View" is selected, and the graph is drawn on the screen. It can be printed, or it can be changed and viewed again. Graphs and all their specifications (type, data, labels, scales, grid lines, and so on) can also be saved in graph files and printed later or revised and printed again.

USING LOTUS SOFTWARE TO DEVELOP PROGRAM RECOMMENDATIONS

In order to recommend domestication as a conservation strategy, I needed to demonstrate that domesticated elephants were well cared for and that elephant owners and keepers do not overwork their elephants. Earlier Smithsonian Institution studies listed the physical requirements for the animals as food, water, rest, and shade (Eisenberg 1972; McKay 1973). In the present study, I framed a question around these requirements. I asked 110 elephant keepers which of four mutually exclusive activities—WORK, BATHE, FEED/WATER, and REST—their elephants performed at each hour of the day. Figures 8.3 through 8.6 are bar charts that illustrate the daily schedules of working elephants.

On each of these figures the vertical axis represents the number of elephant keepers; the horizontal axis represents the hour of the day. Figure 8.3 illustrates the hours of work for working elephants. It shows

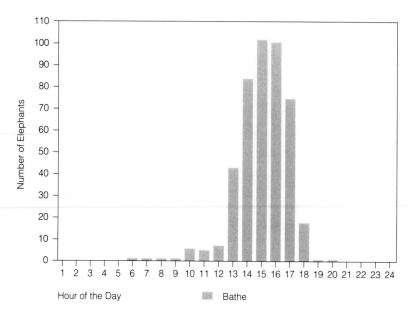

FIGURE 8.4 *Working elephants' daily schedule (bathing)*

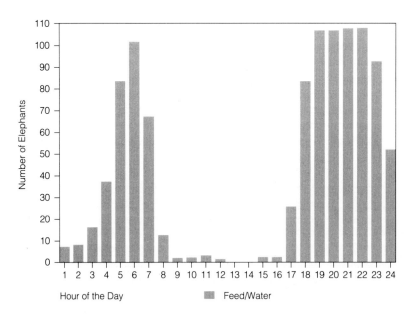

FIGURE 8.5 *Working elephants' daily schedule (feeding)*

7 A.M. and 1 P.M. (1300 hours). Zoo elephants are represented in Figure 8.3 as working between 2 P.M. (1400 hours) and 6 P.M. (1800 hours), when they participate in an elephant show and give rides to the public. Figure 8.4 shows that during the hottest part of the day, between 2 P.M.

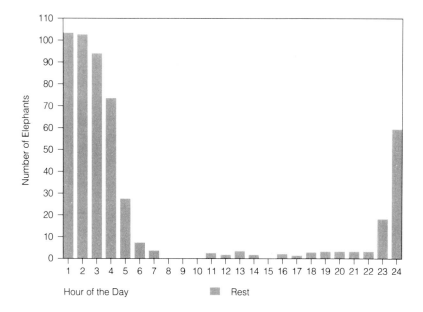

FIGURE 8.6 *Working elephants' daily schedule (resting)*

and 5 P.M., or 1400 and 1700 hours, the keepers surveyed give their elephants a two- to three-hour bath. Figure 8.5 shows that elephants are given adequate time daily to fulfill their requirements for food and water, and Figure 8.6 shows that they are given time to rest.

The tight clustering of results from this fairly large sample suggests that domesticated elephants are not overworked. My own observations at timber camps, the zoo, tourist parks, and other work sites confirmed the activities of elephants during different parts of the day, as shown in Figures 8.3 through 8.6. Participant observation and interviews also confirmed the existence of traditional techniques to tame, train, and manage domesticated elephants. My conclusion was that elephant owners and keepers do not overwork their elephants, and this strengthened the recommendation to domesticate more elephants as a conservation strategy.

USING SAS SOFTWARE TO TEST A HYPOTHESIS ABOUT ELEPHANT OWNERSHIP

Once I had taken a good initial look at the data and completed part of my analysis using Lotus, I wanted to test a particular hypothesis about elephant management. I decided that I needed to use the Chi-square statistic, which can test for a relationship between categories of discontinuous data. Lotus did not allow for the easy programming of a statistical test. Furthermore, I had already entered the data into computer files,

TABLE 8.1 *Distribution of elephant ownership in Sri Lanka,*
1970 and 1985

	NUMBER AND PERCENT OF ELEPHANT OWNERS			
NUMBER OF ELEPHANTS OWNED	OWNERS IN 1970 CENSUS (N)	(%)	OWNERS IN 1985 SAMPLE (N)	(%)
1 elephant	288	(76)	22	(48)
2 elephants	61	(16)	10	(22)
3 elephants	17	(5)	3	(7)
4 elephants	6	(2)	4	(9)
5 elephants	3	(1)	1	(2)
6 elephants	0	(0)	0	(0)
7 elephants	1	(0)	2	(4)
8 elephants	0	(0)	0	(0)
9 elephants	0	(0)	0	(0)
10 elephants	0	(0)	1	(2)
11 elephants	0	(0)	1	(2)
12 elephants	1	(0)	0	(0)
13 elephants	1	(0)	1	(2)
21 elephants	0	(0)	1	(2)
TOTAL	378	(100)	46	(100)

Sources: Jayasinghe, J. B., and Jainudeen, M. R. (1970). A census of the tame elephant population in Ceylon with reference to location and distribution. *Ceylon Journal of Science* 8 (2):66; Moran, K. (1986). Traditional elephant management in Sri Lanka: An ethnozoological perspective for conservation. American Association of Zoological Parks and Aquariums (AAZPA). Annual Conference Proceedings, AAZP. Wheeling, WV.

so it was easier to use a computer to test with Chi-square than it would have been to perform the test by hand. In much larger studies, it would be extremely laborious—to the point of being impractical—to calculate Chi-square by hand. Therefore, I used one of the software packages specifically designed to test hypotheses using inferential statistics. I used a statistical package called SAS, and specifically, a program called PROC FREQ, which displays categories of data in a frequencies chart or table similar to Table 8.3. Unlike Lotus, this software was available at my university only on the large mainframe computer. Because I was a novice computer programmer, SAS was the software of choice because it was recommended to me as "user friendly," and there were instructors and technical assistants available to help me write SAS programs.

I developed a hypothesis based on a comparison of my data with previously collected data. Some of the results from the University of Ceylon–Smithsonian Institution Elephant Research Program, "A Census of the Tame Elephant Population in Ceylon" (Jayasinghe and Jainudeen 1970), are given in Table 8.1. The 1970 census is the only complete record of elephant ownership in Sri Lanka. The left column in Table 8.1 shows

T A B L E 8 . 2 *SAS program to test hypothesis with Chi-square statistic*

```
// EXEC SAS
PROC FORMAT;
    ELSFMT 1=1 ELEPHANT
           2-5=2-5 ELEPHANTS
           6-HIGH=6 OR MORE ELEPHANTS;
DATA KATY;
    INFILE CARDS;
    INPUT CASE 1-3 YEAR 4-7 ELS 8-9;
    FORMAT ELS ELSFMT.;
    IF ELS>1 AND ELS<6 THEN ELS=2;  ELSE IF ELS>5 THEN ELS=6;
CARDS;
001198506
002197009
003198501

{more lines of data here}

422197001
423198504
424197001
;
PROC FREQ DATA=KATY;
    TABLES ELS*YEAR / CHISQ;
    TITLE STATISTICAL ANALYSIS OF CHANGE IN ELEPHANT OWNERSHIP;
```

that before the 1972 land reform, 378 elephant owners had a total of 532 domesticated elephants. The 1970 data are given alongside data from a sampling of elephant owners that I met in Sri Lanka between June and December 1985. I surveyed forty-six owners who had a total of 141 domesticated elephants.

After an initial examination of the distributions in Table 8.1, I wanted to know whether the distribution of elephant ownership had changed between 1970 and 1985. Stated in another way, I wanted to test the Null Hypothesis that elephant ownership had not changed between 1970 and 1985—that is, the hypothesis that there is no difference between the distributions. If the distributions in Table 8.1 were very similar, then a calculated Chi-square statistic would be small because "observed" and "expected" frequencies would be similar. This would suggest no change (see the discussion of hand-calculated Chi-square below). However, if the distributions in Table 8.1 were very different, then Chi-square would be large because "observed" and "expected" frequencies would be dissimilar. This would suggest that change had occurred. It would not "prove" that change had occurred, but it would suggest that change had very likely occurred. Statistical testing only allows statements about the probabilities of events.

I wrote a SAS program to calculate the Chi-square statistic on the mainframe computer (Table 8.2). I grouped the data in Table 8.1 into three groups of elephant owners: those who owned only one elephant, those who owned two to five elephants, and those who owned six or more elephants. SAS software easily handles this kind of grouping in the "Data Step," by recoding the variable ELS, which was the number of elephants owned by each owner (Table 8.2). SAS also allows a researcher to label each new category in the output frequency table, using a formatting procedure called PROC FORMAT (compare the format given in the Data Step in Table 8.2 with the output in Table 8.3).

The Chi-square statistic is rapidly computed by the SAS procedure called PROC FREQ, using the CHISQ option (Table 8.2). The table produced by this procedure is specified by the TABLES statement (Table 8.2). The first variable in the TABLES statement is on the vertical axis of the output table, and the second variable is on the horizontal axis. The results in Table 8.3 suggested that elephant ownership had indeed changed because it had become more concentrated among fewer owners. The Chi-square statistic printed below the output table is relatively large, 37.804. In fact, according to Chi-square tables (which are computed and given as an appendix in most statistics texts), there is only 1 chance in 10,000 that the distributions would be this dissimilar if change had *not* occurred (PROB = 0.0001, in Table 8.3).

It is very easy to lose sight of the mechanics of statistical computations when using a statistical software package. A computer accomplishes in split seconds computations that may take a researcher hours to complete. Programs can be run and rerun many times as a new understanding of the relationships between variables emerges. Correct interpretation of output from statistical packages should rest on an understanding of exactly what a statistical procedure does. In the case of Chi-square, it may be practical for a novice user to compute Chi-square by hand, just to retrace the steps that a computer takes and to understand more fully how Chi-square is derived and what it means. The same is true of all statistical procedures, although, for example, the computation of a stepwise multiple regression can easily take an hour or two, so the practicality of the exercise soon reaches its limits. Some types of statistical procedures have been developed *only* with the availability of modern high-speed computers. When more complex procedures are used, there is no alternative to classroom instruction or tutoring in statistics and practice in writing up statistical results in reports or papers.

With these caveats in mind, the following hand calculations of Chi-square are given as a comparison to, and an explanation of, the computer output in Table 8.3. The Chi-square statistic computed in this research is essentially a comparison between field observations in 1970 and 1985 and what we would expect observations to be if there were no change in elephant ownership in those years. In other words, it is a comparison of Table 8.1 and another, imaginary table of an "expected"

T A B L E 8 . 3 *SAS output*

SAS

TABLE OF NUMBER BY YEAR

NUMBER   YEAR

FREQUENCY
  PERCENT
  ROW PCT
  COL PCT   1970   1985   TOTAL

	1970	1985	TOTAL
1	288	22	310
ELEPHANT	67.92	5.19	73.11
	92.90	7.10	
	76.19	47.83	
2–5	87	18	105
ELEPHANTS	20.52	4.25	24.76
	82.86	17.14	
	23.02	39.13	
6 OR MORE	3	6	9
ELEPHANTS	0.71	1.42	2.12
	33.33	66.67	
	0.79	13.04	
TOTAL	378	46	424
	89.15	10.85	100.00

STATISTICS FOR 2-WAY TABLES

CHI-SQUARE	37.804	DF =	2	PROB = 0.0001
PHI	0.299			
CONTINGENCY COEFFICIENT	0.286			
CRAMER'S V	0.299			
LIKELIHOOD RATIO CHISQUARE	24.688	DF =	2	PROB = 0.0001

distribution if elephant ownership did not change between 1970 and 1985. If the expectations and observations are very similar, then we can conclude "no change" or "no difference." Chi-square summarizes the size of the difference between what is "expected" and what is "observed." The Chi-square distribution is a probability curve that allows a researcher to assess the size of the difference—whether it is a "large difference" or a "small difference." The Chi-square table in most statistics texts is really a compilation of a number of probability curves (one line to a curve). The difference between lines is determined by the "degrees of freedom" that are warranted in the particular research problem at hand. "Degrees of freedom" basically means "random choices." Because the distributions of rows and columns are already specified in a table of observed and expected values, then their midpoints are specified points. Thus, the "random choices" are reduced by one point for rows (r-1) and one point for columns (c-1), and the resulting degrees of freedom (df) is a product of the two (r-1) (c-1).

$$\chi^2 = \sum_{i=1}^{k} \frac{(\text{observed} - \text{expected})^2}{\text{expected}}$$

$$df = (r - 1)(c - 1)$$

Chi-square equals the sum of the observed values, minus the expected values, squared (to convert all negative-sign differences to positive numbers), divided by the expected values. Expected values are determined by multiplying the marginal values and then dividing by Total N, for each cell (see Table 8.3). For example, to obtain the first expected value, calculate the following: $[(310)(378)]/424$. For the data collected in 1970 and 1985, the calculation is as follows:

$$\chi^2 = \sum \frac{(288 - 276)^2}{276} + \frac{(22 - 34)^2}{34} + \frac{(87 - 94)^2}{94} +$$

$$\frac{(18 - 11)^2}{11} + \frac{(3 - 8)^2}{8} + \frac{(6 - 1)^2}{1} = 37.86$$

$$df = (r - 1)(c - 1) = (3 - 1)(2 - 1) = 2$$

In a table for the Chi-square distribution, for df = 2, at p = .001, $\chi^2 = 13.815$. Since 37.8 is greater than this number, Chi-square is significant at, at least, .001.

The COLUMN PERCENTAGES are important in Table 8.3. In 1970, 76.2 percent of the owners had only one elephant, whereas only 47.8 percent owned one elephant in 1985. (These figures also appear in Table 8.1, after rounding.) In 1970, fewer than 1 percent owned six or more elephants, versus over 13 percent in 1985. This shifting away from a dispersed ownership pattern toward a pattern in which people owned larger numbers of elephants is significant at the .0001 level according to SAS output. The Chi-square value is 37.804, which is very high. This suggests that it is highly improbable that elephant ownership has changed merely by chance.

A RECOMMENDATION FOR CONSERVATION
POLICY BASED ON STUDY RESULTS

A likely reason for the change in elephant ownership is that profit was an incentive for entrepreneurs to buy more domesticated elephants from owners who were losing money. Elephant ownership responded to a free-market force and became concentrated in the hands of fewer owners, who recognize elephants as an opportunity for economic profit. The best conservation strategy would be one that recognized these economic motives of elephant owners, but it is essential that an effective strategy also offer farmers some benefits.

Results of this study suggest a conservation approach that will give farmers an investment in elephant conservation as well as a means to rid their fields of marauding elephants. Farmers who live in developed areas can contribute labor and daily on-site information for use in elephant capture operations. They can assess herd composition, location, and migration routes; map paths and local water sources that elephants use; and identify elephant trespassers and damage to human property. Profits from the sale of captive elephants can be returned to farmers in compensation for crop damage and as wages for participation in capture operations.

Domesticated elephants can be absorbed into the local economy, or exported to zoos and circuses in the West, or used for timbering operations in Asia. Elephants could also be used to establish a captive breeding program that would make Sri Lanka a world center for applied and basic research, training, and education in veterinary medicine, elephant husbandry, anthropology, zoology, and a comparison of *in situ* and *ex situ* conservation methodology.

THE DIFFERENCE THAT PACKAGE USE MADE

Development of this strategy for elephant conservation was only possible by combining qualitative and quantitative methods. By themselves, either qualitative or quantitative methods would have been inadequate. Participant observation and interviewing were strongly supported by quantified graphics and finally by a statistical test. On the other hand, the use of quantitative methods alone would have left too many questions about the validity of my observations. Participant observation and interviewing were needed to "double-check" and make sure my conclusions made sense in the field.

The research process began with a conservation problem. A study of present-day Sri Lankan society and government policy revealed that land owners were unhappy, elephants were being killed, and the current policy was not helpful. Ethnohistorical research suggested domestication as a possible conservation strategy. Once this strategy was formulated, then the use of questionnaires in field interviewing allowed the collection of a large amount of semi-organized data that could be used to test the applicability of a "traditional," but new, solution.

The data from structured interviewing were sufficiently organized to be used and manipulated, after being recoded, on both a microcomputer and a large mainframe computer, using appropriate software for each. The use of Lotus allowed me to take an initial look at the data without use of a large computer and without a major investment in learning how to program or create computer graphics. When it became necessary to test a hypothesis, I then switched to SAS. Writing the program for the Chi-square test using SAS was easier than computing it by hand. SAS also made it easy for me to merge files that had already been created. I created files from each questionnaire, then merged the files to analyze relationships between variables. Common variables could be pulled out to analyze a new, merged file. Data were sorted and reaggregated in different ways, allowing me to focus easily on specific research questions as they emerged during the data analysis.

The combination of qualitative and quantitative methods played an integrative role for the natural and social sciences. The result was a proposal to save elephants by addressing the human dimensions of conservation. The conservation strategy offers Sri Lankans access to, benefits from, and participation in the use of their most valued cultural and natural resource. It is an opportunity for economic development through the use of a local natural resource. At the same time, it provides a means to conserve that resource. Most important, it nurtures values that are a motivating force in Sri Lankan society, which is proved by the very survival of elephants in both wild and captive states for over twenty-five centuries on this small island.

CHAPTER NINE

Linear Regression Analysis in Physical Anthropology: A Cautionary Tale

MARC R. FELDESMAN

One of the major tasks in physical anthropology is the proper identification and description of specimens. In this chapter, Feldesman uses linear regression to illustrate the regularities in relationships of bone size. At the same time, his research provides us with a good lesson for the quantitative analysis of all relationships. He warns us that in analyzing sophisticated computer output, no researcher should stray too far from the original data and his or her own good intuition about appropriate research results.

"Gentlemen, you are listening to a machine; do me a favor, don't act like one."

[Stephen Falken, in the movie WARGAMES]

Quantification is an important, if not essential, part of modern research. The modern computer facilitates quantification and enables the researcher to probe data in ways that would be impossible "by hand." This power exacts a price. With it comes the responsibility to know and understand the collected data and the statistical procedures well enough to recognize nonsensical or questionable results.

Unfortunately, many users fail to appreciate the importance of understanding both statistics and their data; misapplications of statistics and of the programs that generate them occur with alarming regularity. The ease with which users lacking the requisite statistical skills can access mainframe statistical packages such as SPSS, SAS, and MINITAB contributes to this problem. Students take courses that encourage (if not require) the use of these programs, but rarely are they told how to use them to recognize data corruption or how to distinguish between legitimate and spurious results. A course such as that outlined by Wood in Chapter 16 of this volume would go far toward remedying this deficiency. My own experience serving on biology, psychology, and sociology MA and PhD committees has convinced me that students need to spend less time on the science and more time on the art of statistics.

Social-cultural anthropology manages to escape much of the aforementioned criticism, not because of its statistical probity but because it approaches virginity in its degree of mathematization. To be sure, Chibnik (1985) concurs that social-cultural is the least quantified anthropological subfield, although use has increased considerably in the last few years.

These preliminary remarks are not meant to criticize those who use the computer as a tool, to castigate those who don't, or to persuade anyone to eschew computer-based statistical analysis. They are meant instead to point out that increased use of computerized statistical packages in social-cultural anthropology is inevitable and that, in consequence, greater care will be required in the analytical process. This chapter illustrates, using linear regression analysis as an example, why prudence and tenacity are dictated in the conduct of this type of research and how proper use of statistics can be facilitated by computer-based packages.

REGRESSION AS AN ANALYTICAL TOOL

When cultural anthropologists use statistics, it is mainly descriptive statistics, nonparametrics, factor analysis, or multidimensional scaling; regression analysis rarely figures prominently in their research designs. Classical ethnographic data do not generally stimulate questions that require regression analysis, so it is not surprising that the only current textbook of anthropological statistics (Thomas 1986) devotes a full chapter to regression but does not cite a single example of its use in cultural anthropology.

There are reasons to believe this situation may change. There has been a renaissance in applied cultural anthropology, with these specialists addressing medical and demographic problems for which regression analysis is ably suited. Given the types of data collected (for example, age structure, measures of modernization, acculturation, health status, ethnicity), there are a number of questions to which regression techniques might be applied (for example, relationships between different kinds and aspects of modernization, relationships between proportions of female labor and severity of puberty rituals, relationships between length of time in a nontraditional society and the degree of acculturation).[1]

Outside of social-cultural anthropology, regression is one of the most popular and important statistical procedures in use today. One researcher conducted a survey at his own computer center and found that nearly 90 percent of the statistical usage was in regression and correlation analysis (Pimentel 1979). These numbers, probably representative of statistical use at most computer centers, attest to the importance of regression procedures in the modern researcher's toolbox. Unfortunately, they offer little assurance that the techniques have been used properly. In naive hands, regression analysis can do more harm than good, and the technique has about as much value as a gift from Zeus to Pandora.

Regression is a technique used to study the functional relationship between two or more ratio or interval level variables. A major purpose of regression analysis is to use at least one (simple bivariate case) of these variables to predict or estimate the value of another. Although this is a paper about regression, except for a brief example of a typical problem for which regression is suited, nothing will be said about the theory and computational details. The interested reader is referred to any popular statistics text (for example, Mendenhall 1986; Wonnacott and Wonnacott 1985) for these details. A simple preliminary example will suffice to illustrate the circumstances under which regression is appropriate. Obese people tend to have high blood pressure. Our interests are in establishing whether this assumption is merited statistically and in determining the precise form of the functional relationship if a significant one exists. To accomplish this we could take a random sample of people ranging from svelte to obese and measure their weights and blood pressures.[2] After "cleaning" the data of obvious errors and computing standard univariate statistics (that is, mean, variance, skewness, kurtosis) for both weight and blood pressure, we could then perform a regression analysis. The regression would establish the extent to which body weight and blood pressure covaried (that is, correlated) and would tell us whether a significant linear trend was evident in the data. If the relationship satisfied statistical criteria for significance (see Mendenhall 1986, Thomas 1986, or Wonnacott and Wonnacott 1985 for the details of this determination), we could then use it to formulate a simple equation that would permit us to predict blood pressure from body weight.

From a computational standpoint, regression is straightforward. From a theoretical point of view, however, regression makes certain assumptions about the data. The degree to which our data satisfy these conditions directly influences the confidence we can repose in the results. First, we must assume that for any value of the predictor variable, there exists a normal distribution of the dependent variable and that we have sampled our dependent variable at random from that distribution. Second, the variances of the dependent variable around each of these normal distributions are assumed to be equal. Third, errors in the dependent variable must be additive, while the values of the dependent variable are themselves assumed to be independent. Finally, the predictor variables must be measured without error (Zar 1984).

PITFALLS OF REGRESSION ANALYSIS

Although least squares analysis is rather robust to violations of these assumptions (Draper and Smith 1981; Zar 1984), especially of the last, it is important for the investigator to assess the degree to which sample data conform to expectations under the model. Serious violations of these assumptions may lead to significant errors of interpretation.

Outliers—data that appear to be inconsistent with the remainder of the data set—can exert a profound effect on regression analyses (Barnett and Lewis 1978). Data that are suspect arise in several ways. Atkinson (1985:2) lists four possibilities:

1. There may be gross errors in either response or explanatory variables. These could arise from incorrect or faulty measurements, from transcription errors, or from errors in key punching and data entry.
2. The linear model may be inadequate to describe the systematic structure of the data.
3. It may be that the data would be better analyzed in another scale, for example after a logarithmic or other transformation of the response.
4. The systematic part of the model and the scale may both be correct, but the error distribution of the response is appreciably longer tailed than the normal distribution. As a result, least squares may be far from the best method of fitting the model.

Few data sets escape one or more of these problems. The effects of these problems differ, as do the approaches for remedying them; however, the process by which a researcher identifies and decides to take action on suspicious data is remarkably similar across the problems.

A PROBLEMATIC APPLICATION OF REGRESSION

The present paper evolved from an analysis a colleague and I conducted to derive stature-estimating equations for South African black tribal populations. Our goal was to use these equations to predict stature in Plio-Pleistocene fossil hominids (Feldesman and Lundy 1987a and 1987b; Lundy and Feldesman 1987). During the early phases of our study, a number of suspicious data points came to my attention. Lundy (1983, 1984) had overlooked these data points in his earlier analyses. On closer inspection, they turned out to be outliers that had a significant effect on our results. Without care in conducting our preliminary analysis, these outliers would easily have gone undetected.

This paper illustrates a simple but frequently overlooked problem in regression analysis. In this regard it is a cautionary tale. It details the process by which we came to identify, isolate, and remove outliers in a regression analysis. In particular, I emphasize the ease with which the microcomputer package SYSTAT permitted, if not encouraged, the analysis. The particular analysis is unimportant to the general theme of this volume. What emerges from this paper, however, is a strategy for conducting a regression analysis that stresses the importance of rigorous screening of data—something that computer-based statistical packages handle with ease and that is difficult to do by hand.

DATA

The data are drawn from a sample of measurements taken on 302 South African black skeletons (177 males, 125 females) drawn from three documented tribal populations: Nguni, Venda, and Sotho. These skeletons are part of the Raymond Dart Collection at the University of the Witwatersrand in Johannesburg, South Africa. Initially, Lundy (1984) collected these data as part of a project to describe skeletal variation in South African black populations. More recently, we used them to derive regression equations for estimating skeletal stature in South Africans (Lundy and Feldesman 1987) and subsequently for estimating stature of fossil hominids (Feldesman and Lundy 1987a, 1987b).

METHODS

We separated the skeletal data described above by gender and then subjected them to ordinary least squares (OLS) regression analysis using SYSTAT's MGLH module (Wilkinson 1986).[3] As part of the analysis, I requested that residuals, predicted values, studentized residuals, and leverage coefficients be saved with the original variables so that they could be analyzed later. I chose the microcomputer package SYSTAT because it is extraordinarily accurate and flexible, and it supports a wide range of data screening functions, including the recommended procedures in Exploratory Data Analysis (EDA) (Tukey 1977; Velleman and Hoaglin 1981). Both SAS (SAS 1985) and SPSS-X/PC (SPSS Inc 1986) offer the same degree of flexibility as SYSTAT; however, I found that the cost of running both mainframe programs was exceptionally high,[4] whereas the PC versions of each did considerably less than SYSTAT for a substantially greater initial price. Furthermore, I found that SPSS-X's regression routines were not as accurate as SYSTAT's (Feldesman 1986).

After completing the OLS analysis, I used the SYSTAT module GRAPH to plot scattergrams of independent versus dependent variables, to plot the OLS residuals versus independent and dependent variables, to draw box plots of independent and dependent variables, and to generate stem and leaf diagrams for independent variables, dependent variables, leverage coefficients, and residuals. The latter analyses (box plots, stem

T A B L E 9 . 1 *SYSTAT command file used to perform the statistical analysis detailed in this chapter. The command file was submitted from inside the SYSTAT executive program called SYSTAT. The text following the semicolons is for illustrative purposes only and would not be included in the actual command file.*

mglh	;invoke the Module MGLH from SYSTAT.
use sfaafeml	;use data file containing male sample
out = sfaaout	;save output to file called SFAAOUT.DAT for later review
model skelht = constant + femurlen	;regression statement, simple linear model
save resid/model	;save residuals and original data in file called RESID.DAT
estimate	;estimate the regression
quit	;quit MGLH
graph	;invoke the Module GRAPH from SYSTAT
out = graphout	;save the pictures to a file called GRAPHOUT.DAT
use resid	;use file containing residuals and original data
plot residual*femurlen/symbol = 'x'	;plot residuals vs. femur length-use 'x' as plot symbol
plot residual*skelht/symbol = 'x'	;plot residuals vs. skeletal height-use 'x' as plot symbol
box femurlen	;box plot of femur length
box skelht	;box plot of skeletal height
stem femurlen	;stem-leaf display of femur length
stem skelht	;stem-leaf display of skeletal height
quit	;quit GRAPH
quit	;quit SYSTAT

and leaf diagrams) are EDA techniques necessitated when it became apparent that there were suspicious cases in the data. Table 9.1 depicts the complete SYSTAT batch command structure to complete one of the analyses reported here.

RESULTS

In conducting my analyses, I focused my attention on the relationship between several different long bone length measurements and the aggregate measurement, skeletal height. My primary concern was to establish the strength of the relationship between these variables and to develop equations that would enable me to predict the skeletal height of an individual from isolated long bone measurements without a complete skeleton.

In our previous studies (Feldesman and Lundy 1987a, 1987b; Lundy 1983, 1984; Lundy and Feldesman 1987), we showed that both femur length and tibia length strongly correlated with skeletal height. I therefore regressed these measurements separately on skeletal height in gender-specific samples to determine the form of the relationship. This paper focuses solely on the analysis of femur length in females; the problems I describe, however, apply equally in males and to our study of tibia length.

Table 9.2 details the results of the initial regression analysis as delineated by SYSTAT. This table makes it appear that there is a strong linear relationship between femur length and skeletal height. Nothing in this listing indicates anything untoward about the analysis. The correlations are quite strong, the R^2 is suitably high, and the standard error of the regression is low. Furthermore, the slope and intercept both are significantly different from zero, and the analysis of variance (ANOVA) shows that the regression itself is significant. Many researchers, having established such compelling evidence for a relationship this strong, would have gone no further.

The request for residuals is an essential part of any regression analysis. Residuals—that which is left over after the model is fit—help a researcher assess the appropriateness of the model. Not coincidentally, they also help a researcher flag aberrant cases. In the present study there are several indications from the residuals that the fit may have been adversely affected by some influential data points. In Table 9.3 SYSTAT flagged three cases with suspiciously high studentized residuals and noted five additional cases with high leverage as possibly influencing the results.

Cases with studentized residuals exceeding 3.0 are immediately suspect. Studentized residuals are those whose distribution is independent of their standard deviation. In this respect, they are like standardized residuals, which result when ordinary residuals are divided by their standard deviation (Younger 1979). Properly calculated,[5] "studentized" residuals are residuals divided by a standard deviation that results when the regression is computed without the case whose residual is being studentized (Belsley, Kuh, and Welsch 1980). Studentized residuals differ little from standardized residuals in cases where samples are large; in small samples the difference may be dramatic. The primary reason for studentizing is that such residuals follow Student's t (hence the name) distribution. Any single residual can therefore be tested for significant departures from an expected value of 0, using the t-distribution with n-p-1 degrees of freedom (Atkinson 1985).[6]

The leverage coefficient for any observation also is useful in determining whether a case is suspicious or not. Leverage is a measure of the remoteness of a particular observation from the remaining observations in the data set (Atkinson 1985). High leverage (values near 1) means that the predicted value of the dependent variable is almost entirely influenced by the dependent variable for that case and is not influenced to any significant degree by any of the other observations in the data set.[7]

T A B L E   9.2 *Output from typical SYSTAT MGLH linear regression (annotated with explanations of all critical output)*

DEP VAR: SKELHT	N: 125	MULTIPLE R: .811[1]		SQUARED MULTIPLE R: .658[2]		
ADJUSTED SQUARED MULTIPLE R: .655[3]		STANDARD ERROR OF ESTIMATE:		4.066[4]		

VARIABLE	COEFFICIENT[5]	STD ERROR [6]	STD COEF [7]	TOLERANCE[8]	T[9]	P(2TAIL) [10]
CONSTANT	29.567	7.501	0.000	1.0000000	3.942	0.000
FEMURLEN	2.725	0.177	0.811	1.0000000	15.379	0.000

ANALYSIS OF VARIANCE[11]

SOURCE	SUM-OF-SQUARES	DF	MEAN-SQUARE	F-RATIO[12]	P
REGRESSION	3909.295	1	3909.295	236.521	0.000
RESIDUAL	2032.982	123	16.528		

1. *In this study, the Multiple R is the simple Pearson correlation between femur length and skeletal height.*
2. *The squared multiple R denotes the proportion of variance in skeletal height explained by the independent variable femur length.*
3. *The adjusted squared multiple R reduces the squared multiple R to a level expected if a new random sample were drawn from the same population.*
4. *The standard error of the estimate is the square root of the residual mean square. It is a measure of the error inherent in any estimate derived from the predicting equation. Hence, the smaller the standard error of the estimate, the better the fit.*
5. *The regression coefficients themselves. The constant represents the y-intercept (B0), and the coefficient associated with femurlen represents the slope of the regression equation (B1).*
6. *The standard error of the coefficients are measures of how much we expect these coefficients to vary from sample to sample. In this case, it tells us that the intercept would vary by (+ −)7.501 with repeated samples of equivalent size drawn from the same population.*
7. *The standard coefficients are standardized regression coefficients (sometimes called beta coefficients in the social science literature).*
8. *Tolerance is not relevant in the case of a simple bivariate linear regression. In multiple regressions (that is, several independent variables), values of tolerance near zero indicate that some of the predictors are highly intercorrelated, an undesirable situation in a typical regression analysis.*
9. *The t-statistics reported here test the significance of the differences between the intercept and the slope, respectively, from zero. A non-significant t (that is, a value with a probability greater than 0.05) would suggest that the true value of the coefficient might really be zero.*
10. *Probabilities associated with the t values. In this case, both the constant and the slope are significantly different from zero.*
11. *The analysis of variance (ANOVA) table summarizes all the useful information about the regression itself.*
12. *The F-ratio is probably the most significant number in this table. Not only is it the square of the t-statistic for the slope, it also is a measure of the significance of the regression itself. It is computed as the quotient Mean Square Regression/Mean Square Residual. Basically it is a measure of the proportion of variation explained by the regression relative to the variation left unexplained by the regression (that is, the residual). In cases such as the one here, the regression explains substantially more variation than it leaves unexplained. The F-ratio is less important in bivariate regression than it is in multiple regressions.*

TABLE 9.3 *Output from SYSTAT MGLH linear regression with information about residuals added*

DEP VAR: SKELHT   N: 125   MULTIPLE R: .811   SQUARED MULTIPLE R: .658
ADJUSTED SQUARED MULTIPLE R: .655   STANDARD ERROR OF ESTIMATE: 4.066

VARIABLE	COEFFICIENT	STD ERROR	STD COEF	TOLERANCE	T	P(2TAIL)
CONSTANT	29.567	7.501	0.000	1.0000000	3.942	0.000
FEMURLEN	2.725	0.177	0.811	1.0000000	15.379	0.000

ANALYSIS OF VARIANCE

SOURCE	SUM-OF-SQUARES	DF	MEAN-SQUARE	F-RATIO	P
REGRESSION	3909.295	1	3909.295	236.521	0.000
RESIDUAL	2032.982	123	16.528		

WARNING: CASE   3 IS AN OUTLIER (STUDENTIZED RESIDUAL =   5.239)
WARNING: CASE   19 IS AN OUTLIER (STUDENTIZED RESIDUAL =   5.531)
WARNING: CASE   32 IS AN OUTLIER (STUDENTIZED RESIDUAL =   4.301)
WARNING: CASE   39 HAS UNDUE INFLUENCE (LEVERAGE =   .060)
WARNING: CASE   62 HAS UNDUE INFLUENCE (LEVERAGE =   .058)
WARNING: CASE   74 HAS UNDUE INFLUENCE (LEVERAGE =   .057)
WARNING: CASE   88 HAS UNDUE INFLUENCE (LEVERAGE =   .055)
WARNING: CASE   96 HAS UNDUE INFLUENCE (LEVERAGE =   .068)

DURBIN-WATSON D STATISTIC   2.043
FIRST ORDER AUTOCORRELATION   -.027

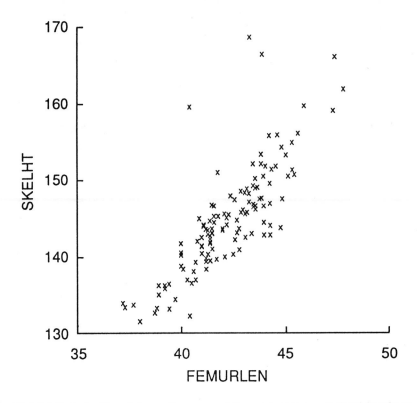

FIGURE 9.1 *Bivariate scattergram of femur length vs. skeletal height in South African females. Note the three outliers in the upper center of the graph.*

Rarely do leverage coefficients reach 1. Researchers have shown that the minimum value is 1/n, where n is the number of observations, and the average value is p/n, where p is the number of variables. According to Belsley, Kuh, and Welsch (1980), observations with leverages exceeding 2p/n may require further attention. Huber (1981) suggests that leverage coefficients above 0.5 are large, and those above 0.2 merit additional review. It should be stated that there is no necessary relationship between values of studentized residuals and leverage coefficients. To be sure, cases in the present data set with high studentized residuals have uninteresting leverage coefficients.

Armed with this information, we can look more closely at the results. Figure 9.1 depicts the bivariate relationships between femur length (independent variable) and skeletal height (dependent variable). The outliers are quite evident here. The renegade points that appear on the scattergram correspond in number and in case to those reported cases of large studentized residuals. The scattergram also suggests that the troublesome variable in all instances is skeletal height rather than femur length.

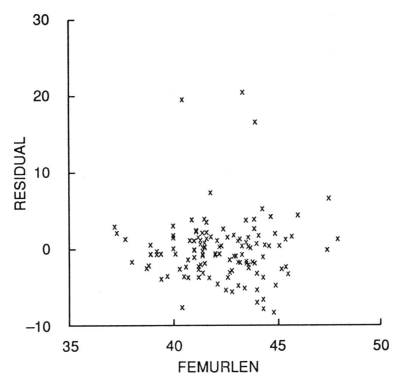

FIGURE 9.2 *Bivariate scatterplot of femur length vs. the residuals from the regression of skeletal height on femur length. Note the three extreme residuals in the upper center of the diagram.*

The residual plot (Figure 9.2) accomplishes two things. First, it clearly isolates the outliers. Second, it assures us that the linear model is appropriate for the data by confirming that the residuals (*sans* outliers) form a narrow band paralleling the x-axis in precisely the manner Draper and Smith (1981:145) require.

If we look at the box plots of skeletal height and of femur length (Figures 9.3a, b) and at a stem-leaf diagram of skeletal height (Table 9.4), the outliers also are clearly evident, and skeletal height stands out as the problem.

The various plots failed to pick up any cases reported to have high leverage coefficients. Because none of the flagged leverage coefficients exceeded 0.07, I paid no further attention to these cases.

The documentation of outliers marks the beginning, not the end, of the process. The fundamental question is, Why are these points outliers? As I pointed out earlier, outliers can exist for a variety of reasons. Most of the time, the problem is due to data entry, coding, or transcription errors. These usually are obvious and are thus exposed when the

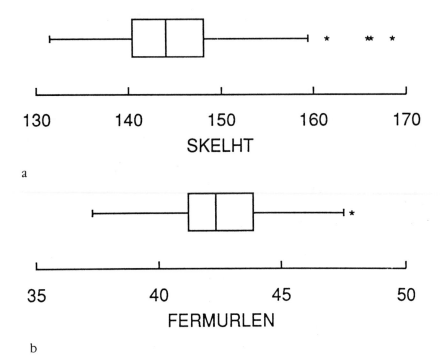

a

b

FIGURE 9.3 *(a) Box and whisker plot of skeletal height. The vertical line in the center of the box represents the median of the distribution of skeletal height; the left and right margins of the box represent the 25 percent and 75 percent quartiles of the distribution (the lower and upper hinges in EDA parlance, the difference between which is called the H-spread). The lines emerging from each end of the box (the "whiskers") represent the inner fences. These are defined to be* lower hinge-(1.5 × H-spread) *and* upper hinge-(1.5 × H-spread). *Note here the four points to the right of the upper inner fence; these are outliers. The innermost point is of no consequence. (b) Box and whisker plot of femur length. The single outlier to the right of the upper inner fence is paired with the innermost outlier of skeletal height.*

researcher scrutinizes the data-entry forms and the coded data. Usually, however, the impetus to investigate these sources comes after computing simple descriptive statistics (for example, means, standard deviations) on the input variables. It is unusual to have a significant coding problem escape this step in the process.

In our study, preliminary computation of sample statistics on the raw data gave no indication of a coding problem. I, therefore, had no reason to suspect these types of errors in the raw data. Both the coding forms and the coded data indicated plausible, if slightly high, values for skeletal height given the femur lengths of the flagged cases.

In studies like this it would have been simple to write these variants off as exemplars of human variability and continue the analysis leaving

TABLE 9.4 *Stem and leaf diagram of skeletal height. This diagram is similar to a histogram. The figures in the leftmost column represent the left-most two digits of skeletal height. Each single digit in the columns to the right represents the terminal digit of skeletal height. Thus, the second row consists of the skeletal heights 132, 132, 133, 133, 133, 133, 133. The letter H signifies a hinge point, and the letter M designates the median. Outliers are those points that exceed the boundaries of the inner fences. Hence the skeletal heights 161, 165, 165, and 167 are outliers.*

STEM AND LEAF PLOT OF VARIABLE: SKELHT   , N = 125

MINIMUM IS: 131.600
LOWER HINGE IS: 140.400
MEDIAN IS: 144.000
UPPER HINGE IS: 148.100
MAXIMUM IS: 167.900

```
        13   1
        13   2233333
        13   455
        13   666666
        13   8888999999
        14 H 0000000111111
        14   22222222222333333333333
        14 M 4444444455555555
        14   66666666677777
        14 H 888888999
        15   0000111111
        15   233
        15   4555
        15
        15   899
   ***OUTSIDE VALUES***
        16   1557
```

in the aberrant cases.[8] Ordinarily I would have done this, but this problem was more complicated and subtle. Skeletal height is not a directly measured quantity. Instead, it is the sum of twenty-eight vertical measurements of the human skeleton. It then became necessary to analyze all twenty-eight component variables, searching for those with aberrant values that might somehow have affected the computation of skeletal height. Normally one would use SYSTAT's STATS module to compute descriptive statistics for all component variables and the GRAPH module for stem and leaf diagrams on each. This step wasn't necessary here, however, as a printout of the component variables made the

T A B L E   9 . 5   *Results of linear regression analysis after outliers have been removed. Note that there are no cases flagged as outliers, and those cases with "undue influence" have leverages below what is usually regarded as significant. Note the dramatic improvement in the multiple correlation, the significant reduction in the standard error of the estimate, and the near doubling of the F-ratio.*

| DEP VAR: SKELHT | N: 122 | MULTIPLE R: | .892 | SQUARED MULTIPLE R: | .795 |
| ADJUSTED SQUARED MULTIPLE R: | .793 | STANDARD ERROR OF ESTIMATE: | | | 2.846 |

VARIABLE	COEFFICIENT	STD ERROR	STD COEF	TOLERANCE	T	P(2TAIL)
CONSTANT	30.426	5.287	0.000	1.0000000	5.755	0.000
FEMURLEN	2.694	0.125	0.892	1.0000000	21.568	0.000

ANALYSIS OF VARIANCE

SOURCE	SUM-OF-SQUARES	DF	MEAN-SQUARE	F-RATIO	P
REGRESSION	3767.172	1	3767.172	465.197	0.000
RESIDUAL	971.762	120	8.098		

WARNING:	CASE	36	HAS UNDUE INFLUENCE	(LEVERAGE	=	.061)
WARNING:	CASE	59	HAS UNDUE INFLUENCE	(LEVERAGE	=	.059)
WARNING:	CASE	71	HAS UNDUE INFLUENCE	(LEVERAGE	=	.058)
WARNING:	CASE	85	HAS UNDUE INFLUENCE	(LEVERAGE	=	.056)
WARNING:	CASE	93	HAS UNDUE INFLUENCE	(LEVERAGE	=	.069)

DURBIN–WATSON D STATISTIC   2.068
FIRST ORDER AUTOCORRELATION   −.044

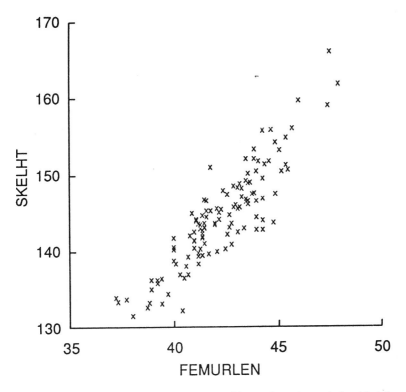

FIGURE 9.4 *Bivariate scattergram of femur length vs. skeletal height with three outliers removed. Note the linearity of the swath of data points.*

problem apparent. I traced the problem to cases where certain critical component measurements were missing and the missing values had been coded improperly. Instead of excluding them from any analysis involving skeletal height, these cases had been included in the analysis, and the miscoded missing measurement had been inadvertently incorporated into the computed skeletal height. Because I had neither collected the data nor analyzed the component measurements, none of my preliminary screening exposed the problem.

Once I eliminated these cases from the analysis, the results stabilized and no further significant outliers showed up. Table 9.5 details the results of the regression analysis with the outliers removed. As can be seen, there is a significant improvement in the fit, in terms of both the increased correlations and the reduced standard errors. Scattergrams and residual plots (Figures 9.4 and 9.5) make the improved fit even more apparent.

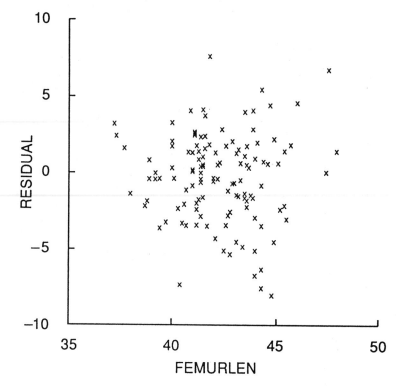

FIGURE 9.5 *Bivariate scatterplot of femur length vs. residuals from a regression of skeletal height on femur length after outliers have been removed. Note that the residuals form a band approximately parallel to the x-axis.*

CONCLUSIONS

Regression analysis is a sophisticated tool that, used properly, is invaluable in research. The personal, mini, and mainframe computers enable researchers to conduct complex analyses with large data sets in seconds or minutes. No rational person would attempt to do these kinds of analyses by hand with a calculator and graph paper—although nineteen years ago I spent two solid weeks chained to a rotary desk calculator during Christmas vacation attempting a discriminant function analysis.

Unfortunately, computer-based statistical analysis removes the researcher from intimate contact with data, allows the investigator to eschew any knowledge of what is happening to the data once it is inside the computer, and then exacerbates the problem by requiring the researcher to develop elaborate coding schemes to trick the computer into ignoring (or not ignoring as the case may be) missing data. In so doing, the probability that subtle errors will creep in unnoticed is increased.

This makes it absolutely imperative that the researcher formulate a strategy for assessing data at every step in the process to guard against its corruption.

Regression analysis is one of a class of multivariable statistical procedures that transform and transmogrify data in a myriad of complicated and sophisticated ways. Because it is not possible for most of us to reproduce the computer's work by hand, except with small and trivial data sets, our first line of defense is to know our data, to employ every technique at our disposal to ferret out inconsistencies, and to be tenacious in questioning anything that doesn't "look right."

Although the computer may insulate us from our data, it can also bring us back in touch with them if we exploit its power and make an effort to properly use the software written for it. None of the analyses described here or elsewhere in this volume is conceptually difficult, and my message isn't negative. Computers make it possible for us to gain insight into our data in novel ways and ask questions that wouldn't have even been considered in pre-electronics days. In the end, though, we need to remember that computers cannot transform sow's ears into silk purses; the adage "garbage in, garbage out" is relevant. Nevertheless, with properly collected and prepared data and with proper choice and use of statistics, the computer can enable a researcher to analyze a data set and "see" relationships otherwise invisible to the naked eye. The only risk is that we may be lulled into thinking that as long as we do everything right, any result reported by the computer must necessarily be significant. At this point we've been seduced—we've let the computer do our bidding. The computer should be seen for what it is—a wonderfully dumb, literal, and faithful servant capable of processing information and performing complex calculations faster and more efficiently than any human. But, humans have to formulate and test the hypotheses and make the decisions about the significance of results. The computer encourages creativity, makes the entire research process go faster, and perhaps even makes complex analyses more pleasurable and, by exposing results that might not otherwise be apparent, easier. For these reasons alone, I am a strong advocate of much greater computer use by anthropologists. But when it comes to deciding what questions to ask, what hypotheses to test, and what results to accept or reject, anthropologists should hold their ground and not surrender to the computer.[9]

NOTES

1. I thank Margaret Boone for suggesting some of these projects.
2. This example ignores factors such as ethnic group, age, sex, and nutritional and health status, all of which exert some influence on blood pressure. If we were to conduct this study properly, we might be inclined to use a

multiple regression approach where we have more than one predictor variable entering into the functional relationship.

3. SYSTAT: The System for Statistics, Systat Inc., 1800 Sherman Avenue, Evanston, Illinois 60201. We used Version 3.0 (MS-DOS), retail price $595.00. Other versions are available for Macintosh, CP/M, and VAX/VMS operating systems. For information call (312) 864-5670.

4. A subset of the analyses reported here was also run in SPSS-X as part of a presentation given at the Society for Applied Anthropology meeting in Oaxaca, Mexico, in April 1987. The actual billed charges to my mainframe account (IBM 4381 under CMS) were $1,350. Given current (August 1987, Portland area) prices for microcomputers, I could have purchased a fully equipped microcomputer and SYSTAT for only $100 more.

5. There is some controversy about the "proper" way to compute studentized residuals. According to Velleman and Welsch (1981), there are two strategies employed. In one case, residuals are "standardized" by dividing them by their standard errors; in the other, they are divided by the standard deviation of residuals based on a regression in which the particular case has been deleted. Residuals computed in the first way follow a beta distribution rather than the preferred t distribution (which is the primary reason for studentizing in the first place). SPSS and SAS studentize their residuals in the first (and possibly improper) way (SAS Institute 1985; SPSS 1986); SYSTAT (Wilkinson 1986) uses the second approach.

6. n represents the number of cases in the analysis and p represents the number of parameters estimated. In a simple bivariate regression that does not pass through the origin, p equals 2 (one for the slope, one for the intercept).

7. One important, but little known, relationship in the algebra of regression diagnostics is that the predicted value can be generated by multiplying each dependent variable for each case by its respective leverage coefficient and summing the products. Thus, cases with high leverage will have a greater influence on the predicted value than will cases with small leverage coefficients.

8. Had these points not been obviously erroneous and removable, we would have considered robust and resistant regression, both techniques designed to deal with the effects of outliers. These techniques are discussed thoroughly in Vellemann and Hoaglin (1981).

9. Thanks are due to my frequent collaborator Dr. John Lundy, U.S. Army Central Identification Laboratory, Ft. Shafter, Hawaii, for permitting me to use the raw data on which this report is based. I also wish to thank Lee Wilkinson, Leah Dorsey, and Chris Soderquist of SYSTAT Inc. for preparing the graphs with their as yet unreleased graphics package SYGRAPH. Finally, I thank Margaret Boone and Bob Trotter for inviting me to present this paper at the Society for Applied Anthropology meeting in Oaxaca, Mexico, in April 1987.

CHAPTER TEN

 # Using Expert Systems in Skeletal Analysis

WILLIAM WILSON

Expert systems provide a computer-assisted mechanism to represent rules and apply those rules to new cases. In this chapter, Wilson demonstrates how computer software can aid in making decisions on the sex of skull specimens. Medical anthropologists, linguists, forensic anthropologists, and kinship specialists will all find expert systems to be a useful type of computer application to illustrate rules, categorizations, and decisions about natural and cultural phenomena. The expert system can be an effective adjunct to componential analysis, as we see later in Chapter 15.

While giving a paper at a conference for forensics experts, a medical anthropologist listed a set of skeletal anomalies and malformations from a recent find. He then requested that the audience indicate what types of diseases were indicated by the traits. After a short period of collaboration, members of the audience listed four to five possible diseases that could be diagnosed with a fair degree of accuracy, whereas the anthropologist listed over twenty diseases that could involve the skeletal anomalies and malformations seen. The twenty diseases had been chosen by an expert system created to help diagnose diseases from skeletal anomalies.

WHAT IS AN EXPERT SYSTEM?

This chapter will explore the concept of an expert system and its application in anthropology. Expert systems can be designed to help anthropologists diagnose, analyze, and advise on specific problems and to document some of their research efforts to understand culture-specific types of decision making. The use of the expert system development package, VP-Expert, will be explored in relation to its applications in medical and forensic anthropology.

An expert system development package is, in the simplest sense, a computer program or set of programs designed to help an expert in any field design a structured environment that will enable a novice to solve a specific type of problem. In anthropology this could include determining the sex of skeletal remains or the cause of death for an individual or analyzing archaeological sites and artifacts to determine their types and functions. Because of the nature of cultural anthropology, it is also possible that the "expert" may be the native resident, so that expert systems can potentially help to diagram how native speakers engage in the "cultural decision making" involved in many types of ritual, linguistic, and other social situations where it is important to make a "culturally correct" decision about some action or expression (Guillet 1989a, 1989b).

A number of packages currently exist to help set up expert systems, including VP-Expert from PaperBack Software, the Personal Consultant from Texas Instruments, and Guru from Mdbs (see Software Appendix). These packages are designed to help a "knowledge engineer" and an expert (or a number of experts in a specific field) create an expert system that can analyze, diagnose, or make a "scientifically" or a "culturally" correct decision. The expert system can then be used by students or novices or by experts to help them in their own work. When used by an expert, the expert system assists in mundane tasks, such as the organizational aspects of one's duties, or in helping to arrive at complex decisions where the knowledge base is widely scattered and/or difficult to assemble, as in worldwide medical diagnosis.

BENEFITS OF USING EXPERT SYSTEMS

Expert systems can provide three basic benefits: reduction of research time, increased work efficiency, and the ability to produce an answer to a question or to make a decision in less time than it would take to research, document, and work a problem out by hand. Most professions today, including anthropology, are concerned with decision making and problem solving. Some applications (including the space program and medicine) require extremely fast decisions that can help avert life-threatening situations. These processes (medical diagnosis, shuttle operation control, and so on) can be improved with the use of expert systems. Expert systems are not a replacement for specialists but are intended to help them to focus their knowledge and to help a novice learn to perform as a specialist.

TYPES OF EXPERT SYSTEMS

Traditionally, expert systems have addressed five different areas: diagnosis, interpretation, prediction, control/monitoring, planning, and instruction. In anthropology, all are potentially useful. In the following example I will concentrate on diagnosis and interpretation.

Diagnosis is the most frequently seen application in expert systems. This type of system may be used to diagnose illnesses or to determine problems with equipment or the reason for general failure. Medical anthropologists and forensics specialists would be the most likely to use this type of system. For example, diagnosing disease in Third World countries, determining cause of death, and ascertaining the sex from skeletal remains would be appropriate applications. The main problem is isolating the "symptoms." If one symptom is masked by another, it can make the diagnosis invalid. Inaccessible or unknown data can also skew the diagnosis.

Systems that interpret or select data are also useful in anthropology. This type of system analyzes data to ascertain their meaning. Interpretive expert systems are currently being used in financial analysis, chemical analysis, and certain types of statistical analysis. In anthropology the applications could include, not exclusively, interpretation of statistical models, testing and interpretation of historical and anthropological social models (Weissman 1987), selection of information sources (Stewart 1987), academic advisement (Klavon 1987). Expert systems could include applications that involve the classification of a wide array of material objects and subjects of study, from artifacts to kinship systems to native diseases.

STRUCTURE OF AN EXPERT SYSTEM

An expert system is composed of interrelated facts that are the "knowledge" necessary to solve a problem. Applications that are likely candidates for expert systems must have readily identifiable characteristics, and there must be a relevant body of knowledge on the subject. This knowledge must be able to be expressed as mutually exclusive questions about the subject at hand. The skill involved in working on the problem must also be able to be taught to a new worker in the field. In the example used later in this chapter, the relevant body of knowledge consists of the skeletal traits that are used to help identify sex. Each trait is a mutually exclusive piece of information that, when used with other traits, helps to identify the sex of an individual skeleton.

If certain general rules are met, then the use of an expert system to solve a given problem will very likely be appropriate. First, an expert in the field of knowledge should be able to come to a conclusion in not less than a few minutes and not more than a few hours without a computer (although in linguistic decision making the time could be much shorter). Second, the benefit of developing an expert system should outweigh the cost of development.

Every expert system must be made up of rules that are based on knowledge about the subject in question. A rule is a specific piece of knowledge. It can also be equated with a two-answer question. The following are examples of "rules": Is a society matrilineal or patrilineal? Is an archaeological site indicative of a permanent or temporary habitation? Is the cranial capacity above or below 1,450 cc? By grouping related questions on a specific topic, an expert system can be set up to answer a specific question.

Traditional programs simply take input and produce a single result with no inference. Expert systems are set up to help a user make decisions and to make inferences or deductions based on the criteria set up for the consultation. An example of the type of deductive process that may take place is determining the sex of an individual using skeletal remains. An expert system is made up of rules, information supplied by the person consulting the expert, and a rule interpreter. The rule interpreter manages the rules and the data supplied by the user and then produces an answer to the problem.

THE PROBLEM OF DETERMINING SEX FROM OSTEOLOGICAL FEATURES

One common problem in medical and forensic anthropology is determining the sex of an individual from existing osteological features. This can be a problem not only for students and new researchers learning the field but also for an expert, given the immensity of the task if the whole skeleton is to be assessed. In the skull itself there are at least nine characteristics that can help a researcher deduce the sex of an individual. An expert system can be created and used to help analyze skeletal remains and, in particular, cranial remains. This type of system can be used to help a novice learn an analytical process, or an expert can use an expert system to help organize his or her work.

SEX DETERMINATION AND EXPERT SYSTEMS

The expert system described in this chapter can be adapted for either instruction or diagnosis. This system—named "Skull"—was created in the VP-Expert expert system development environment. The objective of the system is to assist in determining the sex of an individual based on specific osteological features of the skull. Table 10.1 shows the skeletal features used in the analysis (Gilbert 1985). Sex can be determined by

T A B L E   1 0 . 1 *Skull characteristics*

CHARACTERISTIC	MALE	FEMALE
Size	Large: Cranial capacity CA: 150–200 CC greater, 1,450+ CC = Male	Small: Cranial capacities less than 1,300 CC tend to be female
Supraorbital ridges, temporal crests, nuchal lines, and external occipital protruberance	Medium to large	Small to medium
Forehead	Retreating	Smoother, more vertical
Superior border of orbit	Blunt	Sharp
Frontal, parietal eminences	Small	Large
Supramastoid crests, mastoid processes, zygomatic processes of temporals	Large, rugged	Smaller, more gracile
Mandible	Larger, thicker	Smaller, thinner
Gonial Angle	Less obtuse, with region more everted	More obtuse, angle > 125 degrees, little eversion
Chin	Square, with greater forward projection	More pointed, median

nine skull characteristics—six based in the skull itself and three in the mandible. Depending on which features are still existing in the osteological remains, either a more or a less reliable estimation of sex can be determined. When an expert performs this type of task without an expert system, it is often a tacit, intuitive process. In order for this process to be built as an expert system, the expert must put down in writing the steps involved in making the determination.

TABLE 10.2 *An example of the use of the Skull expert system*

This expert system will help determine sex from skull—skeletal markers. This system computes an index where 100 percent is a perfect fit for either male or female depending on the ratings given. The closer to 100 percent the better the fit.

HIT ANY KEY TO CONTINUE . . .
    IS THE SIZE 1,300 CC OR LESS, OR LARGER THAN 1,450 CC?
    LESS <   MORE

    ARE THE SUPRAORBITAL RIDGES MEDIUM TO LARGE OR SMALL TO MEDIUM?
    SMALL   LARGE

    IS THE FOREHEAD RETREATING OR SMOOTHER AND MORE VERTICAL?
    SMOOTHER <   RETREATING

    IS THE SUPERIOR BORDER OF THE ORBIT SHARP OR BLUNT?
    SHARP <   BLUNT

    ARE THE FRONTAL/PARIETAL EMINENCES SMALL OR LARGE?
    LARGE   SMALL

    ARE THE SUPRAMASTOID CRESTS, MASTOID PROCESSES, OR ZYGOMATIC PROCESSES OF TEMPORALS SMALLER AND MORE GRACILE OR LARGE AND MORE RUGGED?
    SMALLER <   LARGER

    IS THE MANDIBLE SMALLER AND THINNER OR LARGER AND THICKER?
    SMALLER   LARGER

    IS THE GONIAL ANGLE MORE OBTUSE (> 125 DEGREES) OR LESS OBTUSE?
    MORE OBTUSE <   LESS OBTUSE

    IS THE CHIN MORE POINTED OR IS IT SQUARE?
    POINTED   SQUARE

THERE IS A 55.555557 PERCENT CHANCE THAT THE INDIVIDUAL WAS FEMALE.

    Table 10.2 shows a sample session with the expert system program. The expert system is set up to work with the user to help determine the sex of the remains and acts as the consultant for the problem at hand. This process is based on a series of questions about the skull characteristics. The first question involves cranial capacity. There are three possible answers for this (and all the other) features: If the capacity is greater than 1,450 cc, then the sex is more than likely male; if it is less than 1,450 cc, it may indicate a female; or the cranial capacity may be unknown. In this way, the sex of the skull can be determined from the answers to this question and the remaining eight questions. Depending on the answers to these questions, the system will give an estimation and percentage probability of the sex of the individual.

USING VP-EXPERT FOR DETERMINING SEX

VP-Expert programs are composed of three integral parts: actions, rules (the knowledge base), and statements. The action block defines what the goals are for the consultation. This block instructs the inference engine what is to be determined and in what order. The rules compose the actual knowledge. For example, in the Skull expert system, one of the rules helps to determine the size of the cranium (cranial capacity in cubic centimeters). The statement section is used to help assign specific qualities or characteristics to the knowledge variables. In Skull, the ASK and CHOICES statements are used to help query the user for information.

The goals outlined in the action block are found through the FIND clauses. The FIND clause "instructs the inference engine to FIND a value for a given variable" (Paperback Software 1987). This variable is called the goal variable. In this example, there are ten goals that must be accomplished, and the system must "find" answers to the ten goal variables. These variables encompass the decisions as outlined in Table 10.2. In the example, the first goal is to determine the general size of the cranium. When the inference engine has identified size as the first goal, it searches the rule base to find a value for this variable. This process is repeated for each goal, and when an answer (whether known or unknown) is determined for each, the consultation is completed.

Table 10.2 shows a complete consultation. In this consultation, the skull was that of a female. The < symbol indicates the selection, or answer, for the question. In the size question, "less than" the given cranial capacity was the answer to the size "goal." However, a few characteristics were not known. If one of the two choices is not known (that is, if one of the choices is not checked in Table 10.2), then the answer for that goal is not known. Based on all the answers, the expert system calculates an "index of fit." In this example, there was a 55.6% chance that the individual was female.[1]

SUMMARY

VP-Expert is a very flexible tool for creating expert systems that can be used in a lab environment for training or research. An expert system— in conjunction with natural language processing—provides an ability to create a user-friendly program to aid in all types of decision making, including tasks that anthropologists know well: classification and cataloging. The ability to access knowledge, whether in the form of an expert system or in the form of a knowledge base, is a major goal in education. And, for independent consultants in anthropology, this type of tool may also provide suggestions or solutions for a given problem that would not have arisen otherwise. An expert system streamlines decision making into a process that can be consistently duplicated for all users. A more complex expert system that takes a user along a branching structure, and in which each decision point determines the following options, allows a set of complex decisions to be made and to be well documented for future reference or for clients.

The example presented in this chapter could easily be written in a conventional programming language and would probably not be created and used except for classroom instruction. However, the example points the way to the enormous potential use of expert systems by anthropologists. Packages like VP-Expert allow a well-trained expert—but a beginning computer user—to tailor a fairly sophisticated new tool to his or her own professional needs. Expert systems are of most benefit when the questions being asked are branching or hierarchical. The present example provides a stepping stone to further development of full-scale analytical systems.

When looking for this type of development system, a number of factors should be considered. VP-Expert was chosen primarily for its price. It is one of the least expensive expert system development packages on the market. It also interfaces flexibly with other programs. It is in a family of products that, when used together, allow the management of spreadsheet information, database, graphics, and word processing. VP-Expert is able to exchange data with VP-Info or dBASE database files, VP-Planner and Lotus 1-2-3 worksheets, and ASCII text files. It also includes simple English rule construction, confidence factors that are set up to account for uncertainties in the data, automatic question generation, floating point math calculations, a built-in editor, and other useful features.

Expert system development is a new tool for anthropologists. It is growing rapidly among all types of researchers and consultants. The judicious use of expert systems may lend an edge to consultants and anthropology departments, which will help to increase productivity, automate mundane tasks, and simplify complex classification decisions in a way that can be easily documented.

NOTES

1. sexp = (@abs(sexn)*100/9), where "sexp" is the calculated percentage and "sexn" is the number of matching characteristics.

CHAPTER ELEVEN

🐚 GODZILLA: A Simulation Program for Learning Population Genetics

JOHN B. GATEWOOD

Population genetics uses formulas to illustrate changes in gene pools through time. In this chapter, Gatewood describes a simulation program that he wrote, which uses formulas to illustrate the process of genetic drift. As in all computer simulations of natural phenomena (like the weather) or social phenomena (like economic cycles), only some parts of the real system are represented. The Computer Databases Available to Anthropologists section gives several examples of other types of simulations.

SIMULATION PROGRAMS IN ANTHROPOLOGY

Ask anthropologists why computer simulations are useful, and it will not take too long before you hear something like, "That's what you do when you don't have enough data!" There is a grain of truth in this comment, and yet, this kind of assertion may also reflect an unwarranted, overly deterministic view of history and social processes. As long as we imagine that social processes are simple deterministic unfoldings and that history had to happen the way it did, it is easy to agree that simulations are merely stop-gap solutions to problems that will eventually be settled empirically. On the other hand, if the types of processes that we study are truly complex, and/or they can only be understood probabilistically, then simulations enable us to reach a depth of understanding that goes beyond whatever case-specific data we may assemble.

In a complex-probabilistic view of social processes, that which actually happened in any given case—for example, the time it took to settle the New World (Wobst 1974) or the collapse of Classic Mayan civilization (Lowe 1985)—is regarded as only one of several possible histories. Simulation models enable us to identify the full ensemble of possibilities, of which only one became realized in the historical record.

Simulations have other benefits as well. First, when we write computer programs, we must be very clear about the variables that are to be included and how they are interrelated. Second, even if we can write all the equations that govern a system, when we deal with complex processes it is often very difficult to predict system behavior as a whole. However, by doing multiple runs of a program, we can learn the consequences of random fluctuations in the model's variables. Third, by modifying the program—by either increasing or decreasing the number of variables, changing their interrelations, or inserting new initial values—we can see what conditions might lead to different scenarios for the system as a whole.

In what follows, I hope to illustrate some of the virtues that computer simulation may have for anthropology by describing a program dealing with population genetics. It is a reasonably good example because biological evolution is a fairly complex process and some aspects of it are genuinely probabilistic.

BACKGROUND TO A THEORY

Darwin and Mendel lived and wrote in the nineteenth century. However, it was not until the early decades of the twentieth century that Darwin's mechanism of evolutionary change and Mendel's mechanisms of genetic continuity were brought together in the "synthetic theory of evolution." In 1908, mathematician G. H. Hardy and physician W. Weinberg formulated, independently of one another, the Hardy-Weinberg Law. Not long thereafter, treatises by R. A. Fisher (1930), J. B. S. Haldane (1932), and Sewall Wright (1931) laid the mathematical foundations for modern population genetics.

Today, we realize there are four ways the gene pool of a population can change through time; that is, there are four mechanisms underlying evolution: mutation, migration, genetic drift, and selection. The standard undergraduate biology curriculum includes at least one introductory course in population genetics, which covers these cornerstones of evolutionary theory. Students learn the equations for calculating the effects of mutation rates, migration, drift, and selection and also how to determine values from empirical data. In stark contrast, introductory anthropology courses—even the typical "bones and stones" courses in physical anthropology—give only passing mention to these important topics. An unfortunate consequence of this difference between biology and anthropology curricula is that most anthropologists, especially sociocultural anthropologists, never realize that evolution is calculable. They can easily slip into an overly deterministic mode of thinking, which emphasizes selection as the only explanation for evolutionary change and ignores the other, more random, processes.

I heard about Sewall Wright's concept of genetic drift in my first anthropology course. We learned that it had to do with the random effect

of small population size on gene frequencies in subsequent generations: The smaller the population, the greater the random fluctuations.
No equations were mentioned; no demonstrations were performed.
However, we were asked to believe that the overall effect of genetic
drift on a population was increased homozygosity, relative to Hardy-
Weinberg expectations about the stability of a gene pool through
time. The conclusion was not exactly obvious that genetic drift would
increase the similarity of genes in the gene pool and decrease genetic variability. Two years later, I finally encountered the mathematical logic and an explanation of drift in what was for me an elective
course on human genetics (Stern 1960)—and suddenly it made sense!
Similarly, when I discovered how to use genotypes' fitness values
in conjunction with the Hardy-Weinberg Law to compute expected
gene frequencies in subsequent generations, a light dawned. The effects of various evolutionary forces are not a matter of vague faith.
They are precisely specifiable and, in this case, replicable in a relatively modest computer program that simulates some of the processes
of evolution.

The unity of the discipline of anthropology hinges on having a common core of knowledge. Every anthropologist needs to understand the
mechanisms of evolution because culture and language depend on our
evolved species biology. An anthropologist's training, like a biologist's,
should include developing a basic understanding of evolutionary principles through mathematical demonstrations. Evolutionary theory is a
scientific theory, not a cosmology, and its acceptance should be based
on critical evaluation rather than belief.

These are the disciplinary and pedagogical issues that prompted me
to search for better instructional tools in my own "bones and stones"
physical anthropology course. The dilemma was finding demonstrations
that were effective and do not take too much class time. The solution
became clear to me on reading *Armchair BASIC* by Annie and David
Fox (1983), which was my introduction to the previously mysterious
world of computer programming. I had already done some work with
statistical packages on mainframe computers and had given up typewriters in favor of word processors, but until I read their lucid little book,
the very expression "computer program" smacked of high-tech inacces-
sibility. However, armed with some basic knowledge of the BASIC programming language, I set about converting my time-consuming classroom demonstrations of genetic drift and selection into a compact
simulation exercise.

The result was GODZILLA, a program for personal computers that
simulates two of the four evolutionary forces.[1] In what follows, I first
describe the origin and logic of the program and then discuss a set of
computer-aided exercises, which I use to demonstrate the processes of
evolution.

BEFORE GODZILLA, THERE WAS THE BLACKBOARD

In spite of my enthusiasm for computers, it is prudent to remember that we human beings are smarter than they are. Computers only do what they have been instructed, or programmed, to do. Before silicon chips, when circuits could be seen with the naked eye, computers were commonly referred to as "servo-machines"—an expression that properly emphasized their servile nature. However, humans can do anything computers can do, even if it usually takes us longer. Indeed, humans usually have to know how to solve a problem in order to write the series of instructions that will enable a dumb servo-machine to find the solution. Therefore, before describing the GODZILLA program itself, it will be useful to demonstrate genetic drift and natural selection using everyday low-tech instructional props.

A DEMONSTRATION OF GENETIC DRIFT

Genetic drift is one of the most difficult concepts to learn in population genetics. It is not at all clear to most people why, in the absence of any strong selective forces, small populations will tend toward homozygosity, whereas larger populations will not. After several years of trying to demonstrate this subject with only partial success, I stumbled on a new exercise, which eventually led to the computer program GODZILLA.

First, we describe a small breeding population with two genetic varieties having initial gene frequencies of .5 and .5 (for example, five red and five blue poker chips). These gene frequencies represent the proportions of different "alleles" in the breeding population. Next, we imagine that the infamous lizard Godzilla walks through the village where this tiny population lives. As movie buffs know, Godzilla does not care if someone is tall or short, blonde or brunette, red or blue. He steps on whomever is in his way. In this sense, Godzilla personifies random mortality, and we simulate this random element in Godzilla's walk by shuffling a deck of playing cards and dealing one card to each of the ten poker chips. If a spade is dealt, this means that Godzilla has stepped on that chip, and it is removed from the population. Chips receiving a heart, diamond, or club escape unscathed.

When Godzilla has finished his walk through the village, we compute the percentages of red and blue chips in the surviving population, reconstitute the next generation of ten chips to reflect those percentages (rounding off as appropriate), and graph the results on the blackboard. For example, suppose Godzilla has squashed one red chip and two blue chips. In this case, the surviving breeding population consists

In-Class Demonstrations of Drift

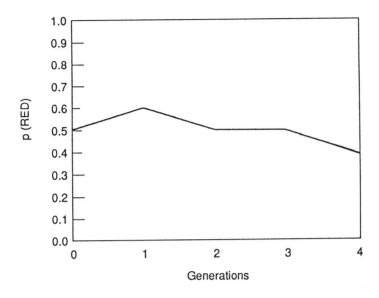

FIGURE 11.1 *Typical results of a four-generation in-class demonstration of genetic drift*

of four reds and three blues, or 57.1 percent and 42.9 percent, respectively. Thus, the second generation will contain, initially, six red chips and four blue chips.

Son of Godzilla then appears and commences his random walk among the second generation, and so forth. Thirty to forty minutes of class time are usually sufficient for us to witness Godzilla's great-grandson wreak havoc among a fourth generation of poker chips. Figure 11.1 shows the results of a typical four-generation, blackboard demonstration.

This demonstration, although much better than simply describing the consequences of genetic drift, is not as effective as it might be, for several reasons. First, the red and blue analogue of genetic varieties is weak because it does not account for the heterozygote condition, where red and blue alleles exist in the same individuals. (There is no purple poker chip.) Second, shuffling cards, dealing them, and computing percentages of survivors takes so long that we seldom see enough generations to witness significant change. Third, even if we continue the number of generations, the resulting graph represents only a single series of possible outcomes, and this reinforces the mistaken idea that drift is a deterministic rather than a random process. Finally, because we deal with only one set of circumstances, the demonstration fails to convey the crucial role that population size plays in drift.

Even with these shortcomings, the demonstration is effective. The card shuffling works particularly well in communicating the random nature of drift.

LEARNING ABOUT NATURAL SELECTION

Selection is also a difficult concept to understand but for the opposite reason that drift is. Natural selection seems to be intuitively appealing and is often accepted as a force in evolution almost without question. However, in a demonstration of natural selection, it is surprising how long it can take for a deleterious recessive trait to be lost from a population, and it is similarly surprising to see that the gene frequency of a trait that is lethal in homozygote individuals may actually increase in a population. In demonstrations of selection, it is often useful to calculate gene frequencies for several generations after the initial gene frequencies and fitness values corresponding to each genotype are given. Eckhardt's two-generation examples illustrate each logical pattern of selection (1979:200–205). More lengthy problems, such as the one in Table 11.1, show the different directions of natural selection through time.

Table 11.1 is useful in understanding the general point that evolutionary forces are calculable. However, it is less effective in developing an appreciation of selection's effects under varying circumstances. As in the demonstration of genetic drift, a single exercise takes a fairly long time to complete. Hence, it is impractical to complete more than one or two for a single introductory course. Still, a single period devoted to teaching the principles and at least one longer demonstration is well justified.

Clearly, it is possible to learn about genetic drift and natural selection using blackboard and chalk. However, the problem with this technique is that the full range of conditions—initial gene frequencies, population size, magnitude of random effects, fitness values, and so on—simply cannot be covered within a reasonable amount of time. This seriously undermines a rapid understanding of evolutionary forces. Drift and selection work differently under different conditions, and it takes time to demonstrate each condition. In an ideal world, lectures would cover principles, demonstrations would illustrate evolutionary processes, and multiple problem sets involving drift and selection would strengthen an understanding of individual processes. However, it is not reasonable to assign twenty or more hours of lengthy exercises on topics that occupy only a week in introductory anthropology.

TABLE 11.1 *A demonstration problem showing the directions of natural selection through time.*

THE PROBLEM:

Calculate the gene frequencies of alleles A and a after four generations, given:
  (1) initially, $p(A) = .500$ and $q(a) = .500$, and
  (2) the fitness values of the three genotypes are:
      $AA = .8$ $Aa = .8$ $aa = 1.0$

THE ANSWER:

[ROUNDED TO 3 DECIMAL PLACES]		AA (p^2)	Aa (2pq)	aa (q^2)	Total
G_0: p = .500					
q = .500					
	CON.	.250	.500	.250	1.000
		× .8	× .8	× 1.0	
		.200	.400	.250	.850
	B.P.	.235	.471	.294	1.000
G_1: p = .235 + (.471/2) = .470					
q = .294 + (.471/2) = .530					
	CON.	.221	.498	.281	1.000
		× .8	× .8	× 1.0	
		.177	.398	.281	.856
	B.P.	.207	.465	.328	1.000
G_2: p = .207 + (.465/2) = .440					
q = .328 + (.465/2) = .560					
	CON.	.194	.494*	.314	1.000
		× .8	× .8	× 1.0	
		.155	.395	.314	.864
	B.P.	.179	.458*	.363	1.000
G_3: p = .179 + (.458/2) = .408					
q = .363 + (.458/2) = .592					
	CON.	.166	.484*	.350	1.000
		× .8	× .8	× 1.0	
		.133	.387	.350	.870
	B.P.	.153	.445	.402	1.000
G_4: p = .153 + (.445/2) = .376					
q = .402 + (.445/2) = .624					

G—generation
CON.—*expected genotype frequencies at conception*
B.P.—*genotype frequencies of the breeding population (after selection)*
*—*heterozygote frequency improperly rounded in order to make the total exactly equal to 1.000*

COMPUTERS TO THE RESCUE

The GODZILLA program was written to solve this instructional dilemma. It harnesses the computational speed of computers to reconcile pedagogical ideal with a practical time constraint. I now continue my classroom demonstrations and assignments as before but augment these with a set of problems to be solved using the computer program. In a couple of hours using the GODZILLA program, the full range of conditions affecting drift and selection becomes comprehensible. The same exercises using pencil, paper, and hand calculator would take days of tedious work.

GODZILLA is an interactive graphics program that is written in GW-BASIC to run on IBM-compatible personal computers equipped with a color graphics adapter (CGA) card. It is not compiled, so users must have their own IBM-compatible Advanced BASIC interpreter. Also, because it is not compiled, users can modify the program as they see fit. The current version takes about 7,550 bytes of disk space for its ninety-nine lines of code.

The program was originally developed to simulate only genetic drift. Later, I revised it to allow drift with or without selection. The code follows essentially the same logic used in the blackboard demonstrations described above, except, of course, that the drift component includes all three genotypes (AA, Aa, aa) instead of just the two homozygote conditions (AA, aa). The following is an overview of how to use the program, after which I describe some details of the code.

HOW GODZILLA WORKS

For any given "run," or simulated outcome of the program, users specify four basic parameters. Of these, only population size and number of generations affect the time required for execution of the program. Larger populations require more computations for each generation.

Parameter 1: Population Size. The range is from 10 to 2,000. The default value is 50.

Parameter 2: Initial Gene Frequencies. These are expressed as the probability, or rate, of one allele, p(A), and the probability or rate of q(a). The range is any fraction greater than 0 but less than 1, where p(A) + q(a) = 1. The default values are p(A) = .5 and q(a) = .5.

Parameter 3: Number of Generations. The range is from 1 to 300. The default value is 30.

Parameter 4: Magnitude of Random Effect. The range is any fraction greater than 0 but less than or equal to .5. The default value is .2. To see the effects of natural selection without drift, the user should set random effects at something like ".0001."

When these four initial conditions have been specified, or their default values accepted by entering carriage returns when prompted, users are asked whether they also want to specify selective forces. If the user responds "NO," then the program begins graphing the effect of drift by plotting the gene frequency of the A allele, that is, p(A), over the specified number of generations. If the user answers "YES" to selective forces, the program asks the user to specify fitness values for each of the three genotypes (AA, Aa, aa) and then graphs changes in the gene frequency of the A allele.

On these graphs, the horizontal axis represents time measured in generations. The vertical axis corresponds to the gene frequency of the A allele, from 0 (bottom) to 1 (top). The gene frequency of the a allele is not shown, for its value is simply 1 – p(A).

After each run, "Again <Y/N> ?" flashes at the bottom of the screen. If the user hits any key other than "N" (for example, the space bar), the program graphs another simulated outcome using exactly the same initial conditions, and the new graph is superimposed on previous ones. This feature allows users to see multiple simulated outcomes under identical conditions and is a very important part of the learning exercises (illustrated in Figures 11.2–11.7 below). If the user responds to the query by hitting "N," the graphs are erased, and the user is given the option of quitting the program or changing the parameters. Hitting a "Q" exits the program; hitting a "P" returns the user to the initial conditions menu.

SOME DETAILS OF THE CODE

One of the ironies of computer programming is that instructions for the computational heart of programs usually require very few lines of code, whereas making the program "user friendly" is often quite complicated. GODZILLA is no exception. The essential calculations for simulating drift and selection compose only about 20 percent of the entire program. The other lines of programming deal with menus for user input and graphics commands for aesthetically pleasing display of output.

There are five user-specified constants that the user can change in order to experiment with the effects of evolutionary processes through time. There are nine other variables that are computed in the program's genetics calculations, using the values of the user-specified constants. In addition, there are three dummy variables (DH1, DHET, and DH2) that are used for temporary bookkeeping in the drift simulation.

USER-SPECIFIED CONSTANTS

POP   population size
GOD   magnitude of the random effect ($0 <$ GOD $< = .5$)
F1   fitness value of the AA genotype (default = 1)

FH   fitness value of the Aa genotype (default = 1)

F 2   fitness value of the aa genotype (default = 1)

COMPUTED VARIABLES

RND   computer-generated random number between 0 and 1

H1C(X)   number of AA individuals in generation X after selection

HETC(X)   number of Aa individuals in generation X after selection

H2C(X)   number of aa individuals in generation X after selection

H1(X)   number of AA individuals in generation X after selection
            and drift

HET(X)   number of Aa individuals in generation X after selection
            and drift

H2(X)   number of aa individuals in generation X after selection
            and drift

P(X)   gene frequency of the A allele in generation X (initial
            value is user-specified)

Q(X)   gene frequency of the a allele in generation X (initial value
            is user-specified)

Table 11.2 shows GODZILLA's heart, that is, the calculating routines that simulate selection and drift. For the sake of clarity, I have deleted graphics and other extraneous commands. Keeping in mind the definitions of variables provided above, let us work our way through the seven stages of the program's logic.

The commands on lines 300 and 310 read the computer's internal clock to determine the seed to be used when generating random numbers. In this way, the sequence of random numbers generated in any given run depends on what time of day (hour, minute, and second) the program is being used. Therefore, random numbers are generated from a different "starting point" in each run.

Line 330 begins a FOR . . . NEXT loop that causes all calculations between 330 and 430 to be repeated a fixed number of times. In this case, each passage through the loop corresponds to one generation, and the looping stops after the user-specified number of generations.

Line 340 contains three commands, one for each genotype, which accomplish two tasks simultaneously. Using the Hardy-Weinberg Law, the previous generation's gene frequencies, P(X-1) and Q(X-1), and total population size (POP), each command computes how many individuals of its respective genotype should be in the current generation. At the same time, these numbers are multiplied by the genotypes' fitness values (F1, FH, and F2), such that the outcome variables, H1C(X), HETC(X), and H2C(X), incorporate the effects of selection. If the user has not specified

T A B L E 1 1 . 2 *Essential "genetics" code in the GODZILLA program, with graphics and extraneous commands deleted*

SUB-SUBROUTINE FOR DRIFT

```
210 DH1 = H1C (X):  DHET = HETC (X) : DH2 = H2C (X)

220 FOR Y = 1 TO H1C (X) :  IF GOD > RND THEN DH1 = DH1 – 1

230 NEXT Y

240 FOR Y = 1 TO HETC (X):  IF GOD > RND THEN DHET = DHET – 1

250 NEXT Y

260 FOR Y = 1 TO H2C (X) :  IF GOD > RND THEN DH2 = DH2 – 1

270 NEXT Y

280 RETURN
```

MAIN CALCULATING SUBROUTINE

```
300 T$ = TIME$:T1$ = LEFT$(T$,2):T2$ = MID$(T$,4,2):(T3$ = MID$(T$,7,1):
    SEED$ = T1$ + T2$ + T3$

310 RANDOMIZE VAL (SEED$)

330 FOR X = 1 TO G

340 H1C(X) = CINT(F1*P(X – 1) ¬ 2*POP):
    HETC(X) = CINT(FH*2*P(X – 1)*Q(X – 1)*POP):
    H2C(X) = CINT(F2*Q(X – 1) ¬ 2*POP)

370 GOSUB 210

380 IF DH1 < = 0 THEN H1 (X) = 0 ELSE H1 (X) = DH1

390 IF DHET < = 0 THEN HET(X) = 0 ELSE HET (X)  = DHET

400 IF DH2 < = 0 THEN H2 (X) = 0 ELSE H2(X) = DH2

420 P(X) = (2*H1(X) + HET(X))/(2*(H1(X) + HET(X) + H2(X))):  Q(X) = 1 – P(X):
    IF P(X – 1) = 0 OR Q(X – 1) = 0 THEN X = G

430 NEXT X

440 RETURN
```

fitness values, another part of the program automatically sets F1, FH, and F2 equal to 1.

Line 370 directs the program to the drift sub-subroutine (lines 210 through 280). Line 210 creates three dummy variables, DH1, DHET, and DH2, whose initial values are equal to H1C(X), HETC(X), and H2C(X), respectively. Then, there are three FOR . . . NEXT loops, one for each genotype, in which each individual runs the "Godzilla gauntlet." This is realized by generating a random number (RND) for each individual of a given genotype, and if the user-specified random effect is greater than this random number (that is, if GOD > RND), then the number of individuals with that genotype is reduced by 1. When all three FOR . . . NEXT loops are completed, control returns to line 380.

The IF . . . THEN conditions in lines 380, 390, and 400 ensure that the number of individuals for each genotype left in the population after selection and drift are never less than zero.

Line 420 extracts the new gene frequencies, P(X) and Q(X), in the surviving population. To speed up program execution, line 420 ends with a conditional command that if P(X) or Q(X) equals zero, the FOR . . . NEXT loop begun in line 330 is to be closed.

Finally, line 440 concludes the genetics subroutine and returns control to the main program.

As written, the program computes selection effects first, then drift. This order can be reversed by removing the multipliers F1, FH, and F2 from line 340 and inserting a line 410, in which the quantities H1(X), HET(X), and H2(X) are multiplied by their respective fitness values. Reversing the order this way makes no difference to the outcome, but it does slow program execution a little.

A final note is that the program occasionally behaves strangely, in the sense that a very low gene frequency persists when we know that, in principle, it should decrease to zero. The reason for such apparent departures from theoretical predictions is that GODZILLA simulates drift using the same basic logic as my blackboard demonstration; that is, individuals run a random number gauntlet, and the next generation is reconstituted at a constant size based on percentages of the previous generation's survivors. This computational procedure requires rounding to the nearest whole integer each generation, because it makes no sense to speak of 1.823 homozygote AA individuals in a population of fifty. Most of the time, rounding to integers does not cause any problems, but users should be aware of the possibility. Instructors may want to pretest lengthy demonstrations to be completed outside of class.

A SET OF PROBLEMS FOR USING THE GODZILLA PROGRAM

Over the past three years, I have developed and pretested a problem set whereby users of GODZILLA can see for themselves the consequences of drift and selection under various conditions. The set contains seven problems, each of which involves comparing simulated outcomes from differing initial conditions. The demonstration, then, requires users to enter the conditions specified in a given problem, take note of what they see on the screen, and write a paragraph about what they have learned from the comparisons. The full problem set is provided in Table 11.3.

The whole assignment takes a couple of hours: about one hour to go through all the situations with GODZILLA and another hour taking notes, drawing conclusions, and writing the interpretive paragraphs. It would take too much space to illustrate GODZILLA's outcomes completely, but a few examples may help the reader's visualization. Figures 11.2 and 11.3 illustrate sample outcomes from Problem 1, Parts A and C, respectively. Comparing these, a user of GODZILLA is supposed to see that drift plays a much larger role in small populations (for example, twenty individuals) than in large populations (for example, 200 individuals).

Figures 11.4 and 11.5 illustrate outcomes from Problem 6, Parts A and B, respectively. These two situations, of course, correspond to the classic case of sickle-cell anemia, where selection favoring the heterozygote acts to increase the gene frequency of a trait that is lethal in its homozygote condition. Figure 11.4 shows what happens when random effects are quite small, and Figure 11.5 shows how drift is held in check by the pattern of selection.

Finally, Figures 11.6 and 11.7 illustrate outcomes from Problem 7, Parts C and D, respectively. Here users see that selection against the heterozygote creates a delicate balance, provided the initial gene frequencies are .5 and .5, respectively (Figure 11.6). But, if there is even a 1 in 20 random factor, the balance will be upset, and the population becomes completely homozygous within about fifteen or so generations. However, which gene frequency increases to 1 and which declines to 0 is completely indeterminate (Figure 11.7).

CONCLUSION

The principal advantage of using a computer simulation program to learn population genetics is the speed with which it performs the calculations. There is nothing in GODZILLA that was not already present, at least by implication, in my blackboard demonstrations. The program is not a "stand alone" tool because lectures on the principles of genetic drift and natural selection are needed to understand the computer output. Nonetheless, GODZILLA can dramatically increase an individual's understanding of population genetics.

Once the card-shuffling/poker chip demonstration of drift has been presented and one multiple-generation selection problem has been worked through, even those individuals who remain adverse to using computers can appreciate that GODZILLA does similar calculations, albeit much faster than humanly possible. It is precisely this speed that makes possible an effective, as well as a reasonable, assignment to be completed outside of class. Now, I can assign a set of problems that take

TABLE 11.3 *A set of problems for using the GODZILLA program*

Numbers appearing within brackets, for example, [3], indicate the number of simulations that should be run for the specified situation.

PROBLEM 1: DRIFT AND POPULATION SIZE

A. Pop = 20	B. Pop = 100	C. Pop = 200
p(A) = .5	p(A) = .5	p(A) = .5
q(a) = .5	q(a) = .5	q(a) = .5
Gen = 30	Gen = 30	Gen = 30
RND = .25	RND = .25	RND = .25
[9]	[9]	[9]
(No Selection)	(No Selection)	(No Selection)

PROBLEM 2: DRIFT AND PROBABILITY OF RANDOM MORTALITY

A. Pop = 20	B. Pop = 20
p(A) = .5	p(A) = .5
q(a) = .5	q(a) = .5
Gen = 30	Gen = 30
RND = .4	RND = .05
[9]	[9]
(No Selection)	(No Selection)

PROBLEM 3: SELECTION AGAINST A HOMOZYGOTE AND THE
               HETEROZYGOTE (TRANSIENT POLYMORPHISM)

A. Pop = 200	B. Pop = 200
p(A) = .4	p(A) = .4
q(a) = .6	q(a) = .6
Gen = 20	Gen = 20
RND = .0001	RND = .2
[3]	[3]
Fitness Values	Fitness Values
AA = .4	AA = .4
Aa = .4	Aa = .4
aa = 1	aa = 1

PROBLEM 4: SELECTION AGAINST A HOMOZYGOTE
               (TRANSIENT POLYMORPHISM)

A. Pop = 200	B. Pop = 200
p(A) = .4	p(A) = .4
q(a) = .6	q(a) = .6
Gen = 20	Gen = 20
RND = .0001	RND = .2
[3]	[3]
Fitness Values	Fitness Values
AA = 0	AA = 0
Aa = 1	Aa = 1
aa = 1	aa = 1

PROBLEM 5: SELECTION AGAINST BOTH HOMOZYGOTES
(BALANCED POLYMORPHISM)

A. Pop = 50
    p(A) = .3
    q(a) = .7
    Gen = 30
    RND = .2
    [6]
    (No Selection)

B. Pop = 50
    p(A) = .3
    q(a) = .7
    Gen = 30
    RND = .0001
    [3]
    Fitness Values
    AA = .8
    Aa = 1
    aa = .6

C. Pop = 50
    p(A) = .3
    q(a) = .7
    Gen = 30
    RND = .2
    [6]
    Fitness Values
    AA = .8
    Aa = 1
    aa = .6

PROBLEM 6: PROPAGATION OF A LETHAL-HOMOZYGOTE TRAIT BY
SELECTION AGAINST BOTH HOMOZYGOTES

A. Pop = 100
    p(A) = .01
    q(a) = .99
    Gen = 30
    RND = .0001
    [3]
    Fitness Values
    AA = 0
    Aa = 1
    aa = .7

B. Pop = 100
    p(A) = .01
    q(a) = .99
    Gen = 30
    RND = .2
    [6]
    Fitness Values
    AA = 0
    Aa = 1
    aa = .7

C. Pop = 100
    p(A) = .23
    q(a) = .77
    Gen = 30
    RND = .2
    [6]
    Fitness Values
    AA = 0
    Aa = 1
    aa = 1

PROBLEM 7: SELECTION AGAINST THE HETEROZYGOTE
(UNSTABLE EQUILIBRIUM, TRANSIENT POLYMORPHISM)

A. Pop = 100
    p(A) = .6
    q(a) = .4
    Gen = 30
    RND = .0001
    [3]
    Fitness Values
    AA = 1
    Aa = .4
    aa = 1

B. Pop = 100
    p(A) = .4
    q(a) = .6
    Gen = 30
    RND = .0001
    [3]
    Fitness Values
    AA = 1
    Aa = .4
    aa = 1

C. Pop = 100
    p(A) = .5
    q(a) = .5
    Gen = 30
    RND = .0001
    [3]
    Fitness Values
    AA = 1
    Aa = .4
    aa = 1

D. Pop = 100
    p(A) = .5
    q(a) = .5
    Gen = 30
    RND = .05
    [9]
    Fitness Values
    AA = 1
    Aa = .4
    aa = 1

E. Pop = 100
    p(A) = .5
    q(a) = .5
    Gen = 30
    RND = .05
    [9]
    Fitness Values
    AA = 1
    Aa = .7
    aa = 1

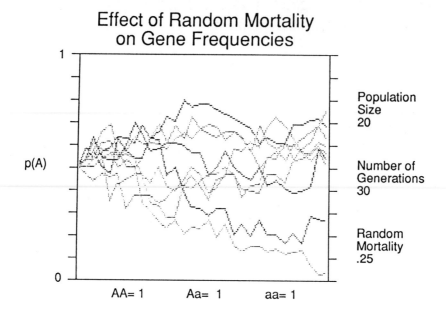

FIGURE 11.2 *Effects of drift in a small population*

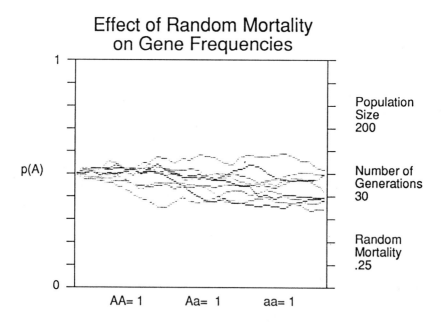

FIGURE 11.3 *Effects of drift in a larger population*

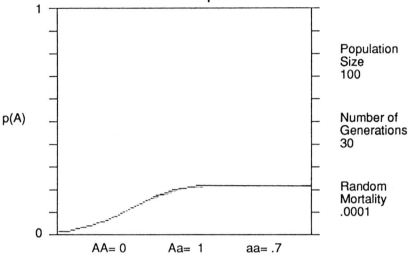

FIGURE 11.4 *Selection causing an increase in the frequency of a homozygous-lethal trait (virtually no random effects)*

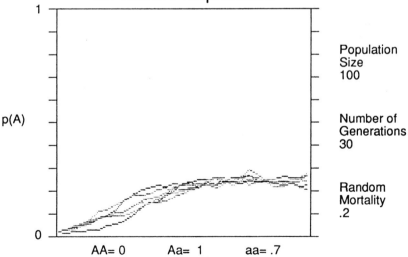

FIGURE 11.5 *Selection causing an increase in the frequency of a homozygous-lethal trait (with random effects)*

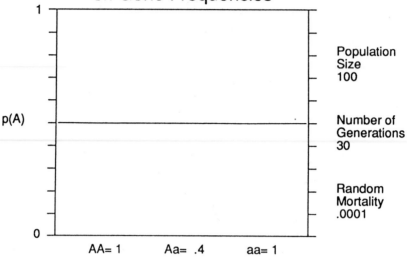

FIGURE 11.6 *Selection against the heterozygote leading to balanced polymorphism as long as random effects are negligible*

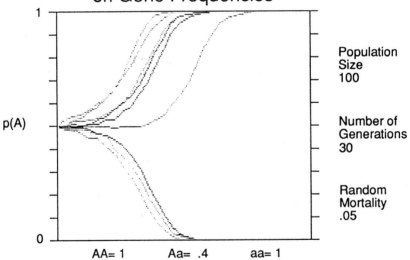

FIGURE 11.7 *Selection against the heterozygote leading to transient polymorphism prompted by random effects*

only a couple of hours to complete and yet cover the range of possible situations. With GODZILLA performing the otherwise time-consuming and tedious calculations, users have the opportunity to experience the excitement of science. Instead of simply believing what an instructor says, they can discover for themselves the effects of drift and selection. This, I believe, is the principal advantage of computer-aided instruction, at least when the topics are truly complex processes such as those underlying biological evolution.

NOTE

1. Copies of GODZILLA (1986, Version 1.1) are available from John B. Gatewood, Department of Social Relations, Lehigh University, Price Hall #40, Bethlehem, PA 18015; telephone 215-758-3814, Bitnet "JBG1@LEHIGH." Please enclose a check in the amount of $10.00 U.S. (includes costs of disks and postage) along with your return address. Within two or so weeks, I will send you the program on an otherwise blank, MS-DOS formatted disk.

CHAPTER TWELVE

A Study of Coastal Fishermen Using Network Analysis and Other Multivariate Techniques

JEFFREY C. JOHNSON
MICHAEL K. ORBACH

Johnson and Orbach analyze social structure with a variety of computer-assisted techniques. They first analyze a social network using a program that calculates social distances between fishermen and displays them graphically in two-dimensional space. They then go on to use two other multivariate techniques to determine the nature and structure of segments in the network and interpret the results in light of theory on urbanization in complex societies.

Many coastal areas in the United States are currently experiencing rapid population growth. This is particularly true in Sunbelt states such as Florida, where people are moving to coastal areas in large numbers. People are attracted by employment and retirement opportunities and by the opportunity to escape climatic extremes (Miller and Ditton 1986). Migrants profoundly affect rural coastal communities, especially traditional fishing communities (Edwards 1986, 1987a, 1987b). This chapter examines the effects of growth on traditional patterns of commercial fishing, using a form of network analysis that relies on a variety of methods, including several computer-assisted techniques, interviews, analysis of secondary data, and participant observation.

METHODOLOGY

The analysis in this chapter uses a number of computer-assisted procedures to determine the structure of social networks and to test hypotheses about actors within the social network of fishermen on Pine Torch Key, 1975–1985 (Figure 12.1). The network of fishermen is represented

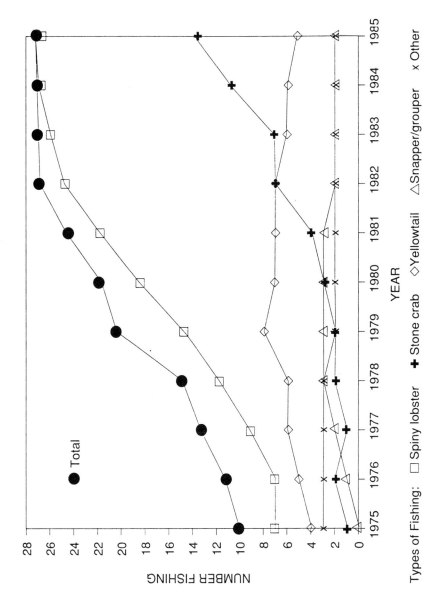

Types of Fishing: □ Spiny lobster   + Stone crab   ◇ Yellowtail   △ Snapper/grouper   × Other

FIGURE 12.1 *Historical participation by Pine Torch Key fishermen*

by a binary sociomatrix derived from a snowball sample and determined by asking fishermen to name persons with whom they talked about fishing. (The matrix is analogous in some ways to the proximity matrix discussed in Chapter 14.) Correspondence analysis (Figure 12.2) is used to explore the structure of social relations within the network. Hypotheses concerning stratification among the actors in the system, due to variation in individual attributes (age and length of residence in the Keys), are tested using discriminant function analysis and canonical correlation analysis (Figure 12.3).

Network analysis is a field within cultural anthropology that has received a great impetus from the development of computer-assisted methods. Network analysis began as qualitative descriptions of network density, intensity, reach, and other characteristics, using simple graphic illustrations like the sociogram. There were efforts to quantify the characteristics of networks of social relationships, for example, calculations of the average number of persons known by the people in a network. These kinds of simple calculations are still performed and remain useful (Table 12.1). Additional techniques are now able to describe and distinguish networks and network segments, using multivariate techniques. The analysis in this chapter makes use of a sociomatrix (a matrix of numbers indicating associations among persons in a network) to uncover the first indications of network segments and then turns to other multivariate techniques to demonstrate the divisions, and characteristics of the divisions, within the network. In the future, combinations of multivariate methods will allow anthropologists to achieve an increasingly sophisticated understanding of social networks. The analysis for this chapter was achieved with the complementary use of ANTHROPAC and SYSTAT (see the Resources Appendix for a summary of ANTHROPAC; refer to the Software Appendix and the Combined Index for information on SYSTAT).

BACKGROUND

Monroe County, Florida, known by most as the Florida Keys, comprises a string of low islands off the southern tip of Florida, just an hour's drive south of the Miami metropolitan area. Commercial, recreational, and subsistence fishing for a variety of fish species, notably the spiny lobster, has been a mainstay of the traditional economy of the Keys. There are now more than 6 million pounds of lobster landed each year, primarily in the Keys, with a dockside value of over $15 million. The lobster fishery has become an economic mainstay for the fishing industry in south Florida.

It is estimated that of the 1,544 permits issued to Monroe County residents in 1985 for commercial fishing of spiny lobsters, only about

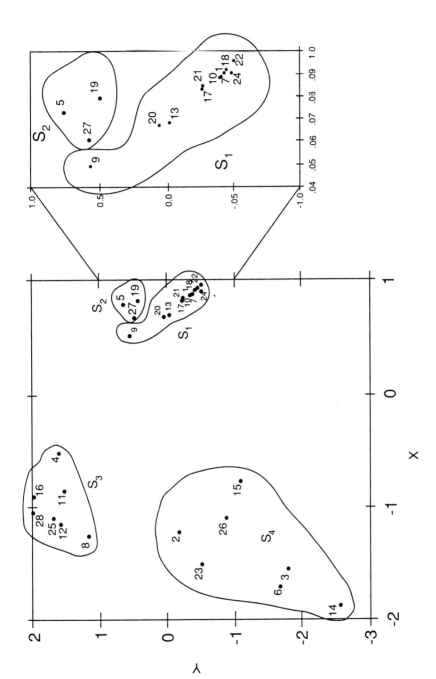

FIGURE 12.2 *Correspondence analysis showing statuses among the fishermen of Pine Torch Key*

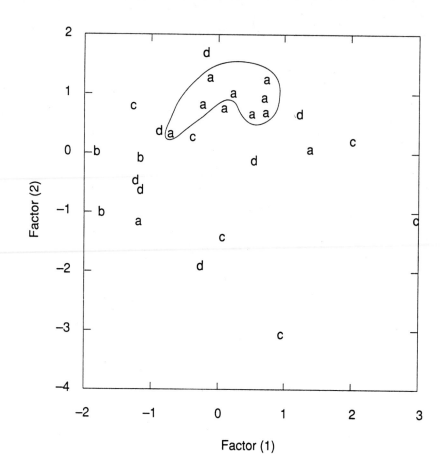

FIGURE 12.3 *Plot of Factors 1 and 2 of the canonical scores with "gentlemen fishermen" encompassed by a circle*

TABLE 12.1 *Mean age and length of residence by status (in years)*

	AGE	LENGTH OF RESIDENCE
Status 1 (n = 11)	$\overline{X}$ = 55.18 σ = 9.95	$\overline{X}$ = 10.27 σ = 3.77
Status 2 (n = 3)	$\overline{X}$ = 33.33 σ = 6.66	$\overline{X}$ = 3.58 σ = 2.45
Status 3 (n = 7)	$\overline{X}$ = 47.33 σ = 14.17	$\overline{X}$ = 18.00 σ = 11.85
Status 4 (n = 7)	$\overline{X}$ = 45.57 σ = 13.69	$\overline{X}$ = 10.00 σ = 5.72

454 are for full-time operations (Johnson and Orbach 1987). The remaining license holders include part-time commercial fishermen, recreational divers, shrimpers, and others who maintain a license in anticipation of possible future restrictions on participation in the fishery. Although the vast majority of spiny lobster are caught in state waters within 3 miles of the shore, the fishery has been under federal management since 1982. Because of the high value of and demand for lobster, and the relative ease of entry into the fishery, the competition and conflict in the fishery have increased substantially in recent years. New regulations have been proposed to address these problems, which, in combination with other factors, constitute a trend toward urbanization.

DEVELOPMENT OF RESEARCH QUESTIONS

Much of the political process surrounding the development and the institution of zoning in the Keys has been influenced by the interaction of several fuzzily bounded social groups or interest groups. These groups generally divide along the lines of commercial fishermen, retirees, developers, and environmentalists. Interactions and alliances among these groups have, in the past, been dynamic in that the groups, who are often in basic philosophical opposition, have joined in a series of on-and-off alliances.

Socioeconomic and class differences have helped to define the boundaries between groups. Most notable among these has been the division, and subsequent differences in views, between commercial fishermen and retirees. Retirees as a group are better off in terms of both temporal and financial capital. The existing social stratification and consequent differences in values and attitudes have shaped the political process and will continue to shape politics in the future. In general, the more affluent retirees do not want commercial fishing neighbors for economic, social, and aesthetic reasons. The processes of change described here will be compounded by the political differences that are consequent to this stratification.

The effect of new zoning laws is to significantly limit the number of places where commercial lobster fishermen can legally operate. The land use plan has been only loosely enforced since its inception in August 1986. However, as recently as winter 1989, several nonresident fishermen renting property in a special fishing district that restricts use to residents only—which we describe in more detail below—have been cited for noncompliance. These fishermen were cited because of continuing complaints by some of the district residents. This kind of contentious behavior is a reflection of stratification among commercial fishermen, as well as between the major groups noted above.

Fishermen have a variety of terms they use to describe different types of fishermen. Many of these terms refer to an individual's commitment to commercial fishing, his "true" dependency on fishing, and his level of skill. Terms such as *full-time part-timers* or, in a derogatory vein, *school teachers* indicate a person's lack of a total commitment to commercial fishing and the fact that they have outside, nonfishing income of some type. The use of such terms is seemingly universal, at least among United States commercial fishermen (Miller and Johnson 1981). Some fishermen can be categorized as semiproletarian. We found evidence of a significant number of economic strategies involving varying combinations of wage labor and small-scale fishing. These part-timers, however, generally do not have the necessary capital to purchase fishing property. In addition, their fishing operations tend to be relatively small (for example, 200 traps versus 1,000 traps on average for a full-time fisherman). Lobster fishing is not a particularly complicated form of commercial fishing. It is relatively easy to learn, although certainly it takes time to reach a high level of proficiency, and it also takes time to acquire the knowledge necessary to develop an effective fishing strategy. Nevertheless, a newcomer with sufficient capital can be fishing in a relatively short period of time with a modicum of success.

One folk classification we found in the lobster fishery was the term *gentlemen fishermen*. Full-time commercial fishermen refer to "gentlemen fishermen" in the Keys as those who (1) tend to have income extraneous to commercial fishing, (2) often have access to investment capital, and (3) may engage in nonfishing activities, often of a recreational or leisure nature, that are viewed as beyond the financial capabilities of most commercial fishermen (for example, African safaris). Such extraneous income is generally in the form of pensions and investment income such as rental property and stocks or bonds. Despite this extra nonfishing-related income, these fishermen genuinely perceive themselves as full-time commercial fishermen, and the size of their operations generally reflects such a categorization.

The emergence of this "class" of fishermen is a process we call the "gentrification" of commercial fishing. Although originally used to describe some European urban neighborhoods and consequential processes (Glass 1964), gentrification has been applied in the United States most recently by Sieber (1987). Gentrification involves the process of replacement of lower-status residents by higher-status residents within declining urban neighborhoods (London 1980). This replacement process has important implications for industrial development and political agendas (Sieber 1987). The gentrification of commercial fishing involves the immigration of a class of financially advantaged or privileged fishery participants in the Keys, resulting in displacement and a new, moderately high degree of social stratification among fishermen. The replacement process influences the social structural character of the political process in terms of industrial, leisure, and housing development.

It is important to clarify the use of the term *class*. Structural or network analysts have argued that the arbitrary determination of class based on income or occupation should give way to more meaningful determinations based on shared relationships over time (Berkowitz 1988), and we therefore view class in terms of social relations, capital, access to the means of production, power, and shared attitudes, cognition, or "consciousness" (Erickson 1988; Ostrander 1980; Tilly 1988). The "oceaned gentry" is a class of individuals who are involved in overlapping social relations, who have access to greater amounts of capital without historical linkage to commercial fishing, who have more ready access to the means of production (that is, commercially zoned fishing property), who may wield more political power, and who share similar attitudes. Members of this class may, as an aside, have higher levels of education or income.

The Pine Torch Key sample illustrates the process of gentrification. Figure 12.1 is a graph of the historical participation of fishermen from the Pine Torch Key sample. Lines below the total show types of fishing activities (SP—spiny lobster; ST—stone crab; YT—yellowtail; S/G—snapper/grouper; and OT—other). Of the twenty-eight interviewed, only ten were fishing in 1975. The greatest influx of fishermen within this sample came in the late 1970s. Many of these fishermen came from midwestern and northern states such as Michigan, Ohio, and Pennsylvania and left other careers in these places to start fishing. Some picked up commercial fishing because they could find no other employment in the Keys. The majority of participants migrated to the area within the recent past, thus meeting one of the requisites of gentrification. The very nature of the term *class* implies the existence of differential statuses among individuals. We would hypothesize the presence of social inequality among fishermen in this community with statuses being occupied by individuals of similar background, circumstance, and attitudes or "consciousness" (for example, we might expect the oceaned gentry to form a status of their own).

THE SAMPLE

The data used in this chapter were generated as part of a larger study of the potential impacts of "limited entry," a management system in which fishing privileges are limited (Johnson and Orbach 1987; Orbach 1980). Several samples were used to produce the primary data and other sources of ethnographic and secondary-source information. Respondents were first interviewed with a common survey instrument designed to elicit a variety of information about them and their fishing operations. A sample (N = 75) was drawn randomly from a list of approximately 1,544 license holders maintaining a Monroe County residence. Their responses gave a representative picture of the fishery. Then, because Hispanic fishermen were known to be a prominent segment of the fishery, a Hispanic sample (N = 25) was drawn randomly from a list of Monroe County license holders with Hispanic surnames. This sample was limited to fishermen who fished with more than 500 traps, in order to maximize the probability of sampling a full-time commercial fisherman. In an attempt to sample fishermen from a major metropolitan area, twenty-five license holders in the Miami area were also randomly selected, of which we were able to contact and interview sixteen.

The sample examined in the network analysis (N = 28) was derived with the use of a snowball sampling technique (Johnson and Maiolo 1986). Ten full-time commercial license holders who resided on Pine Torch Key (a pseudonym), one of the principal industry bases in the Keys, were asked to name five people they talk to most frequently about commercial fishing. Those five were then asked to name five, and so on. The sample was stopped when a high degree of network closure was achieved, that is, when no new names of full-time commercial fishermen who fish out of, or live within, the Pine Torch Key community were being mentioned. Unlike a random sample, the sample for the network analysis constituted a group of respondents who are related to one another in some social structural way. Therefore, we should see some homogeneity with respect to a number of social, demographic, and economic attributes within this group. This is tested in the analysis that follows. The sample was used in order to examine more closely the characteristics of fishermen and a community outside of the two major spiny lobster fishing areas in the Keys, Key West, and Marathon. The city of Marathon and the Key on which it is situated, have a relatively high level of development and are located approximately halfway between Key West and the mainland.

Information was gathered in a large number of informal, ethnographic interviews with commercial fishermen, county officials, fisheries managers, local residents, dealers and processors, and community leaders throughout the Keys and the Miami metropolitan area. One project participant resided in Key West for a period of five months, which resulted in a separate study (Cruz 1987). Key informants, selected with the aid of the snowball sample, were used as a means for cross-validating information.

ANALYSIS

Results of the Correspondence Analysis: Who Talks to Whom

In order to examine the nature of social stratification among the fishermen of this community, sociometric data—of the type, "Who are the five people you talk to most often about commercial fishing?"—were collected for twenty-eight full-time commercial fishermen in a snowball sample as described in the methods section. The data were used to construct a 28-by-28 binary chooser-chosen matrix reflecting the network of relations among these actors. Figure 12.2 is a representation[2] of the binary matrix, showing the relationship among the rows of the matrix, that is, the proximities among fishermen based on patterns of citation—the persons cited as the ones with whom they talked about fishing. Correspondence analysis allows for the representation of relationships among rows and columns of a contingency table or, an (n × m) matrix. Figure 12.2 represents a social topology based on an average linkage clustering of rows using Pearson correlation coefficients as a measure of distance. Fishermen within a circle are structurally equivalent, occupying a particular status/role set (Burt 1982; Johnson 1986). In general, the more that two fishermen have overlapping social relations, the more they are structurally equivalent in Figure 12.2. Statuses are designated by S1, S2, S3, and S4.

In order for our expectations concerning a "class" distinction to be met, first, stratification must be present among members of the community, and, second, gentrified fishermen should form one or more statuses of their own. Figure 12.2 demonstrates the existence of stratification in this system of actors in that there is little disorder in the relations represented there (Burt 1982). Each of the statuses represents reasonably clear subgroupings. There are high degrees of similarity in patterns of relations among members of a status. All of the fishermen who could be termed "gentlemen fishermen" are contained within a single status, S1. Not only do these fishermen form a status of their own, they form one that is highly ordered and cohesive—as demonstrated in the results of the analyses below.

With the exception of fishermen 7, 9, and 18, the remaining actors in status grouping S1 all fit the "gentlemen fisherman" distinction, (see Figure 12.2 at right). With the exception of fisherman 9, all own property in a special fishing district within the community that allows property-owning residents the use of the property for commercial fishing purposes. Most of these gentlemen fishermen have moved to the area since the late 1970s. They are distinguished from other fishermen by their leisure activities, for example, owning an airplane. A fisherman from another status grouping described his attempt to maintain a friendship with one of the "gentleman fishermen" largely out of their mutual interests in hunting. The fisherman stated that he finally had to dissolve the relationship because he could not afford to engage in such things as "African safaris." The fishermen in status S1 tend to be older (late forties and up); to have recently migrated to the Keys; to have already experienced, or retired from, another career; and to have more monetary resources. Some of their former careers include political positions such as U.S. Congressman, county tax assessor, other public service positions, engineers, and corporate executives.

Results of the Discriminant Function
Analysis: Delineation of S1

In order to illustrate how differences in age and length of residence are related to status, and subsequently to gentrification and social class, a discriminant function analysis was performed. Discriminant analysis is a computer-assisted statistical technique used to classify individuals or objects into mutually exclusive and exhaustive groups on the basis of a set of independent variables—in this case, age and length of residence in the Keys. The procedure derives linear combinations of the independent variables (age and length of residence), which discriminate between the groups so that misclassifications are minimized. This is achieved by maximizing between-group variance in relation to within-group variance (Dillon and Goldstein 1984:360). Table 12.1 provides summary statistics (means and standard deviations) for these two variables, for each of the four status groupings, S1, S2, S3, and S4. When status is predicted using age and length of residence, there is little correspondence between actual and predicted membership except for status S1.[3] We would hypothesize differences between status groupings in this case to be more a function of gentrification than status, since members of statuses S2, S3, and S4 would be more likely to share aspects of social class because they are commodity producers.

Results of Canonical Correlation
Analysis: Homogeneity of S1

Canonical correlation analysis is a multivariate technique used to investigate the relationship between two sets of variables simultaneously. In this study it provided a further understanding of status groups. Canonical correlation analysis is the study of the relationship between a set of independent, predictor variables—in this case, age and length of residence—and a set of response measures—in this case, status groups. Canonical correlation seeks two linear combinations of variables, as opposed to multiple regression, which involves only one dependent variable. The procedure computes the linear "variates" or factors from both sets of variables (Dillon and Goldstein 1984:337–339). Figure 12.3 is a plot of Factors 1 and 2 of the canonical scores associated with the hypothesized effect of status membership in this study. The letters represent status membership where a = Status 1, b = Status 2, c = Status 3, and d = Status 4. Gentrified members of Status 1 are encompassed by a circle. Almost all members of Status 1 are close to each other on the plot of the factors. The two fishermen not near the cluster are two of the three not fitting the gentrified distinction. In only one case was a nongentrified fisherman near the cluster of gentrified fishermen. In terms of the two variables, age and length of residence, the gentrified fishermen tend to be a more homogeneous group; that is, there is low variance in their scores. The other status groups reflect more heterogeneity in that there are various combinations of fishermen: old, young, long-time residents, and recent immigrants.

DISCUSSION

For some of the gentrified fishermen, commercial fishing is a lifelong dream finally realized, whereas for others it is simply a productive activity to occupy their time. What is important to note is the fact that the fishing decisions of fishermen in Status 1 are influenced by concerns different from those among "average" commercial fishermen. Because of their unique economic and social circumstances, they share similarities in attitudes as manifested in, for example, political and leisure behavior. Profit, in strictly economic terms, may not be the principal motivation of these fishermen, so the economic relationship between revenues and costs that affects the behavior of most firms may not be at work here. The trend toward gentrification may continue as more people choose to retire from a career at relatively early ages, moving to the Keys to enjoy the weather and life-style.

Although these individuals face the same restrictions imposed by the land use plan that might possibly limit their ability to fish, they often have the necessary capital to purchase the limited amount of residential property that has commercial fishing privileges and therefore have greater access to the means of production. Differences between these and the other groups have led some resident "gentlemen" fishermen to report noncompliance of zoning laws by nonresident renters. These complaints have focused attention on violations in this district that may have otherwise been ignored by county officials. This has also led to resentment between members of the community and the potential for conflict. However, a unique situation stems from the age distribution of this particular class of fishermen. Primarily older, these fishermen will be able to participate in the fishery only for a limited time before advancing age forces them to stop fishing. If, for example, a fisherman who owns commercially zoned residential property stops his fishing operation without selling his property to another fisherman or transferring this property to a son or other relative who will fish, the property may drop out of the pool of the already limited residential commercial fishing properties. This could make a potential commercial fishing land shortage even worse.

The different economic and social classes of fishermen—the full-time "commodity producers," the semiproletarian fishermen who mix wage labor with fishing, and the gentrified fishermen—all represent groups that can engage in competing or cooperative political coalitions. Under some circumstances, expect the gentrified fishermen to share more in common with the retirees than with full-time commercial fishermen. In one case, some of the gentlemen fishermen pushed for and received more exclusionary zoning restrictions in a neighborhood. The neighborhood was changed from a preliminary designation as a less restrictive commercial fishing village that was open to all fishermen (for example, renters) to a more restrictive special fishing district that excluded non-property-owning residents. The potential for political conflict remains, and the class distinctions described above will play a role in its emergence and eventual resolution in the future.

The leisure, tourism, and resort industry has grown dramatically over the past twenty-five years, with the Florida Keys becoming an important leisure and tourism destination. The Sunbelt has become a popular place for people to purchase vacation property or a retirement home, which has increased the price of real estate in the Keys, particularly waterfront property. The amount of canal or waterfront property legally available under the land use plan for commercial fishing is limited. The cost of entering the fishery includes the purchase of property that allows commercial fishing. Further increasing real estate costs have been substantial increases in the assessed value of property. This phenomenon affects not only those wishing to purchase property but also current owners. Tax burdens can significantly increase the cost of doing business.

Johnson and Metzger (1983) recognized a general trend or transformation in coastal areas in the United States from a technical or instrumental focus (for example, commercial fishing, commercial transport) to more of an expressive or leisure focus (for example, recreational boating, recreational fishing, resorts). This trend has become particularly acute in some areas within the last fifteen or twenty years. In many coastal locations, traditionally dominant commercial activities have been forced out by higher costs resulting from the increasing demand for waterfront property by leisure-oriented interests. Conversions of commercially zoned properties to recreational use will further limit the amount of dock space available to commercial operations.

CONCLUSION

All of these phenomena—new zoning laws, the "gentrification" of fishing and its attendant social stratification, rising real estate prices, and the broader cultural trends in the coastal zone (Johnson and Orbach 1986; Meltzoff forthcoming)—are typical of the transformation of an area from rural to urban. In the case of the Florida Keys, this transformation has the clear potential for differential impact on the traditional industries and communities in the Keys—in particular the commercial fishing industry and community.

One group that will probably experience a disproportional amount of these impacts are the smaller-scale fishing operations outside the major Key West and Marathon areas. These fishermen will be initially affected by the land use plan, since many of them are backyard operations on residential property. Most of the fishermen sell their fish for the highest price and do not have the strong connections to any one fish house that might help them in their search for a place to store their boats and traps. The displacement of many fishermen by gentrified fishermen, coupled with escalating land values, will make it difficult for these independents to purchase commercially zoned property. The conversion of commercial areas to marinas will increase the scarcity of commercial space, exacerbating the problem.

All segments of the fishery and fishing community will eventually be affected. It would be safe to predict that these trends will first affect those whose fishing operations are economically marginal and who do not have the industry or community support mechanisms to augment their own resources. Eventually, however, all but the most economically productive and efficient commercial fishermen will be affected, and even they will find significant new constraints on their traditional fishing activity. It is also apparent that the transitions that do occur in the Keys, in fishing as well as other sectors of the culture and economy, will be mediated by the social structures of the Keys communities similar to those described above for the spiny lobster fishermen. These structures form interlocking networks of actors, the interactions among whom will determine the direction of the social, cultural, economic, and political changes in the Keys.

We have demonstrated with the spiny lobster fishermen, that it is possible to trace and document the structure of these networks. Characteristics of the behaviors of fishermen such as those involved in the gentrification process become evident and more easily and clearly definable. The marriage of network methodology and other types of social and cultural analyses can provide a powerful tool both for the assessment of the impact of public policies, such as the Monroe County land use plan, and for social scientific description and explanation.

NOTES

1. This work was sponsored by the Office of Sea Grant, NOAA, U.S. Department of Commerce, and the National Marine Fisheries Service under Grant No. NA86AA-D-SG-046. This is an abridged version of an article that appears in *City and Society* 4(1), 1990. We would like to thank Billy Moore, Ben Holroyd, Mitch Gayle, and the other fishermen in the study for their considerable help and cooperation. We would also like to thank the reviewers for their helpful suggestions.

2. This representation is called an "optimal scaling" (Greenacre 1984).

3. The following figures illustrate the strong relationship between predicted and actual status in S1:

		\multicolumn{4}{c}{Predicted Status}	
		1	2	3	4	Total
Actual	1	8	1	1	1	11
Status	2	0	3	0	0	3
	3	0	1	4	1	6
	4	2	2	2	1	7
	Total	10	7	7	3	27

Using Multivariate Data Reduction Techniques to Develop Profiles of Inner-City Black Patients

MARGARET S. BOONE

Boone uses cluster analysis to explore the nature of poor health in a population of inner-city women, using data from city and hospital records. Her interpretation of the clusters of poor black women from a computer-assisted procedure draws on quantitative results, interviews, and participant observation. The analysis leads to several hypotheses about the relationships between health and life-style among reproductive women—relationships that were not indicated by earlier, simpler statistical tests.

DATA REDUCTION METHODS FOR ANTHROPOLOGISTS

Data reduction methods are useful for anthropologists when a great deal of information has been collected on a group of people and some of it can be coded numerically and entered into a computer data file. In the example in this chapter, cluster analysis (using SAS's PROC CLUSTER) helps to explore and analyze the health-styles of inner-city black female hospital patients.

The broad goal of the research is to understand which variables contribute the most, and in what ways, to the record-high rates of low birthweight and infant mortality in Washington, DC. All the cases in this project were disadvantaged black women who delivered infants at the city's only public hospital. They were chosen specifically because they were so disadvantaged and because Washington, DC.'s low birthweight and infant mortality problems are known to be especially bad in poor, black, inner-city neighborhoods. A comparative research design helped to guide questions about the characteristics that distinguished disadvantaged women who had low birthweight infants and those who did not. From answers to these questions, sociomedical explanations for problem pregnancies were developed and explored.[1] The research data were collected from medical charts and city records and complemented research results gained in interviews and during participant observation. One variable served as the problem indicator for the computer-assisted analysis: the birthweight of the infant each woman delivered during a specific two-year period.

Data reduction techniques such as cluster analysis, principal components analysis, and factor analysis, allow an anthropologist to explore the patterns in a large data base. Data reduction techniques reduce the dimensions of the data by sifting through cases to see which women group together (cluster analysis) and which variables vary together (principal components analysis and factor analysis). Cluster analysis is used here to develop four reproductive profiles based primarily on the clearest clusters of cases. The inductive reasoning used to develop these profiles is much like the reasoning used in qualitative data analysis to sketch cultural patterns, motifs, and "ideal types."

A great deal of caution is necessary in using data reduction techniques because they can allow a researcher substantial freedom in the interpretation of results. Data reduction techniques are not used to test hypotheses in the same way that a Chi-square test or a t-test evaluates a statement in a probabilistic framework. The techniques are misused when researchers are not cautious enough in the interpretation of the "underlying meanings" of factors, components, and clusters, and when new, emerging variables (the components and factors) are then used in further statistical tests using the same database. The techniques are best used when they complement other methods, including techniques based on statistical inference and well-designed, qualitative methods that illustrate and further explore the results of data reduction techniques.

Research results help to explain which aspects of health and life-style affect pregnancy outcome. The separation, reaggregation, analysis, and initial ranking of the importance of the women's characteristics is a research problem that could be approached only with traditional anthropological methods like interviewing and participant observation. In this example, traditional methods are used along with techniques that require a computer.[2] Cluster analysis, principal components analysis, and factor analysis require a good deal of computer space and time—although only seconds compared to the hours and days required for interviewing and participation. The calculations are so extensive that the work is all but impossible without a computer. The numerical results of data reduction techniques can be recombined with qualitative interview material in a final analysis (as in Koons's example in Chapter 7). The results also suggest hypotheses that can be tested using inferential statistics (programs for t-tests, regression, analysis of variance, or categorical data analysis) or further fieldwork.

Data reduction techniques are objective, empirical methods for simplifying the approach to complex, multiple causation in low birthweight and infant mortality among inner-city blacks. The techniques help to form a clearer picture of the relationship between the way people lead their lives and their health status. They are essentially descriptive techniques that use mathematical formulas to group cases (in this case, women) and variables (their characteristics). The purpose of the cluster analysis in this chapter is to see how women grouped together according to variables related to reproductive health. The purpose of an accompanying factor analysis (not presented here) is to identify underlying dimensions that affect pregnancy outcome.

The results of data reduction techniques are open to wide interpretation and have been criticized because they usually do not test relationships between variables using inferential statistics. They have also been questioned because the interpretation of clusters and new, underlying dimensions (principal components or factors) can change, within limits, according to an investigator's biases. However, when several data reduction methods point to the same conclusions, our confidence in them is strengthened. Together, the cluster analysis and factor analysis in the present study went further than the results of the initial, simpler statistical tests, which contrast women with normal-weight and very low birthweight (VLBW) infants (Table 13.1). Interviews and participant observation at an inner-city hospital provide the necessary backdrop to produce a well-integrated, if complex, picture of inner-city black life-style and its effects on reproductive health. There is no simple, single disadvantage that causes low birthweight in the inner city, but there are different assemblages of them. Data reduction techniques allow this complexity to begin to emerge from the data.

The etiology of low birthweight among disadvantaged blacks is complicated. Characteristics that affect reproductive health vary along many dimensions, and factor analysis can be used to search a data set for covariations and to identify a new, smaller set of variables that underlie the original variables. The new factors are qualitative dimensions or bipolar scales along which women vary. "Common factor analysis" searches a data set for linear combinations of variables that account for the variance shared by all the variables. The "extracted" factors should express as much as possible of the variance that is common, or shared, among the original variables. Factor analysis assumes that there is also some variance that is unique to each variable, and this distinguishes factor analysis from principal components analysis (which assumes that all the variance is expressed). There is an indeterminacy in factor analysis because of the assumption that not all of the variance is expressed. Therefore, there are no perfect factor solutions, but there are patterns of different strength that can emerge. After an exploratory factor analysis (or a principal components analysis if there is reason to believe that all the variance is expressed) and a cluster analysis, an anthropologist can return to interview material and case histories to confirm or refute dimensions and case clusters suggested by the analysis.

TABLE 13.1 *Comparison of disadvantaged black women with normal and very low birthweight deliveries*

CHARACTERISTIC	NORMAL-WEIGHT DELIVERIES				VERY LOW BIRTHWEIGHT DELIVERIES				TYPE OF TEST	SIGNIFICANCE LEVEL
	%	(N)*	MEAN	(N)*	%	(N)*	MEAN	(N)*		
Marital status										
Illegitimate births	79.5	(73)			76.4	(72)			Chi-square	Not sig.
Women never married	70.9	(103)			76.0	(104)			Chi-square	Not sig.
Maternal age										
Years at delivery			22.6	(105)			23.2	(105)	t-test	Not sig.
Years at first pregnancy			18.1	(100)			18.2	(94)	t-test	Not sig.
Education										
Years of maternal education			10.9	(55)			10.8	(31)	t-test	Not sig.
Years of paternal education			11.6	(41)			11.4	(17)	t-test	Not sig.
Prenatal care										
Women seeking care at some time during pregnancy	92.9	(91)			77.0	(77)			Chi-square	.01
Ecological distribution										
Women resident in census tracts near hospital	11.4	(105)			25.7	(105)			Chi-square	.01
Migrant status										
Women born outside DC	42.9	(105)			58.1	(105)			Chi-square	.05

					Test	Sig.
Substance abuse						
Women who smoke	44.0	(91)	60.9	(87)	Chi-square	.05
Women with a history of street drugs	25.7	(105)	29.5	(105)	Chi-square	Not sig.
Women who were alcoholics	1.1	(91)	11.5	(87)	Chi-square	.01
Medical/obstetric history						
Women with hypertension history	10.5	(105)	20.2	(104)	Chi-square	.05
Number of previous infant deaths	.05	(97)	.17	(95)	t-test	.05
Number of previous therapeutic abortions	.25	(99)	.56	(92)	t-test	.01
Number of previous miscarriages	.22	(99)	.48	(91)	t-test	.05
Social support						
Women listing female relative as "responsible person"	73.1	(104)	77.5	(103)	Chi-square	Not sig.

*Results based on original comparison of two samples of 105 each, before the single case in the very low birthweight sample was omitted in the follow-up survey. The size of N for Chi-square and t-tests varies according to the number of missing cases. Percentage refers to percent of N in parentheses.

TABLE 13.2 *Programming for cluster analysis (Data and Proc Steps)*

```
//  EXEC SAS
OPTIONS LS = 80;
DATA MYFILE1;
    INFILE RAWDATA1;
    INPUT CASE 1-4 SAMPLE 5 MATCH 7-8 REMATCH 9 CTRACT 11-13 1
        WTLBS 15-16 WTOZ 17-19 1 SSS 21-22 DISAD 23-24 AGEDEL 26-27
        AGECEN 28-29 MOVES 31 MONTHS 32-33 PREVDEA 35 PREVTAB 36
        PREVSAB 37 / QUAD 1 HSTYPE 1-2 OUTCOME 4 GRAVIDA 6-7 AGE1PR 9-10
        IPREGINT 12-14 1;
    TOTOZ = (WTLBS*16) + WTOZ;
    IF QUAD = 1 OR QUAD = 2 THEN PPR = 1; ELSE IF QUAD = 3 OR QUAD = 4 THEN
        PPR = 0;
    IF QUAD = 2 OR QUAD = 3 THEN KIDS = 0; ELSE IF QUAD = 1 OR QUAD = 4 THEN
        KIDS = 1;
PROC SORT DATA = MYFILE1; BY CASE;
DATA MYFILE2;
    INFILE RAWDATA2;
    INPUT CASE 1-4 SAMPLE 2 PERSON1 19-21 PERSON2 23-25 PERSON3 27-29
        PERSON4 31-33 PERSON5 35-37 PERSON6 39-41 PERSON7 43-45 PERSON8
        47-49 PERSON9 51-53 PERSON10 55-57 PERSON11 59-61 PERSON12 63-65
        / PERSON13 1-3 PERSON14 5-7 PERSON15 9-11 PERSON16 13-15
        PERSON17 17-19 PERSON18 21-23 PERSON19 25-27 PERSON20 29-31;
    IF PERSON1 > 0 THEN PERSON1 = 1;   IF PERSON2 > 0 THEN PERSON2 = 1;
    IF PERSON3 > 0 THEN PERSON3 = 1;   IF PERSON4 > 0 THEN PERSON4 = 1;
    IF PERSON5 > 0 THEN PERSON5 = 1;   IF PERSON6 > 0 THEN PERSON6 = 1;
    IF PERSON7 > 0 THEN PERSON7 = 1;   IF PERSON8 > 0 THEN PERSON8 = 1;
    IF PERSON9 > 0 THEN PERSON9 = 1;   IF PERSON10 > 0 THEN PERSON10 = 1;
    IF PERSON11 > 0 THEN PERSON11 = 1; IF PERSON12 > 0 THEN PERSON12 = 1;
    IF PERSON13 > 0 THEN PERSON13 = 1; IF PERSON14 > 0 THEN PERSON14 = 1;
    IF PERSON15 > 0 THEN PERSON15 = 1; IF PERSON16 > 0 THEN PERSON16 = 1;
    IF PERSON17 > 0 THEN PERSON17 = 1; IF PERSON18 > 0 THEN PERSON18 = 1;
    IF PERSON19 > 0 THEN PERSON19 = 1; IF PERSON20 > 0 THEN PERSON20 = 1;
    HOUSTALY = PERSON1 + PERSON2 + PERSON3 + PERSON4 + PERSON5 +
        PERSON6 + PERSON7 + PERSON8 + PERSON9 + PERSON10 + PERSON11 +
        PERSON12 + PERSON13 + PERSON14 + PERSON15 + PERSON16 + PERSON17 +
        PERSON18 + PERSON19 + PERSON20;
PROC SORT DATA = MYFILE2; BY CASE;
DATA MYFILE3;
    INFILE RAWDATA2;
    INPUT CASE 1-4 SAMPLE 2 MCODE 6-7 BDMON 9-10 BDYR 12-13
        MARDEL 15 RESP 17 / SOCSUP 33-34 MIG 36 PNAT 38 HOSP 40 SMOK 42
        ALCOH 44 HYTENS 46 DISAD2 48-49 EDMOM 51-52 EDDAD 54-55 DRUG 57
        PSYCH 59 MOV2 61 MON2 63-64;
PROC SORT DATA = MYFILE3; BY CASE;
DATA MYFILE4;
    MERGE MYFILE1 MYFILE2 MYFILE3;
PROC STANDARD DATA = MYFILE4 OUT = STANDATA REPLACE;
    VAR TOTOZ AGEDEL PREVDEA PREVSAB PREVTAB PNAT HYTENS SMOK ALCOH
        MIG EDMOM EDDAD HOSP REMATCH MOVES SSS HOUSTALY PPR KIDS;
PROC CLUSTER DATA = STANDATA METHOD = WARD OUTTREE = TREEDATA;
    VAR AGEDEL PREVDEA PREVSAB PREVTAB PNAT HYTENS SMOK ALCOH MIG
        EDMOM EDDAD HOSP REMATCH MOVES SSS HOUSTALY PPR KIDS;
PROC TREE DATA = TREEDATA;
```

CODING VARIABLES FOR THE COMPUTER DATA FILE

A data file of nineteen variables for 209 inner-city black women was used. Variables were coded in numerical form: some as categorical measures (for example, alcoholism was 1 for NO, and 2 for YES); some as continuous measures (for example, the number of previous infant deaths); and one as a rank measure (the index of social support). Each woman had a case number and a sample number depending on whether she had a very low birthweight infant (Sample 1), or a normal-weight infant (Sample 4).

Infant birthweight was coded as total ounces and given the variable label TOTOZ. (See variables in programming in Table 13.2.) TOTOZ was used in one cluster program but not another because it "swamped" the results and hid important differences between clusters of women. The type of infant outcome (live at one year, stillbirth, neonatal death, or postneonatal death) was used to interpret the results of the data reduction techniques.

Variables were taken from medical records, coded, transcribed onto data coding sheets, and entered into a computer data file. The woman's age at delivery (AGEDEL) was used because it is considered important in pregnancy outcome. The age when she had her first pregnancy was also used in a later examination of clusters. Measures of obstetric history were transcribed because they are useful in helping a physician predict whether a woman will have a difficult pregnancy: the number of previous infant deaths each woman had (PREVDEA), previous miscarriages or spontaneous abortions (PREVSAB), and previous therapeutic abortions (PREVTAB). The medical records noted whether a woman had any prenatal care (PNAT); whether she had chronic high blood pressure (HYTENS); whether she smoked (SMOK); and whether she was an alcoholic (ALCOH). Birthplace was used and recoded as whether the woman was a migrant from the South (MIG). Southern blacks often have high rates of low birthweight, and they come from different life-styles and environments. The woman's years of schooling were taken from the infant's birth certificate worksheet (EDMOM, or "education woman" in Figure 13.1), as were the infant's father's (EDDAD, or "education man" in Figure 13.1). Education was the only socioeconomic measure found in the medical records and has been shown to be related to birthweight. Information on whether or not a woman lived in the area surrounding the inner-city hospital (HOSP) served as an index of premature labor and emergency delivery—a connection revealed in the medical record review. Medical records also provided two measures of stability of life-style: a residential stability index, coded as the number of household moves each woman had between 1977 and 1984 (MOVES), and a stability social support (SSS) index, coded as a rank measure of the presence and sameness of the "Responsible Persons" listed in a series of three hospital admissions, 1977 to 1984.

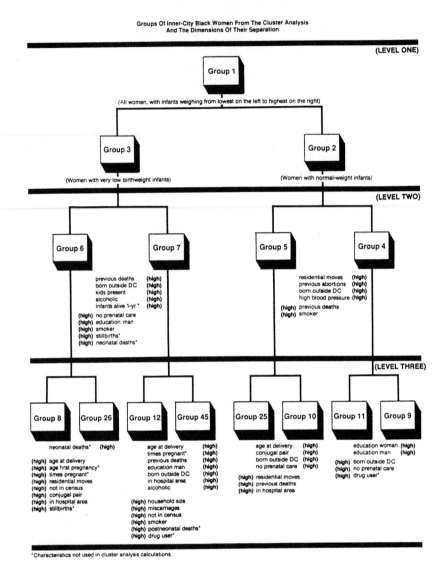

FIGURE 13.1 *Stylized cluster dendrogram in three levels*

A follow-up survey several years after delivery allowed determination of whether or not many of the 209 women were recorded in the 1980 census (REMATCH). This variable represented the general accessibility of their households to outside intervention and inquiry. The same survey also allowed the determination of a woman's household size (HOUSTALY) and composition two to three years after delivery. The latter was recoded to show the presence of a conjugal pair in the household (PPR) and presence of children (KIDS).

Data for all these variables for the 209 cases were typed into a computer file in columnar format for use with SAS programs. The data could be displayed directly after the SAS program in the same file or stored on disk. The file could be viewed on a terminal screen or printed out.

CLUSTER ANALYSIS

The cluster analysis program calculates the "distances" between different women according to the variables, using an algorithm, or formula, in an iterative, hierarchical manner (Aldenderfer 1984). The program used in this research performed successive agglomerations of the cases into increasingly inclusive clusters.

The Mainframe SAS Programs

Table 13.2 shows a SAS program with two basic parts: Data Steps, which name, input, and recode (where necessary) the variables in three files and eventually merge them and Procedure Steps, which include (1) a program to standardize the data (PROC STANDARD), replace any missing data with an average score (the REPLACE option)—although variables were chosen because they had very few missing data[3]—and produce a new data set for the cluster program (the output data set specified by OUT-); (2) a program with a clustering algorithm (PROC CLUSTER), which prints statistics on the clusters and a history of the clustering process in terms of "parent clusters" and "children clusters" and produces another data set for the display of the output with the next program (the output data set specified by OUTTREE-); and (3) a program called PROC TREE, which displays the results of the cluster procedure graphically in a dendrogram. Together, these programs instruct the computer to calculate mathematical distances between women (cases), minimize the variance within clusters, maximize the variance between clusters, and continue in an agglomerative fashion to group cases into successively larger clusters according to the similarities of all their characteristics (variables).[4] The number of the cluster (or group) signifies how inclusive the cluster is. Thus, Group 1 in Figure 13.1 (which includes all cases) is more inclusive than Group 2, which is more inclusive than Group 4. The clustering procedure starts with each case as its own cluster, then groups similar cases, and finally groups similar clusters.

Interpretation of Cluster Output

The cluster procedure has no built-in end-point where clustering stops. Therefore, the first interpretive step is to determine how meaningful the differences between clusters are and where to focus the analysis.

TABLE 13.3 *Cluster output (partial)*

| WARD'S MINIMUM VARIANCE HIERARCHICAL CLUSTER ANALYSIS | | | |
| EIGENVALUES OF THE COVARIANCE MATRIX | | | |
EIGENVALUE	DIFFERENCE	PROPORTION	CUMULATIVE
38.63189	30.35050	0.67669	0.67669
8.28139	4.03115	0.14506	0.82175
4.25024	2.25048	0.07445	0.89620
1.99975	1.13683	0.03503	0.93122
0.86292	0.19734	0.01512	0.94634
0.66559	0.11485	0.01166	0.95800
0.55074	0.06980	0.00965	0.96764
0.48094	0.23205	0.00842	0.97607
0.24889	0.04866	0.00436	0.98043

Table 13.3 shows the first lines of the CLUSTER output when birthweight (TOTOZ) is not used in calculations. The Eigenvalues, difference (between successive Eigenvalues), proportion (of variance explained), and cumulative (variance explained) show that about 95 percent of the variation between cases is explained when there are five or six clusters.[5]

Decisions about whether to continue the analysis are the researcher's. The level and extent of the analysis depend on whether clusters appear to be meaningfully different according to all the data available—not just data in the clustering calculations. I was interested in identifying different kinds of women who had different pregnancy outcomes, and those differences did not appear to be sufficiently clear when there were only five or six clusters. So I made an arbitrary decision to continue examining clusters through three levels of dichotomous branching, until there were a total of eight clusters. This produced some clusters that were large and very inclusive (like Groups 2 and 3 in Figure 13.1) and some that were small and very specific (like Group 45). Continuing the analysis to that point produced useful results. The variables separating groups of women are listed in Figure 13.1 at the branchings.

Important Clusters of Women That Emerged from the Procedure

In many ways all the women were similar. They were all residents of the District of Columbia in 1977 to 1978, and all delivered at the same inner-city hospital. Seventy-five percent of both samples were unmarried at delivery. Twenty-five percent of both samples abused some drug (drugs, alcohol, or nicotine). Women in Groups 2 and 3 were all black and had the same average age. They tended to be young in comparison to reproductive women in the United States. The similarities between Groups 2 and 3 make the differences between them even more striking. When two groups are the same along fundamental dimensions like marriage rate (which often varies with pregnancy outcome), then we must try to understand why marriage seems to be less important for pregnancy outcome among inner-city women. When women with normal and very low birthweight deliveries have the same rates of substance abuse, then we must examine the variables more closely, for example, specific types of abuse.

The First-Level Division. Group 2 women with normal-weight infants (over 5½ lb) represent 84 percent of the disadvantaged inner-city black patients in the analysis; the other 16 percent have low-birthweight infants (under 5½ lb). This was twice the low-birthweight proportion for the American population at the time of these deliveries. The data reduction techniques focused on a smaller sample of women with very low-birthweight infants (from 1 lb to 3¾ lb) because the VLBW rate varies most directly with infant mortality rate nationwide. Group 3 women with very low birthweight infants represent 3 to 4 percent of disadvantaged, inner-city black reproductive women. There were 104 women with very low birthweight infants. These women were matched with 105 women with normal-weight infants, using a sampling scheme that stratified by month of delivery and sex of the infant delivered.

Only four characteristics clearly set apart Groups 2 and 3. The birthweights of the infants of Group 2 women are higher. The mothers in Group 2 have better pregnancy histories with very few infant deaths in their medical histories. When followed up several years after delivery, they were residing in larger households with children. This is not surprising, since many more of their children lived, both from the 1977 to 1978 pregnancy and from others. Perhaps most revealing, they do not drink heavily. The relative absence of alcohol abuse may be the single most important variable in separating the microenvironments of women in Groups 2 and 3.

The 105 normal-weight infants included only one stillbirth, but the 104 very low birthweight infants died at a much higher rate: 27 percent were stillborn; 49 percent died in the first month; 4 percent more died in the remainder of their first year; and only 20 percent lived to their first birthday. The 1977 to 1978 delivery was usually not the first infant death or stillbirth for a woman in Group 3 and would not be her last according to the medical records. They had more chronic physical disabilities and poorer nutritional profiles (based on expected weight gain during pregnancy) and lived in smaller households several years after delivery. Medical records show that their interactions with staff, family, and friends were difficult. Some women left the hospital against medical advice: They simply "stomped out" or left depressed, alone in a taxi. Sometimes they refused medication, wandered the hospital ward, became agitated, fought with staff, disrupted others by shouting and crying, or "threw things." The records of women with very low birthweight infants also had notes about physical assaults and violence. The records of women with normal-weight infants lack notations of this kind.

Second- and Third-Level Divisions.   Group 4 women—especially women in Group 9—have the highest-weight infants. Group 9 consists of only 17 women, and they fared the best. Their infants weighed more than those of any other group of women, averaging 8.4 lb. The women had more years of schooling, as did their infants' fathers. Several years later they were all living with children in relatively large households that often included a conjugal pair and that appeared stable. In 75 percent of the households there was an adult male also living with the woman and children. The presence of these men clearly separates this cluster (Group 9) from the other cluster (Group 11), whose households often lacked both the resident males and the potentially stabilizing influence of a conjugal pair.

Groups 8, 12, 26, and 45 contribute most to low-birthweight and infant death statistics in Washington, DC. The group of 104 women with very small infants can be subdivided into four separate groups using the results of a cluster analysis. Women in Groups 6 and 7 have a mixture of advantages and disadvantages, so their differences become clearest in the third-level divisions. When a variable serves to distinguish groups at both the second and third levels, there is a concentration of the characteristic in the third-level cluster.

Group 45 is a small cluster of only six women who live in households without conjugal pairs, tend to be migrants from the South who abuse alcohol, and have neonatal deaths in their medical histories. Group 12 is a larger group of forty-six women who are set apart because so many of them live in matrifocal households—women living only with children or with children and a female relative in an ascending generation. Their households are relatively large but isolated—if coverage of the woman in the 1980 U.S. Census is used as an index of household accessibility.

The twenty-one women in Group 26 are unique in their concentration of neonatal deaths. They are in their teens and were first pregnant at an early age. Understandably, they have not been pregnant often in the past. The cluster of thirty-one women in Group 8 have the lowest-weight infants. They are older, paired with either a husband or consensual partner when followed up several years later, and have a preponderance of stillbirths. Groups 8, 12, 26, and 45 all contribute to the low-birthweight rate in the District of Columbia but in different ways and because of different disadvantaged life-styles and health histories.

Clustered Health-Styles

A cluster analysis of reproductive inner-city black women is useful in discovering differences between women who at first glance appear the same because of similarities in race, sex, economic status, life-cycle phase, and reproductive difficulties. A cluster analysis explores some aspects of their life-styles and health histories and gives the first impression of separate mechanisms that may lead to the record-high rates of low birth-weight and infant death in Washington, DC.

FOUR PROFILES OF INNER-CITY PATIENTS FROM THE DATA REDUCTION PROCEDURES

Four reproductive profiles emerge using data reduction techniques. The profiles are "ideal types" in that the perfect example of any profile does not really exist. Without confirmation from traditional anthropological methods, their delineation would be much more uncertain.

Profile: Teen Mother

The cluster analysis was more useful than the factor analysis in segregating the effects of youthful age on pregnancy outcome. The best indication of the teen mother was in Group 26, where all the measures of pregnancy history were low. The women are young and have not had many years in which to be pregnant and suffer miscarriages, stillbirths, or infant deaths. In spite of their short pregnancy histories, the women in Group 26 have a disproportionate concentration of neonatal deaths. Although youthful age may be important in inner-city child-bearing, the characteristics of older reproductive women dominate the factor analysis.

Profile: Older Mother

The cluster analysis and the factor analysis that was performed at the same time underscore the importance of the older mother. In the cluster analysis, older women in Group 8 have a preponderance of stillbirths; older women in Group 45 have neonatal deaths. In the factor analysis, age varied consistently with a history of high blood pressure. The clarity of the profile of the older mother is surprising. Still, she does not have a single image but appears to exist in two forms: one in which poor pregnancy outcome is due to age and another in which it is due also to alcohol abuse.

Profile: Mother in a Matrifocal Social Context

Several clusters (and several factors) give clues that social context affects pregnancy outcome in complex ways. All the women in Group 12 had very low birthweight infants, and there is a concentration of women in households with children and no conjugal pairs—the matrifocal household. Yet most groups of women with normal-weight infants lived in matrifocal households several years after delivery. Still more surprising, the women in Group 8 had very small infants, and they tended to be older and living in a household that included a conjugal pair. In the accompanying factor analysis, low social support scores vary consistently with a high rate of abortion and alcoholism. The interrelationships of all these social and health characteristics are complex, and the effects on reproductive health are felt along many different routes of causation. We are left with an open-ended question: Does the woman in a matrifocal household contribute disproportionately to Washington, DC's low-birthweight and infant mortality rates, or does she not? The data reduction techniques are useful in developing a hypothesis that needs further research.

Profile: Mother with Advantages

The variables for the data reduction methods were chosen mainly to understand the disadvantaged quality of inner-city life. We can see, however—either in the absence of detrimental qualities or in the presence of the few beneficial qualities—women who are less disadvantaged than others. The profiles that emerge with the data reduction techniques all point to two different kinds of women: (1) severely disadvantaged women and (2) less disadvantaged women whose reproductive health is good and whose life-styles are stable in spite of an inhospitable environment. Three characteristics have a double-valence quality: household form (matrifocal and traditional households, both of which are connected to groups of women whose reproductive health is good and bad); migrancy from the South (some women with alcoholism but other women who are found more often in traditional households); and abortion (some women who abuse it and some women who have more years of schooling who simply use it). Women with the positive forms of these variables have advantages over the others, and this is reflected in the birthweight of their infants. Yet another SAS procedure, PROC GLM, was used to develop a more specific model of the "advantaged" mother. The factor and cluster analyses were again useful in developing a hypothesis that needed additional work.

SUMMARY

The research in this chapter illustrates that data reduction techniques can, in some ways, replicate the traditional anthropological task of discovering underlying social and cultural dimensions and covert groupings of individuals or other types of cases. Cluster analysis can be used to group many other types of research observations, such as tools, pots, and sites. Principal components analysis and factor analysis can be used to suggest fundamental meanings that underlie the variables in a research project. When these quantitative, exploratory methods are used in conjunction with more qualitative methods, an in-depth understanding is possible that is not possible by using only one type of method.

NOTES

1. The methodology described in this chapter is the basis for a full-length book entitled *Capital Crime* (recently published by Sage) on the etiology of low-birthweight deliveries among inner-city women. Further details are given in that volume.
2. This research used the SAS computer package and a mainframe computer. Data reduction techniques can also be completed using a microcomputer and a statistical package such as SYSTAT (see Software Appendix).
3. Standardizing the data recalculates all values for the specified variables along the same (standard) scale, the "z" scale from -1 to $+1$. This recalculation and the replacement of all missing values with an average score for a specific variable are preferable when using cluster analysis and factor analysis because they both use correlation (or covariance) matrices, which become "unstable" if there are missing values or widely divergent scales of measure for different variables in the analysis. Translation of all variables into the same scale is one aspect of using data reduction techniques that calls for caution in the eventual interpretation of the resulting clusters and factors—especially if there are outlying values for any of the variables (see Chapter 9 for a discussion of the problems of outliers).
4. Ward's method is based on the loss of information resulting from the grouping of individuals into clusters. The program assesses this with a function that minimizes the sum of squared deviations of every observation from the mean of the cluster to which it belongs. At each level of the hierarchical grouping procedure, the groups are reexamined and the clustering proceeds with the least increase in a defined function, that is, the sum of squared deviations (Dillon and Goldstein 1984:172–175). See also, Ward (1963). Other programs like PROC FASTCLUS use formulas that partition cases rather than group them.
5. In both cluster analysis and factor analysis the percent or proportion of "variance explained" gives some idea of the relative strength or importance of the factors and clusters—as does the Eigenvalue, which represents the contribution to the total variance for the entire set of variables. Both give a mechanism for ranking factors and clustering stages.

CHAPTER FOURTEEN

 Multidimensional Analysis of
Perceptions of Ways of Making
a Living among Zapotec Indians
of Southern Mexico[1]

GREGORY F. TRUEX

*Multidimensional scaling allows Truex to hypothesize an
important difference in the emic perceptions of his
informants—a difference that makes all the more sense
because of the nature of modernization and rural-urban
migration in Mexico. Using a sorting technique during interviewing that is widely applicable for both literate and
nonliterate informants, he illustrates how computer-assisted
methods can summarize a great deal of varying information in a compact and meaningful way.*

This chapter explains how multidimensional analytical techniques reveal
the underlying common structure of perceived economic opportunities,
without ignoring the importance of the individual's point of view. By
measuring the acceptance of different, locally relevant ways of making
a living in Santa Maria, a Zapotec town in Oaxaca, Mexico,[2] this research
places both extra community, historical forces (represented by the increasing economic opportunities from state-level intervention) and the
community and individual reaction (represented by individual choices)
in the same analytical context. Data were gathered to investigate the local
perceptions of the relative usefulness of schooling, and other skills and
assets, in making a living in the town. These perceptions both reflect
the townspeoples' attempts to accommodate new opportunities in their
existing life-style and point to the directions that further changes are
likely to take.

The economic development of Mexico, accelerated by the oil boom
of the 1970s, has continued the long history of culture change, which
began with the Spanish conquest, in which native communities must
adjust to conditions that are largely imposed on them from the outside.

National policies and international capitalism provide new economic opportunities while, at the same time, undermining the traditional social and cultural relations of the community. In addition, returning migrant workers have made new economic opportunities for themselves and others by bringing back new skills and technologies and, more important, the capital to use these locally. Both long-term absence and short-term but frequent absence from the community change the social relations of the townspeople and disrupt their normal expectations of their life courses. New economic opportunities, coupled with associated changes in social relations in their communities, directly affect the perceptions individuals have of their life chances. The choice of how to make a living has become increasingly problematical.

BACKGROUND: CULTURAL CHANGE AND DEVELOPMENT

Economic growth and development are integrally connected to social change and cultural development. Economic growth implies increased productivity and, correspondingly, increased per capita income. Economic development generally includes economic growth, but it also implies social and cultural change associated with rationalizing economic decisions, leading to increased well-being. By these measures, much of rural Mexico has undergone growth without corresponding development.

Changes in the capitalist economy, both national and international, have brought about changes, from decade to decade, in state priorities for growth and development. These have led to changes in locally available alternatives supported by the state. Over the last half-century or more, two of the most important state priorities have been to (1) make modern technology available to rural communities by introducing electricity, for example, and (2) change the social structure of peasant communities by opening them to outside influence through intervention on the side of regional or national interests. Development implies changes in the relations among culture elements, as well as the introduction of new ones. Therefore, changes in who uses both old and new technology are central to development. For example, some changes have presented opportunities for community members to become bureaucratic entrepreneurs, brokering both technological and economic (credit) aid to members of their community. In the town of Santa Maria, other changes, such as the introduction of tobacco contracts, have affected those who participate directly and those who do not. Switching household labor resources to tobacco production made many land-poor families more dependent on local production by corn producers, establishing a secondary credit market (producers sold corn and expected returns on tobacco). The relations between landowners and the landless changed from clientage (share-tenancy) to market-and-credit relations.

The most important new economic opportunities that have been introduced to this Zapotec town depend on higher levels of schooling and mechanization. In the Oaxaca region of Mexico, employment as a taxi driver, ferrying people from town to town and into the regional center, is now commonplace. Tractors are now available for rent. High school graduates can get employment (outside the town) in low-paying clerical and service work. Secondary education opens opportunities for "white-collar" work as clerks and secretaries. However, these opportunities are thwarted by failure of the local economy to provide much employment, requiring emigration to take advantage of these new skills. Individuals are faced with various risky choices: Stay in town and do little or no white-collar work (that is, support themselves doing work not related to their training), or move to the city where there is more work but you are far from family and face risks of job loss without support. The payoff from hard work and sacrifice involved in staying in school is not transparently higher than that from traditional ways of making a living.

THE RESEARCH QUESTION

This research focuses on the choices people make within the town. Changes have brought new ways of making a living in Santa Maria, and they have led to changes in the significance of old ways. The cycle of life in Santa Maria remains rural, dominated by the agricultural economy and the seasons, with social institutions still largely functioning and meaningful, although under severe stress because of the economic dislocations. To begin an analysis of the choices the townspeople are making, a basic grasp of their perceptions of alternatives is necessary. Choosing a "way" of making a living is conceived to include, among other things, a person's (1) projection of income and income variation, (2) evaluation of life-style implications such as when you work and with whom, and (3) assessment of locales for work (permanent residence in the town, commuting to work in the regional center, or permanent migration to other cities, states, or countries). These choices are inherently complex. The experiences and community values that people hold are intact, to some degree, even under the duress of change. They do not make choices that are strictly dominated by expected monetary income. Rather, they weigh the expected utility associated with their way of life. They consider how these opportunities fit into existing, even traditional, life expectations and patterns. They consider the impact on their social relations such as networks of friends: If your friends are carpenters (*albaniles*), then choosing a clerk's life-style would be socially costly.

In the midst of change, the need for a community consensus about the "fit" of innovations, particularly those directly related to livelihood, is paramount. In order for individuals to make reasonable choices (in the view of their community), the choices must fit into an overall consensus of "what's going down." However, the community rarely speaks with a single voice. Except on infrequent political occasions, the members of the community do not give expression to a single, communal viewpoint. Rather, it is implicit in the summation of the individual views of the townspeople. Community consensus does not imply homogeneity. The analytical task is to discover the common social and cultural grounding for eminently economic choices without assuming a strong, normative consensus.

This type of analysis is made possible by a computer program for a multivariate technique, multidimensional scaling, which can assist an anthropologist in uncovering, describing, and analyzing emic data. While the computer aids in the analysis by making patterns of perceptions more recognizable, quantifiable, and graphic, the coherence and meaningfulness of the results can be judged only in the context of the culture history, the wider economy, and the external relations of the people—in short, in the ethnographic context of the town, itself.

A METHODOLOGICAL APPROACH FOR MEASURING MODERNIZATION ATTITUDES AND MODERN ALTERNATIVES

The technique described in this chapter can substitute for some of the more laborious aspects of the task of pattern analysis—the sifting, manipulating, measuring, and graphing of relationships between items in a set (that is, any kind of items that can be perceived by a group of individuals). Once the items are presented to native residents by the researcher and reacted to by the native residents, and once the reactions are recorded and entered into a computer file, the computer and appropriate software can manipulate the data about the items' perceived similarities at a far greater speed than can the human eye or hand. The technique used in this chapter would not be undertaken by hand and, if used completely by itself, could lead to erroneous results. Fieldwork involving other methods should always be used in conjunction with any inductive, multivariate technique like multidimensional scaling or cluster analysis (see, Chapter 13).

In 1976, mandatory attendance at the primary school in Santa Maria was enforced for children up to about eleven years of age. Townspeople expressed positive attitudes toward schooling, reflecting community norms. They held school attendance to be a "good thing," all other things being equal. However, informal discussions with townspeople revealed widely varying attitudes concerning these other things. Some criticized the ways the schools were run. Some criticized what was taught in them. Many criticized the teachers and their attitudes toward the town, townspeople, and children. Although most townspeople agreed that good schools are good things, they disagreed about whether the town's school was a good one. The task of measuring the townspeople's attitudes about the local school, therefore, required some care.

Positive evaluations of schooling generally indicate a "modern" attitude. Standard modernization scales, such as Kahl's (1968), are used in measuring the extent to which individuals are socially and psychologically "modern." Such scales emphasize abstract norms and values. Their primary use is in predicting the acceptance or rejection of innovations, based on the degree of modernization of the individual or group under study. For example, Kahl found that the most innovative individuals in Mexico and Brazil had both higher status and higher scores on his scale. Certainly the general attitudes of townspeople indicate the degree to which innovations and change can easily take place. Modernization alternatives involve acceptance and use of fairly concrete innovations such as new crops, potable water, schools, and so forth. These alternatives are evaluated by individuals within the framework of life as it is and not life as it may become. Schooling may be widely viewed as a good thing, but the actual impact of schooling on an individual's life may be limited by the lack of opportunities to apply schooling-based skills in remunerative activities.

In the present research, it was necessary to use data-gathering techniques that took into account the local conditions, particularly the relatively low literacy rate among townspeople. A questionnaire and a sorting task made up the main data-gathering strategy. In a questionnaire, respondents were asked to agree or disagree with statements about the school. In the sorting task, respondents ranked the usefulness (in making a living) of a selection of locally applicable skills and assets. Care was taken in constructing these instruments to exclude, as much as possible, questions and conditions that assumed schooling-acquired skills in formulating and expressing opinions and understandings.

THE QUESTIONNAIRE

A questionnaire was drawn up after extended discussions with my principal collaborator[3] and other townspeople concerning the role of schooling and the ways of making a living in the town. Items for the questionnaire were selected because they represented varying attitudes toward the school and because they were concretely tied to the actual school in the town.

Only men participated in the sample reported in this paper. They were part of a wider study of social relations of kin and had been chosen for that study on the basis of network ties. In 1987, the Educational

Attitudes Questionnaire was administered to a sample of both men and women, but the results are not reported in this paper.

The questionnaire contained tweny-six questions. Each respondent was asked if he was in agreement or disagreement with each statement in the questionnaire.[4] On eight of the items, there was complete agreement among respondents—either all agreed or all disagreed with the statement. As a measure of consensus, the number of agreements was subtracted from the number of disagreements on each item, and this number was divided by the total number of respondents. The absolute value of this measure was taken to be the "index of consensus" among respondents on that item. This index ranged from a low of 0.077 to a high of 1.000 with a mean value of 0.729 and standard deviation of 0.301.

Five of the items were below 0.500 on the index, which is more than one standard deviation below the mean. These five[5] were selected for further analysis because they maximally divided the sample. That is, they produced the least amount of agreement.

A SORTING TECHNIQUE TO EXPRESS "EDUCATIONAL USEFULNESS"

Using Nerlove and Walters's (1977) rank-order sorting technique, respondents rank-ordered fifteen items in terms of "which would be more useful in making a living in the town." The items included the following. (Spanish and English versions are both presented.) Respondents used a sorting technique to express how useful each of the following items was, from their viewpoint.

1. *20 hectareas de terrenos de segunda.*
   Owning 20 hectares of second-class land.
2. *Terminar la secundaria.*
   Completing high school.
3. *Saber trabajar tabaco.*
   Knowing how to work tobacco.
4. *Llevarse bien con gente que puede encontrarle trabajo fuera del pueblo.*
   Getting along with people who can get you work outside town.
5. *10 hectareas de terrenos de segunda.*
   Owning 10 hectares of second-class land.
6. *Terminar la primaria.*
   Completing primary school.
7. *Saber carniceria.*
   Knowing how to butcher.
8. *Llevarse bien con gente del pueblo que puede darle trabajo.*
   Getting along with people from town who can give you work.
9. *5 hectareas de terrenos de tercera.*
   Owning 5 hectares of third-class land.

10. *Saber leer y escribir sin terminar la primaria.*
    Knowing how to read and write without finishing primary
    school.

11. *Tener una tienda.*
    Having a store.

12. *Llevarse bien con los parientes que le puede ayudar.*
    Getting along with relatives who can help you.

13. *No tener terrenos.*
    Not owning land.

14. *No saber leer y escribir.*
    Not knowing how to read and write.

15. *Tener licencia de chofer.*
    Having an automobile driver's license.

The sorting technique uses a stack of cards. On each card is listed one of the (above) items to be sorted. The cards are shuffled for each new respondent. Then, the first pair of cards is placed face up on a table and the respondent selects one (in this case based on which is more useful in making a living, in his view). The one selected is placed face down on the table, and the other one is put on top of it (face down). The next pair of cards is compared, and the one selected is placed face down on the table and the other one is placed face down on top of it. If there is an odd number of cards, the last card is treated as a separate pile (as if it had two cards) in the next set of comparisons.

Comparisons continue through the deck of cards. Then, the first pair is compared to the second pair by turning each pile over and comparing the two exposed items. The one selected is placed to the side face down, exposing the other card previously compared to the one just selected. The two exposed cards are compared, and the one selected is placed face down on the previously selected one. At this point there may be no further comparison because the two already selected came from the same pile. Or, there may be one more comparison, after which the selected card is placed face down as before. The last exposed card is placed face down on the pile, which now has four items in rank order. After the rest of the piles of two's are compared and collapsed into piles of four, the piles of four are collapsed into eight, and so forth until all cards are in a single stack. The stack represents a rank order, for that individual, of all items.

This form of data gathering is particularly useful in field settings because it can be used with nonliterate respondents by simply reading the items to them. The respondent is only required to choose between two items at any given point, simplifying the ranking task. The number of comparisons is held to a minimum (much less than with complete paired-comparisons), so it is less fatiguing for respondents.

DATA REDUCTION THROUGH MULTIDIMENSIONAL ANALYSIS

There are many related, although importantly distinctive, models for data reduction through multidimensional scaling analysis. A. P. M. Coxon provides a very useful and complete review of the various options, including the one used here (1982:176–181). All of the options share the essential feature that they reduce the complexities of a given set of data by representing the relations between items spatially. The relations between points in the data are often easier to understand in a visual "picture" than in the original matrix of numeric data. If the "picture" of the data has as many dimensions as there are data points, then the relations between the data points can be perfectly represented. However, multidimensional scaling algorithms (formulas) reduce the complexity of the data further by representing all of the points in many fewer dimensions. These dimensions are chosen so that they capture the major differentials (the variance) between the data points. The fewer the dimensions, the easier is visual interpretation of the relations between the points. The results of many multidimensional scaling analyses represent data points along only two major dimensions of variation.

THE SAMPLE

Possible selection bias is one of the most serious sources of bias in data analytical work. Because random sampling was not feasible in this research, the respondents (N = 27) were "recruited" from the social network of two key informants whose primary kin reside in the Upper and Lower Barrios of the town, respectively. The constraints on who could be recruited reflected concerns with biases that would affect a different research project. The data for this chapter were gathered in conjunction with research on kinship perceptions (Truex 1981). Therefore, one criterion for recruitment was that the respondents not be "close" relatives: No two respondents in the sample share either a mother or a father or both. Another criterion was that the respondents' domiciles be distributed across the major divisions of the town. Nineteen (70 percent) come from the Upper Barrio, and eight come from the Lower Barrio. This ratio is roughly proportional to the population distribution of the town.

The average age of the respondents was 45.7 years, ranging from 18 to 73. Seventy percent (19 out of 27) claimed some degree of literacy in spite of the fact that six of the 19 (32 percent) had never attended school. Sixty-three percent (17 out of 27) spoke at least some Zapotec; all spoke Spanish. Only four (15 percent) had ever held a position of authority in the town government.[6]

DATA MANAGEMENT THROUGH COMPUTER USE

Some kinds of analyses cannot be done without computers. For example, the reduction of complex data sets to reveal their underlying regularities —such as through multidimensional scaling of preferences or perceptions—would not be attempted by hand. In addition to making such analyses possible, computers also increase the efficiency and productivity of many other research activities. The range of programs that can aid in research is wide. Most of these have been developed and designed for business. When used by a researcher, these programs accelerate the gathering and preparation of data for statistical analysis. They also aid in examination, interpretation, and understanding of results. Throughout my research on perceptions of ways of making a living among the residents of Santa Maria, I have used a number of computer programs, some quite sophisticated and some rather simple.

Because this research spans more than a decade, it reflects the limitations of the state of computers of a decade ago, at the same time that it has benefited from the latest in hardware and software. The original rank-ordering protocols were designed, organized, and printed out with precomputer technology in the field. During the summer of 1987, follow-up work was done on a Zenith portable. With a modern word processor and a simple random-number generating program, the rank-order task (which is only relatively randomized) could have been replaced by a complete paired-comparison design. In recent fieldwork, just such designs have been used. With portable computers in the field, pilot tests of surveys and protocols are possible. When warranted, quick editing and proofreading and integrating new items can be done while still in the field. Discovering a better item or procedure after returning from the field is always disappointing, since nothing can be done until another return trip.

When the data have been gathered, one of the most critical preanalytic tasks is transferring the respondent data (which are usually on paper) to an electronic computer medium. Some statistical programs are better than others because, for example, they have a user-friendly interface. However, most statistically sophisticated programs require setting up restrictively defined commands and data files. The keying-in of many numbers (corresponding to the choices, for example, in a multidimensional scaling analysis), in exactly the format required by the program, introduces a high degree of possible error. In order to assure data integrity, I wrote a simple program that allowed me to directly input the respondents' rank orders, in order to minimize possible error. These rank orders were then reorganized by the program into a matrix of numbers, in which item 1 is in the first column for each respondent, item 2 is in the second, and so on. The corresponding rank given by that respondent is entered into the (rectangular) matrix form required by the scaling program. This simple program helped avoid many of the typographical errors that make data analysis difficult. I also used a spreadsheet (Quattro) and database manager (PC-File, dBase III) for handling descriptive statistical data.

In addition to these relatively major programs, there are a number of very simple "utilities programs" that greatly aid in computer work. For example, the restrictions on the lengths of file names sometimes makes differentiating them, and remembering the significance of the difference among them, virtually impossible. To avoid using the wrong file, I constantly resort to a simple program for "browsing" through files. This lets me quickly look at the content of files and then quickly go on to whatever I need to do. Every experienced computer user has a favorite set of these kinds of utilities.

MULTIDIMENSIONAL ANALYSIS
OF EDUCATIONAL SORTS

There are substantial differences in the rank orderings of different people. In many research situations, psychologists have assumed that these differences reflect "errors" in judgment.[7] In those situations the items are assumed to form a single unidimensional scale. Differences in orderings are assumed to reflect differences in attentiveness and understanding (Torgerson 1958:166–168). They are not assumed to reflect deeper differences in the perceived relations among the items, on the various dimensions. Furthermore, they are not assumed to reflect deeper differences in the meaningfulness or importance of the dimensions, themselves. One standard statistical technique for reducing such rank orderings to a unidimensional scale is called "least-squares scaling" (Gulliksen 1956). The model for an analysis of that type assumes one underlying dimension on which all respondents make their judgments.

In cases where a single underlying dimension is not assumed, multidimensional scaling analyses can be used that systematically take into account interrespondent variation. Such an analysis of rank-order data can be accomplished by using the "point-vector model" (Carroll 1972:107-111), a special case of Coombs's (1964) general "unfolding model."[8] The point-vector model used here implies an "internal" mode of analysis (Carroll 1972:114), in that there is no *a priori,* known set of dimensions that accurately portrays the relations among the stimulus items—in this case, the "ways of making a living." Both the set of dimensions to portray the ways of making a living and the importance of these dimensions to respondents are derived in the same analysis.

Results of an analysis using the point-vector model are calculated by a computer program and can be graphically depicted in the computer output. In the point-vector model, each respondent's ordering of the ways of making a living is represented by right-angle "projections" of the ways (of making a living) onto a "preferred direction" (vector direction) for that individual. The farther away from the subject-point the intersection falls along this vector (this line), the lesser the preference or dominance of that particular stimulus for that particular respondent. The angles that the individual's direction vector make with the reference dimensions (the x-axis and y-axis) define the relative importance or "trade-off" of each dimension to that individual. Thus, a graphic representation depicts the relative perceptions of each of the respondents.

The point-vector model, for the analysis of multidimensional rank-order data in this research, has been implemented using a program called MDPREF (Chang and Carroll 1969).[9] It is one of the options available in PROC ALSCAL in the SAS Supplemental Library (Young and Lewyckyj 1979). The computer program is written to interpret and work with a rectangular matrix of numbers representing a sample of individuals' perceptions. Each respondent's rank orderings were transferred to a matrix in which the (horizontal) rows represented each respondent, and each (vertical) column corresponded to one of the ways of making a living. For example, if a given individual put item 4 tenth in the rank order, then a 10 is placed in the fourth column. If that individual chose item 5, say, to be third in the ranking, then the integer 3 is put in column 5 of the row corresponding to that individual. By examining each column, then, the number of times that a particular way of making a living was chosen first through fifteenth can be calculated. For example, respondent EJR produced the following rank order of the ways of making a living. (Recall that one individual's responses are on one horizontal row in a matrix of numbers.)

Position in rank order = 1 2 3 4 5 6 7 8 9 10 11 12 13 14 15

.   .   .   .

Item chosen = 1 2 5 6 9 7 8 10 11 4 15 12 3 13 14

EJR's ranking is permuted into the matrix as:

Column in matrix = 1 2 3 4 5 6 7 8 9 10 11 12 13 14 15

.   .   .   .

Row data = 1 2 13 10 3 4 6 7 5 8 9 12 14 15 11

The row data are then subtracted from 16, so that the highest-ranking item (that is, item 1) is given the highest score in the row of the matrix (15), and so on to the lowest rank in the row (15), which is given the lowest score (1). This reordering will place the respondents nearest their highest rank item on the plot of (the graphic representation of) the MDPREF solution. This change in numbers has no other effect on the analysis. The resulting matrix has twenty-seven rows—one for each of the twenty-seven respondents—and fifteen columns, one for each way of making a living.

The following card setup illustrates the kinds of directions, options, and manipulations that are specified in a computer program for a multidimensional analysis of perceptions. The term *card* is still used, in spite of the fact that computers do not now use actual physical "IBM cards." Researchers once did input directions and data using stacks of cards that had been physically "punched," or perforated. Today, a "card" typically refers—in much statistical work in the social sciences—to an 80-column line of data in an electronic data file. The term *card* continues in use because it conveys well the notion of a "line of numerical data." An equivalent term is *deck*. A "column" refers to the number of the column on the "card," that is, the specific location in a line of data. Many of the specifications and options illustrated below can be given as simple statements in SAS or SPSS-X or other statistical package instructions. For example, if a plot is desired, then a researcher simply writes "PLOT" at a specific point in the program. Other brief statements specify the type of plot and other standard options.

CARD IMAGE SETUP FOR MDPREF[10]

1. Title "card." This card labels output.

Card:			1	1	2	2	3	3	4	4	5
Columns:	1	5	0	5	0	5	0	5	0	5	0

|----|----|----|----|----|----|----|----|----|----|--

Input: EDUCATIONAL UTILITIES SORT — AYOQUEZCO 1976   7/3/87

2. Parameter "card." This card stipulates the options to be used for this particular analysis.

Card:			1	1	2	2	3	3	4	4	5
Columns:	1	5	0	5	0	5	0	5	0	5	0

|----|----|----|----|----|----|----|----|----|----|--

Input: 27   15   2   2 1   0   0   1

Columns: 1–4 define the number of people (27) who did the sorting task.

5–8 define the number of ways of making a living (15) that were sorted.

9–12 define number of factors (2) to be extracted.

13–16 define the number of those factors (2) to be plotted.

17–20 define the type of matrix that is being used. In this case the data are rectangular with one row for each sorter and one column for each way of making a living. The integer, 1, indicates such a matrix.

37–40 use numbers and letters to label plots.

41–44 label the persons on the plots.

49–52 include a plot where the vectors for people are normalized to unit length.

3. The next card tells the program to read in data by skipping over the first six columns and then reading each three columns as an integer number. (Repeated fifteen times, one for each way of making a living.)

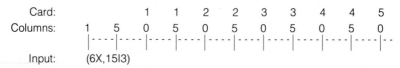

Card:			1	1	2	2	3	3	4	4	5
Columns:	1	5	0	5	0	5	0	5	0	5	0
Input:	(6X,15I3)										

4. The next twenty-seven cards are the sortings of the ways of making a living. Columns 7–9 contain the position of item 1 in the ranking of the individual represented on that row. Columns 10–12 contain the position of item 2 in the ranking of the individual. Columns 13–15 contain the position of item 3 in the ranking of the individual, and so on. Columns 49–51 contain the position of item 15 in the ranking of the individual. Each row represents one individual.

Card:			1	1	2	2	3	3	4	4	5
Columns:	1	5	0	5	0	5	0	5	0	5	0

Input:

```
1 EJR 15  14  3  6 13 12 10  9 11  8  7  4  2  1  5
2 EMC 12  15  4  3 11 14  7  9 10 13  6  8  2  1  5
3 GBM  4  10 12  8  9 15  5 11  7 13  6 14  2  1  3
  :
  :
27 TZJ 10 15  3 13  8  6 12  9  4  5 11 14  2  1  7
```

RESULTS AND DISCUSSION

Output from the Program

A computer program for a multidimensional scaling analysis used the rank-order data for the twenty-seven Santa Maria respondents to develop a summary representation of the variation in perceived differences among the stimulus items. The summary is called a "solution," and it can be expressed in statistical terms and displayed graphically in the output of the program. A researcher uses both statistical measures and the graphic display to develop an understanding of the basic dimensions along which respondents perceive the items. The results are often used to explore intracultural variation, culture change, and culturally specific distinctions.

The two-dimensional solution using MDPREF on the educational usefulness sorts is presented in Figure 14.1. The ways of making a living are labeled with their descriptions. The respondents form an arc on the right of the figure. Each subject-point may actually represent several subjects when their perceptions and responses are very similar. Fourteen

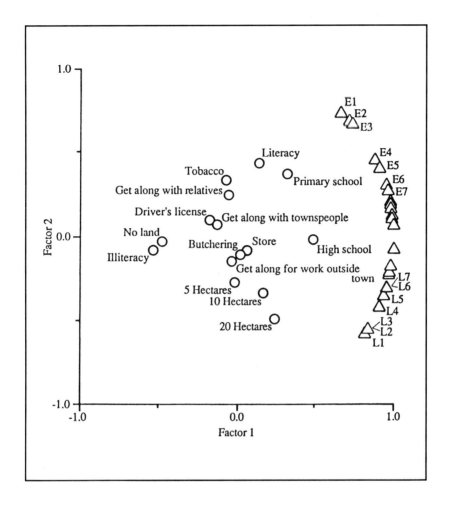

FIGURE 14.1 *Two-dimensional plot of respondents and ways of making a living*

of the subject-points are labeled E1 through E7, and L1 through L7.[11] Each individual's rank order is implicit in the right-angle projections of the item points on a line (called a vector) going from the individual through the origin of the plot (Figure 14.2). Thus, in Figure 14.2 a line (vector) is drawn from individual L1 through the origin. A line (projection) from each item is drawn to L1's vector. These projection lines intersect L1's vector at right angles. The order in which the projection lines intercept L1's vector approximates as closely as possible L1's original rank order. Only two dimensions are discussed here because they illustrate the main conclusions. MDPREF solutions in three and four

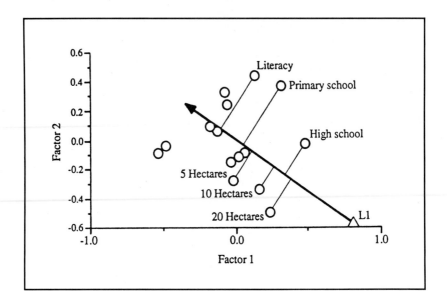

FIGURE 14.2 *Projection of points representing ways of making a living on the point-of-view of subject labeled "L1"*

dimensions were examined. The first dimension of perceived difference accounted for 59 percent of the variance. The second dimension accounted for 10 percent. The third, fourth, and fifth accounted for 7, 6, and 5 percent, respectively. In other words, a large proportion of the variance was captured in one dimension of difference, but people's perceptions varied along a second dimension that exerted some effect. Typically, the results of a multidimensional scaling analysis focus on the first two main dimensions, which often capture most of the variance.

Interpreting the Solution

The relations among the ways of making a living reflect the overall similarity of the individuals' perceptions of their usefulness. Their physical proximity in the graphic display of the output corresponds to the similarities of their perception. For example, items 1, 5, and 9 are relatively close to each other (20 hectares, 10 hectares, and 5 hectares, respectively). (The "ways of making a living" that are discussed here correspond to the fifteen response items listed earlier in the chapter.) Item 2 (High school) is not strikingly close to item 6 (Primary school). The latter, however, is close to item 10 (Literacy), reflecting, perhaps, that literacy is perceived as the most important skill associated with early schooling. Around this central solution are indicated the range of inter-respondent "points of view" concerning the "ways of making a living" in the town. The projection of the points on the vectors corresponding to respondents in the lower right quadrant (such as L1, L2, and L3) indicates that these respondents place owning land as the most important way of gaining a livelihood. They viewed finishing primary school or being able to read and write as somewhat less useful. As with almost all of the respondents, finishing secondary school was viewed as very useful. Respondents in the upper right quadrant (such as E1, E2, and E3) viewed educational attainment, finishing secondary school and primary school, and literacy, as being more useful in gaining a livelihood than even owning large amounts of land (such as 20 hectares).

When compared with the answers on the Educational Usefulness Questionnaire, there appear to be general correlations that warrant further investigation. A comparison of respondents E1, E2, E3, E4, E5, E6, and E7 (the "education-oriented" respondents) with respondents L1, L2, L3, L4, L5, L6, and L7 (the "land-oriented" respondents),[12] in terms of their answers on the five questions that most differentiated respondents on the Usefulness Questionnaire, shows that a statistically significant difference exists.[13] That is, the land-oriented respondents gave twenty-four [mean = 3.429, sd = 0.787] negative responses on these questions, whereas the education-oriented respondents gave fourteen [mean = 2.000, sd = 1.155] negative responses [t = 2.705, df = 12, p < .019].

One interpretation of this result might be that the land-oriented group is less "modern," since they expressed, in general, more unfavorable views about the local school than did the education-oriented group and, in addition, they are more land oriented, which is a traditional peasant trait. However, the education-oriented group had five members who speak Zapotec (a conservative trait), whereas the land-oriented group had only two [Chi-square 2.66, 1 df, p < 11%]. The education-oriented group had served an average of 0.57 years in the military, whereas the land-oriented group had served an average of 1.43 years in the military [t = 1.732, df = 12, p < 11%]. Otherwise, the two groups do not differ markedly in social characteristics such as years of schooling or literacy. The land-oriented group is younger by five years, on average, but this is not a statistically significant difference. The two groups are statistically similar in number of children, service in town offices, and civil status (six out of seven in each group are currently married). All of the respondents described themselves as *campesinos*.[14] Three of the education-oriented respondents and two of the land-oriented respondents said they had some income in the previous year from other occupations, as well.

Access to land, of course, might be a significant predictor of these modernization attitudes. Measuring such access is difficult, and the data on the two groups are too sparse to analyze meaningfully. Respondents were probed about land, but they were generally reluctant to indicate more than whether or not they "owned" some land.[15] All of the respondents in both groups "owned" some third-class land (because the *municipio* has large communal lands for anyone who continuously works the land). None of the respondents is a large landowner.

The land-oriented individuals may not be so much conservative as realistic. Because of the limited opportunities in the town and because of the value of crops such as tobacco, the land-oriented respondents may be correct: In materially objective terms, a livelihood gained in the town is greater when land is owned, and the more land owned, the better. It is true that completing secondary schooling would get one a good job outside of the town. However, completing secondary school would not materially change one's livelihood within the town because there is no work that is related to that kind of education. Nevertheless, both groups consider the completion of secondary school to be a major economic benefit.

The data suggest that the two groups revealed in the multidimensional analysis differ in evaluating other educational opportunities and the usefulness of land. Why they differ is not clear. Perceived life opportunities, based on land access and alternative employment, may be critical. Certainly, the issue is important. Mexico faces serious social dislocations because of the wholesale migration from rural towns, such as Santa Maria, to metropolitan areas. Expectations about the future quality of life in rural Mexico reflect, among other things, the perceived usefulness of ways of making a living there.

NOTES

1. The editors have provided both encouragement and helpful criticism. Dr. Nancy Weber Truex worked in the field with me and has provided both support and insight into the problems this paper addresses. The California State University, Northridge, provided funds for a brief field visit during the summer of 1987 for work on this and related materials. I thank them all.

2. Santa Maria was a town of about 5,000 in 1976 when this research was carried out. Zapotec is still spoken there, and there is historical continuity with the traditional heritage of the town. Nonetheless, the townspeople have adopted rural Mexican Spanish as the language of social, political, and economic life of the town.

3. Sr. Erasmo Jimenez Rodriguez and I have collaborated in ongoing research in Santa Maria for over fifteen years. The term *collaborator* reflects his designation of our relationship, in which he has contributed both to the research agenda and to the actual research. We are currently formulating research protocols on his social concerns about parent-child communication. This collaboration involves input from both of us into a common research enterprise.

4. Some items are implicit comparisons, such as item 10 (What really is valuable for making a living is learned from relatives and not in school). To ensure that the respondent had comprehended and given their actual choice for

each item, these items were rephrased to reflect the respondent's answer and read back for verification. If the respondent hesitated or disagreed, the question was broken down into its components. For example, question 10 (What really is valuable for making a living is learned from relatives and not in school) was first broken down into "Is what is learned from relatives valuable?" and "Is what is learned in school valuable?" Then, respondents were asked to rank the two. The sense of the ranking was then taken as their response. Almost all respondents had some questions so rephrased. For eleven of the respondents, all questions were verified in this way.

5. They are: 10. What really is valuable for making a living is learned from relatives and not in school. 11. During the "seeding season," fathers who do not send their children to school should not be fined (by the local authorities). 16. More religion and not so much science and mathematics should be taught in the schools. 17. The children can get better grades by giving gifts to the teachers. 19. The teachers are late to school almost every day. These five questions have an index of consensus ranging from 0.077 to 0.385 (with a mean of 0.200).

6. The sample is not random, and following the suggestions of Brislin and Baumgardner (1971), this description of the sample is provided.

7. "Some variability of judgment with respect to any given stimulus . . . is true of any measurement procedure" (Torgerson 1958:63). That some differences reflect "errors" induced by the failure of discrimination processes is fundamental to most psychophysical measurement models (cf Torgerson 1958: Chapter 4; Bock and Jones 1968; Coombs et al. 1970:38–60).

8. The point-vector algorithm attempts to find the best configuration of points in a multidimensional space while at the same time finding the best fitting vector for each respondent. The respondent vector is placed in the configuration in such a way that the orthogonal (right-angle) projections of the stimuli points on each respondent vector reproduce the rank order of that respondent. This type of analysis is analogous to factor analysis, where the stimuli configuration is like the factor loadings and the respondents' vectors are like the factor scores. The best solution finds uncorrelated linear combinations of "variables" that may be ordered by the amount of variance explained as in principal axes techniques such as factor analysis. MDPREF does not make the types of distributional assumptions often associated with factor analytical methods.

9. I have implemented the MDPREF algorithm distributed by the Bell Laboratories for the IBM-PC. The analyses were originally run on the CDC 3300 at California State University, Northridge, and replicated on the IBM-PC.

10. The corresponding PROC ALSCAL cards are:

```
DATA = EDUCATIONAL UTILITIES SORT — AYOQUEZCO 1976
SHAPE = RECTANGU
ROWS = 27
LEVEL = ORDINAL
```

T A B L E 1 4 . 1 *Least-squares scaling of ways of making a living*

WAY	SCALE VALUE
2	3.3
3	1.7
4	1.8
5	2.3
6	2.7
7	2.0
8	1.6
9	1.8
10	2.2
11	2.1
12	1.9
13	0.7
14	0.0
15	1.4

```
CONDITION=ROW
SIMILAR
UNTIE
MODEL=EUCLID
PLOT
```

11. A least-squares scaling algorithm (Gulliksen 1956) was applied to the resulting 27 by 15 matrix of respondents' rank orders. The results show that respondents, as a group, judged "finishing secondary school" to be the most useful in gaining a livelihood (with a scale value of 3.3). They judged "finishing primary school" the next most useful (scale value 2.7). These scalings are listed in Table 14.1. The order of the stimuli from this least-squares scaling is replicated (approximately) by the projections of the MDPREF stimuli on the vector direction defined by the x-axis (the first factor of the MDPREF solution, accounting for 60 percent of the variance in the data). The rank correlation between the ranks of the least-squares scaling and the rank order from the MDPREF is 0.988 (see Table 14.1).

12. Because the angles that the individual's direction vector makes with the reference dimensions (x-axis and y-axis) define the relative importance or "trade-off" of each dimension to that individual, the members of the "land-oriented" and "education-oriented" groups were taken to include all those whose cosines were less than 0.97 (which separates roughly the extreme quartiles of respondents). The cosines for the "land-oriented" group range from 0.816 to 0.956. The cosines for the "education-oriented" group range from 0.661 to 0.963.

13. t-statistics are suspect because of unknown bias in the sample.

14. *Campesino* is usually translated as "peasant." It can, however, refer to any of many kinds of agricultural workers in the Mexican system. Characteristically, *campesinos* are those who work their own or communal lands, mainly for subsistence, using family capital and labor resources. The *campesinos* in Santa Maria are not exactly peasants, in the traditional sense, because they commonly raise crops for the market (tobacco) and participate in an international trade in labor (as undocumented agricultural workers).

15. "Owning" land is not a sound basis for judging access to land in Santa Maria Men, for example, may not "'own" land until well into their fifties or sixties (when their parents die), but they have significant access to good land, nonetheless.

CHAPTER FIFTEEN

Computer Representation of Cultural Constructs: New Research Tools for the Study of Kinship Terminologies[1]

DWIGHT W. READ
CLIFFORD A. BEHRENS

In this chapter, Read and Behrens tackle one of the central topics in cultural anthropology: the nature and meaning of "kinship." The authors codify rules of naming in the formulas contained in the computer programs they write, and they display kinship relationships in the graphic representations formed from the computer output. They demonstrate that the interactive capacity of microcomputers can be an integral part of the research process and theoretical development in the discipline.

Programming languages on microcomputers have increasingly made the development of software for anthropological research accessible to the noncomputer specialist. Along with languages and software architecture that emphasize problem definition over solution procedure, this is making it possible to develop sophisticated software that can effectively model both cultural and analytical constructs. Computer-based modeling of constructs opens up the potential of using software as a major research tool and not just a computational device. In this chapter, the potential of software for the modeling of constructs will be examined through computer software applications to the analysis of kinship and genealogical systems. The goal is to understand better the interplay between the formation of native conceptual systems at an abstract level and their implementation as interpretive frameworks for action and behavior.

THE COMPUTER AS A RESEARCH TOOL

Our aim in this chapter is to examine the role that computers can play in our efforts to model the structure of cultural and social systems. We will focus on kinship systems in this task because virtually all of the issues and complexities involved in the general endeavor are found in the study of kinship. The complexities and issues are of two kinds. First, there are three interrelated questions that frame the materials that should be given representation in a computer idiom: (1) What is the problem domain? (2) What are the data for this problem domain? and (3) What theoretical perspective is being used? Second, the answers to these questions affect our choice of an effective computer language and software design to represent the concepts, information, and data of the analysis.

No one of the first group of questions can be singled out as a starting point in this endeavor, since answers to any one of the questions affect the answers to the others. The choice of a problem domain, for example, affects what facts are considered to be "data." Observations about data can challenge previous theoretical perspectives. Change in theoretical perspective may restructure what is considered to be a problem domain, and so on.

In the first part of this chapter we illustrate how a changing theoretical perspective on the nature of kinship terminologies (labels for genealogical positions versus a structured set of kin terms) affects what are considered "primary data"—and hence, the models that are constructed for kinship terminologies. The models, as we illustrate, influence our choice of computer language and software architecture that are used in our work on representing the structure of kinship terminologies.

Next, we briefly review other ways that kinship terminologies have been considered and how these other viewpoints lead to different choices in computer language and software design. The computer programs we review include:

1. Database programs for genealogical data
2. Graphics editors suitable for preparation of kin term charts and diagrams
3. A program for the componential analysis of kinship terminologies (Kronenfeld 1976)
4. A program for the representation of rewrite rules for Crow/Omaha kinship terminologies (Smith et al. 1982)
5. A program for developing algebraically based models of kinship terminology structure (Read and Behrens 1988)
6. A program for the graphical display of the structural implications of systems of marriage rules (Ottenheimer 1986)
7. An example of an expert system program of kin term usage (Read and Behrens 1988; Wilson, Chapter 10 in this volume)

Finally, we suggest that through direct involvement with software design, anthropologists can make effective use of computers in research that goes far beyond the more traditional viewpoint of computers as highly effective computational devices.

THEORETICAL PERSPECTIVE, PROBLEM DOMAIN, AND KINSHIP DATA

We illustrate the interrelationships among theoretical perspective, problem domain, and data, by considering a long-standing controversy over whether kinship terminologies should be viewed primarily as labels for genealogical relationships or as labels for native concepts that may include—but need not be limited to—genealogical relationships. The difference is essentially between viewing a kin term (such as our term *Mother*) as a label for a genealogical position and viewing the term as part of a structured set of categories in which genealogical properties are secondary to the structure. The first perspective considers a genealogical space, or grid, as primary, with kin terms serving as labels for genealogically defined positions. The second perspective considers kin terms as forming a structured set of categories for which genealogical relationships are secondary and a consequence of how the categories are defined. Put another way, the first framework makes genealogical positions the primary data, and the second framework makes kin terms the primary data.

We present below a way to model kinship terminologies based on kin terms taken as the primary data. This reformulation allows us to embed what has been considered, until now, separate analytical tasks into a single framework and provides the foundation for the computer-based modeling of kinship terminology structure that is part of our research. But, before doing so, we trace out in more detail the way in which perspectives on kinship terminologies have been changing.

THE NATURE OF KINSHIP

The formal, scientific study of kinship systems began with Lewis Henry Morgan, who, in his seminal work, *Systems of Consanguinity and Affinity of the Human Family* (1871), recognized kinship terminologies as expressing an essential aspect of human social and cultural systems. It has been argued that kinship terminologies provide the native, conceptual framework for the organization of persons within a society and serve as a means to transform genealogical relationships into a larger, more general, institutionalized framework of social relationships (Leaf 1971). The universality of kinship—in the sense of persons linked through parent-child connections—has been well established. However,

TABLE 15.1 *Kin term analysis based on genealogical grid*

PROBLEM		METHOD
Task 1	Description of terminology	Genealogical method
Task 2	Classification of terminologies	Archetypes based on cousin term labeling of kintypes
Task 3	Formal analysis of terminologies	A. Componential analysis—genealogically based components B. Rewrite rules—universal genealogical grid

exactly what it is that constitutes "kinship," in the sense of a native-defined conceptual system, is still in dispute. It is even disputed whether there *is* a conceptually separable domain in native thought that can be called "kinship" (Atkins 1984; Hirschfeld 1986; Needham 1971; Schneider 1972:42–43, 1984).

The view that kinship terminologies are first and foremost a way to classify genealogically defined positions (Scheffler and Lounsbury 1971:38–39) has been challenged on the grounds that "kinship"—if it is anything—is a native conceptual construct. So, whether or not it is a way of thinking about genealogical relationships must be demonstrated on a case-by-case basis and not assumed (Schneider 1972, 1984). The difference that is being expressed is between assuming that kinship terminologies are universally based on a common genealogical grid and asserting that kin terms refer to native-defined categories that need not be precisely coincident with genealogical positions defined with respect to "Ego."

GENEALOGICAL APPROACHES TO KINSHIP

In Table 15.1 we list a series of tasks that are part of a traditional approach to the study of the terminological aspects of kinship systems—whether or not computers are used. The first task is the description of the basic data: the linguistic utterances used in address and/or reference. Typically, "translation" of terms is provided by associating with each kin term, the "kintypes" (the genealogical positions such as "mother's brother") for which the kin term is applicable. For example, the kin term *Uncle* may be used for the kintype "mother's brother." After this stage, kinship terminologies can be represented by lists of kin terms and their associated kintypes. These data lead to questions about variation and similarity among kin terminologies. The task at the next level is to provide order through classification of terminologies—for example, Morgan's distinction between descriptive and classificatory terminologies (1871) and Murdock's work on kin terminology classification (1949).

Classification (Task 2, Table 15.1) orders the data but does not necessarily provide deeper understanding of the structuring principles of a kinship terminology. Two approaches have been used to analyze structural principles (Task 3, Table 15.1): (1) componential analysis (Goodenough 1956; Romney and D'Andrade 1964; Wallace and Atkins 1960) and (2) rewrite rules (Lounsbury 1964a, 1964b, 1965; Scheffler and Lounsbury 1971). Briefly, componential analysis takes kin terms as embedded in a "genealogical space" (the set of all possible genealogical positions an Alter can have with respect to Ego) and determines a minimal definition for the subregion of this space corresponding to a kin term. For example, the genealogical positions for which the term *Grandmother* is applicable are the kintypes "mother's mother" and "father's mother" (the subregion of the genealogical space), and these can be reduced to a single expression: female, two generations removed from Ego. That expression defines the minimum components (hence the term *componential*)—sex and generational distance—needed to know what genealogical positions are included within the scope of the term *Grandmother.*

Rewrite rules take kin terms as labels for classes of kintypes, as does componential analysis, but then considers the kintypes associated with a kin term as being of two kinds: (1) focal kintypes, which are needed to provide a minimal definition of a kin term as a class of kintypes, and (2) derived kintypes, which can be obtained from the focal kintypes through what are called "rewrite rules." A rewrite rule states that a kintype expression in one form can be rewritten as a kintype expression in another form. The goal is to provide a minimal set of rules that permit a researcher to formally derive the full classification of kintypes from the primary or focal kintype(s) for kin terms.

THE RESEARCH PROBLEM AND THE NEED FOR A COMPUTER PROGRAM

In the sequence of tasks going from data description to the development of models, decisions at one step about data and representation of data had a substantial impact on subsequent steps. One of these choices led to the use of a genealogical grid for both elicitation (Rivers 1910) and representation of kin terms. However, Schneider (1972, 1984, 1986) has argued that the presumed primacy of genealogy as the basis of kinship (assumed explicitly with the rewrite rules), or at least as a proper domain for distinguishing the attributes of kin terms (assumed with componential analysis), is questionable.

Although componential analysis and rewrite rules have both been successful as analytical means of describing kinship terminologies in a way that makes cross-cultural comparison more meaningful, a problem arises because properties of one kind of data—namely, kinship terminology structure—are answered through use of the other kind of data—namely, kintypes and genealogical spaces. For example, Murdock used differences in cousin terms as these are expressed in the form of sets of kintypes—genealogical data—to classify terminologies—terminology data. Therefore, it is unclear to what extent the claimed distinctions or similarities between different terminologies are an artifice of the kintype-based representation that has been used or to what extent the distinctions stem from the structural properties of the terminologies. An alternative to a presumed "universality" of a genealogical grid would be to disentangle genealogy from kinship and to analyze kinship as a cultural construct whose reference may, but need not necessarily, include genealogical relationships (Read 1976, 1984, 1988). This reformulation has been the foundation for developing our computer program to analyze the structure of kinship terminologies.

REFORMULATION OF THE PROBLEM DOMAIN

Disentangling the genealogical space from the kinship domain allows an examination of kinship terminologies as cultural constructs—that is, as structures having a form given by their internal logic. The structure is that of relations among kin terms taken as linguistic utterances, not of relations among persons to whom the kin terms may be applied. The structure is formed directly from objects (kin terms) related through underlying concepts that relate the objects to one another and not secondarily on relations derived from a genealogical space or grid. The distinction being made here is essentially between (1) native knowledge that, for example, in American culture, informs us that "a Mother [kin term] of a Father [kin term] is a Grandmother [kin term]" regardless of any genealogical meaning that might be given to these terms, and (2) the assertion that "mother [kintype] of father [kintype] is father's mother [kintype], and an appropriate term of reference for father's mother is the kin term *Grandmother*."

In our American terminology, this distinction is not as clearly expressed as it is in other terminologies. For example, among the !Kung San (a hunting/gathering people of the Kalahari Desert) people know what kin terms to use for each other even when they do not know their genealogical relationship—if any—since the appropriate kin term can be determined from the term each of them uses for a common relative.

To illustrate using our terminology, if Ego and Alter both know that Ego calls a third person by the term *Father* and Alter calls that same person by the term *Uncle,* then Ego and Alter should use the term *Cousin,* for each other.

Table 15.2 gives the sequence of steps—again going from basic data to analytical construct—but this time keeping the genealogical information separate from the kin term information. These two parallel sequences will be used to frame our discussion of computer programs that have been developed for different tasks in the study of kinship terminologies.

We begin with a step in the genealogical sequence that is not always considered explicitly in the analysis of kinship systems, namely, the raw data of actual persons and their linkages through procreation. We introduce this to make it clear that genealogy that is empirically grounded and structured through the facts of procreation should be distinguished from kinship terminology structure that has its base in the facts of linguistic terms of reference and address and structure as a consequence of how a terminology is constituted as a system of symbols.

In the next step, organization of data (see Table 15.2), we introduce a step prior to classification in which the objects making up the raw data (persons in one case, terms in the other) are empirically linked together in a structure. This gives us a genealogy in the sense of a "family tree" in one case, and in the other case, a structure that has been little used in the literature for kin terms—a kin term map. The kin term map lists each kin term as a single node, and connections are made from one kin term to another to show linkages among kin terms only (Leaf 1971; Read 1984). In a genealogical chart, a researcher would have two genealogical positions (mother's father and father's father, labeled with the kin term *Grandfather*). However, in a kin term map for the American Kinship Terminology (Figure 15.1), the kin terms *Mother* and *Father* each label a single node and are each linked to the single node with the label *Grandfather.*

In the next step, we introduce models that have been used in the analysis of kinship, either implicitly with kintypes arranged in a genealogical space or explicitly in the case of kin terms. For terminologies we distinguish two classes of models: (1) models based on the genealogical space—componential analysis and rewrite-rule models and (2) models of kin term structures taken as structures in their own right—represented by work using algebraic formalism to model kin terminology structure as an abstract, structured system of symbols (Read 1984, 1988).

Finally, we add a step for the implementation of conceptual structures (Table 15.2). Here we are making explicit the linkage between (1) kinship terminology providing a conceptual framework that structures external phenomena and how the framework becomes interpreted in actual usage and (2) how the framework provides the foundation for more extensive structuring of persons. The former leads us into models

TABLE 15.2 *Kin term analysis with separation of genealogical from terminological data*

CATEGORY OF INFORMATION	DATA STRUCTURE	COMPUTER LANGUAGE REPRESENTATION
GENEALOGICAL SEQUENCE		
Raw data		
Person + father, mother, spouse, and so on	Fixed field	Genealogical database
Organization of data		
"Family tree"/genealogy	Pedigree chart	Graphics Editor, genealogical database
Model for genealogical data Kintypes and kintype products	Graph— kintype chart	Graphics Editor
Model for terminology		
A. Analytical model— componential analysis	Character strings; notation system	Procedural language: ALGOL, BASIC, C, FORTRAN, Pascal
B. Conceptual model— classification of kintypes	Strings of kintypes	Procedural language; Symbolic language
TERMINOLOGICAL DATA		
Raw data		
Terms of reference, address	Word list	Word Processor, Text Database Manager
Organization of data		
Kin term map	Graph	Graphics Editor
Model for terminology Conceptual model— structure generated through kin term product	Semigroup	Symbolic language: LISP, PROLOG
IMPLEMENTATION OF TERMINOLOGY STRUCTURE		
Social organization	Marriage rules	Procedural language
Kin term usage	Decision tree, production rules	Expert System Shell

of cultural competence (Wallace 1970) and the latter into models of social organization. With this background on the relations among theoretical framework, problem domain, and data identification, we now turn to the representation kinship data and their analysis with computer software.

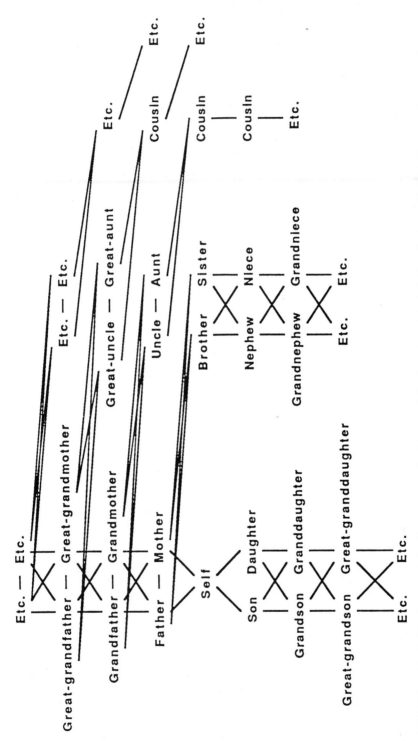

FIGURE 15.1 *Kin term map for the consanguinal terms of the American Kinship Terminology. Each kin term appears exactly once as a node. Vertical connections are derived by taking products with the kin terms Father, Mother, Son, or Daughter.*

COMPUTER APPLICATIONS

The analysis of genealogy and kinship has progressed from description and classification of social data to modeling of these data as embedded within conceptual structures and the analysis of the manner in which conceptual structures are related to behavior. With the availability of microcomputers and the newer developments in computer languages, it is increasingly feasible to use the computer in all kinship analysis tasks, from data management to exploration of the logical consequences of models of genealogical and kinship systems. Although computer applications in research have heretofore generally centered around computational problems, the interactive nature of the computer is making it possible to use the computer as a general purpose tool for the manipulation of all forms of information—text, graphic, symbolic, numeric, visual, or spoken. These diverse capabilities are making computer-based methods increasingly suited to anthropological research on symbolic and conceptual systems.

At the same time, the proliferation of languages and software makes it all the more important that the data domain and structure be well specified, since the selection of a computer language and representation should follow from the formalism used to express the properties of the domain. We now consider examples of going from data specification to formalism to computer representation.

GENEALOGICAL DATABASE MANAGEMENT

The study of kinship has often been linked with genealogical research, and the genealogical method has been used to elucidate the relationship system by asking informants for the terms they use for the members of their genealogy (RAI 1971:79). Typically, the information for the genealogy—name, age or birth date, sex, place name or address, father's name, mother's name—and other important ethnodemographic information were transferred to index or edge-punch cards after the data were collected in the field. These card files were manually sorted to determine genealogical connections, membership in descent groups, marriage ties, residence patterns, and the like.

From the viewpoint of computer representation, recording and sorting data that are structured in this manner is a problem in database management. With the advent of specialized genealogical database management systems (GDBMS), such as "Family Reunion" (Personal Software 1984) and "Roots II" (COMMSOFT 1984), the index and edge-punch cards can be replaced by computer data files. A computerized GDBMS structures genealogical data in fixed-length records, much like an index card file, with each record formed of a fixed number of data fields. A file of this form is often called a "flat" or "rectangular" file. The data fields are used for recording genealogical information in the form of character strings, numbers, paragraphs of text, and, in some cases, graphics or photo images.

The power of a GDBMS derives from its indexing capabilities, as with other computer database management systems. Use of an "index key" for properties of interest such as descent allows the user to create files of record pointers that link lists of informants in the database. Index files, along with Boolean operators ("and," "or," "not"), are used to conduct rapid, restricted record retrieval and database queries. For example, index files can be searched to determine if a consanguineal relationship exists between two individuals within a specified number of generations. In addition, most genealogical systems provide pedigree charts of nuclear and extended families, descendant charts and trees, birth date lists, Ahnentafels (ancestor tables), and maps and pictures in some cases.

A fixed format file is an appropriate data structure for managing genealogical information, since the tasks to be done require manipulation of records according to the contents of the data fields. Because flat files are relatively simple data structures and search speed is important, most GDBMS software is written in Assembler machine language or compiled, procedural languages such as BASIC.

GRAPHIC REPRESENTATIONS OF GENEALOGICAL AND KINSHIP DATA

The graphical presentation of genealogies and kinship data has always been an essential means to communicate relational information. Perhaps the most common graphic in the anthropological literature is the genealogical chart. Guidelines for drawing genealogical charts have been published (RAI 1971), and although different graphical conventions are sometimes used to denote such properties as sibling relationships (Keesing 1975; Cf. RAI 1971), most charts are built from simple geometric forms such as lines, circles, and triangles.

One difficulty in representing the complex relationships embedded in kinship terminologies in a genealogical chart is their "lack of fit." In any terminology there will be terms that seem "exceptional" or relationships that are difficult to communicate with standard conventions for drawing genealogical charts. (These problems are particularly severe when drawing family genealogy charts.) However, computer graphics editor programs such as Dr. Halo or PC Paint make it easy to build graphic templates and files containing all of the geometric forms that might be integrated in a chart. By electronically cutting and pasting these forms and using the different character fonts and sizes available in the editor, customized charts can be created and stored in disk files with modest effort compared to the hand-production of these diagrams.

AUTOMATION OF COMPONENTIAL
ANALYSIS OF KINSHIP TERMINOLOGIES

A genealogical link between Ego and Alter is traced using the kintypes mother, father, son, daughter, brother, sister, and spouse. These kintypes can be represented in terms of sex, generation, and marriage: Mother is female, up one generation; brother is male, sibling (0 generation); husband is male, spouse, and so on. Romney and D'Andrade (1964) symbolically represent these distinctions as follows: a, person of either sex; m, male; f, female; +, one ascending generation; −, one descending generation; 0, sibling link; and =, marriage link. The authors then represent a kintype as a string of these symbols, read from left to right beginning with the sex of the speaker and ending with the sex of the referent. For example, the kintype "father's brother's daughter" (where the sex of the speaker may be either male or female) has the representation a + m0m − f.

Consider the set of kintypes {mother's father, father's father} associated with the kin term *Grandfather* in the American Kinship Terminology (AKT). This set can be restated in the symbolic strings {a + m + m, a + f + m}, and the two strings can be replaced by the single string a + a + m without loss of information. The principle used in this simplification can be stated as a rule: "Rule 1. Rule of Minimum Difference Within Range. Where two kintypes within a range are identical except for a difference in sex markers in the same position, the two kintypes may be written as one with an a in the contrasting position" (Romney and D'Andrade 1964:149). Rule 1 is one of four rules Romney and D'Andrade define for simplifying sets of symbol strings.

Although algorithms are usually associated with numerical procedures, Romney and D'Andrade have provided an algorithmic definition of the componential analysis of symbol strings. A componential analysis first requires rewriting all the kintypes included under a single kin term in symbolic string form; then applying the simplifying rules exhaustively; and finally analyzing the resulting strings for critical distinctions. These distinctions, or components, such as sex of relative, sex of speaker, and relative age, are extracted, and the extracted components are arranged in terms of "common distinctive variables that characterize systems . . . such [as] direct vs. collateral, generation, etc." (1964:152). The distinctive variables then stand as a purported cognitively salient representation of a kinship terminology.

Romney and D'Andrade's algorithmic procedure for the analysis can be specified in a procedural computer language. Kronenfeld (1976) has used the language ALGOL in a program to implement the componential analysis of kin terms. The architecture of his program is built around manipulation of character strings, where the character strings are the set of kintypes associated with a kin term stated in Romney and D'Andrade's notational form. The program proceeds by parsing and comparing strings to see if any of the four rules are applicable. If so, the rule is applied and a new character string is formed. The program continues in this manner until each set of kintypes is reduced to a single model kintype.

As the analysis proceeds, the program associates with a kin term the rules used to reduce its kintypes to a model form, so the procedure can also be reversed. When a model is expanded, the rules associated with a term are applied and "a new kintype is formed from the model. . . . As many new kintypes as possible are formed from each kintype on the list until [all] possibilities are exhausted" (Kronenfeld 1976:48–49).

COMPUTERIZED DEMONSTRATION OF REWRITE-RULE ANALYSIS (CROW/OMAHA TERMINOLOGIES)

The microcomputer program called KINTYPER (Smith 1982) has been developed for demonstrating rewrite-rule analysis of kinship termi-nologies. Rewrite (or extension) rule analysis proceeds by first determin-ing the focal kintype(s) for a kin term and then forming the minimum set of rules required to recreate the full range of kintypes for the kin terms from the focal kintypes (Lounsbury 1964; Scheffler and Lounsbury 1972). The rules take the form of asserting that one kintype, or kintype product, can be replaced by another, for example: "The Half-Sibling Rule: FS→ B; MS → B; FD → Z; MD → Z" (Scheffler and Lounsbury 1972:115).

Using the notation developed by Romney and D'Andrade, KINTYPER simulates the production of kintypes by using rewrite rules that account for the variants of the Crow/Omaha terminology. A user is prompted from menus that give the options of reviewing rewrite rules (for example, merging and skewing rules), of reviewing a kintype chart, or of simu-lating the production of kintypes for any of the Crow/Omaha (Types 1–4) systems. Once the user selects a kin term, KINTYPER finds the focal kintype in a table, and then the user is given the choice of charting all the focal kintype expansions for the Crow/Omaha system that have been selected.

Unlike the componential analysis program, which uses parsing, matching, and substitution in character strings, this program uses table look-ups to simulate rewrite-rule expansions. Wheras the componen-tial analysis program is noninteractive and only produces character out-put, KINTYPER exploits the interactive and graphic capabilities of the computer. The use of graphics display and the sequential presentation of menus make it suitable for being programmed in a procedural language, in this case, BASIC.

ALGEBRAIC MODELING OF KIN TERM STRUCTURE

Whereas the componential and rewrite approaches begin with the genealogical space as an already structured foundation, no assumption about structural form is made in the algebraic modeling approach—which can also be pursued with appropriate computer software. Kin terms are taken as objects (nodes in the kin term map), and the structure of concern is that produced through a kin term product defined as follows: "If Ego (properly) calls Alter1 by the kin term K and Alter1 (properly) calls Alter2 by the kin term L, then the product of K and L (denoted L x K) is the kin term M, if any, that Ego (properly) uses for Alter2" (Read 1984). For example, in the consanguineal space of the AKT, if Ego calls Alter1, Child, and Alter1 calls Alter2, Parent, then Ego properly calls Alter2, Self (since Alter2 would be Ego). This yields the structural equation, Parent x Child-Self, for the AKT. (Kin term products can be glossed using "of" for "x"—read, "Parent of Child equals Self.")

Some of these objects (kin terms) are "atoms" (indivisible), and others are compound (product of atoms). Pairs of terms are directly connected in the kin term map only when there is a kin term product using an atom that maps one term of the pair onto the other. It is not known which terms are atoms in advance, but this is implied through the structure of relationships that terms have with other terms. It is similar for the structural equations. In this way, for the AKT, the algebraic analysis demonstrates that each of the terms *Self, Parent, Father, Mother, Child, Son,* or *Daughter,* is an atom, but the terms *Brother* or *Sister* are compound terms (for example, Brother-Son x Father) (cf. Read 1984). On the other hand, in the Trobriand terminology, the terms *Tama* (= "Father"), *Tuwa* (= "Older Brother") and *Bwada* (= "Younger Brother") are atoms, and the equation "Parent of Child-Self" is not a relevant structural equation (Read 1987). Therefore, neither the choice of terms to serve as atoms nor the structural equations to be used in generating structure are universal.

Several questions are posed in the algebraic analysis: (1) Which kin terms are atoms? (2) What structural equations are necessary for generating the terminology structure? (3) What is the basic underlying structure? (4) What role does reciprocity play in generating structure? and (5) How is the complete complex structure derived from this basic structure?

Unlike componential analysis and rewrite rules, there is no initially specified computational algorithm to implement. Instead, the analysis is inductive and based on postulating atoms and structural equations that are then confirmed or disconfirmed by the structure they produce. If the resultant structure is found to diverge from the target structure (in this case, the kin term map reduced to the simpler form shown in Figure 15.2), then another claim about potential atoms, equations, and

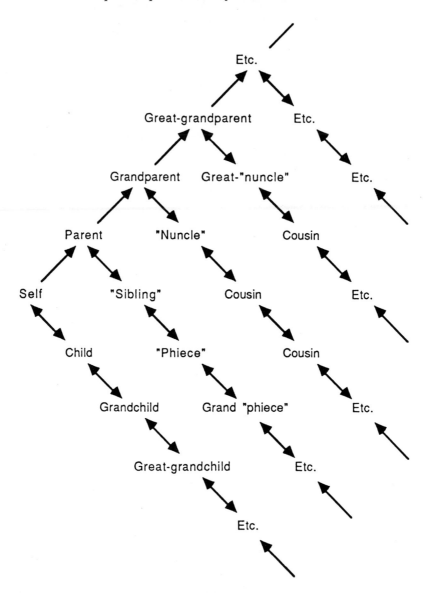

FIGURE 15.2 *Kin term map for the consanguineal terms of the American Kinship Terminology without sex markings*

the like is formulated, and the procedure is repeated until the algebraic structure converges on the target structure (Figure 15.3). In this way, a researcher finds that, for the AKT, Parent and Child are the basic atoms, and not Mother, Father, Son, and Daughter, through assessment of the respective structures produced by these two sets of terms.

This iterative process is dependent on analysis in an axiomatic framework; that is, theorems about structure must be logically deduced from

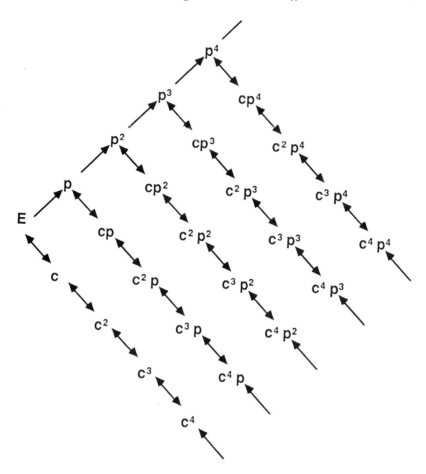

FIGURE 15.3 *Structure of the algebraic semigroup generated from the atoms PARENT, CHILD, SELF, and the equation PARENT (X) CHILD = SELF*

the posited atoms and equations. The question arises of whether it would be possible to take advantage of (1) nonprocedural computer languages, (2) the graphics interface available on microcomputers, and (3) expert system architecture. These capabilities would then be integrated in an environment where the user would "communicate" with an "intelligent" algebraic system via text and graphics input and output. The program KAES (Kinship Algebra Expert System) has been engineered to provide exactly this environment (Read and Behrens 1988). The program design is based on three parts: (1) a module for the production of an algebraic structure in accordance with its specification in terms of atoms and structural equations, (2) a graphics/text interface, and (3) an expert system that guides progress through the program. Each of these three parts has a different architecture to match the requisite tasks.

In the algebraic module, an algebraic structure is constructed in two steps. First, all possible products (called words) of the atoms are formed. Second, equations are applied that will reduce the products (much like rewrite rules) to form an algebra within which the equations are valid. The products, or words, are defined recursively: (1) Each atom is a word, and (2) if w', w'' are already defined words then $w = w'w''$ is a word.

The algebraic module requires a language that can implement a declarative definition of an algebraic structure, and the language selected for this task is PROLOG, a declarative language. PROLOG allows for character strings to be treated as atoms, and it uses predicates with arguments in list form as a basic data structure. If PARENT, CHILD, and SELF are atoms, then the equation PARENT $\times$ CHILD = SELF can be represented in PROLOG as the two-place predicate statement "equation ([PARENT,CHILD],[SELF])," where "equation" is the name of the predicate and the arguments are the lists [SELF] and [PARENT,CHILD].

PROLOG evaluates a declarative statement by searching all branches in a tree structure representation of the solution space. Recursion is a basic aspect of a tree search, and this makes PROLOG particularly effective for the task of constructing an algebra. For example, the PROLOG program corresponding to the recursive definition of words given above would be:

(1) atom (PARENT) .   atom (CHILD) .   atom (SELF) .
(2) word ([X])   IF   atom (X) .
(3) word (W)   IF   word (U)   AND word (V)   AND product (U, V, W) .

The first line declares that PARENT, CHILD, and SELF will be atoms. The second line declares that a list with a single symbol will be a word if the symbol is an atom. The third line declares that if V and U are words, then the word W, which is the product of U and V, is a word (where the predicate "product" has its own separate declarative definition that asserts W will be the list formed from the lists U and V). PROLOG would then find all solutions to this declarative definition: [PARENT], [CHILD], [SELF], [PARENT, PARENT], [PARENT, CHILD], [PARENT, SELF], [CHILD, PARENT], and so on. Translated back to algebraic form these would be PARENT, CHILD, SELF, PARENT x PARENT, PARENT x CHILD, and so on.

The graphics/text interface is guided by information that must be passed either from the user to the program or vice versa. Kin terms and equations must be written by the user, and these must be parsed as symbol strings into their constituent parts and "interpreted" for the algebraic analysis. Conversely, an algebraic structure is transformed from its abstract structure as a list of products into a graphical representation for visual comparison with the kin term map.

Here the representational task depends on manipulating menus, windows within which text may be written, and windows within which graphs may be drawn. One wants to be able to treat a menu, for example, as a single class of objects. Menus differ only in the number of items among which selection can be made and the content of each item. Similarly, it should be possible to treat a graph window as a discrete object wherein a graph may be drawn regardless of the location of the window on the screen or the form of the graph. So-called object-oriented languages provide this capacity. For the KAES program, a combination of TURBO PASCAL and an object-oriented windowing program, METAWINDOWS, has been used. The graphics/text interface is a key aspect of the KAES program that allows for input and output of text (names of kin terms), symbols (equations), and graphics (kin term map, graph of algebras) information.

Control over the interface is provided in a nonstandard way because it is necessary to move back and forth among the parts of the program in an order that is not predetermined. The expert system module maintains control by evaluating the current state of the algebraic construction and deduces what the remaining steps will be and what part of the program should be invoked next.

GRAPHICAL DISPLAY OF MARRIAGE SYSTEM DIAGRAMS

A kinship terminology conceptually defines a universe of relationships between a person and others. It also provides an interconnection between genealogical links created through procreation and institutionalized systems of social organization such as descent systems, residence systems, and the like (Leaf 1971). Rules of marriage, descent, and residence figure prominently in these systems of organization.

One goal in the analysis of these systems is to trace out the consequences of marriage, descent, and residence rules in terms of the descent and alliance alignments that are formed. For example, what will the composition of residence groupings be under, say, patrilateral, parallel, second-cousin marriage, double descent, and uxorial residence? Tracing out the connections by hand is laborious at best, even though the solution is well defined. Laborious and well-defined tasks are especially amenable to computer implementation and graphical display. These tasks are performed by the program KINSHIP AND MARRIAGE (Ottenheimer 1986).

The user is presented with a sequence of menus that offer possible rules for defining a particular system. The first menu offers the user a choice for a marriage rule, such as second-cousin marriage. Then, the user selects whether or not descent, or descent and residence rules, should also be included. If so, further choices are presented, such as unilineal descent based on patrilines with matrilocal residence. Finally, when the system of rules has been specified, the program prepares a diagram that shows the alignments and groupings that would arise. The diagram is based, in the simpler cases, on four "couples"—actually four pairs of kintypes—that are marked according to sex, marriage and descent links, and descent and residence group affiliations.

The user can easily see the different structures resulting from different rules. A switch in rules from a parallel-cousin to a cross-cousin marriage system, within a system of patrilineal descent, immediately shows the different structural effects that distinguish the two systems and that have been the subject of many theoretical discussions. Because the combinations of rules that are possible within the program are not limited by empirical instances, the program allows experimentation in examining potential marriage systems that do not have empirical reference.

The KINSHIP AND MARRIAGE program has been written in BASIC and uses graphs drawn from graphic characters available as part of the extended ASCII character set. The representation problem is primarily one of the graphical display of the kintype structure entailed by a set of organizational rules using the same kind of diagrams found in publications. BASIC serves well as an implementation language for representing marriage systems because it allows for relatively easy manipulation of character strings and the production of line graphics on the screen while executing the program in text mode.

MODELING SOCIAL TERM USAGE
AS RULE-BASED BEHAVIOR

Once a conceptual structure such as a kinship terminology is given a complete formal representation, it is interesting to determine the manner in which information about the terminology is used along with knowledge from other domains, as natives make decisions guiding their social behavior. The suggestion that culture is "rule based" (Chibnik 1981; Keesing 1974) points to the possibility of the production rule as an appropriate data structure for representing information embedded in culture. The potential of so-called "expert systems" for modeling culture has been explored (Behrens and Read 1987) by applying INSIGHT2 (Level Five Research 1985), an expert system shell. This software models elicited decision-making principles about the address terms used by Bisayan speakers in the Phillipine Islands (Geoghegan 1971) as a rule base.

Following Geoghegan (1971), the problem of deciding on a culturally "correct" term of address for another person in Bisayan society might include an evaluation of the ordered set of rules shown in Figure 15.4 (assuming a male Alter and other preconditions). This branch of the full decision tree (cf. Fjellman 1976; Gladwin 1975; Quinn 1975) displays two decision criteria (shown as diamonds) to be evaluated when deciding among the four possible address terms listed as decision outcomes (shown as boxes). For example, if English is the language spoken in the present social situation, then the appropriate term for Alter is

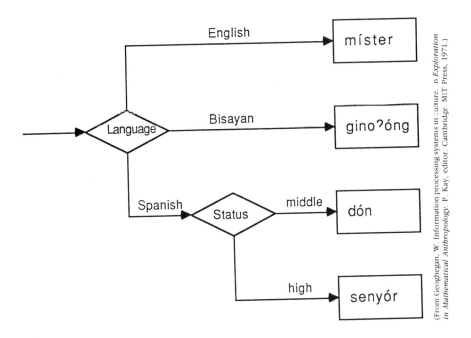

F I G U R E 1 5 . 4 *Part of the decision tree for Bisayan address terms. Shows the decision nodes to determine if the address term should be* míster, gino?óng, dón, *or* senyór.

(From Geoghegan, W. Information processing systems in culture. In *Exploration in Mathematical Anthropology.* P. Kay, editor. Cambridge MIT Press, 1971.)

míster, but the appropriate term is *gino?óng* if Bisayan is the language. When Spanish is used, the choice of terms is also affected by Alter's social status: *Dón* is the appropriate term if Alter is from the "middle class," whereas *senyór* is applied when Alter is a member of the "high" or "wealthy class."

Geoghegan provides, within an axiomatic theory, the formal means for representing the information encoded in cultural rules. In his formalism, an assessment, A, of an entity, E_i, in terms of a categorization, K_p, may be represented by the ordered couple $A = <E_i, K_p>$, where an assessment is the result of determining the correspondence between an object and some value in a relevant categorization. Geoghegan defines an ordered classification rule R^* to be the ordered 5-tuple, $R^* = <A_i, A_o, P^*, S_o, g^*>$, where S_o is the set of all possible output states, or results, of the rule R^*; P^* is the set of ordered paths generated by assessments A_i and A_o; and g^* is a function that maps P^* onto S_o.

For the portion of the decision tree resulting in the four Bisayan address terms shown above, the specific ordered paths P_j^* for the rule

R^* with result S_{oj} for each path obtained from the mapping $g^*(P_j^*)$ are as follows:

P_j^* in P^* for Ordered Rule R^*	$g^*(P_j^*)$
P_1^* = <<Language, english>>	S_{o1} = *míster*
P_2^* = <<Language, bisayan>>	S_{o1} = *gino?óng*
P_3^* = <<Language, spanish>,<Status, middle>>	S_{o3} = *dón*
P_4^* = <<Language, spanish>,<Status, high>>	S_{o4} = *senyór*

Consistent with the tree diagram, the terms *mister* and *gino?óng* are the outcomes of separate paths, each with a single assessment set. But the address terms *dón* and *senyór* are the results of paths that assess the language classification first, followed by the assessment of Alter's social status.

If Geoghegan's "entities" are thought of as objects, his "categorizations" as attributes, and his "categories" as values, then it is easy to translate his formal representation of cultural rules into the idiom of object-attribute-value (OAV) production rules (Buchanan and Shortliffe 1985; Harmon and King 1985; Weiss and Kulikowski 1984). Furthermore, by allowing for the possibility that the output from one ordered rule may be used as input information for another rule (called "recoding" by Geoghegan), a researcher may postulate that chaining—as essential inference strategy in expert systems—is an appropriate algorithm for replicating natives' processing of cultural rules.

With INSIGHT2, as with other expert system programs, rules are collected together in a "knowledge base" or "rule base" and are specified according to explicit syntactical rules. For example, the four rules given above have the following representation in the INSIGHT2 knowledge base:

RULE	Determine if the address term is mister
IF	Language class IS english
THEN	Address term is mister
RULE	Determine if the address term is gino?ong
IF	Language class IS bisayan
THEN	Address term is gino?ong
RULE	Determine if the address term is don
IF	Language class IS spanish
AND	Absolute social status of Alter IS middle class
THEN	Address term is don
RULE	Determine if the address term is senyor
IF	Language class IS spanish
AND	Absolute social status of Alter IS high class
THEN	Address term is senyor

In this knowledge base, rule names, such as "Determine if the address term is mister," have been created to describe the conclusion of a rule.

A production rule consists of one or more condition clauses and a conclusion clause analogous to Geoghegan's assessments and output states. Each clause specifies an object (and may include an attribute of the object) and a value for the clause following the predicate IS. Conditional clauses begin with the reserved word IF. When more than one condition is evaluated in a rule, the words AND or OR are used to join the conditions. Conclusion clauses are expressed in the same manner except these follow the reserved word THEN. This particular production rule format is the correct syntax for INSIGHT2's "production rule language."

The INSIGHT2 knowledge base only provides data to be evaluated by the expert system. Evaluation of rules is performed by a control program, often referred to as an "inference engine." INSIGHT2 uses (in this example) a "backward chaining" search strategy to arrive at conclusions. For instance, INSIGHT2 might set as a goal the task of concluding that the appropriate "Address term is senyor." To draw this conclusion, it attempts to establish the validity of the subgoal "Language class IS Spanish." If this is true, then INSIGHT2 makes the condition "Absolute social status of Alter IS high class" its next subgoal and attempts to establish the validity of this clause. If the language class is not Spanish, then the inference engine hypothesizes another goal, for example, the appropriate "Address term is don," and sets out to infer this conclusion by chaining back through all of its ancestral subgoals. In this manner, the clauses used as conditions at one level of a decision tree are conclusion clauses from a prior level.

There are many advantages of using an expert-system model to simulate social behavior based on the use of cultural rules. As this example demonstrates, formal representations of cultural rule-based decision making can be nicely mapped onto the domain of production systems. The disentanglement of data from program control—a fundamental design principle in all expert systems—makes it easy to revise rules or add new ones to a knowledge base. One need only be concerned with the knowledge-base content rather than the search algorithms, making it possible to simulate extremely ill-structured problems. Using the built-in querying capabilities of an expert system, it is also possible to list the rules that were evaluated or conclusions drawn in the process of establishing a goal. Such a list reveals the underlying cultural logic of a decision and provides the basis for a componential analysis of conclusions drawn by the expert system.

CONCLUSION

As these examples illustrate, computer-based methods are suitable for tasks ranging from the more mundane organization of data to the implementation of complex arguments phrased in a symbolic language. Effective use of computer resources for these tasks requires identification of data structures and systems of formal representation of data structures, so that appropriate programming languages and architecture can be selected in accordance with data structure and representation.

Kinship studies have been characterized by both data redefinition and new analytical approaches. Methodologies that have sought structuring principles for kinship terminologies in procreation have based their models on kin term data embedded in a genealogical grid. However, research aimed at discovering principles that relate kin terms in conceptual structures has found it advantageous to disentangle terminological from genealogical data and to use a structural representation.

Since the content of kinship data has been redefined and alternative analytical approaches proposed, different formalisms have been appropriate. Genealogical approaches to kinship research have made good use of procedural languages because of the ease with which they lend themselves to algorithmic applications—in addition to their graphics capabilities, character-string manipulation, and relatively fast execution speeds. However, focus on the analysis of kinship as a conceptual structure will lead to greater use of symbolic and declarative languages, artificial intelligence software architectures, and object-oriented languages suitable for the development of more transparent user interfaces.

Whereas programs for mainframe computers emphasize computation over presentation, the interactive capacity of microcomputers makes the interface between program and user an important component of program development for both input and output of information in symbolic and graphic form. We have found, in our development of the KAES program, that the interface is a crucial aspect that serves as a means to "translate" information convenient for the user into a form convenient for the PROLOG program. The advent of object-oriented programs increasingly makes the development of an effective interface a simpler task.

Finally, we want to point out that all of the programs discussed here, except for the commercial genealogy programs, have been written by anthropologists, none of whom are professional programmers. Writing software and not just being a consumer of software is feasible and necessary if the full potential of the microcomputer for anthropological research is to be realized.

NOTE

1. Research reported here has been supported in part by the National Science Foundation (Grant # BNS 86 09844) and the IBM Los Angeles Scientific Center.

PART FIVE

 # Teaching Computer Applications

In this part, Wood provides a useful outline for a course in computer applications, along with the rationales for demonstrating different types of analysis. The experience of the contributors to this volume suggests that teaching computer applications—either formally or informally—becomes a normal task for any professional anthropologist who learns to use computer-assisted techniques for his or her work.

CHAPTER SIXTEEN

🦠 Teaching Computer-Assisted Anthropology[i]

J O H N   J .   W O O D

Computing is a powerful and useful addition to the toolkit that anthropologists use to discover, analyze, and communicate knowledge. Statistical computing offers ways of modeling complex relationships and discovering patterns, as well as convenience and accuracy in calculating basic statistics. Computer processing of various kinds of text greatly facilitates the management and analysis of qualitative data. Computers have many other uses. Some applications, like artificial intelligence research, are new to anthropologists; others, such as simulation, have not been used to their full potential.

We are more likely to be convinced of the significance of computing for anthropology when we see the difference it makes with real data and real problems. This process can and should begin in the classroom.

The experience could be part of a research methods class or the subject of a semester or year-long course, or it could be partitioned into several semester segments. Computing can be the major focus of a course, play an important but secondary role, or simply support or extend existing methods. The amount of exposure to computer-assisted anthropology has to be balanced with other curriculum needs, but every program should have some provision for student work with computing.

The kinds of experience may range from programming to modeling and from statistical computing to analysis and processing of text. A cafeteria approach—a series of short introductions to a fairly wide selection of computer applications—might be suitable for acquainting students with what can be done with computers, say, as part of a survey of anthropological research methods. However, the practice of working through a set of data, from coding through analysis and write-up, will maximize the impact.

In this chapter I review general features of a computing curriculum—such as modes of data analysis, student preparation, kinds of computer packages, projects, and expected outcomes—that emphasizes statistical computing and ethnography. I present topical course outlines and make suggestions for adding tools and skills to these or other courses. The References and Suggested Readings section in this book serves as an introduction to the literature, and the Resources Appendix suggests resources for teaching as well as for research.

STATISTICAL COMPUTING

Statistical computing works best when viewed as process of extended engagement with one's data, not unlike the way anthropologists are accustomed to working with their field notes. The primary difference is that in statistical computing we work with coded data and mathematical abstractions to a greater extent, and we have to pay more attention to obtaining complete, comparable, and carefully sampled data. Consequently, statistical computing permits us to model complex relationships and to summarize large amounts of data, as well as to test hypotheses and make inferences about populations from samples using the theory of probability.

Hypothesis testing and estimation are based on assumptions about research design and sampling. The ritual of comparing results with those generated by some random process is so strong in some disciplines that the absence of significance tests in one's research paper may be grounds for a negative comment by reviewers or for rejection of the paper by an editor. This "scientism" and its perpetuation in statistics courses in the social and behavioral sciences probably accounts for the cavalier treatment of assumptions apparent in the published literature.

The problem with violating assumptions of statistical tests is the difficult decision about the significance of one's results: Are the results statistically significant, or are the results unduly influenced by violating the assumptions of the test? Students must be thoroughly grounded in the assumptions of each statistical computing technique we teach them, as well as the consequences of neglecting those assumptions (Chapter 9 in this book is an excellent case study that addresses this point.) They also should be reminded that the most important goal of research is substantive significance and that statistical computing offers avenues other than significance tests toward this end.

GENERAL FEATURES OF A QUANTITATIVE CURRICULUM

Data Analysis Modes

There are three modes of data analysis that can be addressed in the statistical computing curriculum: exploration, estimation, and confirmation. Exploration involves the search for patterns and relationships in data. Estimation seeks reliable and precise estimates of population characteristics from samples. And, confirmation involves testing statistical hypotheses and experimental design.

In practice, inquiry cycles among exploration and discovery, estimation, and confirmation in the process of engagement with one's data. Consequently, all three modes need to be represented.

With Tukey (1969, 1977), I think there is altogether too much emphasis on "sanctification" (producing numbers for their own sake), at the expense of "detective work" (slow, careful work to uncover fundamental relationships) in data analysis. For example, every batch of numbers should be scrutinized carefully using exploratory data analysis methods and reexpressed, if necessary, before doing anything else with them (Good 1983; Hartwig and Dearing 1979).

Student Preparation

Fifteen years ago, when I began teaching statistical computing, very few anthropology students had any experience with computers and the available packages were not complete, so a course in a programming language was essential preparation. Many students today are computer literate, and the packages are better, so a programming course, although still desirable, is no longer absolutely necessary.

A basic course in statistics, preferably taught with an emphasis on theory and assumptions, is essential and should be required as background for courses in statistical computing. Students need a firm foundation in algebra and trigonometry as well. The matrix algebra necessary to understand some of the techniques of multivariate data analysis can be taught in context, intuitively and geometrically.

Kinds of Packages

Most mainframe packages are batch-oriented; that is, the desired procedures are submitted as a job, and the job, along with a batch of other jobs, goes into a queue to be processed. For persons new to computing, the gap between submitting a job and seeing the results can make learning more difficult and discourage creative data exploration.

SPSS-X, BMDP, and SAS, the three most commonly used mainframe statistical packages, have been written for microcomputers, and there are numerous other packages now available for personal computers (Feldesman 1986). The principal advantages of microcomputers are low cost and rapid turnaround, both ideal characteristics for teaching statistical computing. Many students can afford their own personal computer, and, if they cannot, the likelihood of being able to use one on a university campus or in the workplace is good. Rapid turnaround facilitates learning and encourages the kind of involvement with data that can result in rich interpretation. And, if the microcomputer packages are inexpensive or in the public domain, students can take them with them when they graduate.

Projects and Outcomes

Students should be required to work with real data for their class projects. Real data are messy: There are missing values for some variables; samples are often availability samples; there are usually errors of various kinds; and, chances are, conceptualization of the problems and measurement can be improved on, and the problems that the researcher had in mind when collecting the data may not be what students have in mind for their projects. Working with real data teaches students a great deal about research as well as about the strengths and limitations of statistical computing.

In our program at Northern Arizona University, some students have their own research data; others ask faculty for permission to use some of their data; still others use published or archival material.

Outcomes from statistical computing courses should include, in addition to knowledge of data analysis, an understanding of project management, experience writing quantitative reports, and a portfolio of data analysis experience. The portfolio is especially important for demonstrating knowledge to potential employers.

Computer Use in Anthropological Research: An Example

Anthropological research results often include standardized information gathered from large numbers of observation units such as individuals, households, social groups, archaeological sites, artifacts, and burials. The goal of a graduate course that I have been teaching regularly for about ten years, which we call "Computer Use in Anthropological Research," is to acquaint students with computer-based processing, statistical analysis, and modeling of these kinds of databases, beginning with the transfer of data from the data-collecting instrument. A subsidiary goal is an understanding of the necessary steps for successful project management.

Students are expected to obtain a data set for class use drawn from an actual research project comprising a minimum of ten comparable measurements on a minimum of fifty observation units. The data set is used for weekly projects and a final technical report. Students are required to prepare their weekly assignments and their final technical report with word-processing software, which gives them experience with an additional computer application. The technical report is evaluated using criteria for a quantitative research report, such as those found in Hy's *Using the Computer in the Social Sciences* (1977:73–97). Appendixes consisting of assignments from the semester serve as an important component of the student's quantitative methods portfolio.

As may be seen from the list of topics covered in Table 16.1, "Computer Use in Anthropological Research" is a course in the process of statistical computing, which includes getting data ready for analysis, analyzing the data, and presenting the results.

There are three classes of reading materials needed: One class includes information on getting data ready for statistical processing, such as coding, editing, data structures, and variable transformations. The book that covers these topics best, *Survey and Opinion Research* (Sonquist and Dunkelberg 1977), is unfortunately out of print. However, *Handbook of Survey Research* by Rossi and others (1984) and *How to Conduct Surveys: A Step-by-Step Guide* (Fink and Kosecoff 1985) contain useful sections on these topics.

The second class of materials concerns the use of the statistical package or packages chosen for the course. The technical manuals for the package are best, but they are usually quite expensive. The SPSS-X package has available a variety of books at different levels. *Computer Usages for Social Scientists* by Douglas M. Klieger (1984) is a good survey of how to use three packages: SPSS-X, SAS, and BMDP.

Finally, students need reading materials that cover the methods discussed in class. The particular range of topics and the way I approach them are not covered in any one book. I suspect that others may face the same problem. The Sage series *Quantitative Applications in the Social Sciences* has enough variety and quality to put together a good set of reading materials for a number of courses. Moreover, they are written with social science research in mind, and they are reasonably priced.

The course topically outlined in Table 16.1 was taught exclusively on microcomputers. We scheduled a university microcomputer teaching lab for one afternoon a week. No more than two students had to share a microcomputer. Presentations were a combination of lecture and demonstration, followed by immediate student attempts to duplicate the analyses and by question and answer sessions. Homework assignments, to be turned in the following week, covered the methods discussed and practiced in class, using real data (usually their project data).

We used MYSTAT, a personal version of SYSTAT, for all topics up through linear regression. For cluster analysis and multidimensional scaling, we used some public domain programs, originally written for mainframe computers, that I modified for personal computer use.

I was able to cover more topics in greater depth with greater comprehension by the students than in any of the previous years' courses using mainframe computers. And most important, students learned how to get to know their data intimately and felt relatively unconstrained in looking at their data in creative ways.

T A B L E   1 6 . 1   *Computer use in anthropological research*

TOPIC	RELEVANT CHAPTERS IN THIS BOOK

A. Introduction and Overview
    1. Computers and Operating Systems
    2. Word Processing	

B. Quantitative Research Paradigm
    1. Social and Behavioral Science
       Applications
    2. Sampling	

C. Coding	Chapter 7
D. Data Entry, Cleaning, Modification	

E. Data Description
    1. Resistant Measures
    2. Data Presentation
    3. Summary Statistics
	Chapter 7

F. Estimation and Hypothesis Testing
    1. Standard Errors
    2. Wilcoxon, t-test, KS test, Analysis
       of Variance (ANOVA)	

G. Tables I
    1. Reading Tables
    2. Hypothesis Tests
	Chapter 8

H. Tables II, Association Measures	
I. Correlation and Linear Regression	Chapter 9
J. Multidimensional Geometry	
K. Cluster Analysis I	Chapter 13
L. Cluster Analysis II	
M. Cluster Analysis III	
N. Multidimensional Scaling I	Chapter 14
O. Multidimensional Scaling II	
P. Multidimensional Scaling III	

ETHNOGRAPHY

Transcription of interviews, performances, and observations—the primary data of ethnographic research—generates text, usually in large quantities (even a modest project may generate hundreds of pages). Tacit standards of ethnographic research require extended engagement with these data, from collection through analysis. Computing can help the process in many ways.

Ethnographic inquiry is cyclical and context-dependent. We expect the context to guide inquiry, and we return, literally and through our transcriptions, to the context again and again as inquiry proceeds and focuses. Using a computer for transcription of extended ethnographic accounts makes it relatively easy to search, sort, collate, and retrieve text, thus encouraging this cyclical, grounded process. To realize the full potential for assistance, a computer should be taken into the "field" and used for data entry, and the data should be queried and analyzed on a regular basis.

Computer-assisted management and analysis of text can be practiced or simulated in the classroom (Becker 1986), but ethnographic research, including computer-assisted ethnographic research, is best learned by doing it.

Three chapters in this book discuss, in detail, experience with several aspects of computer-assisted ethnography: management of field notes in a multi-ethnographer project (Chapter 4); creating and managing a database (Chapter 6); and field note management using a particular software package, ETHNOGRAPH (Chapter 5). Each of these chapters discusses computer software, and I have reviewed some of the available programs and packages elsewhere (Wood 1987).

GENERAL FEATURES OF A QUALITATIVE CURRICULUM

Data Analysis Modes

Coding. Transcription is the first step in translating discourse and observations into concepts, or coding. Because transcription cannot reproduce a context in its entirety, and because the way things are said or performed is often as important a focus as what is said or performed, students need to learn how and when to code contextual characteristics, discourse features, and other attributes of performance such as proxemics and kinesics.

Codes are semantic domains. They may be attributed to the actors in a social situation; to the ethnographer; or to the joint experience of the situation by the actors and the ethnographer. Lexical codes are perhaps the most common, but there are, of course, many other ways of expressing meaning—in themes, postulates, values, and world view, for example. Students should be sensitized to the implications of these distinctions.

Coding is a critical component of ethnographic description, and the principles and practices need to be strongly emphasized. Coding is a conceptual activity, but a computer can be a powerful assistant. When text is stored in computer accessible form, indexing, searching, concatenation, cutting and pasting, and printing in the service of code building can be done more easily, allowing more time for conceptual work.

Management.   A good word processor is the most flexible and general tool for managing text. With word-processing skills, students can enter, edit, and manage their data in a limited fashion, as well as prepare their assignments and communicate the results of their research.

Other important "assistants" are database managers (see Chapter 6). Database managers have varying features, depending on their targeted use. Some are limited in their text-processing capabilities, and some with good text-processing features cannot count or tally information (Wood 1987). All require some sort of coding of one's data into smaller units: Files, records, or fields are typical designations.

Because word processors are not really designed for complex searches, sorts, reports, and tallies, database managers for text are essential instruments, and they ought to be part of a course on computer-assisted ethnography, along with a word processor and some form of indexing software.

Analysis.   All of the tools for coding and management may be used also for analysis, which is as it should be, since ethnographic research cycles among these phases. Indexing and tallying of codes may help assess salience. Searching for juxtaposition and sequencing of codes and other contextual analyses help embed meaning in text and help students discover unifying concepts such as decision making, plans, scripts, taxonomies, networks, and other schemata, as well as patterns of discourse, such as discourse cycles.

Cluster analysis, multidimensional scaling, and other methods of multivariate analysis can be used to good advantage in searching for structure of domains and schemata. These techniques also serve as a bridge for students between quantitative methods and ethnographic methods. Network analysis is an additional important tool.

Student Preparation

Word processing and work with most database management systems do not require any preparation, in my experience. As long as no programming is involved, students can get started with both kinds of tools in a matter of a week or so. If they are assigned weekly projects that require using the computer, students can become quite proficient in a semester.

Good comprehension of cluster analysis, multidimensional scaling, and network analysis requires some background preparation in mathematics and some time for development. They are relatively complex procedures that require careful interpretation.

Kinds of Packages

Word processors and database managers for personal computers are legion. The primary consideration in choosing a word processor is the ease with which it can write and import files in a standard format (known as ASCII). This feature facilitates the transfer of information from one program to another. Other useful capabilities include searching for strings of text, cutting and pasting text, indexing, and the ability to display text from two or more files simultaneously on the screen (called "windows"). PC-Write, a shareware package that is very easy to use, has all of these features and more.[2]

Database managers usually come in two varieties: those that process records of standard information and those that process text. A few do both well. For ethnographic work, a database manager that processes text is most useful. Three of the latter that are very good are askSam,[3] Notebook II,[4] and ETHNOGRAPH[5] (Chapter 5, this book; Wood 1987). AskSam and Notebook II combine features of both varieties of database managers; ETHNOGRAPH is designed primarily for text.

It is helpful to have an index of the words and symbols in a file of text for ethnographic analysis, and there are several kinds of indexing tools available (Chapter 4, this book; Wood 1987). AL[6] and UCINET[7] are two excellent packages for multivariate analysis and network analysis that are geared especially for social scientists. STRUCTURE, by Burt, is a nearly complete network analysis system.[8]

Projects and Outcomes

Regular assignments, preferably evaluated at least once a week, are necessary for learning ethnographic research methods and for learning how to use a computer to assist. As mentioned in the discussion on statistical computing, I think work with real data is best. For ethnographic research, a single semester's project, followed from the point of establishing rapport to writing a mini-ethnography, is essential. Students benefit most from seeing the cycle through to completion and from learning how to communicate in an ethnographic genre.

Ethnographic Research Methods: An Example

"Ethnographic Research Methods" is a good example of a course where computing could be successfully incorporated in a secondary supportive role.

I have practiced some computer-assisted ethnography, but I have not, as yet, incorporated it in the courses I have taught in ethnographic research methods. I had many years of experience working with computers, but I was unsure how computing would transfer to ethnography, since most of my experience had been in statistical computing. It transfers well, and the next time I teach the course I will add a significant computing component. What follows, then, is how I would teach a course in computer-assisted ethnography. The ethnography portion is a slightly modified version of the approach and topics that I usually cover; the topics in computer use are how I imagine they would fit (Table 16.2).

My approach to teaching ethnography is basically cognitive and phenomenological, so I find Spradley's two books, *Participant Observation* (1980) and *The Ethnographic Interview* (1979) very congenial as basic texts. Most students also find them easy to understand, and many refer back to them in later fieldwork. I use an extensive reading list and require students to read and review one ethnography, selected from a list that represents several different time periods and methods of doing ethnography.

For my revised course I will recommend an expanded reading list covering definitions of culture, theory, ethics, work with informants, ethnographic writing, proxemics, kinesics, the built environment, discourse analysis, schemata, and semantics as ethnographic topics, and I will add two or three of the Sage Quantitative Applications in the Social Sciences Series to cover network analysis, cluster analysis, and multidimensional scaling. Werner and Schoepfle's (1987a and 1987b) new two-volume work is an invaluable reference and source for reading assignments in ethnography, and the authors explicitly discuss and recommend several techniques of computer analysis. The nuts and bolts of using software packages are in the documentation for each package. The ethnographic applications have to be developed, although there is help in the literature in the form of coding schemes.

I plan to pair the introduction to fieldwork with an introduction to computing, covering the basics of word processing and database management, so that when students start taking notes they will be ready to use the computer for transcription. After a few weeks of data collection and transcription, I will introduce coding schemes, indexing, and searching as aids for the analysis of domains. Several weeks later, when students are ready to work with some unifying concepts, coding will have to be reintroduced in this new context. Finally, near the end of the course, when enough data have been collected in the proper format, I will introduce the students to network analysis, cluster analysis, and multidimensional scaling.

This is all very ambitious, and, if past experience holds, I will probably not be able to cover everything I want to cover. Students will probably tell me that this should be a four semester hour course with a

TABLE 16.2 *Ethnographic research methods**

TOPICS IN ETHNOGRAPHY	TOPICS IN COMPUTER USE

A. Introduction and Overview
  1. Culture and Ethnographic Research
  2. Nature of Cultural Knowledge
  3. Ethics and Integrity	

B. Introduction to Fieldwork
  1. Informants/Consultants
  2. Translation/Interpretation
  3. Ethnographic Writing
	A. Introduction to Computing
	  1. Word Processing
	  2. Database Management

C. Description
  1. Observations
  2. Questions
	B. Transcription

D. Analysis of Domains
  1. Semantics
  2. Searching for Domains
	C. Coding and Indexing
	  1. Coding Domains
	  2. Indexing and Search
	  3. Collating Contexts

E. Focusing
  1. Focused Observations
  2. Structured Questions	

F. Unifying Concepts
  1. Schemata
  2. Searching for Schemata
	D. Coding and Indexing
	  1. Coding Schemata
	  2. Indexing and Search
	  3. Collating Contexts

G. Questioning Hypotheses
  1. Selected Observations
  2. Contrast Questions
	E. Network Analysis

H. Unifying Concepts Again
  1. Structure of Domains
  2. Structure of Schemata
	F. Cluster Analysis and Multidimensional Scaling

*Relevant chapters in this book are 4, 5, 6, 10, 12, 13, 14, and 15.

lab instead of a three semester hour course. In fact, there is material enough for several courses in computer-assisted ethnography, especially of an analytical nature, such as material on network analysis and structural modeling. Once students have gone through the basics of a course like I am proposing, they should have little trouble making the transition.

ADDITIONAL TOOLS AND SKILLS

Other promising additions to a computer-assisted anthropology curriculum are simulation and modeling for anthropological research and for computer-assisted instruction in anthropological concepts.

Courtland Smith (1985) describes principles of design and evaluation for computer-aided learning in introductory anthropology courses. There are potentials for computer-aided learning in the graduate curriculum as well, especially in simulation exercises that have implications for research and practice. Chapters 12 and 13 in this book are good examples of the latter.

SUMMARY

In this chapter I have tried to make a case for incorporating computing in anthropology curricula. Many years of experience in teaching statistical computing have convinced me, and many of our graduates, that a solid course of study in statistical computing helps the quality of quantitative research in anthropology and helps students compete in their quantitatively biased work world. The availability of personal computers and inexpensive, powerful software makes it easy to use, and abuse, quantitative methods. Therefore, more than usual care needs to be given to providing students a clear understanding of the limitations as well as the strengths of statistical computing.

Ethnographic research is the hallmark of cultural anthropology. New developments in computer technology have made the use of personal computers in the field an easy choice, and the available software, although not perfect, is good enough to easily demonstrate the advantages of computer-assisted ethnography. Other applications such as simulation and modeling will help us experiment with our nonexperimental data and promise to suggest new ways of looking at patterns and relationships.

NOTES

1. This chapter is a substantial revision of a paper titled "Computers and Statistics in the Graduate Anthropology Curriculum," presented at the Annual Meeting of the Society for Applied Anthropology, Oaxaca, Mexico, April 1987.

2. PC-Write can be obtained through Quicksoft, Inc., 219 First North, Box #224-PMAZ, Seattle, WA 98109. Full registration—$89.00; Shareware Disketters—$16.00.

3. askSam can be obtained through Seaside Software, P.O. Box 31, Perry, FL 32347. Retail price—$295.00.

4. Notebook II can be obtained through Pro/Tem Software, Inc., 814 Tolman Dr., Stanford, CA 94305. Retail price—$189.00.

5. ETHNOGRAPH can be obtained through QUALIS RESEARCH ASSOCIATES, P. O. Box 3785, Littleton, CO 80161. Retail price—$150.00.

6. AL can be obtained from Steve Borgatti, Department of Sociology, University of South Carolina, Columbia, SC 29208.

7. UCINET can be obtained as "A Microcomputer Package for Network Analysis" from Bruce MacEvoy, Linton Freeman, Mathematical Social Science Group, School of Social Sciences, University of California, Irvine, CA 92717.

8. STRUCTURE can be obtained from Reprint Librarian, Center for the Social Sciences, Columbia University, New York, NY 10027. Request a copy of "Technical Report #TR2." Accompany request with a check made out to "Research Program in Structural Analysis." The cost is $20.00 if paid by personal check; $50.00 for institutions.

The Future

Dow looks toward the future to anticipate future applications of computers for anthropologists. Many of the programs and technologies he mentions are already being used by some individuals as this book goes to print. Given the speed and diversification of computer technologies, we can look forward to the applications described here and also to some that we cannot even envision now.

CHAPTER SEVENTEEN

New Directions in Computer Applications for Anthropologists

JAMES DOW

Over the last decade, the large-scale integrated circuit has dramatically lowered the cost and improved the performance of computing machinery by many orders of magnitude. One result of this technology, the microcomputer, has affected anthropology more than any other piece of computing equipment. By itself, the cost-effectiveness of microcomputers has made many new applications possible. In addition, new programs and ideas are creating entirely new areas of application for anthropology.

THE NEAR FUTURE

New computer developments are appearing on the immediate horizon, and anthropologists should be alert to those that they may see very soon. Because the time between the public discussion of a new electronic technology and its commercial development is only a few years, and because the time between the announcement of a new product and the time it becomes available is only a few months, some of the developments mentioned in the following sections will be available at the time of reading.

Field Applications

Computer hardware for the field. More and more data processing is moving to the field. In a few years sophisticated field projects will be doing—and some are already doing—all their data processing in the field. New opportunities will be available to test theories while gathering data. Field computers have the potential of making anthropological field research a continuous process of theory formation and analysis, thus causing some areas of anthropology, particularly those using quantitative data, to resemble more closely the laboratory sciences.

Anthropological fieldwork is carried out in a wide variety of environments ranging from American shopping malls to desert mountains. Several years of experience with field computers in anthropology has shown that most field use places only slightly more strain on the equipment than office use. Relatively inexpensive voltage regulators designed to protect television sets in underdeveloped countries have protected computers from line voltage variations. Humidity has not proved to be as serious a hazard as previously assumed. Floppy disks have been caught in tropical rainstorms, cut open, dried, and copied without loss of data. Computers have purred away in rain forests. Dust is considered to be an enemy of disk drives, but lap-top microcomputers have been used successfully in dusty Sudan locations. Hard disks are internally sealed against foreign particles. Yet, it is not known how long field microcomputers will last in dusty environments. There are physical limitations to everything.

Anthropological field projects of the present and near future make use of two types of computers: (1) small, highly portable computers for direct data entry and (2) larger base computers that receive the data from the smaller computers. These field computers are already being used in some projects to process both qualitative and quantitative data. Several types of microcomputers and minicomputers are now being used in the field for archaeological, ethnological, and linguistic research. Portable, battery-operated computers can be carried to almost any location to enter notes directly into a simple text file or into a portable version of a database. Small hard disks are available for laptop computers, and their storage capacity is increasing.

The larger base microcomputer has a large permanent storage and is capable of sophisticated data processing. The software of the base computer is designed to integrate the data fed to it by the portable computers. It incorporates scanned documents and video pictures as well. The base computer performs a fairly sophisticated analysis of the data on a regular basis and thus informs the field workers of how the research is proceeding. The base computer produces data summaries, interview schedules, and survey forms for field workers. In archaeological research the base computer holds a complete three-dimensional map of a site and a complete artifact database.

Although laptop computer batteries can now be electrically charged from relatively inexpensive solar panels, most base computers still need other generated electricity. It will soon be possible to run a base computer on solar power alone. Flexible, lightweight plastic solar panels are available, and a small solar-powered base computer equipped with a hard disk could weigh around 20 pounds—a weight that would permit it to be carried anywhere by hand, in a canoe, on a small airplane, or on horseback.

Direct data entry in the field is, and will continue to be, enhanced by (1) small data-entry devices and (2) incorporation of audio recordings with digital data. Small hand-held devices have batteries, small keyboards, and small liquid crystal display (LCD) data displays. The data are stored in an electronic memory during recording in the field and then transferred to a portable or base computer later. Adaptation of data-entry devices and small computers to this purpose is a solvable problem of interfacing their output with a larger computer. Similar applications are now being tested and used in field surveys. Another solution to data-recording problems in ethnographic fieldwork is to incorporate audio recordings into a digital database. Audio recording is more efficient than paper and pencil for rapid and complete recording of interviews and can be digitized for storage along with an index that provides computer controlled access to the audio information. As computer memories grow more economical, visual and audio data can be indexed and stored in this way.

The major hazards to computers used in rugged field environments have turned out to be shock (the old nemesis of military electronic equipment) and, surprisingly, insects that invade portable computers much like they invade home television sets. Laptop LCD screens are vulnerable to shock and vibration failure. Hard disks can be ruined by shock and have to be treated carefully, but new, more shock-resistant hard disks are now available, and this problem is being rapidly overcome. The general rule in acquiring computer hardware for field use is to get the most shock-resistant type of equipment available and to pack and transport it carefully.

The insect problem is not as common and is encountered most often in tropical forests. Some of the materials used in the manufacture of microcomputers have proved attractive to insects, but not much is yet known about this problem, and it may be solved in the future by including insect repellents in the microcomputers or by sealing microcomputers more adequately. Anthropologists using microcomputers in tropical forests are advised to use closable disk drives. Yet, in general, field computer equipment has proved no more delicate than field camera equipment and in many cases much less so.

Software for the field. Practically all research projects benefit from storing data in a database from which it can be thoroughly and quickly retrieved. Database software is steadily improving in flexibility and user friendliness. If a research project concentrates on gathering a particular kind of data, and if the method of analysis of the data has already been decided, then the data can be entered directly into the database where it is finally analyzed. However, such mechanically inflexible research designs are not the rule. Usually, the data are entered into a field database from which they are later transferred to other types of analytical databases. Because computers can easily do the tedious work of transforming data, the final form of the data does not have to be decided at the time that they are gathered, and often it is not. A field database should handle both numerical and textual data. It should permit various summaries to be printed for use by field workers. It should also allow the reformatting of data in a wide variety of forms to use as input to later analytical programs and databases. At present there are a number of ways of accomplishing this task.

One solution to the field database problem is to use plain ASCII (American Standard Code for Information Interchange) text files for recording data (see Chapter 4 in this volume). These files are later edited and fed to analytical databases or statistical programs. One program, ETHNOGRAPH (see Chapter 5), is designed to turn field note text into a textual database. Free-form databases and list-processing databases are another solution to the field database problem. A free-form database is one in which the length of fields and records is not limited. A list-processing database is able to transform the database back and forth between an editable ASCII form and a fast processing binary form. A big advantage in using a free-form database over text files in the field is that the data can be more rapidly searched and retrieved while they are still being accumulated. This permits cross-checking and better quality control. Free-form databases can be programmed to output the data to other programs.

Another problem for field projects is integrating the data in the smaller computers with that in the base computer. We can expect to have small versions of database software that will run on the smaller portable computers to create data that will be compatible with the database on the large-capacity base computer. Most of these field databases will be of the free-form type.

Microcomputer spreadsheets can now be used to record data in the field, and their capabilities will improve. They offer the advantage of being able to display data in rectangular matrix form. Spreadsheets are presently designed to present *and* analyze numerical data. When used in the field, spreadsheets provide a means for the immediate analysis of quantitative data. A spreadsheet can represent the analysis in tabular or graphic form (such as the bar and pie charts used by Moran in Chapter 8), and guide the data collection while it is in progress. The problem of exchanging data between spreadsheets and other programs is being overcome by translation software.

Image processing and text scanning are now available for microcomputers. It is possible to input drawings, video pictures, visual outlines, and texts in the field. Foreign language font development has been applied to the problem of text scanning. Documents in Armenian, Coptic, Russian, Old English, Greek, Spanish, and Yiddish have already been scanned (Abercrombie 1987). Some present databases can combine graphic with textual data. The field database of the future will routinely contain not only text but also video pictures and diagrams. An anthropologist will carry a portable field computer and attach it to a video camera for adding pictures to the portable database. Archaeology, which requires accurate site maps and artifact databases, will benefit particularly from combining textual and graphical data in many stages of its survey and fieldwork.

Data Retrieval and Qualitative Processing

Databases and text files. Databases seem to be the best means of storing and retrieving data. What kinds of databases are proving to be the most useful and where will anthropological database software have to be developed in the future? Microcomputer business-oriented databases such as dBase IV, REFLEX,[1] and RBASE-5000 can be useful in storing quantitative anthropological data from time-allocation studies, physical anthropology, and archaeology. The software can be programmed to produce statistical summaries without transferring the information to statistical programs. The programming available in these database systems allows a variety of outputs for later input to other programs.

Databases that can process textual data are fewer and more difficult to program. Therefore, textual data are often processed in a text file rather than in a database. However, the slow speed at which large volumes of text are handled in text files by microcomputers can be a problem. This situation is being improved by faster microcomputer architecture such as processors with virtual paged memory, as well as software techniques for indexing large quantities of text. Field workers anticipating large text files should select the higher-speed microcomputers for their work. Text processing should not be confused with word processing, which can be done on less sophisticated equipment. When coupled with new software, the next generation of microcomputers should be able to handle large texts more efficiently.

Nevertheless, a database system, because of its design, will always be more efficient in processing large amounts of textual data. A variety of free-form databases are emerging that can handle the kind of information that social scientists develop. We can expect an improvement in the quality of free-form databases. Many existing, free-form databases lack high speed, windows, symbolic and graphic fields, sophisticated text editing, fast search capabilities, and so on. The future free-form database will be capable of displaying text in matrix form with blocks of data that can be expanded when needed. The dimensions of the rows and columns can be arranged to reflect different topics of the research.

Specialized editors that are useful for recording field notes are beginning to appear. Complex fonts are available to record languages and other symbolic information. At present, inexpensive microcomputer video systems and editors allow the anthropologist to create new character fonts embracing all the characters needed to record exotic languages. Ideographic writing is also possible. Word processors for Japanese, Thai, Chinese, and Korean are common. Computer scripts for a number of exotic languages are rapidly appearing. Multilingual editors capable of dealing with several languages at the same time now need to be developed. In the future we can expect a standardized system for encoding many languages in one database.

Relational databases.   Relational databases are databases that are linked to each other. These are not new, but their capabilities should improve and their applications should increase dramatically in the future. Relational databases can be useful in quantitatively oriented research. For example, suppose a village population is surveyed and time-allocation studies are made. An anthropologist would want to develop a database containing these observations and might be interested also in the kinship relationships among the persons, their ages, characteristics of their location, and so on. These latter interesting variables need not be encoded each time an observation is made. Instead, they can be put into a related database. One database would contain the observations, another would contain relevant information on each person, and another might contain relevant information on each location. The three databases, the observations, the persons, and the locations would all be related by the main database program in order to produce files for input to a statistical program, for example, to analyze the important measures.

Similarly, an archaeological project might want to keep one database with descriptions of artifacts and another with descriptions of locations within a site. Software exists today that can manage relational databases. The future development of this type of software is driven mainly by business applications. Some commercial software is of great use to research anthropologists. However, the future will probably see relational free-form databases that will better meet the needs of this sort of scientific research.

The standardization effort now taking place in the computer industry is making available database software running on a variety of platforms from microcomputers to main computers. The several open-systems efforts and the UNIX operating system offer a means of integrating databases and communication between portable computers and base computers. The anthropological field system of portable and main computers that has been suggested will make use of the new standards. This will make data and programs developed in the field later transferable to networks and other computers in the university or business environment.

Centralized databases.   Other problems come up in anthropological research that will eventually be solved by centralized databases. A centralized database is a single collection of data that is accessed by many individuals from remote locations. A typical example would be an applied anthropology project employing a dozen field workers and producing frequent advisory reports. Notes and other field data are transferred by the workers to the central database where they are accessed by people guiding the project and developing the reports. Such a system would dramatically decrease the time between fieldwork and final report and would make applied anthropology a more attractive service to clients with limited time schedules. A system of this sort is discussed by Trotter in Chapter 4 in this volume.

Most commercial centralized databases, such as airline ticketing systems, are not designed for social science applications. However, we could speculate on the type of system that is needed. The main database software can reside in a central computer, which could be a micro-computer or a minicomputer. It needs to be accessed by only two or three persons at the same time. Each field worker would be equipped with a portable microcomputer and modem. A field worker would develop a portion of the database as the information was gathered. Periodically, these portions would be transmitted to the main computer by telephone or when the field worker returned to the main computer. Periodic reports, summaries, and analyses would be carried out with the main database. The main computer would also maintain an electronic mail system for communication between all the project personnel. The telephone network is the largest communication network in any country and is the most accessible one to use for this purpose.

Computer networks are growing, and they might be incorporated into this kind of communication scheme. Public packet-switching networks could be used for telephone access to a main computer. Also a research subnetwork for anthropology could be formed with a number of nodes connected via the Internet.[2] Field researchers would access the nearest anthropological research node and through it could contact the node on which their main database is kept. Because the Internet is worldwide, oriented toward research, and adaptable to the greatest variety of computers, it is good computer network for this purpose.

Distributed databases. Distributed databases are more complex and still under development for commercial applications. Instead of keeping all the data at one location, they distribute it over a network of computers that have to be coordinated. The applications for such a system go beyond the type of research project just described. As presently designed, the computers running distributed databases have to be in constant communication. Such configurations would be more appropriate for massive amounts of research data, such as that contained in the Human Relations Area Files. Anthropological research would probably require development of specific types of distributed databases. Their main advantage would be overcoming storage and maintenance problems by having the data stored at different locations. The data would be refined at various locations and called up on a computer network when needed at another location. Noncontributing users could subscribe to the database by means of inexpensive mass storage media such as helical-scan tape recorders or optical disks. The advantage of working with a distributed database is that it contains the very latest information available at any single time. At some point in this development, distributed databases become electronic libraries. In the future it will be possible to browse electronically through articles, books, and bibliographies kept in a giant library physically located at numerous locations around the world.

Graphic, visual, and audio information.   The variety of data that can already be processed by computers is being constantly amplified by new and cheaper devices. Small, fast hard disks, text-reading devices, graphic scanners, video input, and digitizers are declining in cost and increasing in quality. Super-minicomputers are appearing with architectures similar to supercomputers which can handle the high-speed processing required for voluminous graphic data and simulation. These will become more available to more anthropologists in the future.

The possibility of text- and concept-oriented spreadsheets for qualitative data analysis looms on the horizon. Spreadsheets are beginning to work in conjunction with word processors and databases. Miles and Huberman (1984) have developed matrix methods of analyzing qualitative data that are clear candidates for text-oriented spreadsheets. Text spreadsheets will probably appear on large high-resolution video screens, which are now being introduced on high-powered desktop workstations (like Sun workstations) with window interface systems— and these are getting more affordable. A researcher could select key words and fields for each row and each column. The cell at which a row and column intersected would contain the records with both row and column key words in their respective fields. A set of such records could be laid out in adjacent windows for comparison, or parts of the spreadsheet could be expanded in separate windows for other comparisons. The spreadsheet could also convert the textual data into numerical data by responding to individual coding of the records or by following a programmed coding system that responded to different elements in the text. A number of modern databases such as REFLEX already include this coding feature in a spreadsheet-like display.

Databases that store graphic data are already of great use as catalogues of material culture that include hundreds of thousands of artifacts. An entire three-view video image of a museum artifact can be stored in 7 megabytes of digital storage (Sugita 1987:18). Large volumes of video data can be kept on computer-controlled optical disks linked to a main database and called on to produce the images when needed. Visual information can be analyzed by computer to extract information for comparative analyses. Devices that use a VHS video cassette and helical scan recording to store from 2 to 5 gigabytes of information are readily available. Such devices can be adapted to incorporate visual data in a database system. The potential of digital paper recording is even higher, and such storage systems are appearing on the market.

Digital mapping and the graphic display of geographical information is becoming more economical and is now being routinely used by some anthropologists. Microcomputers can be equipped with graphical software that permits the storage and display of large maps and drawings. Archaeological field projects can record all their data in three-dimensional, graphically oriented databases in which the data can be displayed either as drawings or as text. The time has come for archaeologists to use universal coordinates to locate the provenience of artifacts, so that eventually all digitized, archaeological, graphics databases can be joined together as needed to cover large regions and eventually the world.

It is possible to include audio recordings in a computer database or a "multimedia" database. A major problem in traditional ethnography is that the human mind is a poor recording system. It is better used in searching for patterns and meanings in the data. However, it can do this empirically only if the data are accurately refreshed. Computers, which have complete recall but relatively poor analytical ability, can assist in the refreshing process. One way of dealing with the large volume of interview material gathered during the course of an ethnographic study is to record the interviews on audio tape. The audio recordings can be incorporated into a computer database, which is able to retrieve the sound data with complete recall of the original information, by itself or in conjunction with other information.[3]

Computer Analysis

The most traditional and the most exciting uses of computers have been to extend human intelligence beyond its biological limits. Computer science and combinatorial mathematics now have developed computer applications that go well beyond the original numerical analysis applications. The potential for the anthropological use of computers as aids to analysis is unlimited. Only a few applications can be mentioned here.

Artificial intelligence and simulation.   Artificial intelligence is related to cognitive anthropology and provides a fertile area for (1) the creation of new models for understanding the structure of plans, social cognition, and other features of culture and (2) the creation of systems for recording and analyzing qualitative data on, for example, kinship and marriage (see Chapter 15). Because of advances being made in general artificial intelligence research, we can expect to see artificial intelligence models proposed for a wide variety of cultural behavior. Properly speaking, this is an application of computer science, not computers, to anthropology. However, computers are the means for realizing the simulation of cultural behavior in an artificial intelligence model. A series of logical propositions can be tested as the basis for cultural behavior by generating the simulated behavior with a computer-based "inference engine."

Graphical simulation techniques that produce graphics output can be used to test various spatial models of the distribution of markets or of other artifacts of an economic process. Graphical simulation can also be used to illustrate the logical results of marriage rules or of other social institutions. For example, if the pattern produced as a kinship diagram matches real data, then the model can be proposed as a hypothesis.

Simulation methods making use of simultaneous equations can now be perused more economically with the new, inexpensive super-minicomputers, whose speed is beginning to rival the older supercomputers. Parallel processing allows a numerical problem to be split up and worked out by many central processing units working simultaneously, thus increasing the speed at which the computation is completed. RISC (Reduced Instruction Set Computer) architecture increases the overall speed of each CPU (central processing unit) by doing the operations in less time. The software, the chips, and the design of such machines are now in accelerated development. The result will be an easier, more accessible simulation laboratory for anthropologists.

Statistical procedures.   The main effect of computer technology on statistical processing is, and has been, to stimulate the development of more sophisticated statistical techniques. Three main types of statistical procedures have been encouraged—even made possible by—the development of computers: (1) factor analysis and other methods to identify key underlying dimensions in a database, whose mathematical computations include matrix inversions and a great deal of matrix algebra, in general; (2) LISREL, or covariance structure analysis, which combines factor analysis and multiple regression in one procedure; and (3) maximum likelihood estimation procedures such as logistical regression, which approximate initial solutions and then go on, through a large number of iterations, to work toward a solution (see, for example, PROC LOGIST in the SAS Supplemental Library).

The power of microcomputer statistical packages is rapidly increasing. Standard statistical procedures as complicated as factor analysis can now be done economically on microcomputers. More sophisticated procedures for microcomputers will be developed, and super-minicomputers will accelerate this trend. Galton's problem in hologeistic research can now be overcome by network autocorrelation and further refinements in hologeistic and intracultural statistical methods are to be expected.

Electronic Communication

Electronic publishing.   The publishing of anthropological articles and data in electronic form is well underway. Publications on computer disk are being issued by World Cultures and the Human Relations Area Files.

Current efforts encompass cross-cultural codes, codebooks, bibliographies, mapping software, time allocation data, and other quantitative data sets. The publication of quantitative data in the social sciences is a long-standing tradition as evidenced by, for example, the work of the Inter-university Consortium for Political and Social Research.[4] Anthropology is participating more in the development of quantitative data sets, and it is coming into the process at a time that microcomputers are being widely used; therefore, there has been a tendency to release electronic publications on microcomputer disks rather than on computer tape.

We would expect to see this trend continue. As qualitative research becomes more computerized, we will see qualitative datasets and ethnographies in electronic form. This would permit rapid searching and indexing of ethnographic data, which would then be more useful for cross-cultural coding and comparison. Hypertext techniques are well suited to ethnographic data. Hypertext allows a researcher to browse through text on various paths built into the textual presentation by linking different topics and subtopics. Because ethnographic data can be organized in a variety of structures, and because different readers peruse it with different goals in mind, open-ended hypertext presentation of ethnographic data seems to make a great deal of sense. It is possible to record field data (audio, textual, and visual) in a hypertext database and to publish this as a basic ethnography to be used by others with a variety of interests.

Computer networks. As scientific data processing moves to the individual workstation, network connections become an important central resource. Networks, which allow many computers to interact constantly, should be seen at several levels of organization. The most basic level consists of the communication links enabling computers to transfer symbolic data between themselves. The higher levels of organization are composed mainly of software standards that enable the communication to take place without interference.

The computers in a network are linked by digital communication. The main difference between one type of digital communication and another is the speed at which the communication takes place. Most computer users are familiar with the kind of digital communication that uses ordinary voice telephone lines. Two modems at the ends of a line convert the digital data coming from a terminal or computer into audio tones that are carried over the telephone wires. Fortunately, there are now worldwide standards for all modem-to-modem communications.

Another familiar form of digital communication is the local area network (LAN). LANs work at speeds a thousand times faster than modems. At these rates one computer can access files in another computer's memory without loss of processing time. LAN standardization is taking place rapidly.

Public packet-switching networks were an important network development in the 1970s. These reduced the cost of connecting a terminal to a distant computer by sharing communication lines with other digital messages. Long-distance computer communication is inherently cheaper than voice communication because the messages are simple on-off signals and not complex speech waveforms requiring a larger band width. The advantages of digital signals are that (1) they can contain information generated by the switching system, and (2) they can be switched in millionths of a second from one circuit to another. Thus, computer communication is becoming the basic form of electronic communication in Western cultures. College campuses are being interconnected digitally within themselves and with each other, and networks are now reaching some of the more underdeveloped parts of the world.

Personal computers are now able to exchange messages and documents over long distances. Eventually, the entire world will be linked digitally at reduced costs, so that field projects can be coordinated over distances that span the globe. It will probably be some time before adequate digital communication reaches the very remote field locations in which many anthropologists work. However, even today it is possible to upload and download digital messages to amateur radio satellites from any spot in the world. In the future, a low-orbit digital relay satellite might be launched to facilitate scientific communications with small, portable digital transceivers in the field where there are no ground, microwave, radio, or wire communications available.

Computer conferencing originally required a central computer to which public messages were sent to be read by everybody participating in the conference. The first microcomputer conferencing systems were called bulletin board systems (BBS). Computer conferencing allows multiperson discussions to take place at a slower pace than they might occur in a face-to-face meeting but at a pace faster than if the notes were sent by regular mail to all participants. Many new and elegant features are being added to this basic concept to make the conferencing more fluid and functional. Systems are now evolving through which many computers can support the same conference. Simple examples of this are the echomail systems on public BBS and the Usenet newsletters circulated among UNIX computers. There are now scientific conferencing systems on Bitnet. These trends will continue, and computer conferencing will become commonplace.

THE FAR FUTURE

The march of technology continues, and anthropology will continue to benefit from the information age. What can we expect from new developments in computer hardware? Architecture is a key item in computer design. It signifies the way in which basic components are laid out to determine the computational capacities of the machine. There is a tendency for the architecture of the big computers to be transferred to the smaller microcomputers. Four important capacities have now appeared: virtual memory, multitasking, parallel processing, and RISC chip design. Virtual memory unlocks the size limits on programs and data, and multitasking permits the computer to run several programs at once. This means that almost any common computing job that is now run on a mainframe computer can be run on a microcomputer in the future. The critical limitation will be the time it takes for the job to be done.

Parallel processing and RISC chip design are increasing the processing speed of relatively inexpensive minicomputers. The era of the large mainframe computer is passing. The smaller "minicomputer" arriving on the scene can do more computing than can the old mainframe. The implication for anthropology is that simulations of demographic processes, cultural evolution, genetic evolution, social network interaction, and other human processes will be easier to carry out. Students will soon have access to computing power that was once available only to faculty with grants. Many people will be experimenting with simulation designs, and a better theoretical understanding of evolution and culture change should be the result.

The more distant future looks interesting. The reduction in size and cost of computing equipment will continue. The silicon crystal has proved to be one of the most stable and reliable structures in nature. Mechanical and optical devices will continue to provide better and cheaper printers, scanners, and instrumentation. We can expect "supercomputers" to become common. Standardization will also become more widespread, and programs and data will become much more transportable from one computer to another. Computers will be able to communicate with each other more easily. One bad effect of this will be the increasing hazard of computer viruses and worms, against which the users of standardized equipment will have to protect themselves.

Superconductivity and optical computers will stimulate the longest modern technological revolution ever recorded. In computer architecture the advent of neural networks offers some interesting possibilities to social scientists. Neural networks are computers that work more like the animal brain. Instead of processing data sequentially word by word, they process it simultaneously, comparing a million bits of information to another million bits of information and remembering the mapping. Therefore, neural networks, like human beings, develop fuzzy concepts of relationships. They could be used to model the development of human culture as well as the human brain. Neural networks could give us a tool for modeling and understanding culture and its inherently fuzzy aspects that defy precise analysis. Holographic neural computers, whenever they become practical, will have an impact on anthropological theory. Not only do they offer a tool for capturing the imprecise and inconsistent sides of cultural behavior, but they also can model the way in which culture develops as a synthesis of many human experiences.

PROBLEMS AHEAD

A major factor slowing the development of computer methods is software. The operating systems required to run virtual memory and multitasking are difficult to develop and even more difficult to standardize. Anthropology has a current problem in that the numbers of programmers and computer scientists working in the field are small. This fact limits the number and scope of problems that can be solved in any period of time. However, as this book illustrates, there is some very energetic and creative work among those who are active. As problems are defined, it will probably be necessary to write programs that are specific to a small group of related life sciences. Yet, the level of skill required to write really useful programs is difficult to attain and is getting more so, and people who combine the programming skills, mathematical skills, and scientific knowledge required are difficult to find. More sophisticated programming tools that allow less trained persons to write anthropological programs are needed, but students should also be encouraged to develop the needed programming skills within their graduate curricula.

The programs needed in anthropology are generally not unique to the field, so cross-fertilization between software in sociology, economics, computer science, and statistics is very important. The typical professional user is already aware of dozens of programs that could be of use to him or her. Collecting information on existing programs is an important task, and sorting out the useful ones from less useful ones can be difficult. Eventually, anthropologists will have to do this work and some of their own programming, as well.

Anthropology is an international human science that is making special contributions to computer applications that are of interest to people outside the field as well as inside. As is its tradition, this fundamental science is generating many new ideas and techniques. The future promises to see many more new developments in computer techniques. The rise of computer techniques in anthropology has just begun.

NOTES

1. A product of Borland, Inc.
2. The Internet is the cooperative computer network linking many earlier networks such as CSNET and ARPA though standardized protocols and domain

addressing. TCP/IP protocols would allow the nodes on an anthropological research subnet to contact each other.

3. The databasing of audio information is currently limited by digital storage capacity of portable computers and base computers. Respectable fidelity requires a sampling rate of 8,000 cps and eight bit digitization. Thus five minutes of audio interviewing would require 2.4 megabytes of storage. Understandable speech can be produced with a sampling rate of 4,000 cps and four bit digitization, reducing the storage space to 600 kilobytes. Compression to this level still fills up 20 megabytes in two hours and forty-six minutes. With WORM disk, digital paper, or helical scan recording on the base computer, a full-scale digitized audio field project can be carried out. These high-density recording devices are already available, and the costs of a base computer capable of databasing audio from a large field project will soon be within the range of many research projects. Of course, there is still the problem of developing the software to handle the audio information.

4. The Inter-university Consortium for Political and Social Research (ICPSR) has been distributing machine-readable social science data for over twenty-five years. Their mail address is ICPSR, P. O. Box 1248, Ann Arbor, MI 48106, and their Internet address is ICPSR_NETMAIL@UM.CC.UMICH.EDU .

Software Appendix

MICROCOMPUTER SOFTWARE
USED OR MENTIONED
IN THIS VOLUME

Readers should shop around for the best discount prices for microcomputer software. The prices given below are approximate list prices, which can be much higher than those at discount software retailers. Prices also tend to decline over time. For more information, see *The Software Catalog:* Microcomputers, Parts I and II, Elsevier Science Publishing, New York, 1989, which was the source for much of the information that follows. The latest versions in that source are listed.

Program	Information
ABSTAT	Version 5.0
	Anderson-Bell Corp.
	11479 S. Pine Dr. Suite 441
	Parker, CO 80134
	(303) 841-9755
	Approximate price, $295
AL	Steve Borgatti
	Department of Sociology
	University of South Carolina
	Columbia, SC 29208
	(803) 777-3123
AMBUSH	Reference: Howell, N. and V. Lehotay 1978.
	AMBUSH: A computer program for stochastic
	microsimulation of small human populations.
	American Anthropologist 80:905–922.
ANTHROPAC	Version 3.0
	Steve Borgatti
	Department of Sociology
	University of South Carolina
	Columbia, SC 29208
	(803) 777-3123
	Approximate price, $25
ASKSAM	ASKSAM SYSTEMS
	P. O. Box 1428
	119 S. Washington St.
	Perry, FL 32347
	(800) 327-5726
	Approximate cost, $220

ASTAT	Version 83.1 (Educational users only)
	Duke University Press
	Box 6697 College Station
	Durham, NC 27708
	(919) 684-2173
	Approximate price, $25
BIOM-PC	Version 2.0
	Exeter Publishing, Ltd.
	100 N. Country Rd.
	Setauket, NY 11733
	(516) 751-4350
	Approximate price, $55
BISEX	BISEX: Bisayan Expert System
	Unpublished software program, 1987
	C. Behrens (XBEHREN@UCLASSCF) and
	D. Read (RAREAD@UCLASSCF)
	Dept. of Anthropology, UCLA
	Los Angeles, CA 90024
	(213) 825-3988
BMDP	Forty-four separate programs
	BMDP Statistical Software
	1440 Sepulvedo Blvd., Suite 316
	Los Angeles, CA 90025
	(213) 479-7799
BUSINESS STATISTICS MULTIVARIATE ANALYSIS	Lionheart Press, Inc.
	P. O. Box 379
	Alburg, VT 05440
	(514) 933-4918
CRISP	Crunch Software
	1541 Ninth Avenue
	San Francisco, CA 94122
	(415) 564-7337
DASY	Statistical Software Resources
	20355 Seaboard Road
	Malibu, CA 90265
	(213) 456-5150
DATA DESK	Data Description, Inc.
	P. O. Box 4555
	Ithaca, NY 14852
	(607) 257-1000
DBASE IV	Ashton-Tate
	10150 W. Jefferson Blvd.
	Culver City, CA 90230
	(213) 204-5570
	Approximate cost, $695

DBXL

Version 1.2
Wordtech Systems, Inc.
21 Altarinda Rd.
Orinda, CA 94563
(415) 254-0900
Approximate price, $150

DR. HALO III

Media Cybernetics, Inc.
8484 Georgia Ave.
Silver Spring, MD 20910
(301) 495-3305
Approximate cost, $105

ELF

Statistical package, Version 5.2
The Winchendon Group, Inc.
3907 Lakota Road, P. O. Box 10339
Alexandria, VA 22310
(703) 960-2587
Approximate price, $110

EPISTAT

Version 3.3
Duke University Press
Box 6697 College Station
Durham, NC 27708
(919) 684-2173
Approximate price, $20

ESP

Expert Systems International
1700 Walnut St.
Philadelphia, PA 19103
(215) 735-8510
Approximate price, $670

ETHNOGRAPH

THE ETHNOGRAPH
Qualis Research
611 E. Nichols Drive
Littleton, CO 80122
or,
P. O. Box 3785
Littleton, CO 80161
(303) 794-6420
Approximate cost, $150

FAMILY REUNION

Version 3.1
Personal Software Company
P. O. Box 726
1580 E. Dawn Dr.
Salt Lake City, UT 84110
(801) 943-6908
Approximate cost, $75

GODZILLA

Version 1.1, 1986
John B. Gatewood (JBG1@LEHIGH)
Dept. of Social Relations, Price Hall #40
Lehigh University
Bethlehem, PA 18015
(215) 758-3814

GURU

Micro Data Base Systems
P. O. Box 248
Lafayette, IN 47902
(317) 463-2581
Approximate price, $6500

INSIGHT2+

Level Five Research
503 Fifth Ave.
Indialantic, FL 32903
(407) 729-9046
Approximate price, $365

KAES

Kinship Algebra Expert System, 1988
D. Read (RAREAD@UCLASSCF)
and C. Behrens (XBEHREN@UCLASSCF)
Dept. of Anthropology, UCLA
Los Angeles, CA 90024
(213) 825-3988

KEDIT

Version 4.0
Mansfield Software Group
P. O. Box 532
Storrs, CT 06268
(203) 429-8402
Approximate price, $110

KINTYPER

Unpublished software program, 1982
J. Smith
Dept. of Anthropology
University of South Florida
Tampa, FL 33620

LOTUS 1-2-3

Release 1A, 1983
Lotus Development Corporation
55 Cambridge Parkway
Cambridge, MA 02142
(617) 577-8500
Approximate price, $320

MACSYMA

Reference: Mathlab Group 1977
MACSYMA Reference Manual, MIT Computer
Science Laboratory Technical Report
Cambridge: MIT Press

MDPREF	Reference: Chang, J. J., and J. D. Carroll 1969 How to Use MDPREF Murray Hill, NJ: Bell Telephone Laboratories (201) 582-3000
METAWINDOW	Version 3.4, 1989 Metagraphics Software Corp. 269 Mount Hermon Rd. P. O. Box 66779 Scotts Valley, CA 95066 (408) 438-1550 Approximate cost, $145
MICROSTAT-II	Ecosoft, Inc. 6413 North College Avenue Indianapolis, In 46220 (317) 255-6476 Approximate cost, $275
MICRO TSP	Version 6.0 Micro Time Series Package Quantitative Micro Software 4521 Campus Dr., Suite 336 Irvine, CA 92715 (714) 856-3368
MINITAB	E. F. Paynter and Associates 6140 N. College Ave. Indianapolis, IN 46220 (317) 257-7561 Approximate price, $70
MODELING SYSTEMS OF KINSHIP AND MARRIAGE	Version 2.0 Duke University Press Box 6697 College Station Durham, NC 27708 (919) 684-2173 Approximate price, $20
MUSTAT	The Statistical Center Dept. of Mathematical Sciences Agricultural Experiment Station Montana State University Bozeman, MT 59717 (406) 994-5346
NEEDLE IN A HAYSTACK	Aurora Software Drawer A 12591 Beachcomber Anchorage, AK 99515

NOTEBOOK II	Version 3.01
	Pro/Tem Software, Inc.
	814 Tolman Dr.
	Stanford, CA 94305
	(415) 947-1000
	Approximate cost, $140
NUMBER CRUNCHER	Berta-Max, Inc.
	3420 Stone Way N.
	P. O. Box 31849
	Seattle, WA 98103-1849
	(206) 547-4056
	Approximate Price, $20
NWA STATPAK	Version 4.1
	Northwest Analytical, Inc.
	520 N. W. Davis St.
	Portland, OR 97209
	(503) 224-7727
	Approximate price, $370
PARADOX	Version 2.0
	ANSA Software
	1301 Shore Way Rd.
	Belmont, CA 94002
	(415) 595-4489
	Approximate price, $545
PC-FILE+	ButtonWare, Inc.
	P. O. Box 5786
	Bellevue, WA 98006
	(206) 454-0479
	Approximate price, $35
PC PAINT PLUS	Mouse Systems Corp.
	2600 San Thomas Expressway
	Santa Clara, CA 95051
	(408) 988-0211
	Approximate price, $60
PC-WRITE	Quicksoft, Inc.
	219 First North
	Box 224-PMAZ
	Seattle, WA 98109
	Full registration, $89; Shareware Disketters, $16
PERSONAL CONSULTANT PLUS	Texas Instruments
	12501 Research Blvd.
	Austin, TX 78769
	Approximate price, $2950

PLANPERFECT	Version 3.0
	WordPerfect Corp.
	288 W. Center St. Way
	Orem, UT 84057
	(801) 225-5000
	Approximate price, $295
QUATTRO	Version 3.0
	Borland International
	4585 Scotts Valley Dr.
	Scotts Valley, CA 95066
	(408) 438-8400
	Approximate price, $115
RATS	Regression and Time Series
	VAR Econometrics
	134 Prospect Avenue South
	Minneapolis, MN 55419
	(612) 822-9690
RBASE for DOS	Version 2.1
	Microrim
	3925 159th Ave. N. E.
	Redmond, WA 98073-9722
	(206) 885-2000
	Approximate price, $525
REDUCE	Reference: A. C. Hearn 1983
	REDUCE User's Manual, Version 3.0
	Rand Publication CP78(4183)
	Santa Monica: The Rand Corporation
REFLEX	THE DATABASE MANAGER
	Borland International
	4585 Scotts Valley Dr.
	Scotts Valley, CA 95066
	(408) 438-8400
	Approximate price, $90
ROOTS II	Version 2.1
	COMMSOFT
	2257 Old Middlefield Way
	Mountain View, CA 94043
	(415) 967-1900
	Approximate cost, $145
SAS-PC	SAS Institute, Inc.
	SAS Circle, Box 8000
	Cary, NC 27511-8000
	(919) 467-8000

SCS	Instant Statistics 517 E. Lodge Drive Tempe, AZ 85283 (602) 838-7784
SIGSTAT	Significant Statistics 3336 N. Canyon Road Provo, UT 84604 (801) 377-4860 Approximate price, $445
SOCSIM	Reference: E. A. Hammel 1976 The SOCSIM Demographic-Sociological Microsimulation Program Operating Manual Research Series, No. 27 Berkeley: University of California
SORITEC	Version 6.36 The Sorites Group 8136 Old Keen Mill Road, A-309 P. O. Box 2939 Springfield, VA 22150 (703) 569-1400 Approximate price, $70
SPSS-X/PC	SPSS Inc. Suite 3000 444 N. Michigan Ave. Chicago, IL 60611 (312) 329-2400
STAT80	StatWare P. O. Box 510881 Salt Lake City, UT 84151 (801) 521-9309
STATGRAPHICS	Version 2.1 STSC, Inc. 2115 East Jefferson Street Rockville, MD 20852 (301) 984-5488 Approximate price, $480
STATVIEW	Brainpower, Inc. 24009 Ventura Blvd., Suite 250 Calabasas, CA 91302 (818) 884-6911 Approximate price, $35
STATWORKS	Cricket Software 3508 Market St., Suite 206 Philadelphia, PA 19104

STRUCTURE	Reprint Librarian, Center for the Social Sciences Columbia University, New York, NY 10027 Request a copy of "Technical Report #TR2," and send a check for $20 ($50 for institutions) made out to "Research Program in Structural Analysis"
SUPERCALC 5	Computer Associates 1240 McKay Dr. San Jose, CA 95131 (408) 432-1727
SYSTAT MYSTAT	The System for Statistics Version 3.2 Systat, Inc. 1800 Sherman Ave. Evanston, IL 60201 (312) 864-5870 Approximate price, $596
TURBO PASCAL and TURBO PROLOG	TURBO PASCAL, Version 5.5; TURBO PROLOG, Version 2.0 Borland International 4585 Scotts Valley Dr. Scotts Valley, CA 95066 (408) 438-8400 Approximate cost of either, $60
UCINET	A Microcomputer Package for Network Analysis Bruce MacEvoy, Linton Freeman Mathematical Social Science Group School of Social Sciences University of California Irvine, CA 92717
VP-EXPERT VP-GRAPHICS VP-INFO VP-PLANNER PLUS	Version 2.0 Version 1.4 Version 2.0 PaperBack Software 2830 9th Street Berkeley, CA 94710 (415) 644-2116 Approximate cost, VP-GRAPHICS, VP-INFO, or VP-EXPERT, $95 Approximate cost, VP-PLANNER PLUS, $135

WORDCRUNCHER

Version 4.22
Electronic Text Corp.
5600 N. University Ave.
Provo, UT 84604-5634
(801) 225-5000
Approximate price, $225

WORDPERFECT

Version 5.0
WordPerfect Corp.
288 W. Center St.
Orem, UT 84057
(801) 225-5000
Approximate price, $270

WORDSTAR
PROFESSIONAL

Version 4.0
Word-processing software for PC
MicroPro International Corp.
33 San Pablo Avenue
San Rafael, CA 94903
(415) 499-1200
Approximate cost, $370

WORLD OF
KINSHIP

Unpublished software program
Marty Ottenheimer
Kansas State University
Manhattan, KS 66506
(913) 532-6865

Resources Appendix

Anthropologists who are interested in learning more about computer applications can find a wealth of information in print journals and newsletters, electronic journals and bulletin boards, special databases of bibliographic citations that are now on-line and on compact disk, databases of cross-cultural data on diskette, specialized software to analyze anthropological data, and anthropology programs with specializations in computer applications and with special computer resources. Information is also available in continuing education programs of the American Anthropological Association and other anthropological societies and at university computer centers. The following list of resources can serve as a starting point for anthropologists who want to learn more about computer applications. However, this list is by no means complete. New resources are developing very rapidly, and readers should inquire about the latest developments and the latest prices.

RESOURCE: PRINT JOURNALS

Computers and the Social Sciences

This publication focuses on computer applications in the social sciences. A regular section of "Software Reviews" evaluates new programs. Feature articles evaluate and compare programs. (Special Issue: Jan-June 1986, vol. 2, no. 1/2, Statistical Packages.) Computer types: microcomputers. Contact person: Meg Bloch, Managing Editor. Address for subscriptions: Paradigm Press, Inc., P. O. Box 1057, Osprey FL 33559-9990. (813) 922-7666. Publication frequency: quarterly. Subscription rate: $89. [Information from the bulletin board, Information System for Advanced Academic Computing, ISAAC]

Journal of Quantitative Anthropology

The primary purpose of the journal is the advancement of quantitative research in anthropology. The journal will provide a forum for scientific research, methodological developments, computer applications, and other subjects of interest to anthropologists. Although traditional in subdisciplinary breadth, the journal will highlight new developments in quantitative methods and modeling and computer applications in anthropology. Contact person: Jeffrey C. Johnson, Editor-in-Chief, with the Department of Sociology and Anthropology, and the Institute for Coastal and Marine Resources, (919) 757-6220, East Carolina University, Greenville, NC 27858-4353. Bitnet, CMJOHNSO@ECUVM1. Subscription rates are $49 for individuals and $102.50 for institutions. Address for subscriptions: Kluwer Academic Publishers, P. O. Box 358 Accord Station, Hingham, MA 02018-9990. (617) 871-6600. There are four issues per year. [Information from the publisher, and the editor-in-chief]

Social Science Computer Review

This publication is produced by the Social Science Computer Laboratory of North Carolina State University. It is a vehicle for those interested in the exchange of information and software relevant to social scientists. Information on software is presented via lengthy "Software Reviews," which evaluate and compare programs; "News and Notes"; book reviews; and feature articles. The winter issue has reviews of the state of the art in computer use in various disciplines, and anthropology is always represented. Contact person: G. David Garson, Editor, (919) 737-3067. Address for subscriptions: Duke University Press, Box 6697 College Station, Durham, NC 27708. (919) 684-2173. Publication frequency: quarterly. Subscription rates are $28 for individuals and $56 for institutions. [Information from ISAAC and from the editor]

Practicing Anthropology's "Practical Computing" (formerly called "Computer Column for All Seasons")

This column appears in the Society for Applied Anthropology's career-oriented publication. The editor accepts a wide variety of manuscripts from anthropologists who are developing and using computer applications in their professional work. To date, columns have included (1) a report on teaching the use of a microcomputer statistical program SYSTAT to anthropology students (Crabtree and Pelto 1988); (2) a column on the use of computers in development consulting and the introduction of microcomputers in developing societies (Nunn 1988); (3) a piece about the use of E-mail internationally to collaborate in writing a chapter in an anthropology book (Koons 1988); (4) a column about a special computer and printing application to study Native American languages (Edwards 1989); and (5) a report introducing "Managed Anthropological Teamwork (MAT)" as an approach to team ethnography using microcomputers (Erickson 1989). The first issue in 1991 will include reviews of the Centers for Disease Control anthropometric analysis packages "CASP" and "Anthro."

At this writing, columns are planned on original software programs from a wide range of subdisciplines. Two printed copies of manuscripts and ASCII or WordPerfect 5.0 on 3.5-inch diskette can be sent to the column editor: James W. Carey, Department of Anthropology, Georgia State University, Atlanta, GA 30303. (404) 651-2255. Individual subscriptions to *Practicing Anthropology* are $14 per year. Address for subscriptions: SfAA Business Office, Box 24083, Oklahoma City, OK 73124.

RESOURCE: ELECTRONIC JOURNAL ON DISKETTE

World Cultures

WORLD CULTURES is an electronic journal and database published quarterly on microcomputer diskettes. The General Editor is Douglas R. White, School of Social Sciences, University of California/Irvine, Irvine, CA 92717. (714) 833-6801. The journal welcomes articles, brief communications, datasets, programs, comparative research, and instructional material from scientists of any country, dealing with any aspect of human groups. Issues (volume, number) that are available for library, instructional, and research use include:

1(1) on Murdock and White's Standard Cross-Cultural Sample; 1(2) on Murdock's Ethnographic Atlas; 1(3) on Software Supplements for the Electronic Journal (including setting up a cross-cultural workstation, micro statistical packages for cross-cultural research, and social science teleconferencing; 1(4) on standard sample codes (including several topics on kinship and women's status and roles).

2(1) on ethnographic bibliography; 2(2) on standard sample codes (including selections on data quality control, language, climate, women, and so on); and 2(3) on standard sample codes and magico-religious practitioners; 2(4) on the Ethnographic Atlas.

3(1) on standard sample codes (including topics on fertility, war, slavery, agriculture, sex, and enculturation); 3(2) on cultural diversity database (cross-cultural instructional atlas, including Human Relations Area Files (HRAF)-indexed guide); 3(3) on physical anthropology; 3(4) on Western North American Indians. 4(1) will be on cross-cultural sampling frames. Further information on WORLD CULTURES can be obtained through P. O. Box 12524, La Jolla, CA 92037-0650. [Information from materials distributed at the annual meeting of the American Anthropological Association meeting, 1987, Chicago.]

RESOURCE: COMPARATIVE
ANTHROPOLOGICAL DATA ON DISKETTE

The Human Relations Area Files (HRAF) offers data sets on diskette from P. O. Box 2015 Yale Station, New Haven, CT 06520. Telephone David Levinson and Richard A. Wagner at (203) 777-2334. Data sets are available only in ASCII files.

Data sets available in the Quantitative Cross-Cultural Data Series are:

1. General Cultural and Religion Data, edited by David Levinson and Richard A. Wagner (60 societies, 103 variables). $40.

2. Death and Dying in the Life-Cycle, edited by Anthony P. Glasscock and Richard A. Wagner (60 societies, 207 variables). $40.

3. Magico-religious Practitioners and Trance States, edited by Michael Winkelman and Douglas White (115 types of practitioners in 45 societies). $40.

Forthcoming data sets include:

4. Adolescence, edited by Herbert Barry III and Alice Schlegel. $50.
5. Human Aggression and Violence, edited by V. Burbank, D. Levinson, K. Otterbein, and P. Rozee-Koker. $40.

Another series of Cross-Cultural Studies in Time Allocation is planned, and will be edited by Allen Johnson. [Information from HRAF]

Duke University Press offers data sets on diskette, along with hard copy manuals. The data sets are also offered in formats that may be more adaptable than those using Lotus, dBase, and other programs for analysis. Call (919) 684-2173. Address: Box 6697 College Station, Durham, NC 27708. The following are part of the HRAF Research Series in Quantitative Cross-Cultural Data:

1. Cultural Diversity Database, edited by Douglas R. White (186 societies, 177 variables) [from WORLD CULTURES; see, ELECTRONIC JOURNAL, above]

2. *Death and Dying in the Life-Cycle*, edited by Anthony P. Glasscock and Richard A. Wagner (60 societies, 207 variables).

3. *General Cultural and Religious Data*, edited by David Levinson and Richard A. Wagner (60 societies, 103 variables). [Information from HRAF]

Other offerings include:

1. *Ethnographic Atlas*, edited by Douglas R. White (1267 cultures, 127 variables).

2. *Ethnographic Hypertext*, edited by Douglas R. White (tutorials).

3. *Fugawiland*, by T. Douglas Price and Michael J. Kolb (simulated archaeology) (see also, Computer Databases Available to Anthropologists in this volume).

RESOURCE: COMPARATIVE ANTHROPOLOGICAL DATA ON COMPACT DISK

Cross-Cultural CD

CROSS-CULTURAL CD is a collection of databases based on information from the Human Relations Area Files. It is produced by SilverPlatter, which also publishes bibliographic resources such as MED-LINE (see BIBLIOGRAPHIC SEARCHES BY COMPACT DISK, below). CROSS-CULTURAL CD is a series of ten databases, which can be searched with key words. Each database consists of 6,000–12,000 pages of textual data, on a sixty-culture probability sample. Material can be browsed, combined, and limited with Boolean operators, and displayed, printed, or downloaded. At this writing, the first database was due to be published very soon, and two new databases will be published each year. The topics of the databases are (1) Human Sexuality, (2) Marriage, (3) Family, (4) Crime and Social Problems, (5) Old Age, (6) Death and Dying, (7) Childhood and Adolescence, (8) Socialization and Education, (9) Religious Beliefs, and (10) Religious Practices. A single volume (two databases) costs $1,495. For further information contact David Levinson and Richard A. Wagner at HRAF, (203) 777-2334, or SilverPlatter Information, Inc., 37 Walnut Street, Wellesley, MA 02181. (617) 239-0306. References: Wagner, Richard A., and David Levinson, "From microfiche to CD-ROM: HRAF's experience in computerizing a full-text database," *Microform Review* 18(2):98–102, 1989; Wagner, Richard A., "The rise of computing in anthropology," forthcoming in *SSCORE*, winter 1989.

RESOURCE: SOFTWARE PACKAGE FOR ANALYSIS OF ANTHROPOLOGICAL DATA

ANTHROPAC, Version 2.5. ANTHROPAC is the only software package to date designed specifically for anthropologists. A single, varied product provides a set of user-friendly programs to manage and analyze data using some of the most useful methodologies in cultural anthropology. ANTHROPAC meets many of the computing needs that anthropologists have for multidimensional scaling, log-linear modeling, consensus modeling, unidimensional scaling, Guttman scaling, and other methods. Truex notes that, "while these methodologies may be sometimes overused by those who know them, they are certainly always underused by those who don't" (review forthcoming in the *American Anthropologist*, 1990). Along with its appropriately chosen set of techniques, ANTHROPAC provides a menu-driven set of options with a helpful format, useful prompts, and descriptions of selected options. Field workers can run ANTHROPAC on lap-top computers and therefore can begin analysis in the field (see Chapters 4, 7, and 17 in this volume). The figures produced by the package do not require a graphics adapter. ANTHROPAC comes with documentation and can be obtained as shareware, for a $25 handling fee. ANTHROPAC is copyrighted 1988, 1989 by Stephen P. Borgatti, Department of Sociology, University of South Carolina, Columbia, SC 29208.

RESOURCE: ELECTRONIC BULLETIN BOARD

Information System for Advanced Academic Computing (ISAAC)

ISAAC is a bulletin board and a selection of databases. ISAAC contains research abstracts (for example, some of the project descriptions that appear in the Computer Databases Available to Anthropologists Section of this volume), a software catalog, a software information database, and notes from colleagues around the country. The bulletin board is divided into "rooms" devoted to particular topics. Eight rooms are devoted to academic disciplines; four others are devoted to technical exchange, announcements, questions to ISAAC, and information from IBM. Others are used by independent organizations. ISAAC databases include the Advanced Education Projects (AEP) Database; the Special Studies Database; the SoftInfo Database; and the Academic Software Database.

ISAAC is an outgrowth of the AEP Bulletin Board. ISAAC's purpose remains the same—to encourage innovative applications of IBM computers in higher education. In 1984, IBM's Academic Information Systems Business Unit (ACIS) started the Advanced Education Projects (AEP). Nineteen universities received grants, and more than 2,600 projects were funded. In March 1985, IBM funded the AEP Bulletin Board. The purpose of the bulletin board was to allow educators and researchers from AEP universities to share information. In November 1986, the Bulletin Board became accessible via Bitnet (which is how the ISAAC was accessed for the Computer Database Available to Anthropologists section). Membership was opened up to include faculty, staff, and students at all institutions of higher education.

ISAAC is a free computer-based system devoted to information about the use of IBM computers and compatible software in higher education and research. All students, faculty, and staff at institutions of higher education and members of participating societies are eligible to use ISAAC. To request access to ISAAC, send the following information to Isaac Access, m/s FC-06 University of Washington, Seattle, WA 98195; or use Bitnet to send it to ISAAC@UWAEE; or, call (206) 543-5604: (1) Name, (2) Address, City, State, Zip, (3) Phone, with area code, (4) University, (5) Bitnet address. A user may connect to ISAAC in two ways. Each method requires separate authorization. If the user chooses modem access, ISAAC provides the communications. Please indicate which method(s) preferred: Method 1—IBM PC, XT, AT or compatible and a modem (Continental U.S. and Hawaii only); Method 2—Bitnet (Bitnet address must be included). Materials will be mailed to the user. [Information from ISAAC]

RESOURCE: PRINT NEWSLETTERS

Cultural Anthropology Methods (CAM)

CAM is a newsletter devoted to the exchange of information about the use and teaching of research methods in cultural anthropology. The editors of CAM, Russ Bernard (UFRUSS@UFFSC), Bert Pelto (PJPELTO@UCONNVM), and Steve Borgatti (N040016@UNIVSCVM) invite colleagues to share insight and materials related to the use and teaching of research methods. This includes the use of computer hardware and software in the field, lab, and classroom.

CAM is a forum whose development is supported by the National Science Foundation. At this writing there were about 600 "subscribers," and the number was growing. CAM presents news and features on (1) the latest methods for conducting research in cultural anthropology and (2) teaching research methods to students of cultural anthropology, for example:

1. Abstracts of published material on research methods and teaching research methods. If colleagues read an article that would be useful to know about, they should send the abstract (or write one and send it) to CAM. (150-200 words per abstract, and the number of abstracts is open)

2. Descriptions of methods courses. CAM publishes features about people who already teach methods courses. The editors are looking for detailed descriptions of any class exercises and examples for teaching particular methods. (up to 1,000 words)

3. Review of software that is useful in teaching research methods or in collecting and/or analyzing data. (up to 1,000 words)

4. Descriptions of new data-collection and analysis techniques. If readers have developed a new technique for collecting data in the field, or modified an existing technique for a special situation, send the results to CAM. (up to 2,500 words)

5. Book reviews. Most books about social science research methods are written by sociologists and psychologists. Reviews of methods books by anthropologists can be submitted to CAM, no matter how old the books may be. (up to 1,000 words, descriptive and informative)

6. Debate. Letters about particular research methods are welcome. (up to 1,000 words)

CAM is meant to be a useful, fun-to-read forum for sharing information about teaching techniques and the "little things" that make a difference in using data-collection methods in the field. CAM will include detailed descriptions of how anthropologists adapted techniques to field situations. For example: How do you do pile sorts with nonliterate informants? How long does it take to actually conduct a household budget interview? How do you train assistants to be reliable and consistent?

How much should informants be paid? What ethical issues are raised by the use of certain techniques, and how have you dealt with the issues? What are the physical demands of time allocation studies, and how have you dealt with the demands? How have you handled sampling problems in the field? What tips can you offer about the use of still and video photography in fieldwork or the use of specific computers, peripherals, and programs in the field?

Similarly, CAM will provide a systematic way for teachers to learn about successful teaching techniques. For example, how do you teach students to be good interviewers? How can students learn about the problems involved in direct, continuous observation? How do students learn to take good field notes? What kinds of coding schemes do you use for field notes, and how do you teach students about coding? What are some good exercises to show students how to work with their own data and how to interpret results in a valid way? How do you teach students about ethical issues in the use of research methods?

If you have written a computer program, describe it for CAM, and give the details for obtaining it. If you have an unpublished bibliography for a methods course, or if you have data-collection sheets that you developed for a special project, send the materials to CAM.

Send all materials by post, rather than by E-mail. If possible, send it in an ASCII file on 3-1/4 or 5-1/2 inch disks. Send Bitnet addresses of yourself and colleagues, including those in overseas locations. Submit materials to H. Russell Bernard, Department of Anthropology, 1350 Turlington, University of Florida, Gainesville, FL 32611. Telephone (904) 392-2031. Binet, UFRUSS@UFFSC. [Information from the editors]

Computer-Assisted Anthropology News (CAAN)

The *Computer-Assisted Anthropology News* is a newsletter/magazine that publishes news and articles concerning the applications of computer technology to all areas of anthropology. Articles address a wide range of topics and levels of expertise. Because many anthropologists are just becoming aware of CAAN, back issues have been reprinted and are being sold. Subscriptions to individuals are $6 U.S. for one volume with four issues. For institutions the price is $12. Back issues are $1.50 apiece to individuals and $3 to institutions. Volume 3 No. 4 came out in November 1987 and focuses on field note and free-form databases. Each issue is thirty to forty pages in length in a 5.5 by 8.5 inch booklet format. Sample issues will be sent if requested. They also need submissions of news items and manuscripts for future issues. Submit them to the editor, James Dow, at the address that follows. Articles should be submitted electronically if possible, in plain ASCII unformatted style and should be less than 50 kilobytes in size. Five to 30 kilobytes is the preferred range. Address: CAAN, Department of Sociology and Anthropology, Oakland University, Rochester, MI 48309-4401. Bitnet, USERXRB8@UMICHUM.

Items in past issues illustrate the range of articles published: 1(1) managing field notes; apples and archaeology; 3-D archaeology program; data for community workers; demographic programs; using Superfile; management of ecological data in the field.

1(2) Setting up and operating a computer under adverse field conditions; courseware; user supported software; apples and archaeology; hardware; Center for Computer Applications in the Humanities; network models and database management; teaching with computers; visual bracket plotting with SAS/ETS.

1(3) A computer approach to a precolonial language problem; the anthropology of computers; World Cultures Database; electronic networking update; hardware and software; The World of Kinship; bibliographies; computers for other cultures; statistical entailment analysis; package for data analysis and matrix manipulation.

1(4) Archaeological cataloging systems for personal computers; Socnet and Polinet; freeware versus moneyware; computers in human services; Fido; Center for Archaeology Field Training; rugged field computer.

2(1) A review of selected microcomputer statistical software packages.

2(2) Using a computer in the field; database management systems for variable length texts; MINIARC database; statistical packages for microcomputers; cultural anthropology database; electronic mail; glossary of electronic communication terms; NAPA bulletin board; the anthropologist's bulletin board system.

2(3) Statistical programs for the Macintosh; roundtable symposium on microcomputers in anthropology; computers in Southeast Asia; COHORTS; WORDTREE: Needle in the Haystack; Sort Blocks by Fields; DIGSITE: computer simulation of an archaeological excavation. [Information from the editor of CAAN]

RESOURCE: ON-LINE BIBLIOGRAPHIC DATABASE SEARCHES FOR ANTHROPOLOGISTS

On-line searches of bibliographic databases are now an integral part of many research efforts. In addition, completion of the most up-to-date bibliographic search is an important stage in the preparation of proposals for many types of funding and other support. Many databases are now updated quarterly, so that a search can include very recent information. Bibliographic searches are only one type of database search. The Computer Databases Available to Anthropologists section presents an example of another type of search, which focused on project summaries appearing in two databases (SSIE and ISAAC) and searched using the key words *computers* and *anthropology*. Other database searches focus on data coded by culture, type of practitioner, and type of activity (see, COMPARATIVE ANTHROPOLOGICAL DATA ON DISKETTE, and COMPARATIVE

ANTHROPOLOGICAL DATA ON CD, above, and BIBLIOGRAPHIC SEARCHES FOR ANTHROPOLOGISTS ON COMPACT DISK, below).

In bibliographic databases, the information appears in units of citation and can be searched, combined, limited, and printed according to author and topic (coded in various ways, often by key words that appear in the title, in the bodies of the abstract, and/or in a list of key words appearing at the end of the abstract) project information. The citations are usually published, although the database can include unpublished references—such as ERIC. Databases include citations from certain journals (and sometimes from books) and not others. Readers should carefully inquire about the sources of the coded citations if one particular journal *must* be searched. Databases also can have various degrees of cross-disciplinary focus. For example, MED-LINE indexes some social science journals (such as *Social Science and Medicine*), in addition to a wide variety of medical journals—but not *all* medical journals. PSYCHLIT indexes a large number of journals of interest to anthropologists, and ERIC (for educational specialists) indexes some social science journals, including some anthropology journals.

There are a number of different ways to access bibliographic databases, and readers should carefully inquire about the least expensive. Many university libraries now provide on-line searches to their own holdings and sometimes other libraries' holdings. Almost all full-service libraries (as well as many government agencies and private companies— especially research and development and communications companies) provide for on-line database searches at cost, using various vendors who provide access to a variety of databases. The library is usually the contact point to inquire about bibliographic database searches. Researchers can also access databases from their own homes and offices, using their own computers, modems, and printers—although this can become very expensive. Different vendors have different methods for "subscribing," searching, charging, and billing, and readers should address inquiries either to the source of the database or to one of the information system vendors, such as those below. One of the most common ways to bill a user is by time on-line. A university computer center should be helpful with technical details concerning the best communications software, accessing databases, downloading, saving large searches, and printing.

Databases can be most easily accessed through computer networks provided by on-line service vendors such as DIALOG Information Systems, which is the largest with over 280 separate databases on-line. Many public libraries and most university libraries now subscribe to services provided by one of the vendors such as DIALOG, BRS, SDC, or others.

It may be useful for anthropologists to begin by examining a useful type of reference—one of the many database catalogs that are arranged by topical area. A catalog gives a description of the database and the service vendors who provide access to it. Some database references are updated repeatedly as serial subscriptions. The following references are among the best known, although other catalogs may be just as helpful, depending on the purpose and topic of the search:

1. *The North American Online Directory: A Directory of Information Products and Services.* New York and London: R. R. Bowker Company. This catalog is issued yearly. There is no separate section on databases in anthropology, but there is a separate section on the social sciences that includes, for example, discipline-specific databases such as PsycINFO; cross-disciplinary and applied databases such as PAIS (Public Affairs Information Service); and topical, problem-oriented databases such as a database on child abuse and neglect.

2. *OMNI Online Database Directory.* Owen Davies and Mike Edelhart. New York: Collier Books, Macmillan Publishing. This catalog is updated every two years. OMNI has a section on "Social Sciences and Services" but not a specific section on anthropology. It does have listings of databases in disciplines related to the work of many anthropologists, such as biomedicine. There are descriptions of each database, along with the major service vendors who provide access to it.

3. *1987 Encyclopedia of Information Systems and Services*, edited by Amy Lucas and Kathleen Young Maraccio. Detroit, MI: Gale Research Co. This reference is an even more inclusive source that lists most kinds of computer-based products and services, by vendor. There is one volume for U.S. listings, another for international listings, and a third volume of indexes. The reference sections of many libraries now contain this and/or other sources for anthropologists who want to conduct selected database searches.

Isaac Databases

The Information System for Advanced Academic Computing (ISAAC) contains databases that can be searched for project abstracts (the Advanced Education Projects, or AEP Database) and IBM project descriptions (the Special Studies Database). These can be particularly useful for anthropologists who are developing project proposals funding. For example, the following titles were obtained in early 1987, by using the key word ANTHROPOLOG for a search of ISAAC's AEP database. Some of the titles have project descriptions in the Computer Databases Available to Anthropologists section in this volume.

1: QAL Workstation Conversion Project

2: Himalayan History and Anthropology Project

3: Analyzing Quantitative Data Relating to the Evolution of the Brain

4: Strong Museum of Anthropology

5: Upper Mantaro Archaeology Research Project

6: Basic Concepts in Evolutionary Genetics

7: Ya Cores (Yabroud Core Analysis SYStat), Ya Tools (Yabroud Tool Analysis SYStat)

8: Improving and Teaching Research in the Department of Anthropology

9: Words and Worlds of Tamang Women

10: Historical Microsimulation Laboratory

11: Humanities and Social Science Database Laboratory

12: Biological Variability in Human Populations

13: Automation of Anthropological Data Collection

14: Computerized Image Processing of Maya Hieroglyphic Inscriptions

15: Computers as Information Processing in Anthropology

16: Integration of Computers in Undergraduate Physical Anthropology

17: Regional and Localized Distribution Analyses of Archeological Site

18: Nubian Field Note Database for Graduate Training

19: The Application of Image Processing and Analytic Techniques to Archaeology

20: Spatial Analysis of Archaeological Sites and Artifacts

21: Burke Museum Catalog of Ethnology Specimens—MINIARC Database

22: American Indian Linguistics

23: Anthropology Computer Laboratory

A researcher who is searching the ISAAC databases can use these titles and project numbers for selection and full viewing of chosen abstracts. Information is given on the principal investigator, affiliation, address, phone number, and Bitnet address. This is followed by information on the software and hardware used in the project and the numbers of faculty and students involved.

ISAAC is a free computer-based system devoted to information about the use of IBM computers and compatible software in higher education and research. All students, faculty, and staff at institutions of higher education and members of participating societies are eligible to use ISAAC. To request access to ISAAC, send the following information to Isaac Access, m/s FC-06 University of Washington, Seattle, WA 98195; or, use Bitnet to send it to ISAAC@UWAEE; or, call (206) 543-5604: (1) Name, (2) Address, City, State, Zip, (3) Phone, with area code, (4) University, (5) Bitnet address. A user may connect to ISAAC in two ways. Each method requires separate authorization. If the user chooses modem access, ISAAC provides the communications. Please indicate which method(s) preferred: Method 1—IBM PC, XT, AT or compatible and a modem (Continental U.S. and Hawaii only). Method 2—Bitnet (Bitnet address must be included); materials will be mailed to the user. [Information from ISAAC]

Smithsonian Science Information Exchange (SSIE)

Some of the abstracts in the Computer Databases Available to Anthropologists section are based on information from SSIE, a database that goes up only to February 1982. The search for this appendix was conducted using the key words COMPUTERS and ANTHROPOLOGY. Abstracts give project title, principal investigator, affiliation, and address and list the sponsoring institution (for example, the U.S. Department of Health and Human Services, the U.S. Department of Agriculture, or the National Endowment for the Humanities), and the size (dollar amount) of the grant. Abstracts are given with three sections: Objective, Approach, and Progress. [Information from SSIE]

RESOURCE: BIBLIOGRAPHIC SEARCHES FOR ANTHROPOLOGISTS ON COMPACT DISK

Three database products on compact disk may be particularly important for anthropologists: PSYCHLIT, ERIC, and MED-LINE, in the areas of psychology, education, and medicine. Together, these three bibliographic databases on compact disk cover a great deal of the social science literature, including the anthropological literature. Among other journals, PSYCHLIT indexes *Annual Review of Anthropology, American Anthropologist, American Ethnologist, Anthropologica, Anthropos, Current Anthropology, Ethnos, International Journal of Primatology, Journal of Cross-Cultural Psychology, Qualitative Sociology, Social Biology, Social Science and Medicine, Social Forces,* and *Social Networks.* The ERIC educational bibliographic database indexes the *Anthropology and Education Quarterly,* many linguistic journals, journals on computers and education, social policy journals, and science journals such as *Science* and *Scientific American.*

RESOURCE: CONTINUING EDUCATION IN COMPUTING AND METHODS OF ANALYSIS

1. *Summer Institutes on Research Methods in Cultural Anthropology.* In 1987, 1988, and 1989, the Department of Anthropology at the University of Florida hosted summer institutes on research methods for anthropologists, funded by the National Science Foundation. In

1990, the NSF-sponsored institute was held at the Department of Anthropology, Northern Arizona University, in Flagstaff, AZ. Each institute consists of a three-week intensive course in the methods of data construction and analysis, and trains twelve anthropologists per year. The curriculum now specifically includes unidimensional scales such as those used in structured interviews; multidimensional scaling; log-linear analysis; network analysis; kinship mapping; consensus modeling; and computerized text management. The summer institutes make use of the software package ANTHROPAC (see above). For information, write H. R. Bernard, Dept. of Anthropology, University of Florida, Gainesville, FL 32611. Bitnet, UFRUSS@ UFFSC. Preference is given to those who teach research methods. [Information from *Anthropology Newsletter* 30(7):31, 1989].

2. *American Anthropological Association.* Each year the AAA sponsors courses, workshops, and formal academic sessions that focus on anthropology and computing and the use of field methods and types of analysis that make use of computers. Sessions have to date been held to acquaint anthropologists with new types of equipment, new computer programs, new types of applications, and old questions addressed in new ways using computer-assisted methods. Preliminary programs give the earliest information each year on these continuing education activities. The *Anthropology Newsletter* of the AAA also publishes columns and features on other continuing education opportunities, new computerized resources for anthropology, and job listings that require specializations and training in quantitative methods and computers. The AAA also conducts surveys of departments that inquire about their computer resources, and the association also publishes departmental information on computer resources in the yearly *Guide to Departments.*

3. *Society for Applied Anthropology.* The Society for Applied Anthropology provides opportunities for workshops, sessions, and exchange at its annual meetings. Sometimes these activities are focused on a particular type of hardware (for example, lap-top computers) and sometimes on particular software (for example, the statistical computing packages). The society's career-oriented publication, *Practicing Anthropology,* has published a special issue devoted to computers and anthropology (volume 6) and now publishes computer column (see PRINT JOURNALS, above).

RESOURCE: NEW ORGANIZATIONS

At the time of this writing, two new professional groups had begun forming that are related to the methods used in this volume. The two groups have somewhat different emphases, but they both have members with interests in new and improved anthropological methods and computer-assisted anthropological applications. These developments are some indication of the growing interests among many anthropologists in computer applications, quantitative methods, and growing methodological sophistication in anthropology, in general. Both groups have begun to discuss affiliation with the American Anthropological Association.

1. *Society for Scientific Anthropology.* The Society for Scientific Anthropology is being organized as a unit of the American Anthropological Association with the following statement of purpose: "The purpose of the society is to promote anthropology as a science. Our goal is to develop a coherent understanding of human beings drawing on social, cultural, biological, linguistic, and archaeological perspectives. We strive for this goal through the design of research employing systematic and reliable methods of data collection and analysis in all fields of anthropology." All who are interested in the society should attend organizational, business, and subsequent meetings at the annual AAA conventions. Contact person: James S. Boster, Department of Anthropology, University of Pittsburgh, Pittsburgh, PA 15260, (412) 648-7524. Bitnet, BOSTER@PITTVMS. [Information from James S. Boster]

2. Proposal for a *Computer Unit of the AAA.* Another group of anthropologists interested specifically in computer use has discussed the possibility of five subsections of their organization: (1) applications such as simulation, artificial intelligence, graphics, map making, and desk-top publishing; (2) programming and programming techniques, including hypertext construction; (3) use of computers in teaching anthropology; (4) coaching of anthropologists in the use of computers; and (5) use of computers in promoting communication among non-Western peoples. Contact person: J. David Sapir, Department of Anthropology, University of Virginia, Charlottesville, VA 22903. (804) 924-7044. [Information from J. David Sapir]

RESOURCE: TRAINING PROGRAMS
IN APPLIED ANTHROPOLOGY

Many, if not most, academic departments of anthropology now provide access to microcomputers and/or mainframe terminals for student and faculty use. Some applied anthropology programs offer a computer focus or computer training as an integral, optional or required part of their curricula. The following information on applied programs comes from the *1987 Guide to Training Programs in the Applications of Anthropology* edited by John van Willigen, of the University of Kentucky, as a special supplement to *Practicing Anthropology: A Career-Oriented Publication of the Society for Applied Anthropology.* Copies for $3.50

from Society for Applied Anthropology, Business Office, P. O. Box 24083, Oklahoma City, OK 73124. The guide is published every two years. It is edited by Stan Hyland, of Memphis State University.

1. *The American University, Department of Anthropology.* The AU Department of Anthropology lists special applied programs in development anthropology and cultural resources management. The university is committed to building computer literacy. Students have access without charge to mainframe facilities and SPSS and SAS statistical packages and to IBM-PCs. The Department of Anthropology offers training in computer-based data management at several levels. Degrees: BA, MA, PhD. Further information: Director, Graduate Admissions, Department of Anthropology, The American University, 4400 Massachusetts Ave. NW, Washington, DC 20016. (202) 885-1830. [PA Special Issue 1987:2]

2. *Case Western Reserve University, Anthropology Department, Quantitative Skills Certificate Option.* The quantitative skills option is offered with the Department of Epidemiology and Biostatistics of the School of Medicine. It is a course of study for acquiring quantitative skills in biostatistics, computer applications, and research design. It combines training in anthropology and the analytical tools of research and evaluation. Completed coursework leads to awarding the certification in addition to the MA and PhD degrees. The Department of Anthropology has two computer labs for data analysis and word processing and also has computer terminals linked to the university system. The department also lists special programs in medical anthropology and cross-cultural aging. Degrees: MA/S, PhD. Further information: Chair, Department of Anthropology, Case Western Reserve University, Mather Memorial, Cleveland, OH 44106. (216) 368-2264. [PA Special Issue 1987:3-4]

3. *University of Florida, Department of Anthropology, Interdisciplinary Program in Anthropology.* The department lists programs in agricultural research, international development, medical anthropology, transcultural nursing, gerontology, applied linguistics, evaluation, and cultural resources management. The UF department provides access to microcomputers and terminals for the university mainframe. It hires a computer consultant for faculty and students. Degrees: BA, MA, PhD. Further information: Chair, Admissions Committee, Department of Anthropology, University of Florida, 1350 Turlington Hall, Gainesville, FL 32611. (904) 392-2031. See also, summer institutes on methods in anthropology, under CONTINUING EDUCATION, above. [PA Special Issue 1987:7-8]

4. *Georgia State University, Department of Anthropology.* The department offers a masters program in applied anthropology of complex societies, with special foci on medical and urban anthropology. As part of their program, all graduate students are required to take a

course in qualitative methods and research design and another in quantitative methods and computer skills. Students may get further computer-assisted skills from an optional course in epidemiology and anthropology. Undergraduates may take a course in ethnographic methods as an elective. Degrees: BA, MA. Further information: Director of Graduate Studies, Department of Anthropology, Georgia State University, Atlanta, GA 30303. (404) 651-2255.

5. *University of Maryland, Department of Anthropology.* The Department of Anthropology lists special programs in medical anthropology and public archaeology. As part of its professional degree program toward a Master of Applied Anthropology (MAA), the department offers students training in quantitative/computer methods and technical writing. The departmental computer laboratory includes microcomputers and mainframe terminals for student use. Degree: MAA. Further information: Michael Agar, Department of Anthropology, University of Maryland, College Park, MD 20742. (301) 454-5069. [PA Special Issue 1987:11–12]

6. *Northern Arizona University, Anthropology Department.* The department lists a special program in applied anthropology, which requires a course in computer applications in anthropology. In addition, their ethnographic research methods course is computer based. A student could put together a program for an anthropology degree with a computer/methods focus. A parallel emphasis in computer courses outside the department allows a computer specialization. Degrees: BA, MA/S. Further information: Gail Rusnak, Secretary, Applied Anthropology Master of Arts, Anthropology Department, Northern Arizona University, Box 15200, Flagstaff, AZ 86011. (602) 523-3180. [PA Special Issue 1987:15–16]

7. *Rensselaer Polytechnic Institute, Department of Science and Technology Studies.* The department lists a special program in public archaeology. The program offers intensive training in industrial and historical archaeology with concentration in the application of computers to archaeology and the archaeological aspect of historic preservation. Degree: MS. Further information: David R. Starbuck, Department of Science and Technology Studies, Rensselaer Polytechnic Institute, Troy, NY 12181. (518) 266-8503, 266-6574. [PA Special Issue 1987:16–17]

8. *University of South Carolina, Department of Anthropology.* The public service archeology program provides students with training in relevant computer skills (mapping, data analysis) as part of the curriculum. Degree: MA. Further information: Graduate Director, Department of Anthropology, University of South Carolina, Columbia, SC 29208. (803) 777-6500. [PA Special Issue 1987:17]

9. *University of South Florida, Department of Anthropology.* The department lists special programs in applied urban anthropology,

applied medical anthropology, and public archaeology. The requirements for the PhD program in applied anthropology include statistics and computer skills. Students have access to university mainframe terminals, a microcomputer laboratory, and departmental PCs. Degrees: BA, MA, PhD. Further information: Alvin W. Wolfe, Department of Anthropology, University of South Florida, Tampa, FL 33620. (813) 974-2150, 974-2209, 974-3231. [PA Special Issue 1987:17–18]

RESOURCE: COMPUTER EDUCATION IN PREDOMINANTLY ACADEMIC DEPARTMENTS

It is now possible for many anthropology students to pursue their interests in computer-based methods in an increasing number of academic departments of anthropology (in some cases, the same as the above departments that allow applied concentrations). Computer courses, programs, and requirements often depend on the expertise and interests of faculty and on available facilities—which can all change very rapidly. The following information can serve as a starting point, and students who are looking for special programs should inquire as widely as possible, sometimes directly to departments that may not appear below. Information is often given in a context of teaching anthropological research methods, so it may be most useful to inquire about methods courses. The following departments are some of those that are now developing good capabilities for teaching computer applications, but this very short list is by no means exhaustive. The last section in this Resources Appendix lists two programs in Great Britain.

1. *University of California/Berkeley, Department of Anthropology.* The Berkeley department has a special computer facility called the Quantitative Anthropology Laboratory (QAL). QAL is described as one of the projects in the Computer Databases Available to Anthropologists section in this volume and is unique in offering computer workstation facilities. Degrees: BA, MA, PhD. Further information: Department of Anthropology, University of California, Berkeley, CA 94720. (415) 642-3391. [Information from the *1987 AAA Guide to Departments of Anthropology*, pp. 34–36]

The Department of Anthropology at Berkeley offers perhaps the best selection of computer and anthropology courses at its Quantitative Anthropology Laboratory (QAL). However, qualitative analysis of ethnographic materials is important and is taught in Anthropology 169, "Computer-Assisted Analysis of Ethnographic Texts" (using programs such as ETHNOGRAPH, described in Chapter 5 in this volume). UCB also offers Anthropology 190B, "Quantitative Methods in Anthropology," and Anthropology 193, "Practical Computer Use." [Information from the *1987 AAA Guide to Departments of Anthropology*]

2. *University of California/Irvine, School of Social Sciences.* UC/Irvine provides a variety of programs and facilities for students interested in anthropology and computing. The Anthropology Department has an interactive computer system for cross-cultural analysis, the Human Relations Area Files, access to three computer systems, interactive software for regression analysis, and facilities for a program in experimental anthropology. Extensive training in computers, statistics, research design, cross-cultural research, and longitudinal field site research is available. UC/Irvine also allows a concentration in Mathematical Social Science, which requires one year of statistics or an equivalent series of courses in mathematics, computer programming, or formal procedures. Anthropologists are affiliated with that program, as they are with the Program in Comparative Culture, which focuses on minority groups and comparative studies. The Social Networks Program is also an official PhD program at UC/Irvine, which involves anthropologist and sociologists and provides outstanding training in quantitative methods and computing. Degrees: PhD in Social Sciences, PhD in Comparative Culture. Further information: Chair, Anthropology Department, University of California/Irvine, Irvine, CA 92717. (714) 856-6336. For further information on the Social Networks Program, contact Linton C. Freeman. The Computer Science Department at Irvine also has a program in Computing, Organizations, Policy, and Society. [Information from the *1987 Guide to Departments of Anthropology*, pp. 38–39, and from UC/Irvine departments]

3. *University of Pittsburgh, Department of Anthropology.* The program at Pittsburgh includes a cultural resource management program with computer facilities, including a state-of-the-art computer graphics facility. The physical anthropology program has a self-contained computer facility. The department has a complete set of the Human Relations Area Files and maintains the basic documents used by the Cross-Cultural Research Center for the compilation of the ethnographic analysis. The PhD program requires two courses in quantitative methods. Degrees: BA, MA, PhD. Further information: Secretary for Student Affairs in Anthropology, Department of Anthropology, University of Pittsburgh, Pittsburgh, PA 15260 (412) 648-7510. [Information from the *1987 AAA Guide to Departments of Anthropology*, pp. 237–241]

RESOURCE: USERS GROUPS

Users groups are often grassroots organizations, sometimes with wider affiliations, which bring together individuals who use the same hardware or software or who are interested in the same type of computer applications. There are users groups that are located in specific communities, universities, government offices, private industries, and even local neighborhoods. The following example is one of the most widely affiliated users group and is composed of individuals who use SAS software for PCs and mainframes.

SAS Users Group International (SUGI)

One of the most widely organized network of users groups is composed of individuals who use SAS software for PCs and mainframes. There are SAS users groups in the United States, Europe, Latin America, Asia, and Australia and New Zealand. The SAS Institute in Cary, NC, publishes bulletins that give directories of users groups, information on the latest SAS products and examples of their application, and listings for courses offered around the United States. There is also an annual international convention where SAS users present papers, hold workshops, and attend training sessions in use of SAS products and systems. The thirteenth annual SAS conference in 1988 was called "SUGI 13," in Orlando, FL. Local users groups allow more frequent participation. The SAS Institute also offers technical assistance over the telephone for SAS programmers at locations that support SAS software. For further information write SAS Institute Inc., SAS Circle, Box 8000, Cary, NC 27512-8000. (919) 467-8000. [Information from *SAS Communications*, Vol. XIII, No. 1, 1987]

RESOURCE: ANTHROPOLOGY AND COMPUTING IN GREAT BRITAIN

Bulletin of Information on Computing and Anthropology (BICA)

BICA is a newsletter produced irregularly, about three times per year. It is free at present but may not be so in the future. BICA welcomes articles, notes, and bits of information. They should be sent to the editor: Prof. J. Davis, Eliot College, The University, Canterbury, Kent CT2 7NS, England or by E-mail to JHRD@UK.AC.UKC.

Issue No. 6, for example, has items on U-SP, a user-friendly survey analysis package; teaching computing methods to first-year anthropology students; a note on mathematics and computers in Mexican anthropology; computers in the field, Part I, permissions and logistics; and news from Kent and elsewhere. It also has a list of electronic addresses that is updated. [Information from Issue No. 6, distributed at the annual meeting of the American Anthropological Association, 1987, Chicago]

TRAINING PROGRAMS

1. *The University of Kent at Canterbury. MA in Social Anthropology and Computing.* The MA in social anthropology and computing is a flexible program designed for graduates who want a professional qualification or who want to apply computing techniques to further academic study in social anthropology or sociology. The program covers a full range of computing applications to social anthropology, with a strong emphasis on qualitative and symbolic methods.

The aim is to provide students with training and experience in computing; computing applications to social research, particularly in developing societies; and the implications of technology transfer and information technology for developing societies. Students learn to program a computer using high-level languages. They use a range of existing computing applications and learn how these may be applied to social analysis. They use computer modeling techniques to investigate social problems. They examine native models underlying contemporary computer programs and environments. They examine the social environments that develop around computers in organizations. Further information: Contact Michael D. Fischer, Center for Social Anthropology and Computing, Eliot College, The University of Kent, Canterbury, Kent CT1 3PY, United Kingdom. [Information from program announcement from the school]

2. *The University of Kent at Canterbury. Doctoral Programme in Applied Computing (Social Sciences).* The doctoral program is a three-year program leading to the award of PhD. During the first year of the program, students will receive some advanced training in their social science subject, in computing, and in methods of social research, and they will carry out preliminary work on their research project. Following satisfactory completion of the first-year work, students will spend their final two years working full-time on their project.

The doctoral program aims to produce (1) social scientists capable of working in industry, commerce, and administration in a technological environment; (2) computer scientists with sensitivity and knowledge of problems in social sciences; and (3) academic social scientists who can contribute to the development of information technology in their area. Applications are particularly welcome from people whose social science experience is in one of the following fields: accounting; econometrics; economics; management science; social anthropology; social psychology; social statistics; sociology. Further information: Contact Dr. Elizabeth Oxborrow, Director of Studies, Doctoral Programme in Applied Computing (Social Sciences), Computing Laboratory, University of Kent at Canterbury, Canterbury, Kent CT2 7NF, England.

Computer Databases Available to Anthropologists

The Resources Appendix lists a relatively new and major source of information for anthropologists: the database search. There are many different kinds of databases, and they can be searched in a variety of ways using variety of media from diskettes to on-line services to compact disks. This section provides an example of a combined on-line database search, using the same key words to search three databases: COMPUTERS and ANTHROPOLOGY. The units in all three databases were roughly the same: the project unit. The database search was conducted in the summer of 1987. The following project descriptions are representative of the type of projects accessed in this database search. Summaries below are abbreviated versions of information that was accessed on Bitnet.

The abstracts come from three networks that allowed project searches: the Smithsonian Science Information Exchange (SSIE); IBM's bulletin board and collection of databases, the Information System for Advanced Academic Computing (ISAAC); and the National Technical Information Service (NTIS). Projects that had received federal funding were more likely to appear in SSIE and NTIS, and the original summaries of federally funded projects included dollar amounts. The three databases cover different periods of time, so some "projects" are still ongoing, and some are not. Some were finished when entered into the databases, and some were not. Some project directors have moved to other institutions or retired. In some cases a project represents the earlier work of an anthropologist who has subsequently gone on to more advanced applications. Therefore, the information is not always the most current. However, the projects represent portions of the enormous variety of computer applications that anthropologists have developed, and together they add to the breadth of coverage of the major chapters in this volume.

The following selection of project summaries includes a wide range of computer applications in all subfields of anthropology—ethnology, linguistics, physical anthropology, and archaeology. Some computer applications are relatively simple. For example, they involve the use of computers to create easily managed inventories of artifacts, sites, specimens of material culture, body measurements, or human genes. Other applications are more sophisticated and involve using anthropological theory and principles of social organization to create complex models of human adaptation and simulations of human evolution or migration and settlement. Many of the projects involve students, who make use of special programs to visualize and experiment with anthropological data by using a computer.

PROJECT: Words and Worlds of Tamang Women

Abstract: This project (1) completes translation of fourteen women's life history narratives and traditional songs, which were tape recorded and transcribed among ethnic Tamang or highland Nepal, and (2) introduces, annotates, edits, and organizes these stories and songs to portray women's lives. Use of the computer focuses on multiple levels in the translation: first, from the transliterated Tamang (here written in the Devanagri script used by Nepali and Hindi) into Nepali; then, from Nepali into a literal English; and finally, into a final English. Innovation: This is a first step in significantly reducing the redundant steps involved in field ethnography. For example, translations are worked directly from tapes to the computer in one step instead of in two (translation and transcription). Computer searches assist in locating and comparing translations of similar words or phrases in various contexts, not to establish a universalizable "computerized" translation but to assist in refining subtle points of translation. K. March, Department of Anthropology and Women's Studies, Cornell University, Ithaca, NY 14853. [Information from the Information System for Advanced Academic Computing]

PROJECT: Ozette Archeological Project

Abstract: Phase XII (1978) excavations at the Ozette site, a prehistoric and protohistoric Makah village, concentrated on the floor middens of houses 2 and 3 (400 B.P.) and 5 (+400 B.P.). A test coring program outside the houses was partially unsuccessful. All artifact data were computerized for inventory. Several cordage types are found in different areas of the houses and imply different activities and status. Cordage confirms the importance of sea mammal procurement at the site and along with cordage from other sites supports regional cultural trait boundaries previously demonstrated with basketry. Various shapes of wood chips correspond with different wood-working activities and family areas within houses. Bent-wood boxes were constructed with diverse techniques. Single whalebone tool types were used for several different purposes. This project was sponsored by the Heritage Conservation and Recreation Service, Interagency Archaeological Services, San Francisco, CA. Jeffrey E. Mauger, Washington Archaeological Research Center, Pullman, WA 99164. [Information from the National Technical Information Service]

*PROJECT: Regional and Localized Distribution
Analyses of Archeological Site and Artifact Attributes*

Abstract: This project determines the extent of the influence of various foreign political systems on, and the nature of, local political systems within the Cajamarca Basin, Peru. Attributes of sites are plotted relevant to their position in political hierarchy and the distribution of diagnostic ceramic types through time. The project also analyzes the relationship of a hierarchy of population centers to the irrigation and road systems in the Jequetepeque Valley, Peru; studies the range and types of prehistoric settlement and their relation to the natural resources of the Colorado River Basin in Texas; and delineates the activity areas and the function of room blocks in the WS Ranch pueblo. Participants: Faculty/Research—2. S. A. Turpin and R. P. Schaelel, Department of Anthropology, University of Texas, Austin, TX 78712. [Information from the Information System for Advanced Academic Computing]

PROJECT: Upper Mantaro Archaeology Research Project

Abstract: The project analyzes data from archaeological research in the highlands of Peru to recognize and explain economic organization of Wanka society prior to and under Inca rule (A.D. 1350–1460 and 1460–1533). Graduate students do the field research, data collection, and statistical analyses, both at the master's and doctorate levels. Analyses include pattern recognition in spatial distributions and materials characterization. Participants: Graduate Students—1, Faculty/Research—1. Terence D'Altroy, Department of Anthropology, Columbia University, New York, NY 10027. [Information from the Information System for Advanced Academic Computing]

PROJECT: Strong Museum of Anthropology

Abstract: This project is designed to inventory and organize the collections of the new anthropology museum, using Lotus 1-2-3 and dBase III as database managers. Students are actively involved in data recording and computer entry. Once completed, the database serves as a source for instruction in museology and archaeology courses. Participants: Undergraduates—3, Graduate Students—4, Faculty/Research—2. Terence D'Altroy and Nan A. Rothschild, Department of Anthropology, Columbia University, New York, NY 10027. [Information from the Information System for Advanced Academic Computing and from the principal investigators]

PROJECT: A Standardized Cross-Cultural
Time Allocation Database

Abstract: Under a grant from the National Science Foundation, we are preparing a series of monographs presenting time allocation data in cross-culturally comparable form. Each monograph represents a single research project and/or a single community. Time allocation data were in most cases collected by random spot-check (scan sampling) technique and describe activity patterns for all age and sex groups in the community for a year-round period. Because those data are usually difficult to compare between studies, we also convert them into a standardized form that is readily compared between studies.

Monographs also include a "cultural checklist" describing basic features of the community in comparable form, a "User's Guide" describing how to use the data, and other supporting materials, such as maps and censuses. The data are provided in ASCII files on diskettes included with the monograph, as well as in a form ready for dBase III users. The first monographs appeared in late 1987, published by HRAF Press in New Haven, CT. In all, some fifty volumes are planned in the series. Participants: Undergraduate Student—1, Graduate Students—2, Faculty/Research—1. Allen Johnson, Department of Anthropology, UCLA, Los Angeles, CA 90024. [Information from the principal investigator]

PROJECT: Cuyapaipe Indian
Reservation Cultural Resource Inventory

Abstract: An intensive cultural resource survey was applied to an ethnographic study of the 4,100-acre Cuyapaipe Indian Reservation, San Diego County, California. Twenty-three prehistoric and two historic cultural resources were recorded. Following the field survey, a computer-assisted hierarchical cluster analysis of site attributes was implemented. Four types of prehistoric sites were discerned. These included three procurement types and one maintenance type. Subsequent to site re-evaluation and data analysis, three prehistoric archaeological site areas consisting of seven site loci have been determined to be potentially eligible for nomination to the National Register of Historic Places. This project was sponsored by the National Park Service, Western Archeological and Conservation Center, Tucson, AZ 85726, Clifford V. F. Taylor and Richard L. Carrico, WESTEC Services, Inc., San Diego, CA 92121. [Information from the National Technical Information Service]

PROJECT: Sex and Race Determination of Crania by
Calipers and Computer: A Test of the Giles and Elliot
Discriminant Functions in Fifty-Two Forensic Cases

Abstract: Giles and Elliot discriminant functions, diagnosing sex and race from cranial measurements, were tested on a series of forensically examined crania of known sex and race. Of fifty-two crania of known sex, forty-six (88 percent) were correctly diagnosed. Racial diagnoses were correct in thirty (71 percent) of forty-two crania of known race. Analysis of the facial data indicates that most of the errors resulted from the misclassification of Native American crania as white or black. This suggests that the temporally remote and geographically limited prehistoric Indian crania used in developing the functions do not provide a database representative of the present-day U.S. Native American population. Cranial size, age at death, and certain pathological conditions altering cranial form can also contribute to misdiagnoses of sex and/or race by the function. We conclude that, despite some shortcomings, the Giles and Elliot discriminant functions provide a useful tool in forensic anthropology. Clyde C. Snow, Steve Hartman, Eugene Giles, and Fontaine A. Young, Office of Aviation, Federal Aviation Administration, Washington, DC 20590. [Information from the National Technical Information Service]

PROJECT: Quantitative Anthropology Laboratory (QAL)

Abstract: QAL provides c. thirty public Sun 3/50 workstations running Berkeley 4.2 BSD UNIX, networked to four Sun servers, and is the center for a fifty-workstation LAN serving faculty and student lab clusters in anthropology and in demography. It maintains several IBM PC and Macintosh microcomputers for document preparation and uploading field data. QAL provides consulting services to anthropology and other faculty and students. It is the locus for courses in basic computer use on Suns, quantitative and qualitative anthropological data analysis, special research courses in anthropology, other courses in other departments, and tutorial research by undergraduates and graduates. Statistical analysis on the Suns concentrates on the ISP and S languages developed for exploratory data analysis at Princeton and Bell Labs and on UNIX utilities such as grep and awk for qualitative data analysis. QAL does not attempt to provide instruction or detailed consulting for microcomputers.

QAL began in 1974 to introduce anthropologists, historians, and others to computer use in analysis and also to introduce more formal methods of analysis. It has functioned since then as a teaching laboratory for courses in data analysis in anthropology, linguistics, history, nutrition, forestry, botany, sociology, and other disciplines dealing with survey, archival, and other field data. The laboratory began with a Data General NOVA 2/10 and four terminals running time-sharing BASIC as well as single-user operation in FORTRAN and RJE access to mainframes. Over the years as demand increased, it shifted to the DG ECLIPSE C300, then to the C330, and finally to the MV8000. It has now moved all operations to a cluster of about thirty public Sun 3/50 workstations networked to four Sun servers. QAL is the center of a LAN that serves faculty and student lab clusters in adjacent buildings in anthropology and demography; there are now about fifty workstations on the network. QAL began as a minicomputer shop and has moved to advanced workstations, with some provision for microcomputing. About 600 students per year are enrolled in the formal courses that use QAL, and the number of users of the lab is about 1,000 per year. Eugene A. Hammel, University of California, Berkeley, CA 94720. [Information from the Information System for Advanced Academic Computing and from the principal investigator]

PROJECT: Integration of Computers in
Undergraduate Physical Anthropology Courses

Abstract: This project integrates the use of computers into the laboratory setting of two upper division physical anthropology courses: (1) physical growth and maturation and (2) human adaptability. The purposes of this project are to (1) adapt laboratory exercises to computer workstations; (2) integrate the use of computers into the laboratory teaching process; (3) integrate the use of computers into the training of graduate students specializing in physical anthropology; and (4) integrate PCs into the principal investigator's ongoing research. Students use the PC to input laboratory observations and measurements, carry out basic statistical calculations, and prepare graphs, charts, and related laboratory reports. Students are able to note various trends and associations in anthropological observations. Participants: Undergraduates—30/semester, Graduate Students—5/semester, Faculty/Research—1. Robert M. Malina, Department of Anthropology, University of Texas, Austin, TX 78712. [Information from the Information System for Advanced Academic Computing]

PROJECT: Cockpit Geometry Evaluation,
Phase III/Computer Program System

Abstract: The Cockpit Geometry Evaluation (CGE) Program is a development of improved methods for evaluating the physical compatibility of crew members with crew stations. The heart of the program is a 23-joint, three-dimensional man model (BOEMAN) that simulates the motion of humans performing tasks in a given environment. The computer program system (CPS) ties the project together. The system uses an updatable bank of anthropological, environmental, and task sequence data. The final report contains both the historical development of CGECPS and the most recent capabilities and modifications to the computer program system. Robert Katz, Boeing Aerospace Company, P. O. Box 3707, Seattle, WA 98124. [Information from the National Technical Information Service]

PROJECT: Burke Museum Catalog of
Ethnology Specimens—ARGUS Database

Abstract: The Burke Museum's catalog of ethnology specimens is being entered into an ARGUS database using a CIE Systems 150/80 supermicrocomputer. The objectives are as follows. (1) Create a database with information on the approximately 40,000 objects in the Ethnology Division of the Burke Museum, identifying the objects by catalog number, accession number, tribal origin, object type, storage location, donor, collector, and accession and collection dates. The database will eventually include more detailed information on materials, dimensions, motifs, condition, and so on. (2) Link this computerized collection catalog with a laser videodisc containing multiple images of the objects. (3) Train museology students in the use of the computer and database. (4) Make the database available as a research resource to university students, faculty, staff, outside researchers, and the public. Participants: Undergraduates—4, Graduate Students—4, Faculty/Research—4. Patrick Kirch, Burke Museum, University of Washington, Seattle WA 98195. [Information from the Information System for Advanced Academic Computing and from the principal investigator]

PROJECT: The AMRL Anthropometric Data Bank
Library, U.S. Correlations (Data File and Reports)

Abstract: Correlation matrices based on data from U.S. Air Force anthropometric surveys of women (1968, 127 variables), flying personnel (1950, 128 variables; 1967, 190 variables), and basic trainees (1965, 161 variables); a U.S. Army survey of women separatees (1946, 60 variables); the Health Examination Survey of civilian adults (1960–1962, 18 variables); and a survey of law enforcement officers (1974, 23 measurements) are presented for use by engineers who need them in solving design problems and for anthropologists and statisticians whose analyses and understanding of the interrelationships of body size data depend significantly on these coefficients. Sample sizes in these surveys ranged from almost 2,000 upward. Sample means and standard deviations are presented for all variables involved.

The contents of the tape are also described in a report, "Intercorrelations of Anthropometric Measurements: A Source Book for USA Data," by E. Churchill, P. Kikta, and T. Churchill, Aerospace Medical Research Laboratories, WPAFB OH, 1978. Definitions and basic univariate summary statistics are presented for all variables involved. Appendixes contain a glossary of anatomical terms, tables for establishing confidence limits for the correlation coefficients presented here, computer programs used in preparing the report, and an index by name, anatomical type, and anthropometric technique. A bibliography is included. This project was sponsored by the Department of Defense, Washington, DC. Charles E. Clauser and Paul Kikta, Aerospace Medical Research Lab (AMRL), Wright-Patterson Air Force Base, OH 45433. [Information from the National Technical Information Service]

PROJECT: The STICK-MAN Program

Abstract: The STICK-MAN Program was written for the Anthropology Branch (MRHA) of the Human Engineering Division, Aerospace Medical Research Laboratory (AMRL). Its function is to provide a means for studying the interrelationships between the mass and center of mass of the human body segments and the mass and center of mass of their component parts. The program uses an IBM 2250 Display Unit to enable the user to enter and modify parametric equations. The results are displayed numerically and graphically on a "stick-man" view of the human body. Once the study is completed for a given subject, a hard copy printout of the results may be obtained. This program was written for an IBM System/360, Model 40 computer. Both assembler language and Fortran IV were used in coding the programs, and Graphic Programming Services for the 2250 (GPS) was used for the graphics software support. The project was sponsored by the Aerospace Medical Research Laboratory, Wright-Patterson AFB, OH 45433. D. L. Wartluft, IBM Federal Systems Division, Gaithersburg, MD 20878. [Information from the National Technical Information Service]

PROJECT: Computer-Assisted Processing of Ethnographic Data

Abstract: Research in ethnography, a field that deals with the natural history accounts of human behavior, has been very expensive because so much clerical effort is involved in filing and sorting data in order to retrieve a small amount of information. A guide describes the BEDRES package of computer programs, which make possible machine manipulation of natural language, such as ethnographic field data, and thus significantly reduce the enormous clerical job of processing the data. Application is to a study of employment disability among Puerto Rican youths. The report is titled "Anthropological Study of Disability from Educational Problems of Puerto Rican Youths." This project was sponsored by the Social and Rehabilitation Service, Washington, DC. Jacquetta Hill Burnett, Bureau of Educational Research, University of Illinois at Urbana-Champaign, Urbana, IL 61801. [Information from the National Technical Information Service]

PROJECT: Himalayan History and Anthropology Project

Abstract: This project edits and compiles a comprehensive bibliographic database covering the Himalayan region extending from the Hindu Kush to the Highlands of Burma. Coupled with a free-text database management software package, F.Y.I. 3000, the PC-AT is used to create an inverted index of every word in every citation, including key words added by the editors as descriptors. Researchers can design search criteria according to their own parameters, using Boolean logic connectors and incorporating up to sixty-five terms. T. Riccardi, Department of Middle East Language and Cultures, Columbia University, New York, NY 10027. [Information from the Information System for Advanced Academic Computing]

PROJECT: Humanities and Social Science Database Laboratory

Abstract: This laboratory is a joint effort between the several sponsoring departments, the College of Arts and Humanities, and Instructional Computing Programs. The goal of the project is to explore and develop several kinds of database tools and techniques and assess their applicability to many liberal art disciplines, particularly the technology capable of supporting text databases and databases comprising graphics images. These projects, together, explore a common set of core technologies, including text (both full-text and text databases) and graphics database tools, computer-aided design tools, and text and image scanners, including Kurzweil scanners, and their applicability to humanities and social science research and teaching. Chad K. McDaniel, Department of Anthropology, University of Maryland, College Park, MD 20742. [Information from the Information System for Advanced Academic Computing]

PROJECT: Nubian Field Note Database for Graduate Training

Abstract: This project enables graduate students to use the Nubian ethnographic field notes database for research papers. A study was undertaken in 1962 to analyze the traditional life-style of 50,000 people living along the Nile in Nubia, Egypt. This region was flooded following the completion of the High Dam at Aswan. The study included plans for resettlement of the people. A database was created in 1982 from eighteen volumes of field notes compiled during the 1962–1964 survey. The present project transfers the field notes from the CDC mainframe to a PC to facilitate wider use. Participant: Faculty/Research—1. Robert A. Fernea, Department of Anthropology, University of Texas, Austin, TX 78712. [Information from the Information System for Advanced Academic Computing]

PROJECT: Arcospace

Abstract: Arcospace is a software package designed for the study of spatial distributions. The program is intended to facilitate the entry, manipulation, graphic display, and statistical analysis of spatial data. Data entry is facilitated by software for a digitizing table. Keyboard or disc entry is also acceptable. A user-supplied version of Borland's Reflex provides the database for the program. GMS from Quantitative Systems is used for some of the screen display of artifact categories. This program provides access to a number of quantitative techniques for intrasite spatial analysis such as K-Means and Unconstrained Clustering. The goal of intrasite spatial analysis is to make inferences regarding site use based on the location of artifacts in relation to other artifacts of the same type as well as to artifacts of other types.

Graphics programs help students visualize how artifacts were located at an archaeological site. Students are able to see the distribution of tools, houses, hearths, burials, and so on at each excavation, and by looking at several excavations simultaneously, they see patterns of use throughout the site.

A simulation program allows the student to design an excavation and see the consequences of his or her decisions. A data bank on real archaeological sites permits advanced students to conduct statistical investigations to understand prehistoric settlements and their changes over time. T. Douglas Price, Department of Anthropology, University of Wisconsin, Madison, WI 53706. [Information from the Information System for Advanced Academic Computing and the principal investigator]

PROJECT: Fugawiland

Abstract: Fugawiland is an interactive computer exercise for use in introductory courses in archaeology and general anthropology. The software runs on IBM-compatible equipment with a minimum of 256K of memory, a graphics card, and a printer. Students are shown a map of twenty-five archaeological sites on a hypothetical landscape and are asked to select and excavate ten sites from that group. "Excavation" graphically reveals the plan of the site on the computer screen, showing the distributions of artifacts, houses, hearths, and burials. Hard copy of the site maps can be obtained using the Print Screen key.

Through the examination of a number of "excavated" sites and their contents, patterns may emerge that provide information on prehistoric subsistence, settlement, season of occupation, population, and land use. This courseware emphasizes the learning experience by providing a variety of help screens with additional information about maps, artifacts, faunal resources, analysis, and the like. Fugawiland further requires creative problem solving in order to resolve the nature of patterning in the distribution of sites, artifacts, and archaeological features. T. Douglas Price, Department of Anthropology, University of Wisconsin, Madison, WI 53706. [Information from the principal investigator. Simulation program by Price and Kolb now available from Duke University Press. See Resources Appendix]

PROJECT: Historical Microsimulation Laboratory

Abstract: A microsimulation model of population dynamics and social organization makes available to undergraduates, graduate students, and faculty a serious research tool capable of testing many historical and anthropological social models. Users define parameters (age distributions, vital rates, characteristics of the social structure) for one or more populations and observe the interaction among demographic and social structural factors at the level of individual decision making as well as group outcomes. Participant: Faculty/Research—2. Ronald F. W. Weissman, Department of History, University of Maryland, College Park, MD 20742. [Information from the Information System for Advanced Academic Computing]

*PROJECT: Computerized Image Processing
of Maya Hieroglyphic Inscriptions*

Abstract: This project uses a computerized image-processing system for digitizing photographs, drawings, and rubbings of Maya hieroglyphic inscriptions. The digitized images then are transcribed into a standardized coding system for sorting on-screen manipulations. Although the project is primarily research oriented, it does have educational value in that it allows students to bypass much otherwise unavoidable labor and to concentrate on deciphering the text. Participant: Faculty/Research—1. James A. Fox, Department of Anthropology, Stanford University, Stanford, CA 94305. [Information from the Information System for Advanced Academic Computing]

*PROJECT: NUÑOA: A Computer Simulator of Individuals,
Families, and Extended Families of the High-Altitude Quechua*

Abstract: The Quechua Indians of the Peruvian Andes are an example of a human population that has developed special cultural adaptations to deal with hypocaloric stress imposed by a harsh environment. A highly detailed human ecosystem model, NUÑOA, which simulates the yearly energy balance of individuals, families, and extended families in a hypothetical farming and herding Quechua community of the high Andes, was developed. Unlike most population models that use sets of differential equations in which individuals are aggregated into groups, this model considers the response of each individual to a stochastic environment. The model calculates the yearly energy demand for each family based on caloric requirements of its members. For each family, the model simulates the cultivation of seven different crops and the impact of precipitation, temperature, and disease on yield. Herding, slaughter, and market sales of three different animal species are also simulated. Any energy production in excess of the family's energy demand is placed into extended family storage for possible redistribution. A family failing to meet their annual energy demand may slaughter additional herd animals, temporarily migrate from the community, or borrow food from the extended family storage. The energy balance is used in determining births, deaths, marriages, and resource sharing in the Indian community.

In addition, the model maintains a record of each individual's ancestry as well as seven genetic traits for use in tracing lineage and gene flow.

The model user has the opportunity to investigate the effect of changes in marriage patterns, resource sharing patterns, or subsistence activities on the ability of the human population to survive in the harsh Andean environment. In addition, the user may investigate the impact of external technology on the Indian culture. C. C. Brandt, D. A. Weinstein, H. H. Shugart, and B. Simmons, Oak Ridge National Laboratory, Oak Ridge, TN. [Information from the National Technical Information Service.] General information about the NUÑOA population and other computer simulations based on the group may be obtained from R. Brooke Thomas, Department of Anthropology, University of Massachusetts, Amherst, MA 01003. (413) 545-2221 or (413) 545-0697.

PROJECT: Aging Among the Mennonites of Kansas and Nebraska

Abstract: This is a long-term multidisciplinary investigation of aging and longevity in religious isolates of Kansas and Nebraska. The primary goal of this study is to investigate the interaction of genetic and environmental factors that affect aging and longevity. The sociocultural, psychological, nutritional, and demographic data will be used to derive environmental indices. Their effects on differential biological aging and longevity will be estimated by path analytical models. Two splinter communities, Alexanderwohl and Henderson, plus a third more distantly related population of Meridian, have been studied because of their long-term genealogical depth, cultural cohesiveness and homogeneity, and excellent historical documentation. These Mennonite communities resulted from the fission of a congregation in Russia during their transplantation to the United States in 1874. Genetic data, physiological, demographic, anthropometric, medical, biochemical, and sensory data have been collected for 1,300 subjects. Sociocultural, psychological, and nutritional information has been compiled for smaller samples. The first two years of this project were concerned with data collection; the third year will be entirely devoted to data analysis, interpretation, and write-up. This project is sponsored by the National Institute on Aging, National Institutes of Health, Bethesda, MD. M. H. Crawford, W. Bowerman, S. Stull, J. Janzen, J. Quadagno, and W. Osness, Department of Anthropology, University of Kansas, Lawrence, KS 66045 [Summary information from the Smithsonian Science Information Exchange]

References and Suggested Readings

Suggested Readings Selected by
Gregory F. Truex, John J. Wood, and Margaret S. Boone

ABERCROMBIE, JOHN R.
1987   Graphics display of foreign scripts. Perspectives in Computing 7(1):43–51.

AGAR, MICHAEL
1979   Microcomputers as field tools: Some problems in cognitive anthropology. Discourse Processes 2:11–31.
1982   Toward an ethnographic language. American Anthropologist 84(4):779–795.
1983   Microcomputers as field tools. Computers and the Humanities 17:19–26.
1986   Speaking of Ethnography. Beverly Hills, CA: Sage.

ALDENDERFER, MARK S.
1984   Cluster Analysis. Beverly Hills, CA: Sage.

ANDERSON, R. E., AND F. M. SIM
1977   Data management and statistical analysis in social science computing. Behavioral Scientist 20:367–409.

ANDRIOLE, STEPHEN J.
1985   Applications in Artificial Intelligence. Princeton: Petrocelli.

ARNOLD, J. B. III
1982   Archaeological applications of computer graphics. *In* Advances in Archaeological Method and Theory, Volume 5. M. B. Schiffer, editor. New York: Academic Press, pp. 179–216.

ASCH, TIMOTHY, JOHN MARSHALL, AND PETE SPIER
1973   Ethnographic film: Structure and function. *In* B. J. Siegel, A. R. Beals, and S. A. Tylor, editors. Annual Review of Anthropology 2:179–181.

ASCHER, M., AND R. ASCHER
1963   Chronological ordering by computer. American Anthropologist 65:1045–1052.

ATKINS, J.
1984   Comments on "An algebraic account of the American kinship terminology." Current Anthropology 25:440–441.

ATKINSON, A. C.
1985   Plots, Transformations, and Regression. Oxford: Oxford University Press.

BARNETT, V., AND T. LEWIS
1978   Outliers in Statistical Data. New York: John Wiley and Sons.

BECKER, H. S.
1986   Teaching fieldwork with computers: Computing in qualitative sociology. Qualitative Sociology 9(1):100–103.

BECKER, H. S., A. C. GORDON, AND R. K. LeBAILLEY
1984   Field work with the computer: Criteria for assessing systems. Qualitative Sociology 7:16–33.

BECKER, LAWRENCE C.
1985   Notebook II: A database manager for text. Computers and the Humanities 19(1):53–56.

BEHRENS, C., AND D. READ
1987   BISEX: Bisayan Expert System. Unpublished software program.

BELSLEY, D. A., E. KUH, AND R. E. WELSCH
1980   Regression Diagnostics. New York: John Wiley and Sons.

BERKOWITZ, S. D.
1988   Afterword: Toward a Formal Structural Sociology. *In* Social Structures: A Network Approach. B. Wellman and S. D. Berkowitz, editors. Cambridge: Cambridge University Press.

BERNARD, H. RUSSELL
1988   Research Methods in Cultural Anthropology. Beverly Hills, CA: Sage.

BERNARD, H. R., AND M. J. EVANS
1983   New microcomputer techniques for anthropologists. Human Organization 42:182–185.

BERNARD, H. R., P. J. PELTO, O. WERNER, J. BOSTER, AND A. K. ROMNEY
1986   The construction of primary data in cultural anthropology. Current Anthropology 27(4):382–396.

BERNOLD, THOMAS
1985   Artificial Intelligence: Towards Practical Applications. New York: North-Holland.

BOCK, R. D., AND L. V. JONES
1968   The Measurement and Prediction of Judgment and Choice. San Francisco: Holden-Day.

BOONE, MARGARET S.
1987   Inner-city black undercount: An exploratory study on the causes of coverage error. Evaluation Review 11(2):216–241.
1989   Capital Crime: Black Infant Mortality in America. Newbury Park, CA: Sage.

BRENT, E. E.
1984   Qualitative computing: Approaches and issues. Qualitative Sociology 7(1-2):34–60.

1985   Relational database structures and concept formation in the social sciences. Computers and the Social Sciences 1:29–50.

1986   Knowledge-based systems: A qualitative formalism. Qualitative Sociology 9(3):256–282.

BRENT, EDWARD, JAMES SCOTT, AND JOHN SPENCER

1987   The use of computers by qualitative researchers. Qualitative Sociology 10(3):309–313.

BRISLIN, R. W., AND S. R. BAUMGARDNER

1971   Non-random sampling of individuals in cross-cultural research. Journal of Cross-Cultural Psychology 2:397–400.

BRITAN, GERALD M., AND RONALD COHEN

1980   Toward an anthropology of formal organizations. *In* Hierarchy and Society. Gerald M. Britan and Ronald Cohen, editors. Philadelphia: Institute for the Study of Human Issues.

BROD, CRAIG

1984   Technostress: The Human Cost of the Computer Revolution. Menlo Park, CA: Addison-Wesley.

BROWN, MALCOLM

1987   ASKSAM, Version 2.3 (Review). Computers and the Humanities 21(3):200–203.

BUCHANAN, B., AND E. SHORTLIFFE

1985   Rule-Based Expert Systems: The MYCIN Experiments of the Stanford Heuristic Programming Project. Reading, MA: Addison-Wesley.

BUCKLAND, P.

1973   An experiment in the use of a computer for on-site recording of finds. Science and Archaeology 9:22–24.

BULLERS, W. I., R. A. REID, AND H. L. SMITH

1986   Computer oriented hospital systems. Hospital Topics (March/April):16–20.

BURT, R. S.

1982   Toward a Structural Theory of Action. New York: Academic Press.

BURTON, M. L., AND D. R. WHITE

1987   Cross-cultural surveys today. Annual Review of Anthropology 16:143–160.

BURTON, V., A. BONIN, J. LOURIE, AND T. SPISELMAN

1970   The computer and archaeology. American Journal of Archaeology 74:221–223.

BUTLER, C. S.

1985   Computers in Linguistics. New York: Basil Blackwell.

CARROLL, J. D.

1972   Individual differences and multidimensional scaling. *In* Multi-Dimensional Scaling: Theory and Applications in the Behavioral Sciences,

Volume I. R. N. Shepard, A. K. Romney, and S. B. Nerlove. New York: Seminar Press, pp. 105–155.

CHANG, J. J., AND J. D. CARROLL
1969   How to Use MDPREF. Murray Hill, NJ: Bell Telephone Laboratories.

CHENHALL, R. G.
1967   The description of archaeological data in computer language. American Antiquity 32:161–167.
1968   The impact of computers on archaeological theory: An appraisal and projection. Computers and the Humanities 3(1):15–24.

CHIBNIK, M.
1981   The evolution of cultural rules. Journal of Anthropological Research 37:256–268.
1985   The use of statistics in sociocultural anthropology. Annual Review of Anthropology 14:135–157.

CHOUEKA, Y.
1980   Computerized full-text retrieval systems and research in the humanities. Computers and the Humanities 14:153–169.

CLANCEY, W.
1983   The epistemology of a rule-based expert system: A framework for explanation. Artificial Intelligence 20:215–251.

CLARK, G. A., AND C. R. STAFFORD
1982   Quantification in American archaeology: A historical perspective. World Archaeology 14(1):98–119.

CLEVELAND, W. S.
1985   The Elements of Graphing Data. Monterey, CA: Wadsworth.

COLBY, B. N.
1985   Toward an encyclopedic ethnography for use in "intelligent" computer programs. *In* Directions in Cognitive Anthropology. J. Dougherty, editor. Urbana: University of Illinois Press, pp. 269–290.

CONRAD, P., AND S. REINHARZ, EDITORS
1984   Computers and qualitative data. Qualitative Sociology (Special Issue) 9(1–2):Entire issue.

COOMBS, C. H.
1964   A Theory of Data. New York: John Wiley and Sons.

COOMBS, C. H., R. M. DAWES, AND A. TVERSKY
1970   Mathematical Psychology: An Elementary Introduction. Englewood Cliffs, NJ: Prentice-Hall.

COWGILL, G. L.
1967   Computer applications in archaeology. Computers in the Humanities 2(1):17–23.

COXON, A. P. M.

1982 The User's Guide to Multidimensional Scaling. Exeter, NH: Heinemann Educational Books.

CRABTREE, BENJAMIN F., AND PERTTI J. PELTO

1988 Anthropologists learn SYSTAT computer program for applied and research uses. Practicing Anthropology 10(1).18,20,21.

CRUZ, M. L.

1987 The Cuban Fishermen of Key West. MA Thesis, Rutgers University.

DAIUTE, COLETTE

1985 Issues in using computers to socialize the writing process. Special issue: Social Aspects of Educational Communication and Technology 33(1):41–50.

DENNIS, D. L.

1984 "Word crunching": An annotated bibliography on computers and qualitative data analysis. Qualitative Sociology 7(1-2):148–156.

DENNIS, J. RICHARD

1987 Intelligent Computer Assisted Instruction. AEP Database. (See Resources Appendix for AEP Database.)

DILLON, WILLIAM R., AND MATTHEW GOLDSTEIN

1984 Multivariate Analysis: Methods and Applications. New York: John Wiley and Sons.

DORAN, J. E.

1970 Systems theory, computer simulations and archaeology. World Archaeology 1:289–298.

1982 A computational model of sociocultural systems and their dynamics. *In* Theory and Explanation in Archaeology. C. Renfrew, M. J. Rowlands, and B. Seegraves, editors. New York: Academic Press, pp. 375–388.

DORAN, J. E., AND F. R. HODSON

1975 Mathematics and Computers in Archaeology. Cambridge: Harvard University Press.

DOW, JAMES

1983 The combined use of computers and audio tape recorders in storing, managing, and using qualitative verbal ethnographic data. *In* Anthropological Research. M. D. Zamora, editor. Special Issue of the Journal of Northern Luzon 13(1-2):56–80. Nueva Vizcaya, Philippines.

DRAPER, N., AND H. SMITH

1981 Applied Regression Analysis, 2nd edition. New York: John Wiley and Sons.

DRASS, K. A.

1980 The analysis of qualitative data: A computer program. Urban Life 9:332–353.

DRIVER, HAROLD E.
1965   Survey of numerical classification in anthropology. *In* The Use of Computers in Anthropology. Dell Hymes, editor. The Hague: Mouton & Co., pp. 301–344.

DUDA, R., AND E. SHORTLIFFE
1983   Expert systems research. Science 220:261–268.

Du TOIT, S. H. C., A. G. W. STEYN, AND R. H. STUMPF
1986   Graphical Exploratory Data Analysis. New York: Springer-Verlag.

DYKE, BENNET
1981   Computer simulation in anthropology. *In* B. J. Siegel, A. R. Beals, and S. A. Tyler, editors. Annual Review of Anthropology 10:193–207.

DYKE, BENNET, AND JEAN W. MacCLUER, EDITORS
1973   Computer Simulation in Human Population Studies. New York: Academic Press.
1974   Computer Simulation in Human Population Studies. New York: Academic Press.

DYSON-HUDSON, R., AND N. DYSON-HUDSON
1986   Computers for anthropological fieldwork. Current Anthropology 25(5):530–531.

ECKHARDT, ROBERT B.
1979   The Study of Human Evolution. New York: McGraw-Hill.

EDWARDS, ELIZABETH A.
1989   Computer assisted instruction: The American Indian Orthography Project. Practicing Anthropology 11(2):19,21.

EDWARDS, M.
1986   Preserving the working waterfront: Protecting working harbors from "development." National Fisherman 67:2–64.
1987a Dockage struggle in San Diego. National Fisherman 67:8–33.
1987b Florida Keys fishermen are being zoned out of their own backyard. National Fisherman 68:25–28.

EGUCHI, PAUL
1987   Fieldworker and computer: An end user's view of computer ethnology. *In* Toward a Computer Ethnology. Joseph Raben, Shigeharu Sugita, and Masatoshi Kubo, editors. Senri Ethnological Studies, No. 20. Osaka: National Museum of Ethnology, pp. 165–174.

EISENBERG, JOHN E., AND MELVYN LOCKHART
1972   An Ecological Reconnaissance of Wilpattu National Park, Ceylon. Washington, DC: Smithsonian Institution Press.

EL-NAJJAR, MAHMOUD Y., AND K. RICHARD McWILLIAMS
1978   Forensic Anthropology: The Structure, Morphology, and Variation of Human Bone and Dentition. Springfield, IL: Charles C. Thomas.

ELSEVIER SCIENCE PUBLISHING
1989   THE SOFTWARE CATALOG: Microcomputers. Parts I and II. New York.

ERICKSON, B. H.
1988   The relational basis of attitudes. *In* Social Structures: A Network Approach. B. Wellman and S. D. Berkowitz, editors. Cambridge: Cambridge University Press.

FAERSTEIN, PAUL H.
1986   Fighting computer anxiety. Personnel 63(1):12–17.

FELDESMAN, MARC R.
1986   A review of selected microcomputer statistical software packages: A cautionary tale. Computer-Assisted Anthropology News 2(1):3–26.

FELDESMAN, M. R., AND J. K. LUNDY
1987   New stature estimates for some Plio-Pleistocene fossil hominids. American Journal of Physical Anthropology 72:198.
1988   Stature estimates for some African Plio-Pleistocene fossil hominids. Journal of Human Evolution 17:583–596.

FIELDING, NIGEL G., AND RAYMOND M. LEE
1991   Using Computers in Qualitative Research. Newbury Park, CA: Sage.

FINK, A., AND J. KOSECOFF
1985   How to Conduct Surveys: A Step-By-Step Guide. Beverly Hills, CA: Sage.

FISCHER, M. D.
1987   Computer representations of anthropological knowledge. Bulletin of Information on Computing and Anthropology 5:11–24.

FISHER, R. A.
1930   The Genetical Theory of Natural Selection. Oxford: Oxford University Press.

FJELLMAN, S.
1976   Talking about talking about residence: An Akamba case. American Ethnologist 3:671–682.

FOX, ANNIE, AND DAVID FOX
1983   Armchair BASIC: An Absolute Beginner's Guide to Programming in BASIC. Berkeley, CA: Osborne/McGraw-Hill.

FREEMAN, L. C.
1988   Computer programs and social network analysis. Connections 11:2, 26–31.

FREIBERGER, VICKI
1987   Personal interview. Office of Information Services, University Hospitals of Cleveland. April 6.

GABBY, J., AND P. DRURY
1986   Getting the data recipe right. The Health Service Journal (March 20): 388–389.

GAINES, S. W.
1974   Computer use at an archaeological field location. American Antiquity 39:454–462.

GAINES, S. W., EDITOR
1981   Data Bank Applications in Archaeology. Tucson, AZ: University of Arizona Press.

GAINES, S. W., AND W. M. GAINES
1980   Future trends in computer applications. American Antiquity 45:462–471.

GARDIN, J.-C.
1971   Archaeology and computers: New perspectives. International Social Science Journal 23(2):189–203.

GEOGHEGAN, W.
1971   Information processing systems in culture. *In* Explorations in Mathematical Anthropology. P. Kay, editor. Cambridge: MIT Press.

GEPHART, ROBERT P., JR.
1988   Ethnostatistics: Qualitative Foundations for Quantitative Research. Newbury Park, CA: Sage.

GERSON, ELIHU M.
1986   Where do we go from here? Qualitative Sociology 9(2):208–212.

GIFFORD, D. P., AND D. C. CRADER
1977   A computer coding system for archaeological faunal remains. American Antiquity 42:225–237.

GILBERT, J. P.
1971   Computer methods in kinship studies. *In* Explorations in Mathematical Anthropology. P. Kay, editor. Cambridge: MIT Press, pp. 127–138.

GILBERT, J. P., AND E. HAMMEL
1966   Computer simulation and analysis of problems in kinship and social structure. American Anthropologist 68:71–93.

GILBERT, ROBERT I., AND JAMES H. MIELKE
1985   The Analysis of Prehistoric Diets. San Diego: Academic Press.

GILLESPIE, G. W., JR.
1986   Using word processor macros for computer-assisted qualitative analysis. Qualitative Sociology 9(3):283–292.

GLADWIN, C.
1975   A model of the supply of smoked fish from Cape Coast to Kumasi. *In* Formal Methods in Economic Anthropology. S. Plattner, editor. Washington, DC: American Anthropological Association.
1983   Structural change and survival strategies in Florida agriculture. Culture and Agriculture 21 (Fall):1–7.
1989   The case for the disappearing mid-size farm in the U.S. *In* Food and Form: Current Debates and Policies. C. Gladwin and K. Truman, editors. Lanham, MD: University Press of America.

1990   Ethnographic Decision Tree Modeling. Newbury Park, CA: Sage.

GLASS, R.
1964   London: Aspects of Change in London. Center for Urban Studies. London: MacGibbon and Knee.

GLAZER, HOWARD
1987   Telephone Interview. Pharmacy Services, University Hospitals of Cleveland. May 29.

GLUCK, HENRY
1986   Personal interview. Psychiatry Data Center, Hanna Pavilion, University Hospitals of Cleveland. September 23.

GOOD, I. J.
1983   The philosophy of exploratory data analysis. Philosophy of Science 50:283–295.

GOODENOUGH, W.
1956   Componential analysis and the study of meaning. Language 32:195–216.

GRAHAM, I., AND E. WEBB, EDITORS
1982   Computer Applications in Archaeology. London: Institute of Archaeology, University of London.

GREEN, EDWARD C., EDITOR
1987   Practicing Development Anthropology. Boulder, CO: Westview.

GREEN, P. E., AND V. R. RAO
1972   Applied multidimensional scaling: A comparison of approaches and algorithms. Hinsdale, IL: Dryden Press.

GREENACRE, M. J.
1984   Theory and Application of Correspondence Analysis. New York: Academic Press.

GRISHMAN, R.
1986   Computational Linguistics: An Introduction. New York: Cambridge University Press.

GUILLET, D.
1985   Microcomputers in fieldwork and the role of the anthropologist. Human Organization 44(4):369–371.

GUILLET, D., GUEST EDITOR
1989a   Expert systems applications in anthropology, Part 1. Anthropological Quarterly 62(2):57–162.
1989b   Expert systems applications in anthropology, Part 2. Anthropological Quarterly 62(3):107–143.

GULLIKSEN, H.
1956   A least-squares solution for paired comparisons with incomplete data. Psychometrika 21:125–134.

HALDANE, J. B. S.
1932   The Causes of Evolution. New York: Harper.

HALLORAN, E. J.
1985   Nursing workload, medical diagnosis related groups, and nursing diagnoses. Research in Nursing and Health 8(4):421–433.

HALLORAN, E. J., C. PATTERSON, AND M. KILEY
1987   Case mix: Matching patient need with nursing resource. Nursing Management 18(3):27–42.

HAMMEL, EUGENE A.
1976   The SOCSIM Demographic-Sociological Microsimulation Program Operating Manual. Research Series No. 27. Berkeley: University of California.
1979   Experimental history. Journal of Anthropological Research 35:274–291.

HANNEMAN, R. A.
1988   Computer-Assisted Theory Building. Newbury Park, CA: Sage.

HARDY, G. H.
1908   Mendelian proportions in a mixed population. Science 28:49–50.

HARMON, P., AND D. KING
1985   Expert Systems: Artificial Intelligence in Business. New York: John Wiley and Sons.

HARRISON, S., C. JARDINE, J. KING, T. KING, AND A. MACFARLANE
1979   Reconstructing historical communities by computer. Current Anthropology 20:808–810.

HARTWIG, F., AND B. E. DEARING
1979   Exploratory Data Analysis. Beverly Hills, CA: Sage.

HAYES-ROTH, F., D. WATERMAN, AND D. LENAT, EDITORS
1983   Building Expert Systems. Reading, MA: Addison-Wesley.

HEARN, A. C.
1983   REDUCE User's Manual, Version 3.0. Rand Publication CP78(4183). Santa Monica: The Rand Corporation.

HIETALA, H., EDITOR
1984   Intrasite Spatial Analysis in Archaeology. Cambridge: Cambridge University Press.

HIRSCHFELD, L.
1986   Kinship and cognition: Genealogy and the meaning of kinship terms. Current Anthropology 27:217–229.

HODDER, I., EDITOR
1978   Simulation Studies in Archaeology. Cambridge: Cambridge University Press.

HODDER, I., AND C. ORTON
1976   Spatial Analysis in Archeology. Cambridge: Cambridge University Press.

HODSON, F. R., D. G. KENDALL, AND P. TAUTU, EDITORS
1971   Mathematics in the Archeological and Historical Sciences. Edinburgh: Edinburgh University Press.

HOROWITZ, MICHAEL M., AND THOMAS M. PAINTER, EDITORS
1986   Anthropology and Rural Development in West Africa. Boulder, CO: Westview.

HOSLER, D., J. A. SABLOFF, AND D. RUNGE
1977   Situation model development: A case study of the classic Maya collapse. *In* Social Processes in Maya Prehistory. N. Hammond, editor. New York: Academic Press, pp. 553–590.

HOWELL, NANCY
1979   The Demography of the Dobe !Kung. New York: Academic Press.

HOWELL, NANCY, AND V. LEHOTAY
1978   AMBUSH: A computer program for stochastic microsimulation of small human populations. American Anthropologist 80:905–922.

HOWELLS, W. W.
1984   Introduction. *In* Multivariate Statistical Methods in Physical Anthropology: A Review of Recent Advances and Current Developments. G. N. Van Vark and W. W. Howells, editors. Boston: D. Reidel, pp. 1–11.

HUBER, P.
1981   Robust Statistics. New York: John Wiley and Sons.

HY, R. J.
1977   Using the Computer in the Social Sciences: A Nontechnical Approach. New York: Elsevier.

HYMES, DELL, EDITOR
1965   The Use of Computers in Anthropology. The Hague: Mouton & Co.

IHDE, DON
1983   Existential Technics. Albany, NY: State University of New York Press.
1986   Consequences of Phenomenology. Albany, NY: State University of New York Press.

IJEBOR, L. ET AL.
1986   What happens to the strategy debate? The Health Service Journal (October 16):1360–1362.

INTECH, INCORPORATED
1986   In-house private report, analysis of the Division of Psychiatry Information Systems. University Hospitals of Cleveland. International Symposium on Ergonomics in Developing Countries (ISEDC)

1987   ERGONOMICS IN DEVELOPING COUNTRIES. Symposium held in Jakarta, Indonesia, November 1985. Geneva, Switzerland: International Labour Office.

JAYASINGHE, J. B., AND M. R. JAINUDEEN
1970   A census of the tame elephant population in Ceylon with reference to location and distribution. Ceylon Journal of Science (BIO SCI) 8(2).

JOHNSON, J. C.
1986   Social networks and innovation adoption: A look at Burt's use of structural equivalence. Social Networks 8:343–369.

JOHNSON, J. C., AND J. MAIOLO
1986   Communication Networks in the North Carolina King Mackerel Fishery. A Report to the South Atlantic Fisheries Management Council.

JOHNSON, J. C., AND D. METZGER
1983   The shift from technical to expressive: The "play-full" harbors of southern California. Coastal Zone Management 10(4):429–441.

JOHNSON, J. C., AND M. K. ORBACH
1987   Limited Entry Alternatives for Florida's Spiny Lobster Fishery: A Preliminary Analysis, A Report to the Gulf of Mexico and South Atlantic Fisheries Management Councils.

JONES, JEFFREY R., AND BEN J. WALLACE, EDITORS
1986   Social Sciences and Farming Systems Research: Methodological Perspectives on Agricultural Development. Boulder, CO: Westview.

KAHL, J. A.
1968   The Measurement of Modernization. Austin, TX: University of Texas Press.

KEESING, R.
1974   Theories of culture. Annual Review of Anthropology 3:73–97.
1975   Kin Groups and Social Structure. New York: Holt, Rinehart and Winston.

KENWORTHY, M. A., E. M. KING, M. E. RUWELL, AND T. VAN HOUTEN
1985   Preserving Field Records: Archival Techniques for Archaeologists and Anthropologists. Philadelphia, PA: The University Museum, University of Pennsylvania.

KILEY, MARYLOU
1986   Applications of nurse/patient summary information. In Touch (University Hospitals of Cleveland Department of Nursing Quarterly) 2(4):22.
1987   Personal interview. Frances Payne Bolton School of Nursing, Case Western Reserve University. February 9.

KIRK, RODNEY C.
1981   Microcomputers in anthropological research. Sociological Methods and Research 9:395–492.

KLAVON, ROBERT
1987 ADVISE: An Expert System for Student Advising. AEP Database. (See Resources Appendix for AEP Database.)

KLEIN, R. G., AND K. CRUZ-URIBE
1984 The Analysis of Animal Bones from Archaeological Sites. Chicago: University of Chicago Press.

KLEINGARTNER, ARCHIE, AND CAROLYN S. ANDERSON, EDITORS
1987 Human Resource Management in High Technology Firms. Lexington, MA: Lexington Books.

KLIEGER, D. M.
1984 Computer Usage for Social Scientists. Boston: Allyn and Bacon.

KLIMEK, STANISLAW
1935 The structure of California Indian culture. University of California Publications in American Archaeology and Ethnology 37:1–70.

KOCH, DAVID
1986 Personal interview. Information Services, University Hospitals of Cleveland. May 13.

KOHLER, TIMOTHY A.
1987 Statistical packages for the Macintosh. Computer-Assisted Anthropology News 2(3):1–26.

KOONS, ADAM
1988 Electronic mail enhances field communications for anthropological research and collaboration. Practicing Anthropology 10(3–4):31.

KORPMAN, R. A.
1984– Patient care information systems: Looking to the future. Software in
1985 Healthcare (Parts 1–5, Apr/May–Dec/Jan).

KRAUT, ROBERT E., JOLENE GALEGHER, AND CARMEN EGIDO
1987– Relationships and tasks in scientific research collaboration. Special issue:
1988 Computer-Supported Cooperative Work. Human Computer Interaction 3(1):31–58.

KRONENFELD, D.
1976 Computer analysis of skewed kinship terminologies. Language 52:891–918.

KUHMANN, WERNER, W. BOUCSEIN, F. SCHAEFER, AND J. ALEXANDER
1987 Experimental investigation of psychophysiological stress-reactions induced by different system response times in human-computer interaction. Ergonomics 30(6):933–943.

LEAF, M.
1971 The Punjabi kinship terminology as a semantic system. American Anthropologist 73:545–554.

LEHMAN, F.
1985   Cognition and computation. *In* New Directions in Cognition. J. Dougherty, editor. Urbana, IL: University of Illinois Press.

LEMLEY, B.
1985   Artificial expertise: Intelligent software for problem solving. PC Magazine 4:108–112.

LENAT, D.
1983   The role of heuristics in learning by discovery: Three case studies. *In* Machine Learning. R. Michalski, J. Carbonell, and T. Mitchell, editors. Palo Alto, CA: Tioga Publishing Co., pp. 243–306.

LENNOX, RAND
1986   Personal interview. Information Services, University Hospitals of Cleveland. December 22.

LEVISON, M., R. G. WARD, AND J. W. WEBB
1972   The settlement of Polynesia: A report on a computer simulation. Archaeology and Physical Anthropology in Oceania 7:234–245.

LINCOLN, Y. S., AND E. G. GUBA
1985   Naturalistic Inquiry. Beverly Hills, CA: Sage.

LIPKIN, J., AND B. S. LIPKIN
1978   Data base development and analysis for the social historian. Computers and the Humanities 12:113–125.

LONDON, B.
1980   Gentrification as urban reinvasion: Some preliminary definitional and theoretical considerations. *In* Back to the City: Issues in Neighborhood Renovation. S. B. Laska and D. Spain, editors. New York: Pergamon, pp. 77–92.

LONG, J. ET AL.
1983   Introducing the interactive computer at work: The users' views. Behaviour and Information Technology 2(1):39–106.

LOUNSBURY, F.
1964a The structural analysis of kinship semantics. *In* Proceedings of the Ninth International Congress of Linguists. H. Lunt, editor. The Hague: Mouton & Co., pp. 1073–1093.
1964b A formal account of the Crow- and Omaha-type kinship terminologies. *In* Explorations in Cultural Anthropology. Ward Goodenough, editor. New York: McGraw-Hill.
1965   Another view of Trobriand kinship categories. American Anthropologist 67(pt. 2):142–185.

LOWE, JOHN W. G.
1985   The Dynamics of Apocalypse: A Systems Simulation of the Classic Maya Collapse. Albuquerque: University of New Mexico Press.

LUNDY, J. K.

1983   Regression equations for estimating living stature from long limb bones in the South African Negro. South African Journal of Science 79:337–338.

1984   Selected aspects of metrical and morphological infracranial skeletal variation in the South African Negro. Unpublished doctoral dissertation, Anatomy Department, University of the Witwatersrand, Johannesburg, South Africa.

LUNDY, J. K., AND M. R. FELDESMAN

1987   Revised equations for estimating living stature from the long bones of the South African Negro. South African Journal of Science 83:54–55.

MacCLUER, J.

1973   Computer simulation in anthropology and human genetics. *In* Methods and Theories in Anthropological Genetics. M. H. Crawford and P. Workman, editors. Albuquerque: University of New Mexico Press.

MacDOUGALL, DAVID

1978   Ethnographic film: Failure and promise. *In* B. J. Siegel, A. R. Beals, and S. A. Tyler, editors. Annual Review of Anthropology 7:405–425.

MANDON, NICOLE

1981   La bureautique des enjeux sociaux. Connexions 35:83–91.

MARTLEW, R., EDITOR

1984   Information Systems in Archaeology. Gloucester: Alan Sutton Publishing Limited.

McINERNEY, WILLIAM D.

1989   Social and organizational effects of educational computing. Journal of Educational Computing Research 5(4):487–506.

McKAY, GEORGE M.

1973   Behavior and Ecology of the Asiatic Elephant in Southeastern Ceylon. Washington, DC: Smithsonian Institution Press.

MELTZOFF, S. K.

        Forthcoming: The cross-currents of occupation, ethnicity, and class: Conservation and conflict in the Florida Keys. American Anthropologist.

MENDENHALL, W.

1986   An Introduction to Probability and Statistics, 6th edition. Boston: Duxbury.

MICHAELSEN, ROBERT H., DONALD MICHIE, AND ALBERT BOULANGER

1985   The technology of expert systems. BYTE Magazine (Apr):303–312.

MILES, MATTHEW B., AND A. MICHAEL HUBERMAN

1984   Qualitative Data Analysis: A Sourcebook of New Methods. Beverly Hills, CA: Sage.

MILKE, WILHELM
1965   Statistical processing. *In* The Use of Computers in Anthropology. Dell Hymes, editor. The Hague: Mouton & Co., pp. 189–204.

MILLER, CRANDALL
1987   Telephone interview. Nutrition Services, University Hospitals of Cleveland. June 2.

MILLER, M., AND R. DITTON
1986   Travel, tourism and marine affairs. Coastal Zone Management Journal 14:1-21.

MILLER, M., AND J. C. JOHNSON
1981   Hard work and competition in the Briston Bay salmon fishery. Human Organization 40(2):131–139.

MORAN, KATY
1986   Traditional Elephant Management in Sri Lanka: An Ethnozoological Perspective for Conservation. American Association of Zoological Parks and Aquariums Annual (AAZPA) Conference Proceedings. AAZPA, Wheeling, WV.

MORGAN, L. H.
1871   Systems of Consanguinity and Affinity of the Human Family. Smithsonian Contributions to Knowledge, XVII. Washington, DC: The Smithsonian Press.

MOSTELLER, J., AND J. TUKEY
1977   Data Analysis and Regression. Reading, MA: Addison-Wesley.

MURDOCK, G. P.
1949   Social Structure. New York: Macmillan.
1961   Outline of Cultural Materials, 4th edition. New Haven, CT: Human Relations Area Files.

NAISBITT, JOHN
1982   Megatrends: Ten New Directions Transforming Our Lives. New York: Warner Books.
1990   Megatrends 2000: Ten New Directions for the 1990's. New York: Morrow Books. (with Patricia Aburdene)

NANCE, C. R., AND W. K. SMITH
1985   Fitting the ethnographic atlas to the Apple II-E computer. Ethnology 24(1):77–82.

NATIONAL ACADEMY OF SCIENCES
1986   Microcomputers and Their Applications for Developing Countries. Boulder, CO: Westview.

NATIONAL RESEARCH COUNCIL (NRC), BOARD ON SCIENCE AND TECHNOLOGY FOR INTERNATIONAL DEVELOPMENT
1988   Cutting Edge Technologies and Microcomputer Applications for Developing Countries. Report of an Ad Hoc Panel on the Use of Microcomputers in Developing Countries. Boulder, CO: Westview Press.

Gregory F. Truex, John J. Wood, and Margaret S. Boone **343**

NAYLOR, C.
1982   Build Your Own Expert System: Artificial Intelligence for the Aspiring Microcomputer. New York: Halstead Press.

NEEDHAM, R.
1971   Remarks on the analysis of kinship and marriage. *In* Rethinking Kinship and Marriage. R. Needham, editor. London: Tavistock, pp. 1–34.

NERLOVE, S. B., AND A. S. WALTERS
1977   Pooling intra-cultural variation: Toward empirically based statements of community consensus. Ethnology 16:427–441.

NOSEK, LAURA
1986   Personal interview; unpublished sketch. Information Services, University Hospitals of Cleveland.

NOWAK, STEVEN
1987   Telephone interview. Department of Radiology, University Hospitals of Cleveland. May 29.

NUNN, RON
1988   A new frontier in technology transfer. Practicing Anthropology 10(3–4):30–31.

OGILVIE, D. M., P. J . STONE, AND E. F. KELLY
1982   Computer-aided content analysis. *In* A Handbook of Social Science Methods, Volume 2, Qualitative Methods, R. B. Smith and P. K. Manning, editors. Cambridge: Ballinger, pp. 219–245.

OLSEN, MARK
1987   Textbase for humanities applications: WordCruncher (Software Review). Computers and the Humanities 21(4):255–260.

ORBACH, M. K.
1980   The social and cultural effects of limited entry. *In* Limited Entry as a Fisheries Management Tool. J. Ginter and B. Renig, editors. Seattle: University of Washington Press.

OSTRANDER, S. A.
1980   Upper-class consciousness as conduct and meaning. *In* Power Structure Research. G. William Domhoff, editor. Beverly Hills: Sage, pp. 73–96.

OTTENHEIMER, M.
1986   Modeling Systems of Kinship and Marriage. Raleigh, NC: National Collegiate Software Clearinghouse.

PACKER, C. L.
1986   Medical records automation comes up to speed. Hospitals (October 20):98–99.

PALMER, R.
1978   Computer transcriptions from air photographs. Aerial Archaeology 2:5–9.

PAPERBACK SOFTWARE
1987   VP-Expert. Berkeley, CA: Paperback Software.

PERCIVAL, LYNN C., AND THOMAS K. NOONAN
1987   Computer network operation: Applicability of the vigilance paradigm to key tasks. Special issue: Vigilance; Basic and Applied Research. Human Factors 29(6):685–694.

PFAFFENBERGER, BRYAN
1988   Microcomputer Applications in Qualitative Research. Newbury Park, CA: Sage.

PIMENTEL, R.
1979   Morphometrics. Dubuque, IA: Kendall-Hunt.

PINKLEY, CONNIE
1987   Personal interviews. Office of Nursing Management Services, University Hospitals of Cleveland. February 2, March 3.

PISANO, STEPHEN A.
1989   The potential of the word processor for the writing of maladjusted students. Maladjustment and Therapeutic Education 7(1):47–53.

PODOLEFSKY, A., AND C. McCARTY
1983   Topical sorting: A technique for computer assisted qualitative analysis. American Anthropologist 84:4.

POLITAKIS, P., AND S. WEISS
1984   Using empirical analysis to refine expert system knowledge bases. Artificial Intelligence 22:23–48.

POST, ROBERT
1987   Personal interview. Office of Professional Affairs, University Hospitals of Cleveland. February 15.

QUINN, N.
1975   Decision models of social structure. American Ethnologist 2:19–45.

RABEN, J., S. SUGITA, AND M. KUBO, EDITORS
1987   Toward a Computer Ethnology. Senri Ethnological Studies No. 20. Osaka, Japan: National Museum of Ethnology.

RAI (ROYAL ANTHROPOLOGICAL INSTITUTE)
1971   Notes and Queries on Anthropology, 6th edition. London: Routledge and Kegan Paul.

READ, D.
1976   Kinship algebra: A mathematical study of kinship structure. *In* Genealogical Mathematics. P. Ballonoff, editor. Paris: Mouton & Co., pp. 15–60.
1984   An algebraic analysis of the American kin terminology. Current Anthropology 25:417–450.

1986   Comments on "Kinship and cognition: Genealogy and the meaning of kinship terms." Current Anthropology 27:232–233.
1987   The structure of kinship terminologies: The Trobriand terminology as a case study. Manuscript.
1988   The structure of kinship terminologies: The Trobriand terminology as a case study. (Manuscript)

READ, D. W., AND C. BEHRENS
1988   Kinship Algebra Expert System (KAES). Mathematical Social Sciences 16(2):218–220.

RENFREW, COLIN, AND KENNETH L. COOKE
1979   Transformations: Mathematical Approaches to Culture Change. New York: Academic Press.

RICHARDS, J. D., AND N. S. RYAN
1985   Data Processing in Archaeology. Cambridge: Cambridge University Press.

RIVERS, W.
1910   The genealogical method of anthropological inquiry. Sociological Review 3:1–12.

ROBERTS, E. B.
1985   Commentary, Health information systems, management information systems: New challenges to meet changing needs. Medical Care 23(5):672–673.

ROLANDI, WALTER G.
1986   Knowledge engineering in practice. AI Expert (Dec):58–62.

ROMNEY, A. K., AND R. D'ANDRADE
1964   Cognitive aspects of English kin terms. American Anthropologist 66:146–170.

ROMNEY, A. K., R. N. SHEPARD, AND S. B. NERLOVE, EDITORS
1972   Multidimensional Scaling: Theory and Applications in the Behavioral Sciences. New York: Seminar Press. 2 volumes.

ROSSI, P. H., J. D. WRIGHT, AND A. B. ANDERSON, EDITORS
1984   Handbook of Survey Research. New York: Academic Press.

ROTH, E.
1981   Demography and computer simulation in historic village population reconstruction. Journal of Anthropological Research 37:279–301.

SABLOFF, J. A., EDITOR
1981   Simulations in Archaeology. Albuquerque, NM: University of New Mexico Press.

SAS INSTITUTE
1978   SAS Introductory Guide. Cary, NC.
1982   SAS User's Guide: Basics. 1982 edition. Cary, NC.

1982   SAS User's Guide: Statistics. 1982 edition. Cary, NC.
1985   SAS User's Guide: Statistics. Version 5 edition. Cary, NC.

SCHEFFLER, H., AND F. LOUNSBURY
1971   A Study in Structural Semantics: The Siriono Kinship System. Englewood
       Cliffs, NJ: Prentice-Hall.

SCHIFFMAN, S., M. L. REYNOLDS, AND F. W. YOUNG
1981   Introduction to Multidimensional Scaling: Theory, Methods, and Applica-
       tions. New York: Academic Press.

SCHNEIDER, D.
1972   What is kinship all about? *In* Kinship in the Morgan Centennial Year.
       P. Reining, editor. Washington, DC: Anthropological Society of Washing-
       ton, pp. 32–63.
1984   A Critique of the Study of Kinship. Ann Arbor: University of Michigan
       Press.
1986   Comment on "Kinship and cognition: Genealogy and the meaning of
       kinship terms." Current Anthropology 27:234–235.

SEIDEL, J. V., AND J. A. CLARK
1984   THE ETHNOGRAPH: A computer program for the analysis of qualitative
       data. Qualitative Sociology 7(1–2):110–125.

SEIDEL, J. V., R. KJOLSETH, AND E. SEYMOUR
1988   THE ETHNOGRAPH: A User's Guide (Version 3.0). Littleton, CO: Qualis
       Research Associates.

SIEBER, R. T.
1987   Urban gentrification: Ideology and practice in middle-class civic activ-
       ity. City & Society 2:52–63.

SILVERN, STEVEN B.
1985– Classroom use of video games. Special issue: Computers in the Class-
1986   room. Educational Research Quarterly 10(1):10–16.

SMITH, C. L.
1985   Two bits on computer-aided learning in anthropology. Anthropology &
       Education Quarterly 16(4):311–317.

SMITH, C. L., AND D. FUHRER
1976   Computer-assisted instruction using cross-cultural data. Behavior Science
       Research 11(1):1–18.

SMITH, C. L., AND J. M. STANDER
1981   Human interaction with computer simulation. Simulation & Games
       12(3):345–360.

SMITH, C. L., J. M. STANDER, AND A. V. TYLER
1982   Human behavior incorporation into ecological computer simulation. En-
       vironmental Management 6(3):251–260.

SONQUIST, J. A.

1977   Computers and the social sciences. American Behavioral Scientist 20:295–318.

SONQUIST, J. A., AND W. C. DUNKELBERG

1977   Survey and Opinion Research: Procedures for Processing and Analysis. Englewood Cliffs, NJ: Prentice Hall.

SPRADLEY, J. P.

1979   The Ethnographic Interview. New York: Holt, Rinehart & Winston.
1980   Participant Observation. New York: Holt, Rinehart & Winston.

SPROULL, L., AND R. F. SPROULL

1982   Managing and analyzing behavioral records: Explorations in nonnumeric data analysis. Human Organization 41:283–290.

SPSS INCORPORATED

1986   SPSS-X User's Guide, 2nd edition. New York: McGraw-Hill.

STEINWACHS, D. M.

1985   Management information systems: New challenges to meet changing needs. Medical Care 23:607.

STERN, CURT

1960   Principles of Human Genetics, 2nd edition. San Francisco: W. H. Freeman.

STEWART, L., AND J. OLSEN

1987   Expert System for Selecting Information Sources. AEP Database. (See Resources Appendix for AEP Database.)

SUGITA, S.

1987   Computers in ethnological studies: As a tool and an object. *In* Toward a Computer Ethnology. Senri Ethnological Studies No. 20. J. Raben, S. Sugita, and M. Kubo, editors. Osaka, Japan: National Museum of Ethnology, pp. 9–40.

SUNDSTROM, ERIC D.

1986   Work Places: The Psychology of the Physical Environment in Offices and Factories. New York: Cambridge University Press.

TELLO, E.

1985a   Knowledge Systems for the IBM PC, Part I. Computer Language 2:71–83.
1985b   Knowledge Systems for the IBM PC, PART II. Computer Language 2:87–102.

THOMAS, D. H.

1986   Refiguring Anthropology. Chicago: Waveland Press.

THOMPSON, BEVERLY A., AND WILLIAM A. THOMPSON

1985   Inside an expert system. BYTE Magazine 10(Apr):315–330.
1986   Knowledge + control = expert systems. AI Expert (Nov):25–29.

TILLY

1988   Misreading, the rereading, nineteenth-century social change. *In* Social Structures: A Network Approach. B. Wellman and S. D. Berkowitz, editors. Cambridge: Cambridge University Press.

TORGERSON, W. S.

1958   Theory and Methods of Scaling. New York: John Wiley and Sons.

TROTTER, R. T. II

1986a   What electronic bulletin boards are all about. Anthropology Newsletter 27(5):1,15.

1986b   Statistical packages for micro-computers. Computer-Assisted Anthropology News 2(2):15–17.

TROTTER, ROBERT T. II, ANITA WOOD, MARCELLA GUTIERREZ-MAYKA, AND MARY FELEGY

1989   Ethnographic report: An ethnography of migrant farm worker educational opportunities. *In* Recruiting Migrant Students. Leon Johnson, editor. Pennsylvania Migrant Education, Pennsylvania Department of Education, Harrisburg, PA.

TRUEX, G. F.

1981   Kinship and network: A cognitive model of interaction. Social Networks 3:53–70.

TUKEY, J. W.

1969   Analyzing data: Sanctification or detective work. American Psychologist 24:83–91.

1977   Exploratory Data Analysis. Reading, MA: Addison-Wesley.

TURNAGE, JANET J.

1990   The challenge of new workplace technology for psychology. Special issue: Organizational Psychology. American Psychologist 45(2):171–178.

UPHAM, S., EDITOR

1979   Computer graphics in archaeology: Statistical cartographic applications to spatial analysis in archaeological contexts. Anthropological Research Papers No. 15, Arizona State University.

VALDES-PEREZ, RAUL E.

1986   Inside an expert system shell. AI Expert (Oct):30–42.

VAN HOUTEN, T.

1985   Machine-readable records. *In* Preserving Field Records: Archival Techniques for Archaeologists. M. A. Kenworthy, E. M. King, M. E. Ruwell, and T. Van Houten. Philadelphia: The University Museum, University of Pennsylvania, pp. 60–77.

VELLEMAN, P. E., AND D. C. HOAGLIN

1981   Applications, Basics, and Computing of Exploratory Data Analysis. Boston: Duxbury.

VELLEMAN, P. E., AND R. E. WELSCH

1981　Efficient computing of regression diagnostics. American Statistician 35:234–242.

WALLACE, A. F.

1970　Culture and Personality. New York: Random House.

WALLACE, A., AND J. ATKINS

1960　The meaning of kinship terms. American Anthropologist 62:58–79.

WARD, J.

1963　Hierarchical grouping to optimize an objective function. Journal of the American Statistical Association 58:236–244.

WATKINS, M. W., AND J. C. KUSH

1985　An Apple computer program for hierarchical cluster analysis. Behavior Research Methods 17(5):576.

WEINBERG, D.

1974　Computers as a research tool. Human Organization 33:291–302.

WEINBERG, D., AND G. M. WEINBERG

1972　Using a computer in the field: Kinship information. Social Science Information 11:37–59.

WEINBERG, W.

1908　Uber den Nachweis der Vererbung beim Menschen. JAHRESHEFTE VEREIN F. VATERL. NATURK. *In* Wu'rttemberg 64:368–382. (Portions transl. in C. Stern, 1943, The Hardy-Weinberg law, Science 97:137–138.)

WEISS, S., AND C. KULIKOWSKI

1984　A Practical Guide to Designing Expert Systems. Totowa, NJ: Rowman and Allanheld.

WEISSMAN, RONALD F. W.

1987　Historical Microsimulation Laboratory. AEP Database. (See Resources Appendix for AEP Database.)

WERNER, O.

1982　Microcomputers in cultural anthropology: APL programs for qualitative analysis. BYTE Magazine 7(7):250–280.

WERNER, OSWALD, AND G. MARK SCHOEPFLE

1987a　Systematic Fieldwork: Foundations of Ethnography and Interviewing. Beverly Hills, CA: Sage.

1987b　Systematic Fieldwork: Ethnographic Analysis and Data Management. Beverly Hills, CA: Sage.

WHALLON, R.

1972　The computer in archaeology: A critical survey. Computers and Humanities 7(1):29–45.

WHALLON, R., AND J. A. BROWN, EDITORS
1982   Essays on Archeological Typology. Evanston, IL: Center for American Archeology Press.

WHITE, DOUGLAS R.
1973   Mathematical anthropology. *In* Handbook of Social and Cultural Anthropology. John J. Honigmann, editor. Chicago: Rand McNally.

WILCOX, J. D.
1973   The use of remote terminals for archaeological site records. Science and Archaeology 9:25.

WILKINSON, L.
1986   SYSTAT: The System for Statistics. Evanston: Systat, Inc.

WILLIAMSON, MICKEY
1985   The history of artificial intelligence. PC-Week (Oct 1):51–53.

WILSON, WILLIAM E.
1985   Artificial Intelligence Applications and Applied Anthropology. Unpublished paper presented at the American Anthropological Association.

WOBST, H. MARTIN
1974   Boundary conditions for Paleolithic social systems: A simulation approach. American Antiquity 39:147–178.

WOLFF, D., AND M. L. PARSONS
1983   Pattern Recognition Approach to Data Interpretation. New York: Plenum Press.

WONNACOTT, T. H., AND R. J. WONNACOTT
1985   Introductory Statistics for Business and Economics, 3rd edition. New York: John Wiley and Sons.

WOOD, J. J.
1987   Some tools for the management and analysis of text: A pedagogic review. Computer-Assisted Anthropology News 2(4):2–26.

WOOD, M.
1980   Alternatives and options in computer content analysis. Social Science Research 9:273–286.
1984   Using key-word-in-context concordance programs for qualitative and quantitative social research. Journal of Applied Behavioral Research 20(3):289–297.

WRIGHT, SEWALL
1931   Evolution in Mendelian populations. Genetics 16:97–159.

YOUNG, F. W.
1987   Multidimensional Scaling: History, Theory, and Applications. Hillsdale, NJ: Lawrence Erlbaum Associates.

YOUNG, F. W., AND R. LEWYCKYJ
1979   ALSCAL-4 User's Guide, 2nd edition. Chapel Hill, NC: Data Analysis and Theory Associates.

YOUNGER, MARY SUE
1987   A Handbook for Regression. North Scituate, MA: Duxbury Press.

ZAR, J. H.
1984   Biostatistical Analysis, 2nd edition. Englewood Cliffs, NJ: Prentice-Hall.

Index